Ancient Philosophy

In this re-titled and substantially revised update of his *Classical Philosophy* (2003), Christopher Shields expands his coverage to include the Hellenistic era, and now offers an introduction to more than 1000 years of ancient philosophy. From Thales and other Pre-Socratics through Socrates, Plato, and Aristotle, and on to Epicureanism, Stoicism, and Skepticism, *Ancient Philosophy* traces the important connections between these periods and individuals without losing sight of the novelties and dynamics unique to each.

The coverage of Plato and Aristotle also has been expanded. It now includes, for example, updated coverage of Plato's allegories of the cave and the divided line and the metaphor of the sun as well as features of Plato's epistemology. Shields also adds new discussion on Aristotle's theory of virtue and his approach to the Socratic problem of akrasia, or weakness of will.

In terms of its structure, *Ancient Philosophy* is presented so that each philosophical position receives: (1) a brief introduction, (2) a sympathetic review of its principal motivations and primary supporting arguments, and (3) a short assessment, inviting readers to evaluate its plausibility. The result is a book that brings the ancient arguments to life, making the introduction truly contemporary. It will serve as both a first stop and a well visited resource for any student of the subject.

Ancient Philosophy offers a vivid picture of the ideas that flourished at philosophy's long birth and considers their relevance, both to the historical development of the Western philosophical tradition, and to philosophy today.

Christopher Shields is Tutor and Fellow of Lady Margaret Hall and Professor of Classical Philosophy in the University of Oxford. He is the author of *Order in Multiplicity: Homonymy in the Philosophy of Aristotle* (1999), *Classical Philosophy: A Contemporary Introduction* (Routledge: 2003), *Aristotle* (Routledge: 2007), and, with Robert Pasnau, *The Philosophy of Thomas Aquinas* (2003). He is the editor of *The Blackwell Guide to Ancient Philosophy* (2002) and *The Oxford Handbook of Aristotle* (2012). Forthcoming is *Aristotle's De Anima, Translated with Introduction and Commentary*.

Routledge Contemporary Introductions to Philosophy

Series editor: *Paul K. Moser*, Loyola University of Chicago

This innovative, well-structured series is for students who have already done an introductory course in philosophy. Each book introduces a core general subject in contemporary philosophy and offers students an accessible but substantial transition from introductory to higher-level college work in that subject. The series is accessible to non-specialists and each book clearly motivates and expounds the problems and positions introduced. An orientating chapter briefly introduces its topic and reminds readers of any crucial material they need to have retained from a typical introductory course. Considerable attention is given to explaining the central philosophical problems of a subject and the main competing solutions and arguments for those solutions. The primary aim is to educate students in the main problems, positions and arguments of contemporary philosophy rather than to convince students of a single position.

Epistemology
3rd Edition
Robert Audi

Ethics
2nd Edition
Harry Gensler

Philosophy of Science
3rd Edition
Alex Rosenberg

Philosophy of Language
2nd Edition
Willam G. Lycan

Metaphysics
3rd Edition
Michael J. Loux

Philosophy of Perception
William Fish

Philosophy of Mathematics
2nd Edition
James Robert Brown

Philosophy of Biology
Alex Rosenberg and Daniel W. McShea

Classical Modern Philosophy
Jeffrey Tlumak

Philosophy of Religion
Keith E. Yandell

Philosophy of Art
Noël Carroll

Philosophy of Psychology
José Luis Bermudez

Social and Political Philosophy
John Christman

Continental Philosophy
Andrew Cutrofello

Ancient Philosophy
Christopher Shields

Philosophy of Literature (forthcoming)
John Gibson

Free Will (forthcoming)
Michael McKenna

Philosophy of Mind (forthcoming)
3rd Edition
John Heil

Philosophy of Economics
(forthcoming)
Julian Reiss

Metaethics (forthcoming)
Mark van Roojen

Ancient Philosophy
A contemporary introduction
2nd edition

Christopher Shields

 Routledge
Taylor & Francis Group

NEW YORK AND LONDON

Second edition published 2012
by Routledge
711 Third Avenue, New York, NY 10017

Simultaneously published in the UK
by Routledge
2 Park Square, Milton Park, Abingdon, Oxon OX14 4RN

Routledge is an imprint of the Taylor & Francis Group, an informa business

© 2012 Taylor & Francis

First edition published by Routledge 2003

Library of Congress Cataloging in Publication Data
Shields, Christopher John.
 Ancient philosophy: a contemporary introduction/
 Christopher Shields.—2nd ed.
 p. cm.—(Routledge contemporary introductions to philosophy)
 Rev. ed. of: Classical philosophy.
 Includes bibliographical references (p.) and index.
 1. Philosophy, Ancient. I. Shields, Christopher John.
 Classical philosophy. II. Title.
 B171.S52 2011
 180—dc23   2011025321

ISBN: 978-0-415-89659-7 (hbk)
ISBN: 978-0-415-89660-3 (pbk)
ISBN: 978-0-203-80255-7 (ebk)

Typeset in Garamond Three and Gill Sans
by Florence Production Ltd, Stoodleigh, Devon

Printed and bound in Canada

Dedicated with gratitude to Fred D. Miller, Jr.

Contents

Preface		ix
Acknowledgments		xiii
1	**Philosophy before Socrates**	**1**
1.1	Thales and the earliest natural philosophers	1
1.2	Xenophanes	6
1.3	Heracleitus	9
1.4	Parmenides and Zeno	13
1.5	Democritus and fifth-century atomism	21
1.6	Protagoras and the Sophistic Movement	25
1.7	Challenges from the Presocratics and Sophists	30
	Notes	31
	Suggestions for additional readings	32
2	**Socrates**	**35**
2.1	The Socratic elenchus	37
2.2	The failures of Meno and Euthyphro	39
2.3	Socratic ignorance and Socratic irony	46
2.4	Socratic conviction and the Socratic paradoxes	47
2.5	Socrates on trial and in prison	53
2.6	Conclusions	58
	Notes	58
	Suggestions for additional readings	60
3	**Plato**	**61**
3.1	From Socrates to Plato	62
3.2	Meno's paradox of inquiry; Plato's response	63
3.3	Two functions of Plato's theory of Forms	68
3.4	Plato's rejection of relativism	69
3.5	Three arguments for Forms	72
3.6	Plato's general characterizations of Forms	85
3.7	Platonic analysis: a case study	88
3.8	The special role of the Form of the Good	97
3.9	Plato's line and cave: our epistemic prospects	100
3.10	Problems about Forms	106
3.11	Conclusions	111

| | Notes | 112 |
| | Suggestions for additional readings | 116 |

4   Aristotle   **117**

4.1	From Plato to Aristotle	118
4.2	Aristotle's introduction of category theory	119
4.3	The four causes introduced	124
4.4	The four causes defended	127
4.5	The four causes applied: soul and body	140
4.6	The four causes applied: happiness and the human function	144
4.7	The virtues of a happy person	150
4.8	Aristotle's treatment of a Socratic paradox: *akrasia*	154
4.9	Aristotle on philosophical analysis: homonymy	156
4.10	Conclusions	163
	Notes	164
	Suggestions for additional readings	165

5   Hellenistic philosophy   **167**

5.1	The Hellenistic period	167
5.2	The Epicureans	171
5.3	The Stoics	182
5.4	Skepticism	207
5.5	Conclusions	228
	Notes	229
	Suggestions for additional readings	232

| *Suggestions for further reading* | 234 |
| *Index* | 243 |

Preface

Philosophy began in the West in a specific time and place: in Greece, along the coast of Asia Minor, during the late sixth century BC. Though advancing with only small steps forward at first, philosophy flowered quickly, in some ways astonishingly quickly, during and after the life of Socrates (469–399 BC). Somehow this one man seems almost single-handedly to have transformed a loosely knit set of far-reaching questions about the character and direction of human existence into a discipline with its own distinctive aims and methods.

Now, philosophy does not own the questions it pursues; it is, on the contrary, easy to find the great tragedians and epic poets of Greece assaying many of the subjects pursued by philosophers. Still, it seems that Socrates in a single-minded and determined sort of way introduced a distinctively philosophical approach, *an analytical approach*, to questions of concern to every reflective person – questions about the nature of human happiness, about the best form of life attainable by human beings, about the relationship between virtue and self-interest, and about the ultimate value of human life. In adopting an analytical approach to these matters, Socrates almost invariably approached them by posing disarmingly simple questions about the *natures* of virtue or of happiness, of self-interest, or of the human good. We all, we think, know what happiness is; it is, after all, what we all seek. Then someone like Socrates asks: *What is happiness?* Unwilling to accept facile responses, Socrates then demands unassailable answers, a sort whose production requires both searing self-reflection and careful critical acumen. As any student of Socrates quickly learns, it turns out that those who regard the answer to this sort of question as simple or straightforward will have trouble defending themselves when subjected to sustained scrutiny. To this extent, anyone wishing to reflect upon the best sort of life available to human beings will benefit from an encounter with Socrates or someone schooled by him.

Scope and aims

This book aims to provide an encounter of this sort. It is not intended as a substitute for reading the works of the philosophers it discusses. To be sure, there is no substitute for reading the writings of the ancient philosophers; so, it is hoped only that this work will help illuminate some of their enduring contributions by bringing them into clear focus for a contemporary audience. It nowhere assumes that the philosophical contributions made by thinkers of this period have been superannuated or discredited by developments in the discipline's subsequent history. Nor does it strive to repackage the philosophical positions of its authors in modern garb so as to make them palatable to a contemporary sentiment. Instead, it tries to present seminal developments in the thought of the period in a sympathetic though non-slavish way, in terms accessible to someone with little or no formal training in philosophy. Moreover, it proceeds upon the conviction that what is philosophically defensible in the views of the authors it treats should be stated and defended as such; by the same token, it does its subjects the service of criticizing their theories where they have been shown false or have been inadequately defended. Throughout, the goal is, simply, to understand and assess their views as live philosophical points of view, rather than as exhibits in a museum of intellectual history.

This book's subjects include not only Socrates, though he is certainly a pivotal figure in the story it tells: it begins before Socrates with the earliest philosophers, the natural philosophers, called the *Presocratics* by scholars, a term which itself already reflects a judgment about the towering importance of Socrates in the development of classical philosophy. It also considers the contributions and challenges set by a loose collection of intellectuals and teachers, the *Sophists*, whose views were of great concern to Socrates, and especially to his immediate successor, Plato (429–347 BC). Plato receives extended treatment, because he is the first philosopher in the West to develop systematic positive theses regarding some central topics in the sub-disciplines of philosophy which came to be known as metaphysics and epistemology. His student and fellow researcher, Aristotle (384–322 BC), receives similar treatment. After studying some twenty years with Plato, Aristotle emerged, like Plato, as a towering figure in the entire history of philosophy. Where their views diverged, Plato and Aristotle have lent their names to orientations which endure today. Thus, for example, we call *ante rem* realists about universals – those who believe that there are necessarily existing abstract mind- and language-independent properties – *Platonists*. Other sorts of realists, *in rebus* realists – who maintain that properties exist only when instantiated – we call *Aristotelians*. To some extent, these labels may be at best only partly accurate, viewed, that is, from the standpoint of the actual views promulgated by Plato and Aristotle. One purpose of this book is precisely to uncover and evaluate the actual views held by the authors who have lent their names to these permanent intellectual factions.

Moving beyond the classical period of Socrates, Plato, and Aristotle, we find other philosophers who have lent their names to our present-day diction, but in ways that have crept more widely into popular discourse. In the Hellenistic period beginning after the death of Aristotle in 323 BC, three distinct movements or schools emerged onto the philosophical scene in Athens: the Epicureans, the Stoics, and the Skeptics. There was a tendency not so very long ago to regard these schools as inferior, as reflecting a serious decline in philosophical quality relative the undeniable achievements of the philosophers of the classical period. Over the last generation or so, however, such judgments have been sharply and rightly revised: renewed interest in the philosophers of the Hellenistic age has stimulated a wide-reaching reappraisal of their influence and value. Today it is much more widely appreciated that the Epicureans, Stoics, and Skeptics developed systems and advanced doctrines rivaling those of the classical philosophers, certainly at least to the point of offering consequential challenges to their points of view. This book closes with a first introduction to the Hellenistic philosophers who developed these systems and mounted these challenges. As we shall see, when today we speak of "epicureans" or "stoics," we are using words which derive in understandable ways from these Hellenistic movements, but not always in ways that accurately depict the actual beliefs of the original Epicureans and Stoics.

The treatment of ancient philosophy offered here has, of necessity, been highly selective. It sets aside many issues of critical importance, a lack, it is hoped, which will be remedied by students who upon reading this book will begin to read more widely in the relevant primary and secondary literatures. To this end, an annotated bibliography of recommended readings follows the text. At the end of each chapter there follows an abbreviated list to which students might wish to turn first. At the end of the volume, a more comprehensive bibliography is assembled. Students' treatments of ancient philosophy in addition to wishing further study will do well to consult this one. In that way, they will come to appreciate and – it is hoped – to enter into the lively scholarly controversies which surround the interpretation and evaluation of the ancient philosophers.

Intended audience and methods

Throughout, the text focuses on the *arguments of the philosophers*, while neglecting much else of value in their writing. Thus, for example, little is said of the literary or dramatic dimensions of Plato's prose. The approach adopted does not reflect the judgment that these features of his writings can be safely ignored while mining his works for their philosophical pay-dirt. On the contrary, in order to understand Plato's views, or the views of the other philosophers discussed here, it is imperative to attend to their own manners of presentation. Still, the discussion in the text for the most part presupposes resolutions to exegetical issues which it leaves unreproduced. In some cases, this is because there is wide scholarly consensus on points of interpretation; in other cases, the interpretations advanced are more controversial. In either case, though, this book will have served its purpose if it has helped students to enter into the writings of the ancient philosophers in order to understand and assess for themselves the central philosophical positions they advance.

In keeping with other volumes in the series in which it appears, this introduction presupposes only a little familiarity with philosophy, and also undertakes to define technical terms as they are introduced. It considers issues of central importance to the philosophers it investigates, in the hope that a mastery of the issues discussed will equip students to range further first, and most importantly, into the principal writings of the ancient philosophers, and, second, to begin working through the professional secondary literature which investigates and assesses their lasting philosophical contributions. To this extent, the work takes seriously the charge of presenting the philosophy of the ancient philosophers to a contemporary audience – an audience which in all likelihood will find reading Plato or Aristotle or the Stoics for the first time somewhat alien, if also in other ways engaging and challenging. In the end, this work accepts as something more than platitudinous the contention that the ancient philosophers have a fair bit to teach a contemporary audience: they present views, and arguments for those views, which demand careful consideration not because they are the views of great philosophers now dead, but because they are views which, if false, are nonetheless instructive, or views which, often enough, are plausibly regarded as true and so as worthy of adoption even today. At any rate, such is the challenge this book seeks to lay before its contemporary audience.

Acknowledgments

This book is reworking and substantial expansion of *Classical Philosophy: A Contemporary Introduction* (Routledge, 2003), most of which forms a proper part of its successor. In producing both works, I benefited enormously from the many students who investigated the philosophers discussed in them with me. Precursors of several sections have been presented to students at the University of Colorado at Boulder, Stanford University, Yale University, and the University of Oxford. Students at all these institutions provided me valuable feedback and assistance, often simply by demanding clarity and forthrightness in our discussions. Their reactions and observations have improved the final version immensely.

Additionally, two sets of anonymous referees for Routledge have offered valuable guidance. Not only have they saved me from more substantive gaffes than I care to contemplate, but they have provided judicious pedagogical advice as well.

Otherwise, I am deeply indebted to the many friends and colleagues who have influenced my thinking about how best to present the topics covered in this work. Doubtless there are many more, but I can detect the salutary effects left by encounters with Thomas Ainsworth, Dominic Bailey, Jeremy Buxbaum, Paolo Crivelli, Richard Cameron, Jane Day, Gail Fine, John Fisher, Cissie Fu, Richard Geenen, John Gibert, Terence Irwin, Rusty Jones, Gareth Matthews, Phillip Mitsis, Brian Noone, Graham Oddie, Robert Pasnau, Dave Robb, Stefan Sienkiewicz, William Simpson, Rachel Singpurwalla, Nicholas Smith, Nathanael Stein, Paul Studtmann, and Ellen Wagner.

I am singularly grateful to Colin Shields for taking the time to read and comment upon the material on Hellenistic philosophy, even while he was busy revising for his final examinations at the University of Cambridge.

As I reflect on the process leading to the production of this book, I am also aware of a longer-term debt, to one with the status of a *sine qua non*, my first teacher of Greek philosophy, who is also indeed my first teacher of philosophy, Fred D. Miller, Jr. I dedicate this book to him with an enduring and affectionate gratitude for the gift in life he has given me.

1 Philosophy before Socrates

1.1 Thales and the earliest natural philosophers

Early in the sixth century BC,[1] a man named Thales looked around at the world in which we live and decided that *everything is water*.[2] This man had eyes and all of the other senses belonging to a normal human being; there is no record of his having been deranged, diseased, or insane. Instead, he is regarded by an ancient tradition, one extending down to the present day, as the first philosopher.

What makes him the first philosopher is not his having a perverse predilection for saying things which are obviously false – though we are bound to regard his most famous dictum as just that. Rather, Thales stands at the head of a long tradition of investigators and speculators willing to make bold pronouncements about fundamental features of the universe which are not, and could not be, immediately accessible to sense experience or common sense. In some ways, then, he has a fair bit in common with scientists today who tell us that if we were to move very quickly in a straight line, we would, in due course, end up back where we began, only a bit younger than we would have been had we never made the journey. That is not only non-commonsensical: it is an assault upon common sense, something which seems at first blush, and in a strict sense of the term, *incredible*. We will come to believe it, if at all, only by being given compelling reasons which override our initial impulses to the contrary.

Any such reasons would take us beyond the immediate deliverances of the senses, would take us beyond the realm of common conception, would force us to conclude that the world is not as it initially seems. Such reasons would in general induce us to believe that the world has inner workings uncovered only by research and reflection, and that consequently the manifest image of the world needs to give way to a scientific image which corrects and overcomes our first, naïve conception of it. These are the sorts of reasons to which Thales must appeal if he wants to convince us that everything is water. It certainly does not seem to be the case that this is so. Why should we think otherwise?

Based upon some ancient testimony, it is plausible to assume that Thales' remarkable conjecture derives from two distinct sources, one broadly methodological and another more empirical in character. In the first instance, Thales evidently presumes a form of *material monism*: he thinks that the universe consists ultimately of some one stuff, that there is some one

underlying material from which everything derives and into which everything resolves. The two parts of this commitment, its *materialism* and its
monism, are fully distinct, but complementary.

In committing himself to a form of materialism, Thales rejects a picture
of the universe found in the Homeric poems, one which posits, in addition
to the natural world, a supernatural quadrant populated by beings who are
not subject to such laws as may govern the interactions of all natural bodies.
If all things are composed of matter, then it ought to be possible to explain
all there is to explain about the universe in terms of material bodies and
their law-governed interactions. This simple thought already stands in sharp
contrast to a world supposed to be populated by supernatural immaterial
beings whose actions may be capricious or deliberate, rational or irrational,
welcome or unwelcome, but which as a matter of basic principle cannot be
explicated in terms of the forms of regularity found in the natural world. In
Thales' naturalistic universe, it ought to be possible to uncover patterns and
laws and to use such laws as the basis for stable predictions about the direction the universe is to take; to uncover causes and to use that knowledge to
find cures for illnesses or to develop strategies for optimizing our well-
being; and, less practically, to find broad-based explanations to fundamental
questions which crop up in every organized society. Such questions persist:
Where did the universe come from? What, ultimately, is its basic stuff?

It is perhaps these explanatory features of Thales' materialism which gave
rise to some anecdotes about him told and repeated in antiquity. Because he
understood a fair bit about cosmology, it was said, he was able to predict an
eclipse of the sun which occurred on 28 March 585, a power which would
have distinguished him from just about all of his fellow citizens. For the
same reason, he was able to predict long-term weather patterns, knowledge
which he turned to profit by renting all of the olive presses early one year
when he realized, on the basis of his meteorological predictions, that a
bumper crop was to be expected. Aristotle later observed that this maneuver
demonstrated that philosophers are capable of making money, even though
they are disinclined to spend their time on such pedestrian pursuits (*Politics*
1259a9–18).[3] However that may be, the anecdote also has a methodological
moral not lost on Thales' successors: naturalistic explanations given in terms
of the lawful regularities among material bodies can be explanatorily potent
by delivering predictive powers unavailable to supernaturalistic explanations
given in terms of the whims of the gods and their occasional predilections
and fickle caprices.

If a materialist explanation carries predictive power in its wake, this must
be due to its having uncovered some regularity in nature which obtains
between the features of material systems. If so, it is easy to infer that predictive
power results from our discovering laws of nature, that rational and empirical
inquiry leads to the detection of laws which capture basic causal and
explanatory features of the universe not written directly upon its surface for
all to read. If we learn that the presence of streptococcus causes infection, and

that antibacterial agents neutralize streptococcus, then we can also predict that infections can be cured by administering appropriate antibiotics, because we have isolated a law which was earlier obscure to us. The mere presumption of Thales that such regularities or laws could be uncovered and enshrined in material explanations already puts him in the methodological camp of natural scientists and distances him from those who would explain strep throat and its attendant pain as something visited upon unworthy mortals by vindictive gods bent upon punishing them for their misdeeds.

In a second way, too, Thales' materialism should strike a methodological chord in the scientifically inclined: he is a *monist*, someone who supposes that, ultimately, the universe is composed of some one stuff. This idea does not seem itself to be immediately or obviously empirical in character. Still, it is a deep impulse driving a fair amount of empirical inquiry: physical scientists have often assumed that there is some one ultimate building block, some basic and irreducible stuff, atoms or molecules or strings or super-strings, in terms of which everything is ultimately to be explained. What is the basis for such an assumption?

Although their motivations have been varied, many scientists hold in common a commitment to *parsimony* in scientific explanation. They seek to reduce the broadest and most diverse range of cases to the smallest number of explanatory laws and postulates. It is a fact that men and women of a variety of ages, races, nationalities, political affiliations, and social proclivities contract lung cancer. Scientists try to look beyond the superficial to determine what range of carcinogenic agents are at play in an effort to isolate the causes and explanations of their common condition. As a methodological precept, parsimony in fact serves us well in such cases. If we then extrapolate upon our successes, we can come to expect naturalistic explanation as such to be parsimonious, and even to use parsimony as a criterion for choosing between competing theories which are otherwise explanatorily equivalent. Extrapolating still further and more precariously, we may also come to hope or expect that the final and complete account of the natural universe will be parsimonious in the extreme, postulating ultimately some one basic stuff in terms of which all else is to be explained.

Thales thought this stuff was water. He holds in common, then, with a great many materialist researchers a commitment to there being a single ultimate explanatory factor, one whose discovery could unify all explanations given at higher levels. But why water? We do not know, though it is clear enough that water has at least some of the features we expect the basic stuff to have — that is, if there is a basic stuff. After all, water is *plastic*, in the sense that it can move rapidly between various states (liquid, solid, gas). Moreover, in its various states, it is hardly clear on the basis of gross sense perception that we even have a single stuff: water vapor or steam hardly appears to be the same stuff as ice. So, water at least has the ability to take on different forms, an ability necessary to the basic stuff, whatever it might be. Further, water is implicated in all living systems in one way or another.

Virtually all living things require water for life. Moreover, it turns out that many human systems, including human beings, are in fact composed largely of water. While this discovery does not exactly vindicate Thales' material monism, it does tend to validate his instincts with respect to water. Given that we need to explain the existence and activities of living systems in explaining the natural world, we ought to look for something common to them all. Here too water seems at least a reasonable first guess.

Now, we do not think that water is the basic stuff; nor do we suppose Thales ultimately justified his commitment to material monism. We do, however, find ourselves in various ways like him in our own methods of explanation and prediction. We are, as he is, prepared to tolerate a rejection of sense perception and common sense where scientific systematicity requires us to do so; we are, again like him, disposed to seek out projectible explanations given in terms of lawlike correlations between otherwise disparate material phenomena; and we are, finally, inclined toward parsimony in both local and global theorizing, just as he is. Although we do not think the basic stuff is water, at least a fair number of us hold out hope that Thales was after all right in form if not in content. We hope that his commitment to materialist monism will after all be shown to be justified, if not by water, then by some other stuff whose exact nature continues to elude us. And even if we are skeptical that there will come a time when we identify the basic building block of the universe, we will nevertheless continue to join with Thales, without apology, in seeking parsimonious and law-governed explanations on a more local scale. As the first philosopher, a natural philosopher, Thales set us on a course from whose essential trajectory we have not really deviated.

Thales was joined in his earliest investigations by other natural philosophers, some of whom were also materialist monists. One of the most striking of these was Anaximander, who was regarded in antiquity as Thales' principal successor in naturalistic investigation. Like Thales, he was credited with investigating a range of natural phenomena, including eclipses and meteorological events, but was understood to have taken his inquiries further, into such questions as the origin of life. His form of monism is noteworthy for its willingness to identify as the basic stuff not one of the familiar elements, like water or air, but a postulated stuff altogether lacking in essential intrinsic features, called the *apeiron*: equally, the *boundless*, the *indefinite*, and the *eternal*. This stuff was, he thought, neither wet nor dry, nor any color in itself at all. Anaximander's basic stuff is so utterly lacking in intrinsic characteristics that it at least initially defies comprehension.

Anaximander's reasons for positing such a primordial stuff may have been in some ways akin to Thales' motivations for promoting water but in some other ways a bit more subtle. In fact, it is reasonably easy to see different sorts of reasons why Anaximander may have postulated a stuff more basic than any of the traditional four elements (earth, air, and fire, in addition to water), reasons which correspond directly to the three meanings of *apeiron* already identified. In the first instance, however malleable water may be, it has some readily identifiable intrinsic characteristics which seem to make it unsuited as a basic stuff for some of the things we observe. It is difficult, for example, to think of water as the basic stuff of fire. By contrast, nothing prevents something *boundless* and *indefinite* from playing such a role. Indeed, whatever the basic stuff may be, if there is a basic stuff, it had better be able to underlie the contrasting features so easily observable at the macroscopic level: things are wet and dry, hard and soft, black and white, hot and cold, liquid and solid and gaseous. Something which could constitute all such things is unlikely to be positively characterized in any such terms itself.

In another way, Anaximander might well have assumed that any basic stuff would need to be *infinite* in two distinct dimensions: in space and in time. First is the obvious thought that there has to be enough of it to go around at any one given time. If we suppose that the universe goes on indefinitely, then so too must the stuff of which it is made. Along another dimension, if our structured world originated in time out of the *apeiron*, as Anaximander supposes it did, then the *apeiron* itself must have preceded our world. It must, it seems, extend infinitely backward in time; and, on the common assumption that whatever is without a beginning is also without an end, it is easy to see why the *apeiron* would also be infinite in time. So, in both ways Anaximander's *apeiron* would have been infinite.

If these speculations are correct, we find in Anaximander, as in Thales, a willingness to engage in a form of *a priori* reasoning even while conducting natural philosophy.[4] Some data appears to him as manifest; some methodological precepts emerge as attractive; and some explanatory postulates intended to account for the manifest data are advanced in line with those precepts. It strikes him, that is, that something or other underlies the change we observe at the macroscopic level. Various precepts, including a commitment to parsimony and explanatory simplicity, appeal to him as attractive. That such postulates are *in principle* unobservable hardly troubles him: if we need such a stuff to explain what needs to be explained, then that is reason enough to accept its existence as rationally grounded. His mode of inference here is hardly alien or facile. On the contrary, however much empirical confirmation we rightly demand, we arrive at many of our first scientific hunches in much the way Anaximander and Thales arrived at theirs, by relying on an admixture of the *a priori* and the *a posteriori*. (It is often reported that Crick and Watson were governed in their search for the DNA molecule in part by the conviction that it would turn out to be something beautiful, as in fact the double helix is. Whether apocryphal or not, the report captures the thought that not every methodological precept in natural science is strictly empirical.)

This is said not to absolve the earliest natural philosophers of their obvious mistakes and missteps. Rather, it is to highlight a feature of their activity which is genuinely philosophical in its orientation. If we regard their forms of explanation against the backdrop of another kind of explanation satisfying to many, one given in terms of the whims and proclivities of the unpredictable gods (for example, that spring returns to us each year because Persephone is released from the underworld for an annual respite of six months), we understand that an exciting change had taken place with the arrival of Thales and the other early natural philosophers.

1.2   Xenophanes

If the materialist monists favor naturalistic over divine and mythological explanations, then they also implicitly favor one form of evidence over another. Broadly speaking, they prefer both the evidence of their own senses and the power of their own minds over putative divine revelation. Whereas it had been customary for Homer and Hesiod to call upon muses for inspiration which might yield cosmogonic and cosmological data inaccessible to most mortals, Thales and his fellow travelers evidently eschewed recourse to such sources of information. Still, at least in the surviving sources, they stopped short of criticizing Homer and Hesiod by name.

Things are different with Xenophanes (c. 570–478), an irreverent itinerant poet and philosopher who made explicit what was left implicit in the work of the earliest naturalist philosophers: he mocks the forms of explanation offered in Homer and Hesiod and openly subjects those who rely upon them to caustic ridicule. He points out, for example, that people habitually make their gods in their own glorified images. The Thracians think that their gods are blue-eyed and red-haired, as they themselves are; the Ethiopians, by contrast, make their gods dark-skinned with broad noses, as, to be sure, they themselves are.[5] Indeed, quips Xenophanes, if horses and oxen could draw, they would no doubt draw gods after their own self-conceptions, and those gods would, unsurprisingly, look like horses and oxen.[6] What is worse, the Greeks do not even idealize their gods: Homer attributes to the gods conduct which is disgraceful even to humans: theft, adultery, and deceit.[7] In short, observes Xenophanes, humans are remorselessly anthropomorphic when it comes to their gods. Surely there is a lesson in this.

There is, thinks Xenophanes; but the lesson is not the simple one which these observations might be taken to commend. Xenophanes does not infer that, since humans evidently conceive their gods in their own likeness, theism is a silly human invention. On the contrary, like the naturalists before him, Xenophanes promotes a form of theism, evidently a form of monotheism, according to which there is one god who seems to be pure mind, a being who thinks, sees and hears, and who does only what is fitting.[8] In a certain way, then, Xenophanes shares the tendency of the earliest natural philosophers to look behind the manifest image in order to uncover what stands behind what is given in sense perception and common sense.

Still, he departs from them in one highly significant way. Implicit in the rejection of mythological explanation is a commitment to a superior form of explanation, one resting not on divine revelation, but on the plain data of our senses and our own reasoning processes. Implicit in this rejection, then, is a claim that non-mythological forms of evidence are not only available but preferable. Until Xenophanes, no one, at least in terms of our surviving evidence, took the next step, a step deeply rooted in the philosophical temperament, of turning such critical attention homeward. Xenophanes asks a simple, far-ranging question absent in his predecessors but which will rightly trouble philosophers for generations upon generations following him: how do we know? This simple question carries in its wake a series of more detailed questions which must be addressed before we can offer an adequate answer. What sources of evidence should we trust? Should we privilege the *a priori* over the *a posteriori*? Vice versa? Is either form of justification ultimately defensible?

Strikingly, Xenophanes does not simply raise an open-ended question about the sources of our claims to knowledge. Instead, he packages his question within a skeptical challenge, general in scope and rooted in an entirely plausible conception of human knowledge. He invites us to reject Homer and Hesiod and to join him in believing that there is one god. Even if we see that he is right when he complains that Homer portrays the gods as engaging in shameful conduct, that he is right about individual cultures when he observes that each manufactures its gods to suit its own self-conception and that in so acting humans betray an arbitrary subjectivity in conceptualizing even the most central features of their worlds, why should we then suppose that Xenophanes is any better off? Why, that is, should we suppose that Xenophanes has alighted upon a more secure vantage point from which to think about such matters?

One of the most arresting features of Xenophanes' philosophy is that he himself wants to caution us from accepting his own pronouncements too readily. He recommends that his own views not be taken as true, but rather as somehow truthlike.[9] This he does for perfectly principled reasons. How, after all, are mythological explanations lacking? The simple reason is easy enough to state: there is no sure evidence to support their hypotheses, however satisfying they may seem to some. So, even if such beliefs turned out to be true, we could not say that the mythologists had knowledge; for knowledge requires more than true belief. In addition to true belief, Xenophanes notes, a knower must have evidence or justification.[10] So much is surely correct. If a detective believed that the butler committed the murder, and it was indeed true that the butler committed the murder, we would be hard pressed to ascribe knowledge to her if we learned that she came to believe that the butler did it because she takes herself to be in para-normal contact with the spirit of the deceased. Instead we would say that though she believed what was true, the detective got it right by accident. She had a true belief; but she did not know. The detective who had the belief based upon conclusive forensic evidence, by contrast, had not only true belief, but knowledge.

What, though, is conclusive evidence in the domain where Xenophanes dwells? What tells us, at the highest level, that rationalistic or naturalistic explanations provide secure justification for our beliefs about the gods, about cosmology, or about the nature of knowledge itself? Having raised his skeptical challenge, Xenophanes retreats. Even if we land upon the truth, he says, we will not know that we have done so; belief, he concludes, reigns over all human inquiry.[11] Still, in raising so clear and general a skeptical challenge, Xenophanes instituted the field of epistemology, and consequently set a course of inquiry for many subsequent philosophers. This inquiry may for our purposes be divided into two sub-inquiries: (1) epistemology narrowly construed, which analyses the nature of knowledge itself in its most general features (Xenophanes, again, plausibly understood knowledge to be justified true belief); and (2) epistemological features of claims to knowledge in various disciplines, including inquiries into the types and standards of justification (a topic which commanded the interest of both Plato and Aristotle).

That said, it must also be acknowledged that Xenophanes gives us little reason to adopt a strident or sweeping skepticism. In the first instance, he gives us little reason to suppose that justification is as a matter of general principle unavailable to human beings. The one grounding for skepticism plausibly attributed to Xenophanes hearkens back to his mockery of popular religious belief. It is easy to see that different peoples project themselves – their hopes and fears, their fretful desires, and their self-conceptions – into their deepest convictions; and it is easy to conclude that in so doing they rely upon a transparent and arbitrary subjectivity. Still, why suppose that awareness of this tendency cannot itself prove a corrective? And why suppose that there is anything arbitrary or subjective in our claims to knowledge in some other domains, such as natural science or mathematics? It is hard to appreciate why I should suppose that my belief that $2+2 = 4$ is in any way arbitrary or subjective. On the contrary, it appears utterly necessary. In general, where is there an entrance for the arbitrary and subjective into mathematical or logical knowledge, or into the *a priori* more broadly conceived? Why, then, should we be moved by Xenophanes' skepticism? So far, at least in this area of inquiry, Xenophanes seems to have nothing very forceful to say.

Even so, his skeptical stance is an important development in Presocratic philosophy. If we are confident that we escape the blinds of an arbitrary subjectivity in, say, mathematics or chemistry, there is little reason to suppose immediately that we are equally free in politics, morality, or aesthetics. At the same time, we evidently want to be able to say, as Socrates will say, that there are some things which we know to be wrong, where we do not suppose that our beliefs about their wrongness are simply arbitrary. Nor do we think that every belief about morality is a belief whose justification must forever elude us.

Here, though, a cautionary note is in order. Although concerned with the foundations of our claims to knowledge, Xenophanes nowhere espouses any form of relativism. That is, he never claims that such truth as there may be depends in any way upon the attitudes or beliefs of individuals or groups. Instead, he assails the possibility of our *justifying* our claims to know what is in fact true. In proceeding in this way, he reveals himself to be a skeptic and never a relativist. On the contrary, insofar as he supposes there is a truth to be known, he distances himself from relativism, which will want to challenge precisely this commitment.

Xenophanes has issued a simple challenge with long-ranging repercussions. If knowledge is true belief plus some form of justification, then whenever I claim to know something, I also claim to be justified in believing what is true. So, if I claim to know that naturalistic explanation is superior to mythological explanation, I must regard myself at least in principle as capable of producing an adequate justification for this belief. Actually producing justification for these sorts of high-level claims proves alarmingly difficult; and to the extent one cannot produce the requisite justification, it is appropriate to feel chastened by Xenophanes' skeptical challenge.

However potent they may be, though, Xenophanes' skeptical worries find no explicit argumentative backing in his surviving fragments. Instead, it is necessary to supply arguments suggested by his remarks concerning our perspectival limitations. In one sense, his main form of support, that humans are constrained by an arbitrary subjectivity in offering a wide range of their judgments, is a way of saying that any evidence we might have concerning, e.g., belief in the gods, is inescapably tainted. If we seek objective justification for our claims but find ourselves at every turn bumping up against the limits of our own perspectives, then we may be forced to acknowledge that such evidence as we may take ourselves to find has already been polluted by our own inescapable limitations.

This sort of motivation for skeptical doubt is highly general and successful only to the degree that our judgments in a given domain are plausibly regarded as ineliminably bound by perspective. Xenophanes does nothing, however, to show that we are *necessarily* bound in this way. Consequently, Xenophanes' worries have only the twin effects: (1) of encouraging us to be cautious about the soundness of our individual appeals to bits of evidence when offering any of a number of specific judgments; and, more generally, (2) of goading us to reflect in an abstract way upon the acceptable varieties of evidence as such.

1.3 Heracleitus

The enigmatic and oracular figure Heracleitus (born *c.* 540) provides some additional reason for supposing that the sorts of perspectival limitations invoked by Xenophanes really are insurmountable. Although not a skeptic,

Heracleitus draws attention to the epistemological weaknesses of others. He says, for example, "the knowledge of the most famous persons, which they guard, is but opinion."[12] These famous people include Homer, the most revered of the Greek poets, whom he criticizes by name on more than one occasion, and Hesiod, another canonical source of comfortable mythology, whom he also derides.[13] People go wrong, no doubt, because they do not always appreciate that appearances are not always reality, since obscure connections are superior to manifest ones,[14] but cannot be ascertained without effort. He agrees, then, with the Milesians that the manifest image of the world can be misleading. As he says, simply, "Nature loves to hide."[15]

Its hiding takes on a special significance for Heracleitus, because he thinks that our approach to the natural world is conditioned by the perspectives and preferences we bring to it. What is more, even if we become aware that we are bound by our perspectives and preferences, this by itself will do little to free us of them. As he notes, asses prefer garbage to gold, pigs like mud more than water, and birds clean themselves with ash, something which humans find filthy.[16] If I am an ass, then I prefer garbage to gold for the perfectly good reason that I can eat garbage but not gold. This will not change for me if, contrary to possibility, I come to be aware that humans prize gold for its luster. In general, how I view and value the world is at least in part a function of who and what I am. If I seek to transcend my subjective self to attain objective knowledge, I am bound to fail, because I cannot become something I am not merely by willing that this be so.

Indeed, as I view the world, suggests Heracleitus, I can appreciate that I am radically cut off from it, in two related ways. In his most famous pronouncement, Heracleitus insists that it is not possible to step into the same river twice.[17] In light of this sort of claim, Heracleitus became known as the philosopher of flux; and for this he exerted an enormous influence on some of his successors, most notably Plato.[18] His idea seems to have been that the material world is forever changing in time. When I bathe in a river today, I enter a river which has renewed itself since yesterday, so that I am not in fact bathing in the same river that I bathed in yesterday. It is new today and will be new again tomorrow. The river is a synecdoche for the natural world as a whole: it flows. Before we can familiarize ourselves with the material world, it has changed and changed yet again.

The significance of Heracleitus' conception of flux can best be appreciated by understanding how it was understood in antiquity to apply to more than rivers. Plato connects Heracleitus with a comic playwright, Epicharmus, who offered an amusing parody of a then current philosophical puzzle, Heracleitean in character.[19] The title of his comedy is unknown, as are the names of its main characters. In it, Alpha approaches Beta, asking for payment of his portion of a debt owed. Beta, out of funds, responds by resorting to a cagey dodge: "If you had an odd number of pebbles – or for that matter an even one – and then chose to add or subtract a pebble, do you think you would have the same number?" "No," says Alpha. Or again, "If you had a measure of one cubit and chose to add or cut off some length of it, that measure would no longer exist, would it?" "No," allows Alpha. Beta then drives home the moral: "Well now, think of a human in the same way: one human is growing and another is diminishing. All are constantly in the process of change. But what by its nature changes and never stays put must already be different from what it changed from. You and I are different from who we were yesterday, and by the same argument will be different again tomorrow." The result is then clear: Beta is not the same man as the debtor. Sadly, that debtor seems to have perished, leaving Alpha no way to collect what is owed him. Alpha, though, is a quick learner. In view of Beta's reasoning, Alpha can and does, in his exasperation, strike Beta. Beta protests. Alpha is now at liberty to feed Beta some of his own medicine. "Why are you angry with *me*?" he can ask. "As someone nearby just demonstrated, it was not I who hit you, not I at all, but someone else altogether."[20]

This passage contains a spoof of what later came to be known as the *growing argument* (GA), which was much in play in the interscholastic dialectic of the Stoics and the Academics in the Hellenistic period. It can be represented quite simply:

1   If we add (or subtract) one pebble from a pile of pebbles, the resulting pile of pebbles is not identical to the original pile.
2   A human being is like a pile of pebbles.
3   So, when a human being loses or gains a particle, the resulting human being is not identical to the original.

Obviously, many will object to (GA-2), though it is not easy to specify precisely the relevant difference. More to the point, it is not easy to see why a Heracleitean is wrong to compare a human being to a river: both sustain continual material replenishment, so much so that in time the particles flow through a human being the way molecules of water flow through a river until they have been completely replaced and the process has begun again. Both are in flux.

Heracleitus does not call attention only to this form of flux, *diachronic flux*, which is change through time, but also to a comparatively attenuated notion of flux, *synchronic flux*, which is, so to speak, change at a time, relative to a context of comparison. Although at first a bit difficult to discern, Heracleitus' second notion of flux is both more interesting and more important for the subsequent development of classical philosophy than is the comparatively straightforward notion of diachronic flux. He says, for example, that "the road up and down is one and the same."[21] Similarly, he contends, sea water is both drinkable and not drinkable – drinkable to fish but destructive to humans.[22] Again, the wisest human appears no wiser than an ape in comparison with a god. So, humans are both wise and not wise, depending upon the point of comparison.[23] This notion of synchronic flux sounds peculiar if it is thought to be a kind of change, since change is normally thought to require the passage of time. Heracleitus supposes that it is nonetheless a kind of change, but a sort of change which results from a shifting perspective rather than the flow of time. This, though, is the key to understanding his conception of its importance. We might characterize a forty-pound sack of potatoes as heavy or light, depending upon who is doing the lifting. It is neither, so to speak, absolutely light or absolutely heavy. Its being light or heavy is determined by the faculties brought to bear upon it. What holds for strength holds for perception and thought as well: what we see and think is partly determined by the perspectival framework we bring to the situation.

If that is so, then Heracleitus has a way of moving beyond Xenophanes, by showing not merely that our perspective tends to infect the way we experience the world but also that we are *necessarily* perspectivally bound. The facts of flux, both diachronic and synchronic, show that none of us can adopt a god's-eye perspective on the world. Indeed, perhaps not even a god could adopt a god's-eye perspective, suggests Heracleitus, since that would be a perspectiveless perspective, a view which is not a view.

Still, importantly, Heracleitus does not exploit the facts of flux to motivate skepticism. Instead, he wants to show that our senses, when properly interpreted, may help us orient ourselves towards the regularities in nature. He does insist that those with "barbarian souls" have bad witnesses in their eyes and ears.[24] This leaves the impression that those without such souls do not suffer under this deficiency, and so may come to know after all.

This impression is confirmed by Heracleitus' repeated injunction that humans should adhere to the *logos* – a multiply ambiguous word meaning, among other things, "word," "story," "account," and "structure."[25] This word will be familiar to some from the first sentence of the Gospel of St John, "In the beginning was the Word [the *logos*]," where the English rendering is intended to have much of the pregnant suggestiveness found in Heracleitus. In Heracleitus, at any rate, the *logos* is evidently meant to comprise all of these meanings and more. Minimally, though, Heracleitus wants to convey that there is an underlying *order* to the universe, and that by attending to his words, humans, with effort, can come to understand that "the *logos* holds always."[26] It is difficult, though, to attend to his words with an earnest appreciation when he insists that "the same thing is both living and dead, and waking and sleeping, and young and old, since these are transformed into those and those back again into these."[27] Perhaps he means only that all things form a unity, one discovered by investigation. Perhaps, then, this is why he says, in a different mood, "Listening not to me but to the *logos*, it is wise to agree that all things are one."[28] How literally we should take this claim is a matter of some dispute. As we shall see, a philosopher who followed Heracleitus intended that it be taken very literally, and very seriously indeed.

1.4   Parmenides and Zeno

Parmenides (*c.* 515–450) is like Xenophanes and Heracleitus in that he expects us to think hard about the cogency of our habitual sources of evidence; but he is unlike Xenophanes insofar as he never endorses any form of skeptical attitude with respect to our evidence. Some evidence, Parmenides supposes, is rubbish, and can be shown to be so. Other forms of evidence, he maintains, provide secure knowledge, utterly immune from skeptical doubt. He also distinguishes himself from Heracleitus, however, in the manner he sets out his contentions. He is not content merely to signify them with vexing, if intriguing, aphorisms. Instead, unlike his predecessors, Parmenides takes it upon himself to *argue* directly and self-consciously for his conclusions. Indeed, in a certain way, he aims to throw down a gauntlet of sorts. He presses direct arguments whose conclusions are effectively incredible, only to challenge those who would doubt him to point out their flaws. Absent such flaws, he expects his readers to join him in abandoning common sense not only in the piecemeal way found in the earliest materialist monists. Rather, and much more radically, Parmenides expects us to reject altogether, in even its most general features, the manifest image of the world delivered by sense perception and ingrained in common sense. He expects us as well to give up all claims to knowledge by experience, insisting that all knowledge is had by the resources of reason alone.

What he denies is this: that there is change of any sort; that entities come into and go out of existence; that there is plurality; that what exists ever had a beginning or will have an end; that we can ever mention or even think of what does not exist. What he affirms is this: it is.[29]

If we focus on just one of Parmenides' startling claims, that there is no change, we can come to appreciate both the radical nature of his thought and the surprisingly good reasons for the enormous influence he exercised on the philosophers who followed him.

If anything is manifest to sense experience, it is precisely that there is change. I see a crow fly; it changes position. I hear a symphony develop; it changes key. I smell the onions burn; they change from sweet to acrid. I taste some sour milk; my own sensations move from a neutral position to detecting something putrid. In all such cases, nothing could be more immediately obvious than that *something has changed*. Initially, at least, it hardly seems reasonable to demand that I provide evidence for such a belief.

Parmenides has little patience for such an attitude. He derides those who maintain these sorts of commonplace views as, well, common. In fact, Parmenides regards such views as effectively bovine: any human can learn, by using resources of pure reason, that not only *is* there no change, there *can be* no change. Change is impossible. Hence, if we think we perceive change, we must be systematically deluded. His view is roughly analogous to the attitude a parent might take toward a child who insists that she *sees* the sun moving around the earth. The parent knows that it will seem so to the child; but he will also know that the child is simply mistaken. If the child is as yet unable to learn the principles of planetary motion, then it will perhaps be best for the adult simply to patronize her until she is capable of mature understanding. If, by contrast, the parent encounters an otherwise normal adult who insists that the sun moves around the earth, or that the earth is flat, despite clear and patiently delivered evidence to the contrary, the parent might well deride that person as foolishly stubborn or imbecilic. Here too the attitude of the parent finds a counterpart in Parmenides: those mired in the manifest image of sense perception are befuddled and bedazed, wandering about the earth without the foggiest appreciation of how the world is and must be.

The world as it *must* be is incompatible with the world of sense perception, because whatever else we know *a posteriori*, we know that the world exhibits change and plurality. In effect, Parmenides means to reject *all* forms of *a posteriori* justification in favor of what can be known *a priori*. That is, if we say that some proposition *p* is known *a posteriori* if, and only if, its justification ultimately makes recourse to the data of sense perception, then we can easily appreciate that Parmenides simply means to deny that we have any such knowledge. Any knowledge we have is knowledge *a priori*.[30]

It is worth emphasizing that Parmenides is not at all skeptical about the possibility of *a posteriori* knowledge. Rather, he thinks that the very idea of such knowledge is incoherent. His reasoning is best reconstructed as follows. He begins by employing a general principle which he supposes is not only true, but necessarily true. He then deploys this principle in what he calls his "battle-hardened proof."[31] The principle is a *relational theory of thinking*:

> (RT) Every instance of thinking involves a thinker standing in relation to something thought.

The idea is that thinking is like touching. Each time I touch something, there is something touched by me. If I try to touch you, but you move, then I have not succeeded in touching nothing; rather, I have not succeeded in touching at all. Again, to use an example a bit closer to Parmenides' own formulation, if I try to express something but fail, perhaps because I simply lack the requisite linguistic abilities, then I have not succeeded in expressing nothing; instead, I have not expressed anything at all. Maybe, for example, I know only a little Korean and when I try to say something sophisticated in that language out comes only gibberish. Have I achieved the assertion of nothing? No, it is better to say that I have not asserted anything at all but have only emitted unintelligible sounds. The same, according to Parmenides, holds for thinking: if I try to think of something, but fail, then I have not succeeded in thinking nothing; rather, I have not thought.

One might want to counter that I can think *of* nothing. For example, I might think that nothing in the bank is worse than something in the bank. Or, again, I might think more abstractly that nothingness is a topic about which only philosophers and mathematicians think; everyone else thinks about something or other. But in that case, philosophers and mathematicians *do* think about nothing; and indeed I too am thinking about it in thinking about their thinking of it. A defender of Parmenides will now aver that if they have actually thought at all, then somehow they have thought of the *concept* of nothingness, which is something after all. If every thought really does involve a relation between a thinker and something thought, if every thought must be contentful, then in these cases we are not really imagining someone who thinks nothing. Instead, if we are thinking, we are thinking something or other.

At any rate, armed with (RT), Parmenides supposes he can derive a sort of corollary, which serves as a *bridge principle* between thinking and existing:

(BP) It is possible to think any arbitrary x if, and only if, x exists.[32]

Note that (BP) says more than (RT). (BP) makes two distinct claims: (1) for any x which exists, it is possible to think x; and (2) for any x which can be thought, x exists. It would follow from (BP), together with Parmenides' claim that *nothing does not exist*, that it is impossible to think nothing. So, if I catch myself seeming to think nothing, then I must be mistaken. The case is similar to this one: if I catch myself supposing that I am just now thinking of a prime number between 14 and 19 other than 17, then I am not only wrong, but necessarily wrong. What seems to me to be true is false, and must be false. It is not a contingent matter that 17 is the only prime number between 14 and 19. So, if I think I am thinking about some number with the specified features other than 17, I am mistaken about what I take myself to be thinking. Similarly, if I think I am thinking nothing, then I am mistaken – and simply confused.

Now, with this much in place, Parmenides can conduct his assault on *a posteriori* knowledge (AAPK). He argues as follows, in two stages:

1   If we have any *a posteriori* knowledge, then we are able to know that there are plurality and change.
2   We are not able to know that there are plurality and change.
3   Hence, we have no *a posteriori* knowledge.

The argument is simple enough and clearly valid. (AAPK-1) seems plausibly true. It seems reasonable, that is, to suppose that if we know anything *a posteriori*, then we also have an ability to detect change and to observe the discreteness of things. After all, if I know that I am now perceiving something blue, then I also know that there is some *region* in my visual field; or we are at least able to know that what is blue is not some other region in my visual field which is black, and not blue. What if, though, my visual field were a sea of undifferentiated blueness? Even then it seems plausible to suppose that I could focus on one half of my visual field and to distinguish it from the other half. Similarly, if I come to know that a leaf has fallen, then I am also in a position to know that the leaf has changed its position. Because these examples are more or less randomly selected, Parmenides is able to think, by extension, that for any given bit of *a posteriori* knowledge you might consider, you will find that your ability to have such knowledge implicates you in one way or another in the ability to know that there are plurality and change in the world of sense perception. So, we can grant (AAPK-1).

It is in any case (AAPK-2) which is the startling and preposterous-sounding premise in this argument. Why should Parmenides think that we cannot know that there are plurality and change? Can we not simply *see* a variety of distinct things, a plurality, changing at virtually every moment we look out into the world? It is here he thinks that *a priori* knowledge trumps *what seems to be a posteriori* knowledge. It is here, in defense of (AAPK-2), that he offers a startling argument, one which relies crucially on (BP), his bridge principle between thinking and existing. There seem to be two sorts of change, generation and simple alteration. Generation involves something coming into existence which has not formerly existed. Alteration, by contrast, involves something which already exists changing from one state into another. Putative examples of generation and alteration are the birth of a new human and that boy's getting a stylish haircut at age 17. Of course, Parmenides thinks that these are merely *putative* examples of alteration, since he thinks, for related reasons, that both of these notions are incoherent. His argument against change is this (AAC):

1   It is not possible to think nothing.
2   It is possible to conceive of generation only if it is possible to think nothing.
3   Hence, it is not possible to conceive of generation.
4   It is possible to conceive of alteration only if it is possible to conceive of generation.
5   It is, by (3), not possible to conceive of generation.
6   Hence, it is not possible to conceive of alteration.

With that much shown, Parmenides needs only to add two simple thoughts to derive half of his preposterous-sounding claim, that we are not able to know that there are plurality and change:

7   All change is either an instance of generation or of alteration.

8   If it is possible to know that there is change, it must be at least possible to conceive of generation and alteration.

9   Hence, by (3) and (6), it is not possible to know that there is change.

This is then half of Parmenides' claim.

If this argument is successful, a parallel argument may be taken to show that there cannot be plurality, since plurality implicates us in thinking that there is *nothing* separating a proposed pair of distinct entities. Together these arguments will yield precisely Parmenides' (AAPK-2), that we are not able to know that there are plurality and change. If we accept (AAPK-2), then given the plausibility of his (AAPK-1), that if we have any *a posteriori* knowledge at all we are able to know that there are plurality and change, Parmenides seems licensed to draw the conclusion that we in fact have no *a posteriori* knowledge at all. He would have effected a triumph of the *a priori* over the *a posteriori*.

How successful is this argument? As a historical matter, it was successful enough to command considerable attention in antiquity, eventually receiving different sorts of refutations from Plato and Aristotle. As a more purely philosophical matter, it will suffice for the present to sketch how Parmenides might have some surprisingly good backing for his crucial moves. To begin, all of the important argumentation comes in the argument against change, since if it is sound, then (AAPK-2) will be established, which with (AAPK-1) really does yield Parmenides' conclusion. (AAC-1) receives such support as it has from Parmenides' wholly defensible commitment to (RT), the relational theory of thinking, coupled with his more problematic bridge principle (BP). So, the argument has initially however much credibility these claims have.

The second premise of this argument (AAC-2) requires comment. According to this claim, it is possible to think of generation only if it is possible to think of nothing. The idea here is this: if we are thinking of real generation, and not just a covert case of alteration, then we are thinking of something *coming from nothing*. We are thinking, that is, of generation *ex nihilo*. Now, it may or may not be possible for *something* to suddenly pop into existence from absolutely nothing, though Parmenides rightly wonders how this could be so. Still, even if it were possible, we could not conceive of its being so, since in that case we would have to think of something coming from *nothing*. Thinking of nothing, however, is something we cannot do, if at any rate (BP) is correct. For that principle holds that we can think only of what exists, of what is, then, something or other; nothing, though, is, well, nothing. Nothing does not exist. So, we cannot think of genuine generation.

As a matter of fact, are we not tempted to say that when we conceive of ourselves as thinking of generation, we are really thinking of instances of alteration? A table is generated. What really happens is that some wood is put into a table shape. That is, what really happens is that some wood is altered in a certain way. So too with the "generation" of an infant. What happens in that case is rather that an egg and sperm join and begin to divide and grow along a largely programmed path by the accretion of ambient matter. Here too we have not generation, but alteration by addition. So, perhaps we cannot conceive of real generation. This is a case in which, upon reflection, we have not been thinking about what we thought we were thinking about. More to the point, we did not realize that in thinking about generation, real generation, we must have been thinking about nothing, which, we now know, we cannot do.

Surely, then, if we grant the interim conclusion (AAC-3), we will not want to go along all the way to (AAC-6). If generation is really alteration, then we can think of generation by thinking of alteration. After all, alteration is the very sort of change to which we have just reduced generation.

Parmenides thinks otherwise. He evidently supposes we have effected no such reduction. Instead, we have seen that generation is inconceivable. Now we see something additional, that for the same reason, alteration is inconceivable, because, as (AAC-4) asserts, it is possible to conceive of alteration only if it is possible to conceive of generation. That is, it is not generation which reduces to alteration; on the contrary, all alteration is really disguised generation. When a woman learns to play the piano, something new comes onto the scene, a piano-playing woman where there had been none before. Looked at in Parmenides' way, each time we have a seeming instance of alteration, we have the generation of something new, something which had not been before. But that too lands us in a problem, since in that case we can conceive of alteration only if we can conceive of generation, something we have just seen we cannot do. If that is correct, then we are after all stuck with the result that we cannot even conceive of alteration. With that conclusion, Parmenides would be entitled to his most radical and revisionary conclusions.

Naturally enough, there are quite a few places where one might want to scrutinize this argument. Beginning with (RT) and (BP), questions arise. Other sorts of questions might give us pause regarding a number of other premises, including most notably (AAC-2) and (AAC-4), premises about which we have only begun a conversation. We have not completed this conversation because there are different and non-equivalent ways of challenging these premises, each with their own advantages and costs. In fact, as indicated, different philosophers in antiquity responded in different ways. We shall see, in due course, how Parmenides' striking and strident argument met with several different refutations at the hands of Plato and Aristotle, refutations which in their turn occasioned some surprising and highly valuable positive developments.

For now, though, it is worth reflecting upon what sort of attitude one ought to adopt to this sort of argument in general. In a certain way, it is like a series of arguments owing to another philosopher from Elea, a bit younger than Parmenides, Zeno (born *c.* 490), who was thought in antiquity to be Parmenides' student and defender. Zeno left four paradoxes of motion, preserved by Aristotle, each with the arresting conclusion that motion is impossible. In one way, then, Zeno may be taken as supporting the Parmenidean contention that we have no *a posteriori* knowledge; for, again, if we cannot know even that anything moves, then we can hardly rely on our senses to know anything at all.

The simplest of these paradoxes relies on two uncomplicated thoughts. First, before I go anywhere, I must go halfway there. That is, whenever an object traverses a distance from point A to point B, it first traverses half the distance. Second, for any distance D, I can divide D in half. So, for the distance D, from A to B, there is a half distance, 1/2 (D); and there is a half of that distance, equal to 1/4 (D); and so on into infinity. There is, it would seem, no minimal distance which cannot be divided yet again. Taken individually, neither of these thoughts seems problematic. Still, together, they seem to yield the absurd conclusion that I can never arrive anywhere: I will forever be on my way, first traversing half of the distance to my destination before arriving, and then again traversing half of the distance to my interim destination before arriving there, and then again traversing half of the distance before to my new interim destination … and so on without end.

Similarly, suppose Achilles is in a race with a tortoise. Realizing that he is much faster than the tortoise, Achilles decides to make things interesting by giving the tortoise a head start of ten meters. That, contends Zeno, was a mistake. For now he can never overtake or even catch him, so long as the tortoise keeps moving. Before he catches the tortoise, Achilles must arrive at position p_1, the position at which the tortoise began. By that time, however, the tortoise will have moved on to p_2, which now Achilles must reach before reaching the tortoise, who is now at p_3. With the altogether humble thought that so long as the tortoise is moving, he does not remain in the same position, this series of events will carry on forever, and Achilles will never catch the tortoise.

It is tempting for many simply to set these paradoxes aside as obviously flawed. In response to Zeno's first paradox of motion, for example, the reader might hope to refute him by simply setting down this book and walking to the door. That shows, it seems, that motion is possible, because it is actual; so, Zeno's paradox of motion must be mistaken.

If a reader adopts this sort of response to her own satisfaction, she will have satisfied no one other than herself. Zeno's paradoxes are paradoxical because they force us to accept a conclusion we cannot bring ourselves to accept, and to do so on the basis of premises we find fully acceptable, even irresistible. When we walk across the room, we affirm something we cannot easily bring ourselves to deny, namely *that motion is possible*. Zeno's conclusion to the contrary, however, derives from just two very simple claims, each of which is intuitively plausible: (i) it takes time to walk anywhere, or more generally to traverse any distance whatsoever; and (ii) whenever one traverses any distance from location-1 to location-2, one must traverse half the distance to location-2 *before* one arrives at location-2. It is easy to see that the second principle can be applied repeatedly, without end, generating an infinite number of distances to be traversed before anyone can arrive anywhere. Armed with just these two theses, consequently, Zeno is able to argue for the impossibility of motion (IM):

1   If motion is possible, then it is in principle possible for a runner to traverse the finite distance of a racecourse, that is, from the start to the finish, in a finite amount of time.
2   In order to traverse the distance from the start to the finish, the runner must *first* traverse half the distance to the finish line, and half the distance to the halfway point, and half the distance to the halfway point of the halfway point, and so on to infinity.
3   If (2), then in order to traverse the finite distance of a racecourse from the start to the finish, the runner must traverse an infinite number of distances in a finite amount of time.
4   It is impossible for the runner (or anyone else) to traverse an infinite number of distances in a finite amount of time.
5   Hence, motion is impossible.

A reader does not refute Zeno by putting down this book and walking away: that is, rather, a way to *ignore* Zeno.

It would be a pity if everyone had elected to ignore Zeno rather than to take up the task of attempting to refute him, because those who did so in fact inspired some extremely sophisticated mathematics, in set theory and in theories of the infinite, much of which has had striking and unanticipated applications in computer science and elsewhere. Indeed, sophisticated variants of Zeno's paradoxes of motion continue to present formidable problems for mathematicians down to the present day.[33] In the present context, however, we need only focus on a striking feature of his intended result. In arguing for his counterintuitive conclusions, Zeno, like Parmenides before him, is prepared to rely on the resources of reason alone, to set aside the easy dictates of what is given, or seems to be given, in sense perception. He urges us to accept only what can be shown, to set aside what merely seems to be the case in favor of what can be demonstrated. In so doing, Zeno parts company with the manifest image of the world in a rather spectacular way.

In these and other such paradoxes, we are invited to reflect on the tenability of widespread assumptions, often deeply intuitive, about space, time, and motion. If we respond with self-indulgent derision, by demanding that if Zeno is so sure that Achilles *cannot* overtake the tortoise then he ought to be willing to bet his life savings on the tortoise, we will certainly miss what the paradoxes have to teach us about actual and potential infinities; about the infinite divisibility of space and time; about infinite sets and their relations to the infinite divisions of finite lengths; about convergence;

and about the summing of infinite series. Indeed, insofar as there are completely satisfactory solutions available to these paradoxes, they were not developed until the twentieth century, some 2,500 years after their first formulations. It is surely noteworthy that these paradoxes were first formulated in the wake of Parmenides' doubts about plurality and change.

In the same way, then, if we are to reject Parmenides' argument as somehow obviously incorrect, then we ought to be in a position to point to those obvious failures. It will turn out that by uncovering its weaknesses – and it does have several – we will at a minimum have learnt something about the nature and limitations of *a posteriori* knowledge, a form of knowledge whose principles of justification turn out to be abidingly elusive. Perhaps Parmenides' argument, despite such flaws as it may have, does after all succeed in showing that we would be mistaken to privilege *a posteriori* knowledge as unassailable or even as somehow more surely secure in its justificatory moorings than is *a priori* knowledge. Is it after all so clear that we *see* plurality and change?

1.5   Democritus and fifth-century atomism

The question of what is immediately evident to sense perception took on a new dimension and an added importance with the advent of fifth-century atomism. Whatever one makes of Parmenides' arguments against *a posteriori* knowledge, it remains true that their conclusions are incredible: it is difficult even to fathom how one might come to believe that there is absolutely no plurality, or that nothing has ever changed. It seems, on the contrary, that the person who is reading this book began to read it at some point in time, and so changed in at least one respect at that moment, or that (so long as the author refrains from reading his own book) the person who is reading this book is not the same as the person who wrote it, and so there is at least that much plurality. Insofar as Parmenides means to deny these commonplaces, his reasoning is bound to seem radically divorced from the data of our lived lives. Of course, he may well want it that way; but that hardly makes his conclusions more palatable.

Parmenides' remarkable contentions might be less jarring if he were at least to explain why it is that the manifest image of the world differs so sharply from the world as it is in fact, in itself. He makes no such effort, however. Instead, one finds in his writings only a stern and uncompromising castigation of those unable or unwilling to follow his lead. On this score, at any rate, some philosophers who followed in his wake fare better. The atomists of the fifth century, Leucippus and Democritus, held views akin to Parmenides in the sense that they all agreed with him in maintaining that the world described by science and philosophy differs sharply from the world of common sense and sense experience. At the same time, according to some ancient accounts, they seemed keen to explain why there should be so great a divergence between what we sense and what we come to believe about the world behind our image of it. They offered *atomism* as a conceptual palliative to Parmenidean monism: although the phenomenal world does not represent the world as it is in itself, there are good reasons why the world should appear as it does. The phenomenal world results from the imperceptible interactions of tiny atoms swirling in the void.

Among the atomists, Democritus (*c.* 460–360) is best represented by a surviving corpus of works. We can understand his views most easily by noting something conciliatory in his attitude towards Parmenides. He agrees with Parmenides on *a priori* grounds that it is not possible for there to be generation *ex nihilo*. So, whatever comes into existence comes from something already existing; and whatever goes out of existence resolves into something, not nothing. Starting at the macro-level, we can see that this is so: a table comes to be from some wood and, if destroyed by an axe, resolves into wood. Looked at this way, a table is simply a temporary modification of some already existing more basic stuff, wood. The same, however, holds for the wood itself, relative to some still more basic stuff, out of which it comes and into which it resolves. This process can either go on indefinitely downward, or it can stop at some basic stuff or stuffs. Democritus took the second alternative: at the bottom are tiny atoms, which are themselves indivisible and so never come into or go out of existence. (The Greek word *atomos* just means "undivided" or "indivisible.") Each little atom is seamless, without beginning or end, and an absolute unity. Each one is, in a certain way, a miniature Parmenidean One unto itself.

There is not merely, however, one all-encompassing atom, as Parmenides had urged. Rather, claim the atomists, there are countless atoms, all swirling in the void. Without really meeting Parmenides' arguments head-on, the atomists sought to sidestep them by first agreeing with him that if change and generation are genuine, then there must be non-being, at least in the minimal sense that it must be possible to say that this is not that, but then to insist on the reality of change, with the ultimate result that there must be non-being. As Democritus claims, "Non-being is no less than being is."[34] Identifying this non-being with the void, Democritus concludes that atoms move in the void, and that their motion accounts for the change we experience in the phenomenal world. His atoms apparently had size, shape, and weight in terms of which observations at the macro-level might be explained. Thus, bitterness might be thought to be a function of a prevalence of sharp atoms in some kinds of food, or sweetness due to a preponderance of smooth and silky spherical atoms in others.

Now, it might be tempting to read this atomistic response to Parmenides as a triumph for common sense. While it turns out that the world as it is remains divorced from the world of common experience, at least the world as it is experienced is grounded in – and explained by – a world of atoms inaccessible to sense experience. Our experiences are both coherent and explicable. We need not fear Parmenidean exhortations or censures.

This easy assurance would be premature, for two related reasons. First, it should be clear that nowhere have the atomists succeeded in directly refuting Parmenides. He has, after all, given a detailed argument for thinking that it is not possible to think of what is not; nothing in the atomistic response addresses this argument directly. At this juncture, it is fair to say that Parmenides would be unimpressed; and it is also fair to say that the atomists have given him nothing much to be impressed about. Second, by being conciliatory, Democritus may have conceded too much, by holding in concert with Parmenides that there is ultimately only one kind of change. We saw that Parmenides implicitly wanted to reduce all instances of alteration to generation (in premise AAC-4). If that seemed unwarranted then, it may seem no less so now to effect the opposite reduction, of all generation to qualitative change. On the Democritean picture, everything is ultimately a modification of atoms in the void. What seems to come to be is, in reality, a new configuration of atoms, one which is a temporary arrangement or modification of them, but which is as such transitory, and, in a certain way, illusory.

This last point was not lost on Democritus himself. In one fragment, he distinguishes sharply between what he terms the "bastard" judgments of the senses and another, legitimate form of judgment, one not based in sense experience but in the workings of reason.[35] In this way, at least, he sounds practically Parmenidean. Bastard judgment belongs to sight, hearing, taste, smell and touch. The judgments of reason, which concern atoms and the void, are in principle impervious to the claims of the senses. That is, however congenial the postulation of atomism may sound to contemporary ears, Democritus seems hardly motivated by the sorts of empirical evidence or data which underscore contemporary atomism. Moreover, he understands his atomism to render great stretches of sensory data non-objective and merely conventional. He says directly that in reality there are *only* atoms and the void; whatever else exists does so only by convention, as a sort of convenient fiction. All of the following, he maintains, exist merely by convention: sweetness and bitterness; hot and cold; and even color.[36]

In contrasting what exists in reality to what exists merely by convention, Democritus evidently relies on a powerful argument, one which will have a long legacy in philosophy. The argument starts with a simple fact, that different people report different sense experiences when interacting with the same objects, and tries to conclude that, as a consequence, there is no objective fact of the matter about what is perceived. It is the Conventionality of Perception Argument (CPA):

1   If S_1 perceives some object x to be F (e.g. a bucket of water to be warm) and S_2 perceives the same x to be not-F (that is, the same bucket of water to be cool), then neither F nor not-F is a property of x in itself.

2   It often happens in perception that S_1 perceives x to be F and S_2 perceives x to be not-F.

3   Hence, perceptual qualities are not in objects themselves.

(CPA-2) is hardly disputable. If someone has just come out of the sauna, the pool will seem cool to her. If someone else has just come out of an air-conditioned house, the pool will seem warm to him. Similarly, it seems a plain fact of experience that in some cases what seems sweet to one person will seem sour to another. Perhaps a glass of lemonade strikes one drinker as tart and another as sweet. This may happen when one perceiver is sick or otherwise abnormal; but it may equally happen when both are perfectly normal healthy people who simply happen to have different frames of reference or different sensibilities.

It follows, then, that if (CPA-1) is true, (CPA-3) follows directly. Why suppose that (CPA-1) is true? It is easiest to understand Democritus' entire argument, and (CPA-1) in particular, as attacking *naïve realism* about sense perception, the view that sensory qualities are intrinsic properties of perceived objects. It is the lemonade which is sweet, the car which is red, or the pool which is warm. These are all real properties, intrinsic to the objects which have them, waiting in the world to affect us when we encounter them. The naïve realist supposes that we simply experience these qualities by interacting in the normal ways with the objects which manifest them. If (CPA-1) is correct, then the naïve realist is wrong.

There is at least some reason to suppose that (CPA-1) is indeed correct. If we are naïve realists, we might evidently need to suppose that if the pool seems cool to some subject S_1 but warm to S_2, then only one of four circumstances must obtain: (1) S_1 is right and S_2 wrong; (2) S_2 is right and S_1 is wrong; (3) they are both right; and (4) they are both wrong. It is difficult to countenance alternatives (1) and (2). Nothing gives us any reason to suppose that either S_1 or S_2 enjoys some superior position relative to the other. Nor does anything from the standpoint of naïve realism commend (4), the view that they are both wrong. That leaves only (3), that they are both right. Yet how is it that the pool can be *in itself* both cool and not-cool and warm and not-warm? This third alternative seems to contradict itself twice over.

Now, it may seem natural to say at this point that neither S_1 nor S_2 is absolutely or objectively wrong or right: both are right as far as each is concerned. That, though, will be just Democritus' point: each is correct only as far as things seem, not as far as how things are in fact, *in themselves*, independent of and prior to our experiences. If it now turns out that each perceiver is an authority over how things appear, and it is not possible for the objects of perception to be objectively, in themselves, as they appear, then naïve realism must be false. It will not be the case that things in the perceptual realm are, to use Democritus' own expression, *in reality* any one way rather than another. Things are hot and cold only *by convention*.

Democritus takes this argument a step further by including colors among the properties which are relative to perceivers. Not even colors, he maintains, are properties of objects in themselves. In varying conditions of lighting, and with differences among perceivers, one and the same object will seem blue to one perceiver and purple to another. At an extreme, red–green colorblind people will mistake what normal perceivers perceive as red for green. Now, if one is tempted to respond by pointing out that the colorblind person is in an obvious way abnormal, Democritus will then simply respond that this talk of normalcy is already talk of conventional *norms*, and so already concedes his point, which is that naïve realism is false. This is, however, just to say that given (CPA-1), (CPA-3) follows. Hence, we are wrong to invest too much significance into our bastard judgments. They tell us how the world seems; but they do not tell us how the world is. In reality, the world is atoms and the void.

Thus construed, atomism preserves some elements of the manifest image by undermining others. There are in fact change and plurality; but all change is merely alteration and not generation; and all plurality is a plurality of atoms swirling in the void. We do perceive the world; but our perceptions yield only bastard judgments which cut us off from all that exists in reality, atoms in the void. Even so, reason can uncover what is in fact the case. All the same, Democritus reflects an enigmatic awareness of the delicate interplay between the mind and the senses – and by extension between *a priori* and *a posteriori* knowledge – in an amusing fragment in which he portrays the senses as addressing the mind: "Wretched mind, do you take your own evidence from us and then overthrow us? Our overthrow is your downfall."[37] The senses here point out that the mind receives its evidence from them and that consequently any attempt on the part of the mind to undermine their authority ultimately serves only to undermine the mind itself. It was clear enough that Parmenides had wanted to undermine the claims of the senses altogether. An intriguing question remains regarding Democritus' self-critical reproach: to what extent does the relativity of perception argument represent an attempt on the part of the mind to undermine the reliability of sense perception as such?

1.6   Protagoras and the Sophistic Movement

Atomism's willingness to postulate a realm of reality beneath the threshold of sense perception puts it into a somewhat precarious epistemic position, especially given (CPA), according to which the qualities experienced in sense perception are not even intrinsic to external objects. Even so, despite such skeptical worries, Democritus never doubts that there is an underlying objective reality. On the contrary, this is precisely what he accepts when he contrasts what exists by convention with what exists *in reality*. If he finds himself in some ways cut off from a reality inaccessible to the senses, then this can only be due to the fact that there is a reality independent of his encountering it in sense perception, one which exists objectively and prior to his experiences of it.

Things take a radical new direction with the advent of the Sophistic Movement, especially given the tendencies of its most famous and formidable practitioner, Protagoras (c. 485–414). Although there is very little to connect all those called "Sophists" in antiquity or since to any one particular doctrine or creed, it remains true that there was a social phenomenon associated with this label, one aptly, if loosely, called a movement. This movement owed its origins mainly to the surprisingly long-lived and entrenched democratic institutions of Athens, which extended, with interruptions, from the reforms of Cleisthenes in the early sixth century until the abolition of democracy at the hands of the Macedonians in 322; even thereafter, during the Hellenistic age, democracy was restored several times, though not for long periods.

Democracy created opportunities for political power denied to many of those disenfranchised under oligarchies and monarchies. These opportunities were most readily exploited by citizens schooled in effective public speaking and the arts of persuasion, a consequence of democracy roundly criticized by families of wealth and privilege. Still, even under democratic rule, power was effectively concentrated among the well born, since only those in the leisure classes could afford to train their sons in rhetoric and public speaking. Here Sophism made its entrance into Athenian life. Many Sophists boasted, with considerable justification, that they were uncommonly capable public speakers; and given their abilities, many were sought out as teachers by families eager to equip their sons with the tools of social success. Given their social aims, these families understandably paid the Sophists handsome sums for their services as teachers.

Still, attitudes toward the Sophists were ambivalent, in some ways mirroring contemporary attitudes toward lawyers: people love to hate them, but want the best money can buy when they find themselves in need of legal services. In the same way, Athenians sometimes lampooned the Sophists as shameless charlatans, but nevertheless engaged their services for a premium. Some Athenians, including some philosophers, criticized them for the pernicious and destabilizing effects of their teaching on traditional morality. These criticisms were in certain ways justified, at least in the sense that recognizably Sophistic teachings really did undermine comfortable and traditional forms of moral thinking and decision-making. Most notably on this score, Protagoras preached a variety of relativism which threatened to abolish any form of concentrated moral authority whatsoever. His teaching could reasonably have been regarded as dangerous by those seeking to endorse the notion of a moral authority independent of individual practices and beliefs. Even so, his teaching found its adherents; indeed, to judge by large stretches of public and academic opinion, many people continue to find his views highly congenial. In some circles, Protagorean relativism is assumed as obviously or even unquestionably correct to the point of unassailability.

His views were, however, assailed in antiquity, most forcefully by Plato and Aristotle. It is perhaps easiest to appreciate why they were so concerned about them by understanding Protagorean relativism as an extension and non-skeptical revision of atomistic concerns about the reality of sense perception. Protagoras held, most famously, a Measure Doctrine (MD), according to which humans are themselves the measures or standards of what is beautiful and ugly, of what is right and wrong, of what is real and unreal. "A human being is the measure," maintains Protagoras, "of what is, that it is, and of what is not, that it is not."[38] Put simply, (MD) holds that humans determine what is the case for humans; they do not discover what is given by the world prior to their interaction with it. For at least some range of qualities, this may strike many as perfectly apt. It is not that it is a mere matter of convention that wine tastes sweet: it *really is* sweet, at any rate it really is sweet to the one who tastes it as such. The phenomenon is the same as the one noticed by the atomists, that different people experience the world differently; the attitude adopted toward this phenomenon is, however, strikingly different. Protagoras will not allow that there is a reality standing behind appearances. Rather, appearances are reality. What appears to me to be so, is so, for me; and there is no reason to doubt either the reality of what appears to me or my ability to know that reality directly.

The Measure Doctrine thus finds its support in precisely the phenomenon noticed by the atomists, that there is variability between our perceptions. Now, however, that observation is extended to another domain: morality. The easiest way to conceptualize this extension is to consider a simple variation on (CPA), the atomists' conventionality of perception argument. Now, however, instead of ranging over perceptual qualities, the argument deals with putatively moral qualities, yielding a simple argument for Protagorean Relativism (APR):

1   If S_1 perceives some action x to be F (e.g. euthanasia to be morally permissible) and S_2 perceives that same x to be not-F (euthanasia to be morally impermissible), then neither F nor not-F is a property of x in itself.
2   It often happens in perception that S_1 perceives x to be F and S_2 perceives x to be not-F.
3   Hence, moral qualities are not in actions themselves.

Here again (APR-2) seems almost undeniable. Plainly, people have moral disagreements. Different cultures, times, and groups diverge in their assessments of the morality of the same sorts of actions. It is now commonplace for Americans to denounce slavery as unconscionably immoral; it was not long ago when Americans held slaves. The first historian in Greece, Herodotus, reports with wonder the astonishing customs of the Egyptians, who do just about everything backwards, the Persians, who marry their daughters, the Indians, who eat their dead, and the Scythians, whose nomadic ways preclude their building temples or engaging in agriculture. About these last, Herodotus admires their ability to escape Persian domination by nimble flight; but in virtue of their other traits he says, "I do not like them." Herodotus even provides a general explanation for his disdain. Those who know a fair bit about cultures other than their own, he observes, habitually regard their own culture as superior. So, Herodotus decides, "Convention is king over all."[39]

Protagoras will no doubt find this congenial, but not merely in the atomistic way, where convention is contrasted with what exists in reality. Protagoras' Measure Doctrine suggests that any such contrast is pointless. Rather, *what is right for the Persians* differs from *what is right for the Greeks*. End of story. There are no further facts to prove that the Greeks, who, as Herodotus says, feel themselves superior, are in fact superior. Nor, by the same token, are there facts to prove the Indians superior, even though they too, no less than the Greeks, regard themselves as superior to those foreign to them. What they do is *right for them*, though not *right for the Greeks*. Moreover, there seem to be no facts which prove some Greeks superior to other Greeks, when they have internal disagreements. Herodotus reports that the Greeks cannot stomach the irreverence of the Indians towards their dead. When he speaks this way, Herodotus forgets about Heracleitus, who holds that "corpses are more fit to be cast out than dung."[40] If there are no non-conventional facts to prove the Greeks superior to the Indians, it is difficult to see why there should be such to prove some Greeks superior to others. Fairly clearly, Heracleitus is not much impressed by the "facts" of convention.

Returning to (APR), then, we can see how Protagoras has extended the atomistic conventionality of perception argument in three ways, each of which signals a difficulty for him. The first extension, one noted by Plato, concerns the very notion of *perception* employed (APR-2). As in English, it is easy in Greek to slide from speaking of narrow sense perception to a more intellectual form of perceptual judgment. (From: "She perceived blue" to "He perceived her lack of comfort in being the only woman present" to "He perceived early in the fiscal year that the GNP would shrink in the months to follow.") Democritus was primarily concerned with disagreements about instances of sense perception, narrowly construed. It is not so immediately obvious that we perceive in every case the moral disagreements that we take ourselves to perceive. It may be that the Indians and Greeks agree about the moral principles governing burial of the dead. All parties may after all agree that morality requires an expression of piety toward the dead; their disagreement will then concern how best to express that piety, with the result that their disagreement will not be best understood as concerning moral principles at all.

The second extension is a bit more complex. Suppose that (APR-2) is just true, as in the end seems plausible: there are disagreements about morality and these extend to disagreements about moral principles. Let us then grant

(APR-2) in just this sense. That much, however, tells us less than some have imagined. (APR-2) asserts only that, as a descriptive matter, there is moral disagreement. How, though, does Protagoras hope to move from the bare fact of moral disagreement to the rejection of traditional morality, which holds that some actions are right or wrong independently of and prior to our judgments about them? That is, as stated, (APR-2) is a simple assertion about cultural or individual differences. If we are to avoid equivocation between the premises of the argument, the first premise must be taken to hold that the bare fact of moral disagreement suffices to show that there are no perceiver-independent moral qualities. Now, there may be no such qualities. Perhaps there are good reasons for doubting their existence. At the moment, however, we are wondering whether Protagoras has given us any such reason. So far, he has not. To establish that moral relativism is true he will have to do more than appeal to the bare fact of moral disagreement. When, for example, there is scientific disagreement, we do not immediately infer that there are no facts of the matter in science. Instead, we try to learn what the facts are in order to settle our disagreement in one direction or the other. Again, if – as some even today may be tempted to do – Protagoras responds that moral and scientific matters are wholly disanalogous, he may be on firm ground. Here too, though, his asserting that this is so does not by itself make it so. In order to *establish* moral relativism – as opposed to merely *asserting* it – Protagoras and his fellow travelers will need to provide an argument. This argument will clearly have to rely on more than the indisputable but pedestrian fact of moral disagreement.

This becomes all the more pressing when we focus on Protagoras' third and final extension of the atomists' argument for conventionalism. This extension concerns his attitude towards his own ultimate conclusion. The atomists evidently wanted to hold that what we perceive is not, so to speak, really real. What is objectively real lies beneath the realm of perception and to some degree helps to explain our experiences. This is what Democritus understood by his rejection of naïve realism: he concluded that perceptual qualities are not intrinsic features of objects, but instead result from our interactions with imperceptible atoms swirling in the void. Protagoras has a much less chaste view. He does not deny the reality of perceptual or moral qualities. Instead, he holds that they are really real. It is just that they depend for their existence on our judgments. He is no sort of skeptic. I know what is *right for me*; it is precisely what I believe to be *right for me*. Nor does he take such judgments to be conventional, if what is conventional is to be contrasted with what exists objectively in a non-conventional reality. Where the atomists had thought that the same object could not be both sweet and not sweet, and inferred that sweetness existed not in reality but by convention, Protagoras concluded that some things really are sweet for me, even if they are not sweet for you. According to Protagoras, what holds for sweetness holds for moral properties; indeed, if we understand the Measure Doctrine to be completely unrestricted, as evidently Protagoras intended it to be, then what holds for perceptual and moral qualities holds for qualities generally. A human being is the measure of what exists.

Looked at this way, the Measure Doctrine seems wildly extreme. It might be given a positive or a negative formulation:

(MD_{pos}) For any arbitrary proposition p, if S believes p, then p is true for S.

(MD_{neg}) For any arbitrary proposition p, if S_1 believes p and S_2 believes not-p, then there is no fact of the matter as to whether S_1 or S_2 is correct.

Put thus, (MD_{pos}) is difficult to believe. If in elementary school a child believes that $3+2 = 6$, then she is wrong and is rightly corrected by her teacher. If, though "true for S" merely means "is believed to be true by S," then (MD_{pos}) is obviously trite, claiming only that if S believes p, then S believes p. One hopes that relativism comes to more than just that. It must, if it is to be at all worthy of our attention.

Now, there may be a tendency here to move to help Protagoras by explicitly constraining the range of propositions under the province (MD_{pos}). It concerns not mathematics or empirically decidable matters but, rather, morality. When we have disagreements in that domain, some will say, there is no fact of the matter as to who is right or wrong. This then slips into what is essentially a restricted version of the negative formulation of the Measure Doctrine, (MD_{neg}). The first and most obvious point is that we have now parted company from Protagoras, who is not interested in any such restriction. Moreover, when we offer such a restriction, we incur an obligation to offer a principled reason to endorse it. This reason will, clearly enough, need to show why we are justified in thinking that relativism should be rejected as a general doctrine, even while it is reserved in some fields of inquiry. As we have already seen, appeals to the bare fact of moral disagreement will not suffice. So, those who wish to press this restriction owe the world an argument.

1.7   Challenges from the Presocratics and Sophists

Protagoras and the other Sophists leave a challenge to those who follow them. Even if we agree that Protagoras has not established the Measure Doctrine, we must concede that we have so far not been given a conclusive reason to reject it either. Moreover, taking into account the atomists upon whom Protagoras builds, we may observe that we face a danger cagily side-stepped by Protagoras himself: skepticism. If we side in the beginning with the naturalists as against the mythologists, we need, as Xenophanes observed, to offer not only justifications for our sundry explanations, but a more general form of justification for our own preferred explanatory framework, one we have self-consciously introduced as superior to that of our predecessors. If we favor *a priori* justifications, then we risk siding with Parmenides and Zeno in adopting some fairly bizarre-sounding conclusions. On the other hand, it is difficult to see how we can in any non question-begging way offer *a posteriori* justifications for our *a posteriori* methods. Perhaps at this stage we are left with Democritus, with our faculties wrangling with each other for justificatory supremacy. At any rate, without the easy and unmotivated expedient of Protagorean relativism, we find ourselves in search of a method sufficient to the task of escaping skepticism without utterly divorcing ourselves from the phenomenal world. These challenges were all in turn taken up with varying degrees of success by Socrates, Plato, Aristotle, and the Hellenistic philosophers. In that same period, skepticism returns with a vengeance.

Notes

1 All dates in this book are BC unless otherwise specified.

2 This observation of Thales, like all of the information we have for philosophy before Socrates, survives only in the testimony of later authors. In this case, the later author is Aristotle, the first book of whose *Metaphysics* relays the views of many of his predecessors. The remark about Thales occurs at *Metaphysics* 983b6–18. It is customarily referred to as DK 11 A 2, a reference to the great work of the German scholars Diels and Kranz [13], who first collected the fragments of the Presocratic philosophers into a usable single volume. Diels and Kranz list two sorts of testimony: A-entries, which record testimony held to be (1) periphrastic or (2) simply the work of a later author recounting something about a Presocratic philosopher; and B-entries, which are judged to be actual quotations of the Presocratics preserved by later authors. Thus, e.g., "DK 11 A 2" refers to the second fragment in Chapter 11, in the A section. It is thus an ascription rather than a direct quotation. The number in the brackets "[13]" corresponds to an entry in the Suggestions for Further Reading at the end of this volume. Students will find an excellent comprehensive presentation of the fragments of the Presocratics in Greek with English translations in [15]; a clear exposition of their main contributions is to be found in [16].

3 DK 11 A 10.

4 Philosophers distinguish two forms of knowledge: the *a priori* and the *a posteriori*. One has *a priori* knowledge concerning a proposition *p* if, and only if, one knows *p* by reason or conceptual resources. *A posteriori* knowledge is knowledge that is not *a priori*. Typically, we think that mathematics and logic are *a priori*, while empirical science is *a posteriori*. To know that it is necessary that squares have interior angles equaling 360 degrees, we do not need to conduct an experiment. Indeed, some would say, it is impossible to know this proposition on the basis of empirical research. This proposition is known *a priori*. By contrast, if we want to know whether vitamin C helps prevent the common cold, then we need to design and execute a controlled experiment in order to collect and evaluate the relevant data. This proposition is known, if at all, *a posteriori*. The distinction between *a priori* and *a posteriori* knowledge as it has developed in the last two centuries corresponds in all essentials to a distinction employed by the philosophers discussed in this volume in terms of what is *known by reason* and what is *known by experience*. Note that both distinctions pertain to how knowledge is *justified*, not how it is *acquired*. Though a student may learn that 2+2 = 4 from her elementary school teacher, her knowledge that this proposition is true, indeed necessarily true, is not justified by appealing to what her teacher told her. Instead, it is justified by appeal to the nature of the plus function. It is known *a priori* or *by reason*.

5 DK 21 B 16.

6 DK 21 B 15.

 7 DK 21 B 11.
 8 DK 21 B 23, DK 21 B 24, DK 21 B 25, DK 21 B 26.
 9 DK 21 B 35.
10 DK 21 B 34.
11 DK 21 B 34.
12 DK 22 B 19.
13 DK 22 B 56, DK 22 B 42.
14 DK 22 B 54.
15 DK 22 B 123.
16 DK 22 B 9, DK 22 B 4, DK 22 B 37.
17 In fact, there were various, non-equivalent formulations of this maxim current in antiq-
     uity, DK 22 B 12, DK 22 B 91a–b, DK 22 B 49a. The text discusses an amalgam of
     them.
18 For Heracleitus' influence on Plato, see 3.2 below.
19 *Theaetetus* 152a–e.
20 This exchange is speculatively reconstructed from DK 23 B 2 = K 170b = DL iii 10–11.
21 DK 22 B 60.
22 DK 22 B 61.
23 DK 22 B 83.
24 DK 22 B 107.
25 DK 22 B 1.
26 DK 22 B 1.
27 DK 22 B 88.
28 DK 22 B 50.
29 DK 28 B 8.
30 On *a priori* vs *a posteriori* knowledge, see note 4 above.
31 DK 28 B 7.
32 (BP) is formulated to capture Parmenides' suggestion that what is and what can be
     thought are co-extensive. See DK 28 B 8.
33 Those interested in pursuing some of the fascinating history and developments of Zeno's
     paradoxes of motion would do well to begin with the excellent collection edited by
     Wesley C. Salmon, *Zeno's Paradoxes* (Hackett, 2001).
34 DK 68 B 156.
35 DK 68 B 11.
36 DK 68 B 9.
37 DK 68 B 125.
38 DK 80 B 1.
39 See Herodotus, *Histories* iii 38.
40 DK 22 B 16.
41 Numbers in brackets refer to the comprehensive Suggestions for Further Reading
     compiled at the end of this book.

Suggestions for additional readings

Primary text

For common reference to the Presocratics and some of the Sophists, scholars
use the following collection of Greek fragments, most of which have accompanying German translations:

Diels, H., *Die Fragmente der Vorsokratiker*, sixth edition, revised by Walter Kranz (Berlin:
    Weidmann, 1952).

Students will find English translations in:

Sprague, R. (ed.) *The Older Sophists: A Complete Translation by Several Hands of the Fragments in Die Fragmente der Vorsokratiker*, edited by Diels–Kranz. With a new edition of Antiphon and of Euthydemus (Columbia, South Carolina: University of South Carolina Press, 1972).

For a selection of Presocratic fragments in Greek with English translations and helpful commentary, the best source is:

G.S. Kirk, J.E. Raven, and M. Schofield, *The Presocratic Philosophers*, second edition (Cambridge: Cambridge University Press, 1983).

Secondary literature

For clear and accessible introductions to the Presocratics consult:

McKirihan, R., *Philosophy before Socrates: An Introduction with Texts and Commentary* (Cambridge, MA: Hackett, 1994).
Hussey, E., *The Presocratics* (London: Duckworth, 1972).
Burnet, J., *Early Greek Philosophy* (London: A. and C. Black, 1932 [1892]).

A full and lively though somewhat less accessible treatment can be found in:

Barnes, J., *The Presocratic Philosophers* (London: Routledge, 1982).

Additionally, students will find a wealth of information about the Presocratics in [1], [2], and [3].[41]

2 Socrates

When he was 70 years old, the philosopher Socrates (469–399) was tried by the Athenians for being impious. At the trial's end, he was convicted by a majority of a jury consisting of 500 of his fellow citizens. His punishment: death by poisoning. Although Socrates left no first-hand account of the proceedings, his associate Plato offers dramatic reconstructions in dialogue form of Socrates' defense speech at his trial, of his period of imprisonment after the trial, and of his final conversations on the day of his execution.[1] Although often at variance with the portrayals of Socrates offered by some others among his immediate contemporaries,[2] the presentation of Socrates found in Plato's writings is both captivating and complex: Socrates could be charming or unrefined; caustic or conciliatory; coy or transparently sincere; determined in his beliefs or avowedly agnostic. Through this complexity emerges an unmistakable portrait of a man with a formidable intellect and an uncompromising character.

Plato's writings also contain some explanation of why Socrates might have been disliked, even intensely disliked. He was in the habit of engaging his fellow citizens in sometimes uncomfortable discussions in which they would be forced to reveal surprising forms of ignorance concerning the very topics about which they professed to have expert knowledge. Typically, Socrates began a discussion by posing a direct and unadorned question about the nature of some simple, familiar moral quality. His interlocutors would claim to know a fair bit about that quality, but would eventually crumble under Socratic questioning, most often by lapsing into painfully obvious self-contradiction.

In one characteristic instance, Plato recounts how Socrates, on the way into his own life-ending trial, runs into an acquaintance named Euthyphro, who had himself just completed some legal business. Asked by Socrates what that business concerned, Euthyphro reports that he had just initiated a trial against his own father on a charge of impiety, the very charge which Socrates was himself about to face. Although Socrates is surprised, Euthyphro is nonplussed: as far as he is concerned, his father has committed a crime and so needs to be brought to justice. Even if other members of his family blame him, Euthyphro can remain confident, even sanctimonious, in his self-righteous expression of his own secure knowledge. He knows that it is appropriate to bring charges, because he knows that his father has been impious.

Despite his own distressing circumstances, Socrates cannot resist the opportunity to pose a question which is at once both simple and revolutionary. The question is this: what is piety? The question is simple for the obvious reason that it merely asks Euthyphro to explain what he says he already knows. It is revolutionary because no philosopher had yet asked this sort of question in so naked a form. Although Xenophanes had implicitly relied upon an analysis of knowledge when issuing his skeptical challenges, he had never stepped back and asked in a direct way: what is knowledge?[3] Similarly, Parmenides denied the existence of change and plurality; but he did so by relying on an unarticulated understanding of each and never demanded an account of either. Even Protagoras championed relativism about value without first inquiring into the nature of value as such. By contrast, Socrates indulges in an *impulse for analysis*. He wants to know, for example, *what piety is*; and he seems genuinely delighted when someone like Euthyphro comes along claiming to have that knowledge.

In requesting such an analysis, Socrates does not seem at all concerned with the *concept* of piety, at least not if this is understood as confined to Euthyphro's particular take on piety. Rather, Socrates wants an analysis of the quality or property *being pious* or piety, that very thing, he says, whose presence makes all pious actions pious (*Euthyphro* 6d). So, he is not at all interested in what some later philosophers called *conceptual analysis* where this is restricted to a consideration of the deep structure of our conceptual scheme; instead, he wants the very thing sought analyzed so that its nature can be displayed. If a chemist wants a chemical analysis of sodium, then she does not want an account of how someone happens to conceive of the stuff; she wants the stuff itself investigated so that its nature may be learned. Socrates wants the chemistry of piety, not its sociology or psychology.

Sadly, though, Euthyphro proves unable to deliver the goods. When questioned by Socrates, he ends up offering a view which cannot withstand scrutiny. At the same time, despite his subjecting Euthyphro's assertions to investigation, Socrates claims that he himself lacks knowledge of the answer he seeks. Although he can see why Euthyphro's answer fails, Socrates has nothing himself to offer in its place. In this way, Socrates' method seems primarily destructive. Thinking that no one really wants to be self-deluded about their own epistemic defects, he means to reveal the ignorance of others as a benefit to them. He even seems to expect his inter-locutors to thank him for helping them to uncover their previously undetected ignorance. For the most part, they do not thank him. Instead, they are embarrassed, humiliated, and sometimes enraged. At the end of his questioning, Euthyphro does not become enraged. In fact, he seems hardly to appreciate what has just happened to him. In his encounter with Socrates, Euthyphro is plainly unable to explain what he says he knows. Nonetheless, at the end of their discussion, when it is pointed out that they have made no progress at all, Euthyphro simply slips away, eager to carry on with some pressing affairs.

In many ways, Socrates' encounter with Euthyphro is deeply character-istic of his method and mission. Most centrally, it reveals three consistent

Socratic traits: an impulse towards analysis; a profession of ignorance; and a method of inquiry used over and over again in his encounters with others, the method of *elenchus*.

2.1   The Socratic elenchus

In an elenchus, Socrates poses a series of questions designed to elicit a statement of the nature or essence of some important virtue. In every case, the questions eventually uncover an inability on the part of his interlocutors, most often by revealing a contradiction lurking within their thinking on the topic. In the abstract, a typical elenchus is a six-stage process:

1   Socrates asks a question of the form: What is F-ness? (What is courage? What is justice? What is virtue?)
2   The respondent answers: F-ness is G. (Courage is standing firm in battle. Justice is helping one's friends and harming one's enemies. Virtue is the ability to acquire good things.)
3   Socrates elicits additional beliefs from his respondent. (Is it possible to stand firm in battle because of being frozen by fear? Is it just to help one's friends when they have themselves been unjust? Is virtue always just? Cannot one acquire good things unjustly?)
4   Socrates shows his interlocutors that their views are internally inconsistent. (It is not possible to hold simultaneously, e.g.: (a) virtue is the acquisition of good things; (b) virtuous activity is always just activity; (c) the acquisition of good things is sometimes unjust.)
5   Socrates' interlocutors realize that they have endorsed an inconsistent set of propositions and so must give something up. They almost invariably give up their initial response to Socrates' request for an analysis.
6   Socrates professes to share their ignorance and recommends a renewed search for the essence of the moral quality under consideration.

Naturally enough, those thus refuted by Socrates sometimes find him vexing; it hardly mollifies them to hear Socrates protest that he too is ignorant.

More to the point, when Socrates professes both ignorance and a renewed desire to analyze the quality in question, he seems to place himself in an awkward position. It is in the first instance difficult to appreciate how – though Socrates sometimes claims more on its behalf – the elenchtic method is anything but destructive.[4] Socrates asks his customary question, the *what-is-F-ness question*. His interlocutors hazard a response. That response is shown to be inadequate, because it is inconsistent with other things believed by the interlocutor. So, the original response is rejected. Why suppose that this process of refutation will not go on indefinitely? As a matter of fact, all of Plato's Socratic dialogues are *aporetic*:[5] they end in puzzlement with an expression of ignorance. Given the method they employ, this may seem perfectly predictable. Moreover, from a purely formal point of view, it is not easy to understand why Socrates and his fellows so readily give up their original responses to his what-is-F-ness questions. That is, when a contradiction emerges under the force of Socratic questioning, all that is rationally required of the interlocutor is that one of the offending beliefs be withdrawn. Nothing from the standpoint of logic recommends that the original response, the attempted analysis, be rejected over any other belief in the inconsistent set.

Perhaps Socrates and his fellow seekers presuppose a shared conception of what successful analysis will accomplish; and they may also think that they have available within themselves the resources to determine when an attempted analysis has failed. At any rate, this much is accepted in Plato's *Charmides*, where the what-is-F-ness question concerns the nature of the virtue temperance. When invited to investigate its nature by using whatever method suits him best, Socrates notes that if temperance is present in someone, it will give its bearer a clue not only to its presence, but will also indicate to them the contours of its undisclosed nature.[6] By extension he seems to hold, then, that if someone is pious, piety itself will provide evidence about its own nature. So, if Euthyphro really is pious, he ought to be able at least to make some progress toward characterizing its nature.

Judged in its most general terms, the suggestion that possession breeds awareness seems absurdly optimistic. (If I am a habitually self-deceived person, there is no reason to suppose that I have any special access to the nature of self-deception.) Still, Socrates may be expressing a more modest optimism, that if we are acquainted with piety, then with enough hard conceptual work we should at least be able to move to a deeper understanding of its nature by analyzing it. Looked at from this remove, the Socratic impulse to analysis assumes only that the philosophical analysis of at least some core qualities can in principle be successful. Presumably, the suggestion that we have the resources within ourselves to conduct the sort of inquiry necessary for genuine progress is primarily a way of saying that the methods of philosophical analysis are largely or exclusively *a priori*.

However that may be, the strengths and weaknesses of the elenchtic method are best appreciated by reflecting on some substantive examples. For this purpose, two different sorts of illustrations are needed, because Socrates demonstrates the inadequacies of his interlocutors' views in two importantly different ways. In the first kind of refutation, Socrates seeks to show only that the view under examination is not even extensionally adequate. That is, Socrates seeks to show how the proposed analysis does not even capture the uncontroversial examples of the quality under investigation by providing a simple or straightforward counterexample.[7] The second form of refutation is subtler: in some instances, Socrates intends to show that though a proposed analysis may be extensionally adequate, it fails nonetheless. In this sort of refutation, Socrates demands more than extensional adequacy for successful analysis.

The illustration of the first form of refutation is drawn from Plato's *Meno*, where Plato and Meno jointly illustrate the nature of virtue, or *aretê*. For an illustration of the second type, there is nothing better than the aporetic investigation of the nature of piety conducted by Socrates and Euthyphro.

2.2   The failures of Meno and Euthyphro

When Socrates bumps into the Thessalian aristocrat Meno, who has come to Athens for some unspecified business, he engages him in a question made significant by the activities of the Sophists. The Sophists had claimed to teach virtue, or *aretê*, and had charged a fee for their services.[8] Given that *aretê* extended not just to moral virtue narrowly construed but to the forms of excellence associated with distinguished ability in the crafts or in the conduct of life generally, there were fair questions about what they taught and whether what they claimed to teach was in fact teachable. The problem can be understood in this way. We might speak of a doctor's primary virtue as consisting in her diagnostic technique or of a certain lawyer's virtue as residing more in his rhetorical abilities than in his fastidious research, but we also speak more narrowly of virtues of character associated with moral probity. So, the doctor is excellent in one way, the lawyer in another, and exceptionally moral persons in still another. If a man now claims to teach excellence as such, one might well want to know before offering him payment exactly what that payment will purchase. These are the sorts of questions Socrates asks Meno, not because Meno is himself a sophist but because of an alleged Thessalian admiration for the Sophist Gorgias, who did profess the teachability of *aretê*. Given the Socratic impulse for analysis, these questions give way rather quickly to another. What is virtue? Or, what is excellence? Socrates professes ignorance; Meno claims to know.[9]

Meno claims first that the virtue of a man consists in his ability to manage civic affairs and to benefit his friends while harming his enemies; the virtue of a woman consists in her managing her home well while being submissive to her husband; and the virtues of children, the elderly, and slaves are different again. Indeed, there is a virtue "for every action and every age."[10]

Socrates' response to this first attempt has both methodological and substantive consequences. He quips that although he had asked for one virtue, he has been beset by an entire swarm by Meno's response. Meno had responded to a what-is-F-ness question by characterizing a plurality of virtues. In reply, Socrates insists that even if there are various distinct virtues, they must all have one and the same form, something whose presence *makes* all virtuous actions virtuous. Just as men and women can be healthy in different ways, what it is to be healthy is the same for them both. So, if we want to know what health in general is, we will want to uncover what men and women have in common when they are healthy. Socrates assumes, then, that unified analyses are possible for the qualities whose natures he investigates. That is, he adopts a *univocity assumption*, according to which there is a single unified definition or analysis for the qualities of concern to him. He recognizes that both a lion and a soldier can be brave. Nonetheless, when investigating the nature of bravery, when answering the question, *What is bravery?*, Socrates hopes for an account which will capture what all and only instances of bravery have in common. Even if there are various types of virtue, then, there should be one thing, virtue, whose general nature we can understand and display. Socrates goes so far as to suggest that virtue is like shape. Although squares and circles are both shapes, pointing to neither answers the question, *What is shape?*[11] Only an analysis of the quality *being a shape* will display what all and only shapes have in common.

In the face of Socrates' univocity assumption, Meno finally determines that virtue is simply the ability to acquire good things. This may seem an odd suggestion. Still, if it is recalled that *aretê* extends beyond moral virtue, Meno's proposed analysis need not seem at all peculiar. It is as if someone, when asked what an excellent kind of life might be, responds that an excellent life would be a life in which one had the ability to acquire all of the good things one wants. Whether correct or incorrect, that claim at least merits a hearing.

The hearing from Socrates is brief; he swiftly and easily reduces Meno to contradiction. Socrates points out that it is plainly possible to acquire good things unjustly, by stealing or lying. Yet, as Meno agrees, the expression of virtue can never be unjust. So, we have an inconsistent triad: (1) virtue is the ability to acquire good things; (2) an expression of virtue cannot be unjust; and (3) one can acquire good things unjustly. Moreover, if we amend (1) so that we treat virtue as the ability to acquire good things justly, we have lapsed back into our earlier problem of trying to define virtue by appealing to just one of its kinds, since justice is only one form of virtue, as if we were to define shape as any figure relevantly like a circle.[12]

Socrates' refutation of Meno illustrates more than a simple reliance on a univocity assumption. It also highlights how a successful Socratic analysis must be at least extensionally adequate. Meno fails because he includes in the class of virtuous actions some things which are manifestly not instances of virtue, like stealing. When he tries to rule such actions out, he fails in a different direction by being too specific. For now he suggests that virtue is the ability to acquire things justly. Unfortunately, he had already agreed that there are many virtues beyond justice, including moderation, wisdom, and munificence.[13] So, Meno has once again failed even to get the extension of virtue right. In different ways, then, Meno's failures illustrate not only Socrates' univocity assumption, but also his perfectly reasonable demand that any proposed analysis be at least extensionally adequate.

Now, in response to Socrates, Meno might simply have listed all of the agreed-upon virtues. He could then have claimed that an action of any one of the listed types would qualify as virtuous. He might then have at least claimed to have specified the extension adequately. Had he done so, Socrates would still not have been satisfied. This much is clear from Socrates' treatment of Euthyphro, who not only gets the extension of the quality he investigates right, but evidently goes a step further by identifying a class which is *necessarily* co-extensive with that quality. Yet even then Socrates remains dissatisfied. This implies that extensional adequacy is not sufficient for Socratic analysis: a successful instance of analysis, Socrates implies, must be *more than* merely extensionally adequate. To see that this is so, it is necessary to consider a stronger, subtler form of elenchtic refutation than the one we find in the *Meno*.

When asked by Socrates to characterize piety, Euthyphro makes his first misstep. He asserts that piety is doing just what he is doing, prosecuting a wrongdoer even when that wrongdoer is a relative. Socrates is not pleased, because Euthyphro has given the wrong sort of answer altogether. Socrates wants a general account; Euthyphro provides an example — or a possible example. Even if his action is in fact pious, his pointing that out does not constitute an analysis of piety. Both Socrates and Euthyphro agree that all pious actions are pious "through one form" (6e). So, a successful account had better capture that commonality. Euthyphro's first response fails on these grounds. Moreover, Socrates insists on an account which will be epistemically serviceable in the sense that it will be possible to look upon it as a model and use it as a standard to judge whether putative cases of piety are in fact instances of piety or not. Socrates wants an account that will guide him when matters are grey, as they seem to be in Euthyphro's own case.

Euthyphro comes to appreciate the force of the univocity assumption and so responds with an appropriately general account: an action is pious just in case it is loved by the gods. Socrates is much happier with this approach, though he does elicit a significant qualification from Euthyphro, that the gods will have to speak with one voice on such matters if the proposal is to have a chance of succeeding. When he concedes this point, Euthyphro implicitly also rejects Protagoreanism, since he now allows that it cannot be the case that one and the same action can be both pious and impious, depending upon which god has it in view. At any rate, Euthyphro's proposal is now at least of the right form.

Indeed, the theory thus articulated has an important history, one beginning before Plato and extending down to the current day. For it is reasonable to view Euthyphro's attitude toward the nature of piety as a natural response to Protagorean relativism, one as widespread today as it was in antiquity. Under Socratic questioning, Euthyphro articulates a realist conception of piety which seems a special case of a more general attitude towards morality espoused, for example, by Antigone, who held that the gods have immutable laws which are superior to transitory human laws, and that, consequently, divine law trumps human law when they come into conflict.[14] Euthyphro's conception of piety is, then, easily viewed as an instance of the Divine Command Theory of Morality, according to which: an action A is morally required if, and only if, A is commanded by the gods; and an action A' is morally forbidden if, and only if, the gods command that A' not be done. On this theory, some actions must be done, others cannot be done, and still others are indifferent from the standpoint of morality. A familiar account from the book of Exodus in the Old Testament has it that honoring one's parents is morally required and that stealing is morally forbidden; but as far as those commands are concerned, driving a red car as opposed to a blue car is a matter of moral indifference.

Given that it is an instance of the Divine Command Theory, Euthyphro's final analysis of piety takes on an added significance, as well as some advantages and disadvantages relative to his first attempts at analysis. It can claim as an advantage at least that it satisfies a demand for univocity: according to Euthyphro, to be pious is to be loved by the gods. Still, although he is happy about this much, Socrates proceeds to raise a devastating problem for Euthyphro's analysis. He asks a simple question: Is the pious loved by the gods because it is pious, or is it pious because the gods love it? (The question also has a more general form: Are moral actions moral because God commands them, or does God command them because they are moral?) This question contains the seeds of a dilemma for Euthyphro, one which emerges in a frightfully complex and subtle exchange whose ultimate conclusion is that Euthyphro has failed to capture the nature of piety because he has instead succeeded only in specifying one feature or quality of piety, namely that the gods love it.[15]

Importantly, this conclusion already permits us to glean the standards Socrates sets for successful analysis. Factoring in the univocity assumption already encountered, these are three. A successful analysis must be: (1) fully general and univocal; (2) epistemically serviceable; and (3) more than extensionally adequate. We have already encountered the first two of these constraints in Socrates' treatment of Meno. The third is new and requires elaboration. Socrates expects an analysis of piety to show what is essential to piety; this in turn requires that its intrinsic nature be specified. It will consequently not suffice merely to capture a feature of piety, even if that feature is something it has non-contingently. That is, even if it is true that the qualities *being morally mandatory* and *being commanded by God* are instantiated by all and only the same actions, and even if this is necessarily the case, it will not follow directly that *being commanded by God* provides any form of analysis of the quality of *being morally mandatory*. In the same way, from Socrates' point of view, neither *being triangular* nor *being trilateral* provides an adequate analysis of the other, even though, necessarily, every triangle is trilateral and every trilateral is triangular. For an example unavailable to Socrates: *being a recursive function* and *being Turing-computable* are necessarily co-extensive, though they are distinct qualities and neither is an analysis of the other. In general, Socrates demands more than necessary co-extension.

This is why he complains that Euthyphro failed to make the *nature* of piety clear when asked to do so. Euthyphro failed to provide an analysis because he merely identified one of its qualities, that it be dear to the gods.[16] The argument for this conclusion, Euthyphro's Problem (EP), is both complex and intricate. It proceeds in two stages:

EP Stage One:

1   Whenever x is affected by some y, x acquires the quality of being affected because y affects it; it is not the case that y acquires the quality of affecting something because x is something affected.
2   Being loved is a way of being affected.
3   Hence, when x is loved, x acquires the quality of being loved *because* some y loves it; it is not the case that y acquires the quality of loving x *because* x is something loved.
4   The pious is loved by the gods.
5   Hence, the pious acquires the quality of being loved *because* something, namely the gods, love it.

So far, Socrates has elicited the thought that something's being god-loved is explained by an activity of the gods, namely their loving what it is that they love. Thus, what explains the pious being loved is precisely that the gods love it. The thought here is that whenever something is affected in a certain way, its being affected in that way is explained by the activity which brings about its being so affected. This much seems utterly unproblematic. If Larry loves Sally, then what explains the fact that Sally has the quality of being loved is precisely Larry's loving her. By contrast, the fact that Sally is loved does not explain Larry's loving her. In this way, Larry's loving Sally is *explanatorily prior* to Sally's having the quality *being loved*. Socrates also establishes in this phase of the argument that explanatory priority is asymmetric. If x explains y, then y does not also explain x. (If a partially blocked coronary artery explains someone's shortness of breath and persistent fatigue, then it is not also the case these symptoms explain her having a partially blocked coronary artery.)

Now the question becomes whether what explains an action's being pious can be its being loved by the gods. Socrates legitimately wants to know this, since on Euthyphro's proposal being pious and being loved by the gods are really the same thing. Indeed, an analysis of piety, on his proposal, reveals its nature to be just this, *being loved by the gods*. Hence, if correct, Euthyphro's view would entail that anytime we wanted to explain why something was pious, we could, or indeed would need to, appeal to its being loved by the gods. This, contends Socrates, we cannot do: the qualities of being pious and being god-loved are at best necessarily co-extensive.

The second stage of the argument, which is a bit more difficult than the first, is intended to show why this is so:

EP Stage Two:

6 An arbitrary action A is pious because it has the quality of being pious.
7 If A is also loved by the gods, that is because A is pious.
8 If (7), then A's being pious is explanatorily prior to A's being loved by the gods.
9 So, A's being pious is explanatorily prior to its being loved by the gods.
10 If Euthyphro's proposed analysis were correct, one could analyze (6) as (6'): an arbitrary action A is pious because it has the quality of being loved by the gods.
11 If (6'), then A's being loved by the gods is explanatorily prior to its being pious.
12 Given (9), it is not possible that then A's being loved by the gods is explanatorily prior to its being pious.
13 Hence, (6') is not an acceptable analysis of (6).
14 Hence, Euthyphro's proposed analysis of piety is incorrect.

This is a complicated argument, in need of explication and defense. Its very complexity in the elenchtic context already demonstrates an intellectual nimbleness on the part of Socrates unexemplified by any of his predecessors.

Crucial to this entire argument is a notion of explanatory priority. Socrates assumes in (EP-12) something he takes himself to have established in the first phase of the argument, that explanatory priority is asymmetric. Armed with this assumption, Socrates has an easy time drawing Euthyphro into contradiction: Euthyphro holds both that being pious is explanatorily prior to being loved by the gods and also that being loved by the gods is explanatorily prior to being pious. He thus violates the asymmetry of explanatory priority. Hence, Euthyphro's analysis fails.

It fails, that is, on the assumption, granted by Euthyphro, of (EP-7), that if an arbitrary action A is loved by the gods, that is because A is pious. For it is here that Euthyphro agrees that being pious is explanatorily prior to being loved by the gods. Perhaps he has made a mistake here? Perhaps he should simply deny (EP-7), and maintain that the gods might love just any old action. That would, after all, permit him to reject (EP-9) and so affirm (EP-11) and conclude that (EP-6') is the correct analysis of (EP-6). That, to be sure, is the purport of his view, which, again, is simply a special case of the Divine Command Theory of Morality.

In fact, Euthyphro does not step back and reflect on whether he should have conceded (EP-7), when it would have been at least consistent for him not to have done so. Presumably, then, Euthyphro also shares a further assumption with Socrates, one not defended or even articulated by either of them. It is this: it is possible that there are some actions so intrinsically impious that no god would ever love them. Put more generally in terms of the Divine Command Theory, the assumption is that there are some actions so intrinsically despicable that an all-good God would never, indeed *could* never, command them. Defenders of Euthyphro, or proponents of the Divine Command Theory, might want to query this assumption. In the context of the *Euthyphro* itself, however, Socrates is content to point out something which would provide an impediment to anyone wanting to defend Euthyphro. Certainly, he concludes, whatever the essence of piety turns out to be, it will be something intrinsic to piety itself. By looking to something outside of piety, Euthyphro guarantees his own failure: he identifies something extrinsic, when he was asked to identify something intrinsic, something essential.

It is a subtlety of Socrates' method that he nowhere denies that the gods will love what is pious, or by extension that God will command what is moral. On the contrary, he seems to allow that it is reasonable to expect the gods, of necessity, to love the pious, or God, of necessity, to command what is moral. His worry is simply that establishing necessary co-extension of this sort is insufficient to answer the what-is-F-ness question. His interaction with Euthyphro reveals why Socrates maintains this. Necessary co-extension by itself does not capture explanatory priority. This is why a successful analysis must be more than extensionally adequate. This is also why the demands Socrates places upon Euthyphro turn out to be interrelated and mutually supportive. By being fully general and univocal, a successful analysis must capture the essence of the quality investigated; if an essence is to be displayed, the analysis must capture what is intrinsic and explanatorily prior; but if it does this much, the successful analysis will also be epistemically serviceable. It will allow Socrates to look to the analysis to determine whether the form of the quality is present in any given action. Knowing that much would enable him to know also whether a putative instance of piety, even one which is disputed, as Euthyphro's own action is, in fact qualifies as an instance of the kind.

In different ways, Socrates' interactions with Meno and Euthyphro reveal distinctive features of his philosophical method. When he indulges in an impulse for analysis, Socrates expects his interlocutors to meet a high standard. He brings with him a univocity assumption which conditions his expectations regarding answers to any given what-is-F-ness question. A successful analysis must be fully general and univocal; must be epistemically serviceable; and must be more than extensionally adequate. On this last point, Socrates' treatment of Meno shows that a proposed analysis must be *at least* extensionally adequate; his treatment of Euthyphro reveals further that a successful analysis must indeed be more than extensionally adequate, with the result that not even necessary co-extension suffices for Socratic analysis.

2.3   Socratic ignorance and Socratic irony

At the end of his discussion with Euthyphro, Socrates reports a profound disappointment. Had he learned the nature of piety from Euthyphro, he could have escaped the charges of impiety leveled against him by demonstrating that he had at last acquired wisdom about the divine, with the result that his ignorance would no longer cause him to be careless and inattentive about such matters. In fact, he laments that with such knowledge, "I would be better for the rest of my life."[17]

Given the obvious dexterity of his examination of Euthyphro, it is difficult to appreciate how Socrates could be as ignorant as he says he is. Nor is this profession of ignorance at all uncommon.[18] Indeed, some of the principal skeptical figures of later antiquity came to claim Socrates as their intellectual progenitor.[19] They thought that Socrates was perfectly skeptical, that he professed ignorance because he realized that knowledge was impossible; and that he had defensible reasons for maintaining such a posture. It is for this reason that some of his interlocutors accuse him of disingenuity or of a kind of caustic and cruel irony.[20] In this way, accusations of irony and professions of ignorance tend to go hand in glove for Socrates. Given that he must know the answers to some of what he asks, his critics suppose, Socrates must also be insincere when he insists that he does not. His insincerity reveals itself in the way he mocks and toys with the likes of Euthyphro, whom Socrates very clearly outclasses intellectually – so very clearly in fact that Euthyphro does not even recognize how thoroughly he has been refuted. Other interlocutors are not so obtuse; they feel the sting of the Socratic elenchus and respond with shame-driven anger.

This view of Socrates as a remorselessly ironic intellectual gamesman primarily interested in his own amusement has found its champions. Still, it is easy to see that nothing in Plato's presentation of Socrates warrants it. To begin, there is no reason at all to suppose that Socrates really must know the answers to the what-is-F-ness questions he poses. What one must suppose is merely that Socrates has a facility for exposing contradictions in the belief sets of his interlocutors. Surely it is possible for someone who does not know whether Fermat's last theorem is true or false to recognize an unsuccessful attempt to prove its truth or falsity – especially if that attempt can be exposed to contain internal inconsistencies. So, someone who does not know whether a given proposition p is true can nevertheless know that someone else who claims to know p in fact does not. There is no reason, therefore, to convict Socrates of disingenuity or malicious irony on any such general grounds.

The question then becomes whether he could possibly manifest his ability to uncover contradictions without ultimately having the knowledge he says he lacks. Clearly he could. He might well have some knowledge, but lack *certain* knowledge; or have common knowledge but no *expert* knowledge; or he might have knowledge in some spheres but not in others. For the most part, he seems only to deny that he commands knowledge of a complete and successful analysis of any of the qualities he investigates. His lacking this sort of *analytical* knowledge would reasonably and defensibly prompt him to characterize himself as ignorant in the context of philosophical analysis. It would also be compatible with a fair bit of elenchtic success, since complete analytical knowledge is not required for elementary progress. Nor is it required to refute those who go badly and obviously astray. (A non-scientist could legitimately correct someone who thought that uranium was a gas, even if she could not specify its place on the periodic table.) Accordingly, without first exhausting all of these possible explanations for Socrates' indisputable elenchtic success, there is absolutely no reason to suppose that he *must really* know the answers to the questions he poses; and without that conclusion, there is in turn absolutely no reason to convict him of disingenuous irony. So far, Socrates may be perfectly sincere. Indeed, it seems plainly correct to insist, as he does, that the impulse to analysis begins in ignorance, in *aporia* even; it is precisely when we feel befuddled that the impulse to philosophize takes hold. In this sense, Socratic ignorance is a pretty common and reasonably widespread sort of phenomenon; it is when we do not know, not when we know, that we engage in analysis.

Moreover, the suggestion that Socrates is *completely* ignorant simply does not square with Plato's portrayal him. Plato does represent him as claiming that he is crucially ignorant in analytical contexts. Even so, he equally represents him as a man with deep moral convictions which are sufficiently entrenched that they govern his personal conduct and character. These convictions are sometimes commonplace; but they are also sometimes perplexing, so much so that they have even seemed paradoxical.

2.4   Socratic conviction and the Socratic paradoxes

If Socrates claims to lack the knowledge required to produce successful analyses of key moral qualities, he does not also claim that he lacks knowledge of important action-guiding moral principles. Moreover, he expresses confidence that certain sorts of moral claims will always succumb to an elenchus, presumably because he knows that they are flawed. Sometimes his views sound like commonsense moral platitudes. He insists, for example, that perpetrating injustice with impunity can never be a good thing; and he claims that it is never in the end just to harm another person and that in general it is never acceptable to do evil. At other times, however, he advances views that are deeply counterintuitive, which therefore require defense if they are to be taken seriously. In some cases, his defenses lie surprisingly close to his moral platitudes. Thus, for example, after noting that it is never just to harm another, he infers first that one should therefore never return harm for harm, and, ultimately, that it is better to suffer than to perpetrate evil or harm. Here Socrates moves from an innocuous-sounding claim, one which may appear utterly unproblematic, to a claim which many will have some difficulty endorsing.[21] In other cases, Socrates' defenses are more obscure and his views more difficult to fathom.

In these other cases, having to do mainly with the relationship between knowledge and virtue, Socrates advances views which are so counterintuitive that they have come to be known as the *Socratic paradoxes*. Still, we should be cautious about regarding Socrates' central moral theses as properly paradoxical, in the sense in which Zeno's views were paradoxical. When putting forth his paradoxes, Zeno had shown each of two mutually incompatible propositions to be motivated by seemingly inescapable premises.[22] Although some of what Socrates says may seem initially outlandish, an outlandish belief is not in itself a paradox, even if it offends common sense. At any rate, one of the most famous of the so-called Socratic paradoxes does not take the form of a paradox properly so called. It is, rather, a striking and surprising thesis which if defensible requires us to adopt some revisionary attitudes about our commonsense moral psychology.

This thesis is Socrates' claim that weakness of will, or *akrasia*, is impossible.[23] Most people, says Socrates, believe that they are sometimes weak-willed. They believe that even when they know what is best, they sometimes fail to do it. In such cases, they are overcome by the prospect of pleasure, with the result that their knowledge is dragged around like a slave by their non-rational passions and desires. For example, sometimes a student knows that she should study for an important examination but finds the possibility of socializing with her friends simply too enticing. Although she will later regret her action – and may even realize ahead of time that she will later come to regret her action – she decides to party and not to study. She does this even though, it seems, she recognizes that it is not in her own best interest to do so. She does not do what she believes, or even knows, to be prudential.

More common still is the experience of failing to do what one knows to be moral. A preacher may sincerely believe that prostitution is wrong. Nonetheless, when confronted with an opportunity to indulge in some taboo sexual practices which would be otherwise unavailable to him, he succumbs. Maybe he even does this every Friday evening, just after he has prepared Sunday's sermon. Later, when he is caught, he cries a river on television while begging forgiveness; he says that he deeply regrets his actions, that he was weak, that we are all sinners. Socrates does not doubt his sincerity; but he does doubt the accuracy of his self-characterization.

These two scenarios seem to illustrate related failures. The student is *prudentially weak*. The preacher is *morally weak*. What they have in common is that both know that all things considered they should do action A; but neither does A; instead, each does some other action B, which they come to regret. They differ in that the student judges primarily on prudential grounds, while the preacher judges primarily on moral grounds. Still, they can both describe themselves as having been overcome by pleasure. Each has a weak will. Each is akratic.

Socrates thinks that somehow the student and the preacher have misdescribed their own experiences. For weakness of will, he contends, is simply impossible. So, those who claim to suffer from it must be mistaken. Of course, it is in principle possible for us to be mistaken about some of our experiences and motivations. We may, for example, fail to realize that we are experiencing jealousy or that we are acting upon it, even until long after we have done so, if then. We may even need to depend upon a perceptive and sympathetic friend to point out the motives of our actions to us. We can be in these ways opaque to ourselves. Even so, as Socrates realizes, we will need a special reason for coming to believe that we have never been weak-willed, or that neither the student nor the preacher has accurately described what has transpired in their own lives.

Socrates' reasons are most easily understood by focusing on prudential *akrasia*, the sort which the student seems to experience, though with certain adjustments his reasoning will apply to putative cases of moral *akrasia* as well. Socrates thinks prudential *akrasia* is impossible because its falsity is entailed by certain other theses which most people accept. Indeed, in the *Protagoras*, where his principal discussion of *akrasia* occurs, Socrates expressly ascribes these background theses to "the many," the untutored masses, in order to show them that given their own beliefs they are constrained to agree that they have misdescribed their own experiences when they claim to have been akratic. The theses are these:

Psychological egoism (PE)   Everyone always acts so as to maximize their own perceived good.

Hedonism (H)   The ultimate good for human beings is pleasure.

(PE) is a descriptive claim; it does not prescribe how people should act. Instead, it simply holds that everyone, as a matter of fact, always acts so as to maximize their own perceived good. It does not specify what that good is, however. Nonetheless, if the many understand both (PE) and (H), and can grasp the connection between them, then they also appreciate that the good everyone seeks is their own pleasure. That is, if the many agree that everyone always seeks their own good, and if they suppose that everyone knows that the good just is pleasure, then the many will also agree that the good everyone seeks is simply their own pleasure. So, according to the many, human beings are egoistic hedonists.

As Socrates notes, most people find (H) and (PE) congenial. Still, once they are granted, he is able to mount the following *reductio* for the impossibility of *akrasia* (IA):

1   (H) and (PE). (Assumed on behalf of the many.)
2   If (H), then "pleasure" and "good" name the same thing.

3   So, if S determines that A is *better* than B, S has in fact determined that A is *more pleasurable* than B.

4   If (PE), S always acts so as to maximize S's own perceived good (which is, according to (H), S's own perceived pleasure).

5   If S always acts so as to maximize S's own perceived pleasure, then it is not possible for S to determine that A is more pleasurable than B, but to do B (knowingly and willingly) nonetheless, because of the perceived pleasure B affords.

6   So, it is not possible for S to determine that A is more pleasurable than B, but to do B (knowingly and willingly) because of being overcome by pleasure.

(IA-6) is simply the denial of the possibility of *akrasia*, as construed in the *Protagoras*. For there, *akrasia* is reasonably characterized as the view that some people sometimes, having determined what is better, are overcome by the desire for pleasure and fail to do what they believe to be best. Some people are prudentially weak; others are morally weak. In fact, most people, at some points in their life, think of themselves as both. If (IA) is sound, they are wrong.

Some people assail (IA-3), because they think that it relies upon a false substitution principle, that if N and N' are co-referential singular terms, N and N' can be substituted *salva veritate* in any context whatsoever. That general principle is obviously false. (Maria can deny that her husband Burt is a transvestite, even though she knows that Bertha is a transvestite, because she does not know that her husband Burt is Bertha. Here "Burt" and "Bertha," though co-referential singular terms, cannot be substituted *salva veritate*.) Even so, it is not at all clear that (IA-3) requires any such unrestricted principle. In the context of the argument, we are assuming that S is a committed hedonist. S therefore thinks that the best course of action among the relevant alternatives is the one which affords the most pleasure. For S, *being better* simply means *being more pleasurable*. In general, S will never be in a position to determine that alternative A is all things considered better than alternative B without also maintaining that, all things considered, A affords more pleasure than B. Nothing about (IA-3) seems problematic, then, for reasons having to do with illicit substitutions of any form.

Once (IA-3) is in place, however, the rest of the argument flows fairly easily. (PE), the claim that people always act so as to maximize their own perceived good, suggests that everyone seeks to maximize their own perceived pleasure – assuming, again, that they have accepted (H), as the many in fact have done. So (IA-4) seems problem free. (IA-5) may seem to commit a modal fallacy, moving as it does from what people *always* do to what it is *possible* for them to do. Presumably, though, the proponents of (PE) do not think it is a random or contingent fact that people always act so as to maximize their own perceived good. Instead, they presume that the truth of

(PE) is rooted in some deep fact about human beings, perhaps some essential fact about human nature. Hence, whatever modality attaches to (PE) carries over: if it is true, then people cannot but attempt to maximize their own perceived good. So, (IA-5) is also in place. With that, the ultimate conclusion (IA-6) follows. So, at least relative to the premise set endorsed in common by Socrates and the many, *akrasia* is impossible.

What is especially impossible, according to Socrates, is the description of *akrasia* offered by the many. They think they can willingly do what is suboptimal because of being overcome by pleasure. Now that seems nonsense. If S wants to maximize her overall pleasure, and she reckons that A is the way to do that, then her suggestion that she pursues B nonetheless because of her being overwhelmed by pleasure amounts to her claiming that she seeks less pleasure rather than more on behalf of pleasure itself. Socrates seems on firm ground to question any such explanation. In fact, the explanation seems incoherent, embracing three mutually exclusive propositions: (1) I always maximize pleasure; (2) I judge that A affords more pleasure than B; (3) I choose B. If I now plead that I choose B because of pleasure, then since I also accept (2) I surely reject (1). Socrates insists that the common attitude toward *akrasia* is in this way incoherent.

So, what of the phenomenon? It surely *seems* that I have been weak-willed on occasion. How am I deceiving myself? This is best considered by returning to the case of the student who knows she should study but decides to party nonetheless. If she really thinks studying is preferable, then given (H), this is because she thinks that studying affords her, all things considered, the most pleasure. She believes, for example, that a life with a good job affords more pleasure than a life without financial stability; and she rightly believes that studying is instrumental to securing such a life. So, then, how can she party instead of studying? Socrates nowhere denies the obvious, that she can do precisely that. What he is denying is rather *her description* of the case, that she did this because she was weak-willed. She could not have been. Instead, she must have made a miscalculation, perhaps one induced by the propinquity of the party pleasure. However induced, though, her miscalculation is just that: a miscalculation. The student came to believe, falsely, that partying would afford her greater pleasure overall. If she was wrong about that, she was not therefore weak-willed. Instead of being akratic, the student had a cognitive failure.

This last point bears emphasizing for Socrates. He conceives the case of the student as akin to a man calculating the best way to maximize the value of his investment portfolio. No one willingly chooses to lose money in the market. Yet someone might divert a part of his portfolio to a moderately risky, short-term stock venture in the hopes of maximizing profits quickly instead of allowing the money to sit in secure and predictable long-term bond funds. His goal in either strategy remains the same: he wants to maximize his overall earnings. It is simply that he regards the short-term strategy as the best way to accomplish that goal. Now, suppose he loses money in the risky venture. Has he been akratic? It seems not; instead, he has made a miscalculation. One way of appreciating that is this: had the man had all the relevant information available to him, he would have preferred the bonds to the short-term stock. He has, as Socrates is fond of saying, acted out of ignorance. Ignorance, though, is a cognitive failure rather than an instance of weakness of the will. Of course, there will be a further question as to whether some forms of ignorance are willful, or whether we are culpable for some forms of ignorance and not others; but these questions already grant the basic point that Socrates has wanted to establish, that failures to maximize pleasure result from cognitive errors. Such failures also therefore require cognitive solutions.

Is Socrates' denial of *akrasia* a paradox? It is so only if we persist in believing that we can choose sub-optimal courses of action due to some form of non-cognitive weakness, perhaps because we are simply overcome by pleasure. Socratic cognitivism suggests that this is a self-indulgent description of our own behavior, that we are somehow passive in the face of our own choices. Really when we do something bad, he suggests, we do so as a result of intellectual slovenliness rather than a weakness in our wills, as if our knowledge were able to be dragged about like a slave and made to do the bidding of a part of ourselves determined to harm us against our own better judgments. If our judgments were secure, then we would not falter; and if we do falter, we should not blame pleasure, or the weakness of our wills. Instead, we should realize that we lack the knowledge of how to secure what is best for us. In this sense, Socrates is demanding that we describe our failures accurately. We ought to prefer explanations which capture the root causes of our misdeeds over those which misleadingly direct our attention to non-causes, self-exonerating though they may be. However uncomfortable, then, Socrates' recommendation is not in itself paradoxical.

That said, the Socratic denial of *akrasia* is bound to seem eccentric. It will eventually be questioned and partially rejected by both Plato and Aristotle. It is, consequently, worth reflecting briefly on its evident strengths and weaknesses. To begin, Socrates seems concerned only with first-order *akrasia*, that is with individual episodes of putative weakness of will. He is not immediately concerned with relatively vexatious questions regarding will-formation as such, including, for example, whether we are cognitively culpable for the development of our own dispositions and standing desires. Moreover, he has structured his argument against the backdrop of both (H) and (PE), each of which as stated certainly admits of challenges. Still, it is a strength of Socrates' argument that it can be adapted to deal with more nuanced varieties of hedonism, and even to various other non-hedonistic conceptions of our final good. As for (PE), it is either false or vacuous. (Either it admits of obvious counterexamples or else it is rendered trivial by stipulation.) To the extent that Socrates and the many rely upon it, the challenge to *akrasia* is in jeopardy. Nonetheless, the argument can easily be restructured so as to dispense with (PE) altogether. One particularly forceful restructuring rejects (PE) in favor of a kind of rational egoism, which is normative in character, insofar as it maintains that an ideally rational agent always act so as to maximize the agent's good. With that thesis in place, one which Socrates fairly clearly also accepts, the Socratic challenge to *akrasia* becomes more forceful still. Looked at this way, Socrates' argument against the possibility of *akrasia* is a sort of template which can be altered and adapted in quite a number of ways. Given how initially counterintuitive its conclusion seems, (IA) turns out be an argument with a surprising force and resilience.

2.5   Socrates on trial and in prison

Socrates holds his convictions firmly and unwaveringly. He is mainly immune to the sorts of social pressures many others feel. In this sense, he is a non-conformist who does not shrink from distinguishing himself sharply from his fellow citizens, whose moral principles he probes and whose moral improvement he seeks. In his defense speech, Socrates says that his zeal to improve himself and others is divinely inspired, that he is on a mission partly instigated by a personal god who speaks to him, giving him negative directives.[24] He also reports that he is led to question others because he wants to understand what the Oracle of Apollo at Delphi could have meant when he proclaimed – as he is reported to have done by Socrates' friend Chaerephon – that no man was wiser than Socrates. Socrates, conscious of his own profound ignorance, set out to quiz others in order to show that they were wiser than he, so that he could come to terms with the Oracle's intended riddle. He reports, for good reason, that he discovered that those with the greatest reputations in the city were the most intellectually deficient. Others too were ignorant, but understood themselves to be wise; Socrates, by contrast, was unwise but had at least the advantage of appreciating his own ignorance. As he reports, though, his persistent questioning caused him to become unpopular and to be slandered by those whose reputations for great wisdom had been deflated courtesy of a Socratic elenchus.[25]

Socrates never reports doubts about the probity of his own mission. He recognizes that even his own defense speech is likely to cause a stir, but consonant with his moral convictions, he warns the jury that their killing him will harm them more than it will harm him. Indeed, he goes so far as to say that his accuser Anytus *cannot* harm him at all, since it is not permitted "that a better man be harmed by a worse."[26] In advancing this sort of claim, Socrates seems to portray himself as morally superior to Anytus, and to others as well. Perhaps this is because he also regards himself, at least to the degree he mentions, as intellectually superior to others, those who are not even cognizant of their own ignorance. Given the connection between moral knowledge and virtuous action that we have seen maintained by Socrates, it is hard to escape the conclusion that his virtue and knowledge travel together.

If he comes across as brash or as unduly uncompromising in his own defense, Socrates seems unconcerned. Instead, as he points out repeatedly, he will act in service of the god, even when this puts him at variance with others in his city. He recounts how he refused to engage in actions he regarded as illegal or unjust, as when he rebuffed those who insisted that members of his council prosecute ten generals who had failed to rescue the Athenian survivors at the battle of Arginusae due to a violent storm, or when, after the Athenian democracy fell to the oligarchs in 404, he refused to obey their direct commands. In these instances, Socrates acts in ways consonant with his moral principles, in ways that we would expect him to act. In particular, when justice demands something incompatible with civic law, for Socrates the demands of justice take precedence, even if his meeting them will result in his own execution. So, it is unsurprising that Socrates states directly that he will not accept acquittal on the condition that he no longer practice philosophy; obedience to that sort of decree would be unjust. Socrates will obey the god rather than the city.[27]

It is, however, surprising that after having been convicted and imprisoned, Socrates refuses to escape, as he might customarily have been expected to do. Or, rather, it is surprising that he should refuse to escape for the reasons he gives in the *Crito*, a dialogue which recounts conversations conducted by Socrates while in prison awaiting his execution. For those reasons seem incompatible with the crisp distinction Socrates is prepared to draw in his defense speech between the dictates of justice and the dictates of human law. Given his oft expressed desire to improve himself and others, it seems appropriate to determine whether Socrates himself advocates an inconsistent set of beliefs regarding justice and its relation to civic law.

The case against him can be put rather simply. While in prison awaiting his execution,[28] Socrates receives a visit from his associate Crito, who tries to cajole him into escaping. Crito initially appeals to the attitudes of the many, who will likely regard Crito as having been too cheap to spend the money required to bribe the guards so that Socrates could escape and flee beyond the reach of Athenian law. As Crito notes, most people will regard him as a dishonorable man, since there is no worse reputation than to be thought to care more about money than one's friends. Unsurprisingly, Socrates chides him for his concern. We should not, he explains, care at all about what the majority thinks; instead, we should determine the counsel of the most reasonable men, the wise. That, after all, had been their custom in the past. Nothing in the present circumstance warrants abandoning their habitual reliance on reason and argument.[29]

This much seems appropriate. The problem arises when the wise counsel Socrates not to escape, evidently because civil disobedience is never justifiable. They go so far as to advise Socrates that he "must either persuade or obey" the state's orders, and abide by its decrees even unto death if he is unable to persuade the state as to the nature of justice.[30] If the wise really counsel so extreme a view, then Socrates himself acted unwisely when, as he reports in the *Apology*, he disobeyed the oligarchs. He also claimed directly in the *Apology* that he would have disobeyed any order that he cease philoso-phizing if he were to be acquitted on that condition. It is sometimes noted that the oligarchs did not constitute a legitimate government, and that Socrates in fact only threatened to disobey a duly enacted Athenian edict, but never really did so, with the result that, strictly speaking, he never contradicts himself. This sort of response is unhelpful, since it skirts the issue at hand.

That issue is this: Socrates repeatedly endorses the following simple claim:

(AJ) One must always do what is just.

The argument of the *Crito* seems to entail that:

(NCD) Civil disobedience is never justifiable.

So far, (AJ) and (NCD) are compatible – so long as the dictates of justice and the laws of society always and everywhere perfectly overlap. But, as Socrates himself notes, they do not: there are sometimes unjust laws. Given that simple fact, (AJ) and (NCD) cannot both be true. So, if he maintains them both, Socrates has contradicted himself. Borrowing an argumentative technique from the Socratic elenchus, we can see directly that *what is just* and *what is legal* are not even co-extensive. When we find something which is just, but not legal, we expect Socrates to favor (AJ) over (NCD), as, for example, Martin Luther King did in his moving *Letter from a Birmingham Jail*, when he urged non-violent civil disobedience in the service of justice, a policy which King says he derived in part from Socrates. In that letter, written to his fellow Christian ministers to explain his support of civil disobedience, King claims, in a Socratic spirit, that unjust laws *must* be broken, precisely because they are unjust. King's Socrates is the Socrates of the *Apology*; yet the Socrates of the *Crito* seems at variance with King's Socrates.

The question, then, is whether Socrates ever endorses anything so extreme as (NCD). The argument of the *Crito* begins in a familiar vein. Socrates says that it is never just to wrong someone willingly, and infers that it is therefore never just, even when wronged, to retaliate by wronging someone in return.[31] This much may seem unproblematic, but it is in fact already controversial. A proponent of retaliation might simply reject Socrates' baseline principle, by maintaining that since retaliation against an unjustified harm is permissible, it is in some circumstances just to wrong someone willingly. It is just when the person to be wronged deserves to be wronged, because of their own bad deeds. Although he realizes that some people will think this way, Socrates remains secure in his baseline principle. He invites Crito to reflect upon its defensibility, intimating that it may have some far-reaching consequences. Crito does so and reaffirms his own commitment, thus paving the way for the main argument in favor of (NCD).[32]

The main argument against civil disobedience (ANCD) is advanced by the personified Laws, who give voice to the state's point of view:

1 If S has a justly made contract with S', then S willingly harms S' if S knowingly breaks that contract without having been released from it.
2 Socrates has a justly made contract with Athens either to persuade it as to the nature of justice or to obey its laws.
3 Socrates has not persuaded Athens as to the nature of justice.
4 Hence, Socrates can break his contract with Athens only if he has been released from it.
5 Athens has not agreed to release Socrates from his contract.
6 Hence, Socrates will willingly harm Athens by escaping.

(ANCD-6) simply affirms that escaping is a form of disobedience, and so is contractually proscribed. Given that it has been agreed that willful harm is never just, it follows that since breaking one's binding contracts is a form of willful harm, escaping from prison turns out to be unjust. In a sense, then, instead of seeing that (AJ) and (NCD) jointly create conflicts, Socrates actually wants to use (AJ) as a premise in an argument whose eventual conclusion is (NCD).[33]

This is surprising, given that (AJ) and (NCD) are incompatible, so long as it is allowed that the just and the legal are not co-extensive. Since this is also something Socrates has allowed, it is hard to appreciate how he can argue for (NCD) as he does. This tension commends a closer look at (ANCD).

There are many *prima facie* problems with this argument. (ANCD-1) already seems too strong, unless it envisages liberal conditions of release. As Socrates himself elsewhere argues, we are justified in breaking some of our agreements, as, for example, when we are faced with returning a weapon, as originally agreed, but discover that the man from whom we borrowed it has since gone insane.[34] On the other hand, if conditions of release are liberal, then it may be asked why it does not suffice to nullify a contract that one party has treated the other unjustly. Socrates seems unhappy with that conclusion, since he maintains that the matter of past injustice is irrelevant to the question of future cases of willful harming.

(ANCD-2) receives its own argument, one with a rich subsequent history. The Laws note that although Socrates has never signed an official contract with the state, he has surely tacitly consented to some such contract by freely receiving the many benefits it has provided him.[35] Socrates is in this way like most of us: we have never signed a contract of any form with our governments. Hence, if such contracts exist, and we are bound by them, we have tacitly consented to their terms. Assuming he is right about that (though one may well doubt that he is), a thorny question immediately arises: what are the terms agreed upon? Socrates specifies some surprising terms: persuade or obey. Again, there seems little reason to suppose that any such terms could have been specific to Socrates' local circumstances and time. Those deciding whether they wish to endorse (ANCD) may therefore want to reflect whether they have themselves agreed tacitly or otherwise to any such terms. Here there has sometimes been an attempt to relax such stringent terms by noting that in Greek "persuade" is not always a success verb, so that it may mean merely "attempt to persuade." (Something similar is true of the English adjective based on this verb, as when it is said that "Although the defense attorney was very persuasive, she ultimately failed to win over the jury.") This may be so, although it seems unlikely that the weaker notion is at play in the *Crito*. In any case, if it is, it mainly relocates the question: why does Socrates' defense speech not qualify as an attempt to persuade the Athenians as to the nature of justice? Indeed, is there not a sense in which his entire elenchtic mission is precisely that?

Our understanding of "persuasion" clearly affects our attitude to (ANCD-3) as well. Some of these same questions will consequently arise with respect to it, along with one other. If we apply the weaker standard, and suppose that the only contractual obligation placed upon a citizen is that she attempt to persuade her state as to the nature of justice, then one needs to wonder why Socrates has not wanted even to make such an attempt. In raising such a question in the current context, we are not inquiring into features of Socrates' psychological biography. Rather, we are raising yet another possible tension in his presentation in the *Crito*. If Socrates has not even attempted to persuade the Athenians as to the nature of justice, then he seems to have abdicated a central portion of the divinely inspired mission he claimed for himself in the *Apology*.

At any rate, with these premises in place, the Laws have their interim conclusion in (ANCD-4). Subject to the provisions regarding contractual release discussed in the context of (ANCD-1), the Laws are free to stipulate (ANCD-5) and so can derive their ultimate conclusion, which is simply a specific application of their general ban on civil disobedience. That is, they seem now in a position to affirm (NCD), the claim that civil disobedience is never permissible. Because Socrates endorses their conclusion, he too seems bound to accept this conclusion in what appears a fairly strong form.

There are various ways of restricting the range of (NCD), some of which *may* be consistent with the arguments of the *Crito*. Students and scholars are right to look for some such restrictions, given that in its unrestricted form, (NCD) seems at odds with the spirit of much of Socrates' own positive philosophy, including especially (AJ), the claim that one must always do what is just. Students may gauge Socrates' dominant dispositions by determining his likely attitude towards such courageous civil rights campaigners as Gandhi or King or The White Rose, the daring student group whose members were executed by the Nazis for their subversive activities. The Nazis were right that these students were subversives; it is difficult to believe that Socrates could regard their subversion as anything other than an exemplary attempt to secure justice in desperate circumstances.

These inquiries into the force of Socrates' arguments in the *Crito* are, then, not undertaken in an effort to convict him of internal inconsistency. Rather, they are meant to illustrate that in view of Socrates' trenchant commitment to justice, whenever there is a threat of inconsistency, (NCD) must yield to (AJ). In keeping with Socrates' own announced mission, it seems altogether appropriate to ask him to demonstrate how this is to be accomplished, and so to justify himself by showing that his own views are elenchus-proof.

2.6   Conclusions

The Socrates who appears in Plato's dialogues is an arrestingly complex and forceful figure. From a narrowly methodological point of view, two features stand out: (1) Socrates' impulse for analysis, which resulted in his posing the what-is-F-ness question concerning a wide range of desirable moral qualities; and (2) his elenchtic method, with its attendant high standards for success. According to these standards, an instance of philosophical analysis is successful only if it is fully general and univocal, epistemically serviceable, and more than extensionally adequate. If he found himself incapable of meeting his own high standards, Socrates never veered from the course of trying. This is because he held that "the most important thing is not living, but living well,"[36] where living well consists in living nobly and justly. Living in this way, for Socrates, requires a commitment to sustained intellectual inquiry, not merely as an abstract directive, but as an intimate and personal action-guiding principle. This is why he says, with his characteristic and piercing candor, that "an unexamined life is not worth living."[37]

Notes

1 The defense speech is given in Plato's *Apology* (*apologia* is simply the Greek word for "defense"). The *Crito* contains Socrates' conversations concerning justice and civil disobedience, conducted while in prison; and the *Phaedo* presents Socrates' final conversations, mainly about the immortality of the soul. Though it is controversial in the scholarly community, although these three dialogues present a dramatic unity, it is likely that the first two of them strive to present a more or less accurate portrait of the historical Socrates, while the *Phaedo* presents Plato's own views, using Socrates as a mouthpiece. On the character of the Socratic versus the Platonic dialogues, see 3.1 below.

2 Socrates himself wrote nearly nothing. Scholars therefore confront the "Socratic problem": how are we to determine the views of the historical man, Socrates, as opposed to the various non-equivalent portrayals of him and his views? In addition to Plato, the other main sources for Socrates are: (1) the comic playwright Aristophanes, who lampoons Socrates as a Sophist in the *Clouds*; and (2) the detailed portrayals of Xenophon, who wrote an *Apology of Socrates*, as well as various other works in which Socrates features, including the *Memorabilia*, the *Symposium*, and the *Oeconomicus*. In terms of their philosophical content, these works are pedestrian in comparison with the dialogues of Plato. I accordingly focus on the presentation of Socrates in Plato's so-called Socratic dialogues.

Although it would be imprudent to be overly secure about doing so, it is nonetheless reasonable to regard Plato's Socratic dialogues as intended to represent the views of the historical Socrates. (On the order of Plato's dialogues, see Chapter 3 note 5 below.) All references to the *Apology* are to Plato's *Apology*, unless otherwise noted.

3 By contrast, Plato asks and answers this question at length in the *Theaetetus*. See 3.2, 3.3, and 3.5 below for a discussion of his approach to knowledge and its objects.

4 Socrates occasionally claims that the elenchus can reach the truth: *Gorgias* 497e, 480e, 508e–509b, though such claims never arise in the shorter, fully aporetic dialogues which pose the what-is-F-ness question. Cf. also *Laches* 196c and *Charmides* 166d.

5 On the Socratic versus the Platonic dialogues written by Plato, see 3.1 below. Note 5 to 3.1 provides a partial list of the Socratic and Platonic dialogues.

6 *Charmides* 159b–c.

7 An account is *extensionally adequate* if, and only if, it captures all and only the instances falling within the extension, or class, of the quality in question. Thus, for example, an account of a square as "a four-sided closed plane figure with interior angles equaling 360 degrees" is not extensionally adequate since it admits rectangles into the extension. In the other direction, an account of a swan as "a large white water bird with a long, slender neck" is not extensionally adequate because it excludes the black swans of Australia (*cygnus atratus*).

8 On the Sophists, see 1.6 above.

9 *Meno* 70a–71d.

10 *Meno* 71d–72a.

11 *Meno* 72a–b, 72c–d, 74b–76b.

12 *Meno* 78c–79e.

13 *Meno* 74a.

14 Sophocles, *Antigone* 450–9, 1065–8, 1270.

15 *Euthyphro* 10a–b.

16 *Euthyphro* 11a–b.

17 *Euthyphro* 16a.

18 Socrates professes his ignorance often, though in differing ways: *Apology* 20c, 21d, 23b; *Charmides* 165b, 166c; *Euthyphro* 5a–c, 15c; *Laches* 186b–e, 200e; *Lysis* 212a, 223b; *Gorgias* 509a; *Meno* 71a, 80d.

19 The head of the skeptical Academy, Arcesilaus, is reported to have acquired his thorough-going skepticism from studying Socrates: Cicero, *De Oratore* 3.67; *De Finibus* 2.2, 5.10; *Academica* 1.43–4; *De Natura Deorum* 1.11; Numenius ap. Eusebius, *Praeparatio Evangelica* 14.6.12–13. See 5.4 below.

20 Accusations of Socratic irony by his interlocutors: *Gorgias* 489e, *Republic* 337a, *Symposium* 216e; joined by Aristotle, *Nichomachean Ethics* 1127b22–6.

21 *Gorgias* 472e, 507b–c, 508e–509b; *Apology* 30b; *Crito* 48b.

22 On Zeno's paradoxes, see 1.4.

23 A second Socratic "paradox" is the claim that the canonical virtues of his time (courage, piety, justice, temperance, and wisdom) were somehow unified, minimally in the sense that one could never have one without the others, though sometimes a stronger doctrine is evidently intended, that these virtues are one and the same. See *Protagoras* 329c–d and 332a–333; and Laches 198a–199e. The two paradoxes are connected by Socratic cognitivism, since Socrates suggests that moral virtue is simply moral knowledge (in support of the unity of the virtues) and that knowledge is thus sufficient for virtue (against the possibility of *akrasia*).

24 *Apology* 31c–d; cf. Xenophon, *Apology of Socrates* 12, *Memorabilia* 1.1.2.

25 *Apology* 21a–24b.

26 *Apology* 30d.

27 *Apology* 32a–d, 29d–e.

28 Socrates spent approximately one month in prison before his execution, because his trial occurred just after the departure of an official Athenian religious mission to Delos. No

executions were permitted while the ship conducting that mission remained away from Athens. We learn at the beginning of the *Crito* that the ship is nearing Athens on its return voyage (*Crito* 43d).

29 *Crito* 44b–d, 46e–48b.
30 *Crito* 51b.
31 *Crito* 49a–c.
32 *Crito* 49b–e.
33 *Crito* 49e–51c.
34 *Republic* 330c–d.
35 *Crito* 52a–d.
36 *Crito* 48b.
37 *Apology* 38a.
38 Numbers in brackets refer to the comprehensive Suggestions for Further Reading compiled at the end of this book.

Suggestions for additional readings

Primary text

The best collection of translations for Plato's presentation of Socrates is available in:

Cooper, J. (ed.) *Plato: Complete Works* (Cambridge, MA: Hackett, 1997).

All of the individual dialogues discussed in the text are also available in less expensive formats than [22].[38] A relevant selection of the texts regarding Socrates in [22] can also be found in:

Plato, *Five Dialogues* (*Euthyphro, Apology, Crito, Meno, Phaedo*) (Cambridge, MA: Hackett, 1981).

Secondary literature

Wading through the vast secondary literature on Socrates can be somewhat daunting. Good places to begin, in addition to [4], are:

Smith, N. and Brickhouse, T., *The Philosophy of Socrates* (Boulder, CO: Westview, 2000).
Vlastos, G., *Socrates: Ironist and Moral Philosopher* (Cambridge: Cambridge University Press, 1991).
Santas, G., *Socrates: Philosophy in Plato's Early Dialogues* (London: Routledge, 1979).

Also good are the following anthologies, which contain excellent articles on a variety of topics in Socratic philosophy:

Benson, H., *Essays on the Philosophy of Socrates* (Oxford: Oxford University Press, 1992).
Vlastos, G. (ed.) *The Philosophy of Socrates* (London: Doubleday, 1971).
—— *Socratic Studies* (Cambridge: Cambridge University Press, 1994).

3 Plato

Plato (429–347) is a constructive and systematic philosopher of astonishing range and depth. Unlike Socrates, he does not confine himself to matters of ethical conduct. Instead, he investigates issues in metaphysics; in epistemology; in philosophy of mind; in aesthetic theory; in morality, including moral metaphysics and moral epistemology; in political philosophy; and, in a new and abstract way, issues pertaining to philosophical method. So sweeping has Plato's philosophical influence been that the eminent British philosopher Alfred North Whitehead was able to claim, with an evident and sincere reverence, "The safest general characterization of the European philosophical tradition is that it consists of a series of footnotes to Plato."[1] Here we begin an investigation into Plato's most lasting contributions to philosophy, not by looking first to his astonishing influence, but by engaging his own texts directly in an effort to determine whether we should ourselves accept his principal philosophical doctrines as true. It is, of course, possible that we will come to regard some of his main contentions as false and indefensible. This much, though, would be giving Plato the treatment he seeks: it seems clear in reading Plato's dialogues that he expects us to come to dissenting conclusions where they are warranted, but, by the same token, to join him where they are not.

Key to understanding Plato's philosophy is an appreciation of his coupled commitments to the defensibility of *a priori* knowledge and the existence of abstract entities he calls *Forms*. Plato is not the first philosopher to suppose that human beings have a facility for *a priori* knowledge.[2] Certainly, before him Parmenides held the same view, though in a radical and extreme way, inasmuch as he maintained that the *a priori* exhausted all of human knowledge. While he agrees with Parmenides about the existence of *a priori* knowledge, nothing in Plato's writings suggests that he would be inclined to join him in his immoderate presuppositions about its scope. Nor would Plato side with those contemporary philosophers who are radical in the other direction by holding that human knowledge is restricted to the *a posteriori*. Instead, he positions himself between them by allowing for the existence of both forms of knowledge. This may seem to be the moderate centrist position, at least if we are willing to allow that some knowledge, in mathematics for example, is *a priori*, while some other kinds of knowledge, including knowledge in the natural and social sciences, is largely *a posteriori*.

Plato's epistemological tenets become contentious and controversial, however, when he yokes them to some metaphysical commitments which many regard as extravagant or somehow extreme. For he thinks that the range of *a priori* knowledge extends well beyond mathematics: Plato argues that there is a distinctive kind of *a priori* philosophical knowledge which takes as its subject matter objects akin to the objects of mathematics. He calls them Forms. Forms are to philosophy what numbers are to mathematics and shapes are to geometry. When we discover the relations between numbers, we discover something necessary and inalterable. So, too, when we learn that the interior angles of a triangle equal 180 degrees, we come to appreciate something which could not be other than it is. It is not a contingent or conventional fact about triangles that they have these sorts of features. In the same way, argues Plato, when we come to learn the nature of Justice or Beauty, we discover something about Justice itself which is not the product of convention, something which is not relative to a time or a place, something which cannot be other than it is. This claim is bound to surprise even Plato's most sympathetic readers. Our goal will be to introduce his motives and arguments for maintaining it. We will also begin, but only begin, the fascinating process of assessing the soundness of these arguments. If we are in the end persuaded that this process has been one well worth engaging, then we will have lent at least that much credence to Whitehead's reverential assessment of Plato's towering accomplishment.

3.1   From Socrates to Plato

Socrates professed analytical ignorance: he did not know the correct answers to the calls for analysis he initiated. Since his interlocutors regularly failed to illuminate him, Plato's Socratic dialogues characteristically end in an admission of failure punctuated by a cheery optimism to the effect that renewed philosophical effort might yet reap rich philosophical rewards. There is, however, no clear record of an agreed-upon success. In this sense, Plato's Socratic dialogues are primarily destructive, rather than constructive, even though nothing about the elenchtic method as such requires that they be so. Moreover, despite his clear and sophisticated criteria for analytical achievement, Socrates did not turn his attention to epistemology or metaphysics as special subjects in their own right. Instead, as Aristotle observes, Socrates concerned himself exclusively with moral qualities, focusing for the first time on their universal and definitional features.[3] Plato, by contrast, again according to Aristotle, concerned himself with the whole of nature and with metaphysical matters left untouched by Socrates.

If we rely on Aristotle's judgment, as it seems reasonable to do,[4] we can begin to differentiate the dialogues of Plato in which an effort is made to present the views of the historical Socrates from those in which Socrates features as a mere character dedicated to the expression of Plato's own positive theories. Although there are scholarly controversies about the relative datings of Plato's dialogues,[5] it is reasonably easy, and relatively uncontroversial, to separate them thematically into the Socratic dialogues,[6] which formed the basis of our discussions of Socrates, and the Platonic dialogues, which themselves seem readily divisible into earlier and later periods. These Platonic dialogues are the sources of our investigation into Platonic philosophy.

Whatever our attitudes toward the relative datings of Plato's dialogues, we must be struck by an important shift in Socrates' self-presentation across the Platonic corpus. The Socrates we have met so far, the historical Socrates, professes his analytical ignorance. He is also agnostic about such important matters as *post-mortem* existence. Indeed, in his defense speech, Socrates claims directly that he does not know whether there is life after death. Even so, he can see that death is one of two things: nothingness, in which case it is not a harm; or a relocation of the soul from one place to another, in which case it is a positive blessing, since it will afford opportunity for pleasant conversation with such immortal poets as Homer and Hesiod.[7] (We are left to imagine the Socratic elenchus with Homer on the topic of *aretê*!) This contrasts starkly with the Socrates of the *Phaedo*, who has a perfectly secure belief in *post-mortem* existence. Indeed, he retails proof after proof of the soul's immortality, each intended to establish beyond a reasonable doubt that earthly death is the separation of the soul from the body, and not the end of our existence. Assuming that the Socrates of the *Phaedo* now represents Plato's views rather than those of the historical Socrates, we can identify a first major Platonic departure from Socrates. Plato, unlike Socrates, has not only positive convictions, but is prepared to argue for them at length. He is not content to engage others in elenchtic investigation. Instead, he argues directly, in a constructive manner, for positive theses and theories which range widely beyond the moral matters of primary concern to Socrates.

In so doing, Plato also exhibits a willingness to engage the sorts of epistemological issues which invariably accompany metaphysical investigation, including those into the metaphysics of morality. Plato, unlike Socrates, is perfectly willing to offer an analysis of moral qualities, including most centrally the nature of justice, the main topic of his *Republic*, whose ancient subtitle was in fact *On Justice*. When he does, he presents himself as being familiar with the natures of essences or such qualities. Understandably, questions about his epistemic access to these natures never lag far behind. In general, when someone claims to know the nature of justice, or of virtue, or of right and wrong, or that the soul is immortal, or that relativism is false, an interested party will inquire of him *how* he knows what he claims to know. Since he never claimed such knowledge on his own behalf, Socrates did not face such questions. Plato, by contrast, must face them; and he does not shy away from engaging them when it is appropriate for him to do so.

3.2   Meno's paradox of inquiry; Plato's response

One of Plato's earliest and most noteworthy forays into epistemology occurs in a dialogue we have already encountered, the *Meno*. That dialogue begins with a paradigmatic Socratic elenchus.[8] Socrates asks Meno what virtue is.

Under Socratic tutelage, Meno respects the univocity assumption, offers an analysis, and is promptly reduced to contradiction. Socrates, as is his manner, confesses his own ignorance and encourages a fresh start, in hopes of capturing their elusive analytical prey.[9] So much is standard Socratic fare.

Things take an unexpected turn when Meno abruptly refuses to play along. Instead, Meno raises an epistemological question unprecedented in the Socratic dialogues. There comes, all at once, a Platonic moment: Meno calls Socrates on his profession of ignorance by demanding to know how he can make progress toward a goal he cannot even recognize. How is it possible to seek out the analysis of virtue when the correct analysis is unknown to all of the parties of the discussion? Meno's question in one way recalls Xenophanes' complaint that even if we were to happen upon the whole of the truth, we would lack knowledge because even then we would have no way of knowing what it was that we had stumbled upon.[10] But Meno's question moves beyond Xenophanes, inasmuch as Meno is prepared to argue that inquiry as such is impossible by more elaborate means.

Meno's paradox of inquiry (MPI) takes the form of a simple dilemma:

1   For all x, either you know x or you do not.
2   If you know x, then inquiry into x is impossible, since you cannot inquire into what you already know.
3   If you do not know x, then inquiry into x is impossible, since you cannot inquire when you do not even know what to look for.
4   So, for any x, inquiry into x is impossible.

Meno's idea is simple enough. (MPI-1) seems to be a straightforward appeal to the principle of the excluded middle. (MPI-2) suggests sensibly that it is not possible to inquire into what is already known, provided that one knows all there is to know about the topic in question. I cannot, for, example, inquire into whether $2+2 = 4$. I know that it does; there is nothing more for me to ascertain. (MPI-3) is a little less straightforward and so requires a bit more amplification. The idea is that it is not possible to inquire into something about which I know nothing. For example, if a completely uneducated person were asked what a *cosine* was, she would not even be able to choose between three possible answers: (1) a vessel in which bread consecrated for Holy Communion in religious ceremonies is kept; (2) the ratio of the length of a side adjacent to one of the acute angles in a right-angled triangle to the length of the hypotenuse; or (3) a special form of a national flag flown by military ships. In short, if we knew nothing at all, then inquiry would be impossible, since we would never know where to begin or to end.

Plato immediately characterizes (MPI) as an "eristic argument," or a "debater's argument," where the clear purport is that it rests upon some tricky fallacy. Surely he is right about that. As presented, (MPI) employs an equivocal sense of knowledge, since if (MPI-2) is to be true, knowledge must mean *know everything about*, whereas if (MPI-3) is to be true, knowledge must mean *know anything at all about*. If we hold either one or the other of these meanings fixed, then (MPI-2) or (MPI-3) will be false and the argument unsound. If we understand knowledge differently in (MPI-2) and (MPI-3) so that each is true (or has a chance of being true), then (MPI-1) will no longer be an instance of the excluded middle, but will instead be false, since it will now read: for all x, either you know all about x or you do not know anything about x. Clearly, that is false, since there are plenty of things about which we have only partial knowledge. Equally clearly, then, Plato is right when he insists that his argument contains a slippery fallacy, one which will not seduce anyone who reflects on it even briefly.[11]

Surprisingly, however, after noting that the argument is fallacious, Plato does not go on to expose the fallacy. Instead, he uses it as a launching pad for one of his most distinctive and notorious theses, *the doctrine of recollection*. Plato introduces this doctrine initially by citing the authority of poets and holy men and women, but then, in his characteristic fashion, offers an engaging argument in its defense. The doctrine of recollection consists of the following theses: (1) the soul is immortal; (2) there is nothing which the soul has not learned; and (3) what humans call learning is actually recollection. Thus, when we come to "learn" something, such as the nature of virtue, in fact what we are doing is prodding ourselves to dredge up knowledge already available to us, because it is already in our souls. If asked now to reproduce the Gettysburg Address, which I learned as a boy, I may have to struggle to piece it back together. If I am successful, then I have recollected it. I did not learn it all over again, even though, at first, I was unable simply to recite it. By analogy, if Meno wants to "learn" the nature of virtue, he needs only look within, to dig into what he in fact has available to him, and to jog his memory until he meets with success. Consequently, says Plato, we should pay no heed to the debater's argument (MPI). Instead, we should remain keen and energetic in our analytical quest.

Given the impetus for its introduction, it is difficult to know how to respond immediately to the doctrine of recollection. That impetus is an argument which Plato recognizes to be fallacious, (MPI), but whose fallacy he does not deign to display. Moreover, it is a fallacy whose exposure obviates the need for the introduction of a response with anything even vaguely approaching the metaphysical extravagance of the doctrine of recollection. To make matters worse, it is not even clear precisely how the doctrine of recollection, even granted in its entirety, responds to (MPI). It does not bring to light its debater's trick; it does not refute its conclusion directly; and it does not even seem directly to engage its terms. In a certain way, it seems even to grant its conclusion, since it evidently allows that what humans *call* learning is really something else, namely recollection, which is not the acquisition of new knowledge but the rekindling of the old. If that is right, then inquiry – if that is to be construed in terms of an attempt to discover what one does not know – really is pointless.

Presumably Plato is sensitive to this last point, since it is an open question as to what inquiry itself consists in. One component of Plato's doctrine of recollection, that there is a sense in which what seems to be learning in some cases is really rather an instance of accessing what is already available to us, may not be so extravagant after all. Indeed, one way to understand Plato's responding to (MPI) as he does, with the doctrine of recollection instead of with a curt exposure of Meno's equivocation, is to suppose that he sees a formidable point standing behind Meno's paradox. In any event, he would be right to do so, since Meno's paradox does admit of formulations to which Plato's doctrine of recollection would provide an appropriate response. One might well ask, in the spirit of (MPI), what sort of progress is possible in philosophical analysis. If philosophical analysis merely specifies the deep structure of a quality being analyzed, then, if correct, it merely displays that very property. If correct, that is, someone might contend that it merely tells us what is already known by us at some level, and so can hardly be informative. Yet even Socratic analysis seemed informative, at least in the minimal sense that it revealed to some that they did not know what they thought they knew. By the same token, if they had in fact known what they claimed to know, then they would have made no progress towards knowledge in the process of analysis. They would have learned nothing. To use Plato's metaphor, the best they could have done was to recollect what they already knew. So, maybe Meno has a point after all, that philosophical analysis of the sort practiced by Socrates and Plato is completely pointless and a real waste of time. Each episode of analysis is either unnecessary or incorrect.

In view of these sorts of concerns about analysis, Plato's argument for the doctrine of recollection, as opposed to his initial citation of poetic and religious authorities, has a legitimate claim to be heard. The argument is presented discursively, in the form of a dialogue with an unnamed slave who has never been trained in geometry but seems to contain within himself, in some manner of speaking, the answers to geometrical questions which initially stump him. When asked how to form a square twice the area of an original square ABCD, the slave makes two false starts, but eventually comes out with the correct answer. The square which is twice the area of ABCD is not the one whose sides are twice as long as those of ABCD, nor again is it the one whose sides are half again as long, but is rather the square based on the diagonal of ABCD.[12] The slave thus has some success, although, Plato insists, the success cannot be attributed to what he has learned in this life. For, although he learned Greek, he has never studied geometry.[13]

Plato infers on the basis of this presentation that "the truth about reality" is always in our souls and that the soul is immortal, the two most important components of the doctrine of recollection. As for the third, Plato points out that it does not much matter whether we call what we do learning or recollection, since what we want to do is to move toward clear and manifest knowledge in philosophical analysis, the sort of knowledge which can be taught.[14] Already, however, one component of the doctrine of recollection, that the soul is immortal and has existed before its current incarnation, seems hardly established by the argument expressed in the slave passage. That argument is simply that since the slave never learned the truths in his soul during this life, he must have acquired them some time before he was born, which would entail that his soul enjoyed some form of pre-natal existence. Fairly clearly, the slave could have had the success he had without any such existence. He could, for example, simply have *a priori* knowledge regarding the truths of geometry; or perhaps such knowledge is simply innate. In either case, for some range of truths, justification is available to any rational creature willing to engage in disciplined reflection, with the result, as Plato says of the slave, that we can move from true belief to knowledge via a process of inquiry.[15]

That result, however deflationary when set aside the full doctrine of recollection, commands considerable interest in its own right. For as Leibniz and some other later philosophers recognized, the slave passage carries within it an interesting and important argument for the existence of *a priori* knowledge. The argument is suggested in various ways in the passage, beginning with the kind of knowledge Plato selects for illustration. That kind of knowledge is *knowledge of necessary truths*, such as geometrical knowledge, a kind of knowledge Plato implicitly contrasts with the sort of contingent knowledge the slave manifests by speaking Greek. Although taken this way the slave passage suggests something modest by comparison with the doctrine of recollection, what it does suggest is something significant nonetheless, that knowledge of necessary truths, if we have it, cannot be justified *a posteriori*. That is, Plato seems to argue that for any proposition p, if p is necessary, then p can be known only *a priori*. This suggestion is really two-fold. First, if p is necessary, then it can be known *a priori*; and second, if p is necessary, it cannot be known in any way other than *a priori*. So, in this sense, if the slave knows the geometrical proposition that the square twice the area of an original square is the square formed on the diagonal of the original square, then he must know that proposition *a priori*.

Plato's reason for believing this claim is not obscure, however controversial it may since have become. The point is this: not only did the slave not learn geometry in this life, but he *could not* have grasped the necessity of the truths of geometry by appeal to sense perception. No matter how many figures he sees drawn in the sand by Socrates or anyone else, he will never be in a position to appreciate that the proposition he knows *must* be true unless he grasps something about the nature of squares themselves. The fact that p holds true of each representation of a square he has seen thus far does not, and cannot, by itself justify another claim, which the slave is also in a position to know, that p will, because it must, hold true of any square he might ever encounter. Since he does in fact know this, and could not know it *a posteriori*, the slave must know the geometrical proposition he knows *a priori*. There seems to be no point in denying that he knows it; so there seems to be no point, Plato implies, in denying that he knows it *a priori*. If that is correct, then there is no point in denying that there is *a priori* knowledge. As Plato says later in the *Meno*, echoing the analysis of Xenophanes, knowledge is simply a true belief together with a rational account, where a rational account is one which provides the requisite form of justification.[16] If the slave passage is correct, however, Xenophanes was wrong in his ultimate skeptical conclusions: for some range of propositions, necessary propositions, justification is possible *a priori*.

3.3   Two functions of Plato's theory of Forms

Plato believes that the range of necessary propositions extends well beyond geometry, into moral and metaphysical matters which, as Socrates before him maintained, have immediate consequences for how we should conduct the business of our lives. Many people may be willing to follow Plato when he suggests that the truths of geometry are both necessary and known only *a priori*.[17] Still, many among them will hesitate when Plato appeals to *a priori* justification in morality. There are two motivations for such hesitation. The first derives from relativistic intuitions. Because Plato is a realist about value, he denies Protagoreanism and seeks to establish the existence of mind- and language-independent transcendent values which are apprehended by discerning minds but in no sense created or constituted by them.[18] The second motivation for hesitation is not relativism but skepticism, both about the existence of such values and about our epistemic access to them, should they exist. Again in virtue of his realism, Plato seeks to provide good reasons for believing that the values he posits ought to be accepted by anyone capable of appreciating the arguments he offers on their behalf.

Plato addresses both skeptical and relativistic concerns with his theory of Forms. He supposes that those who think that we have secure knowledge in such domains as mathematics and geometry are in an unstable position if at the same time they deny that we have such knowledge available to us in morality. For the objects of such knowledge are the same in both cases: they are precise, fixed, necessary, unchanging abstract objects which have all of their intrinsic properties essentially. Just as a genuine, abstract scalene triangle is perfectly scalene in a way in which no physical representation of a scalene triangle could ever be, so justice, taken itself on its own terms, alone and by itself, as Plato frequently says, is an ideal which just institutions and individuals approximate but never equal. If Plato is correct in postulating objects of knowledge in the realm of values corresponding to the sorts of objects many people accept in the domain of geometry, then he has a good reason for believing that relativism about value is indefensible. He will also, however, incur a special debt to skeptics, who will legitimately demand good arguments for the existence of such qualities, as well as some account of the epistemic access we are supposed to have to them. Unsurprisingly, Plato will argue that our knowledge of them is *a priori*.

3.4 Plato's rejection of relativism

If Plato is right, then Protagoras is wrong.[19] We have seen that Protagoras has a tidy response to skepticism about values: we know which things are good or bad, just or unjust, or beautiful or ugly, because each of these qualities is determined or constituted by our own attitudes. If I believe that the fourth movement of Mahler's Fourth Symphony is beautiful, then it is beautiful *for me*, and I have no difficulty knowing that; I need only consult my own attitudes. Similarly, if I believe that, all things considered, slavery is a just institution, then it is just *for me*, and there is no further question as to whether or not I might be mistaken. Here again there is little opening for the skeptic. Since I know how things seem to me, and I am aware that slavery seems just to me, I have no grounds for doubting that it is just for me. So, if Plato has a good reason for rejecting relativism, he loses whatever advantages relativism may offer in terms of its response to skepticism about value.

This is a price Plato is willing to pay, since he thinks that whatever its epistemological advantages, relativism is indefensible. His most developed criticism of relativism occurs in the *Theaetetus*, a dialogue which investigates the nature of knowledge. In a strikingly Socratic fashion, Plato poses a what-is-F-ness question, though not one about a moral quality. Instead, he wants to know: *What is knowledge?* In the course of the *Theaetetus*, Plato considers and rejects three proposed accounts of knowledge (*epistêmê*). The three definitions he considers are:

1   x is an instance of knowledge $=_{df} x$ is an instance of perception.[20]
2   x is an instance of knowledge $=_{df} x$ is (a) a belief; and (b) x is true.[21]

and

3   x is an instance of knowledge $=_{df} x$ is (a) a belief; (b) true; (c) accompanied by an account.[22]

Plato finds all three of these analyses defective, with the result that the dialogue ends, again in Socratic fashion, aporetically.

Plato's response to Protagoras occurs in the context of his refutation of the first of these definitions, according to which knowledge just is perception. This definition may seem wholly unpromising; and, in fact, Plato has little trouble refuting it. Along the way, however, Plato rather surprisingly characterizes the suggestion that knowledge is perception as a bit of Protagoreanism,[23] which in its turn is identified as of a piece with Heracleiteanism.[24] This may seem a far stretch, but within the context of the *Theaetetus*, Plato's transformations seem fair enough. If knowledge is perception, then since the objects of perception are forever in flux, so too are the objects of knowledge. If that is correct, then Heracleitus had a point. What is more, if knowledge is perception, then things are as they seem. What appears to me to be the case really is the case, for me. As we have seen, it is easy in Greek, as it is in English, to move from a narrowly perceptual sense of "appears" to a more cognitively rich notion (e.g. from "In dim light maroon appears purple" to "It appears that the monarchy is in jeopardy"). So, it is natural to treat the suggestion that "Things are as they appear" in both a broader and a narrower sense.

The broader sense is tantamount to Protagoras' Measure Doctrine, his principal formulation of relativism. The Measure Doctrine (MD) as formulated by Plato in the *Theaetetus* holds that "a human being is the measure of all things: of things which are, that they are, and of things which are not, that they are not." Understanding the doctrine predicatively, as seems warranted by Plato's treatment of it, we have:

(MD$_p$): If a human being S believes that some x is F, then x is F, for S; and if S believes that some x is not F, then x is not F, for S.

So, for example, if Rodrigo believes that his glass of Riesling is sweet, then it is sweet, for Rodrigo. Similarly, if he believes that infanticide is justifiable, then it is justifiable, for Rodrigo. Again, since as stated (MD) is unrestricted in its domain, then if Rodrigo believes that $(2+2)$ has the property of equaling five, then it does equal five, for Rodrigo. As we have seen,[25] it is a bit difficult to understand that this last suggestion is intended to be understood as anything beyond the triviality that if Rodrigo believes that $2+2 = 5$, then Rodrigo believes that $2+2 = 5$.

Something similar pertains to another of Plato's formulations of (MD). Plato also appropriately, though non-equivalently, treats (MD) as a doctrine about truth:

(MD$_T$) If a human being S believes that some proposition p is true, then p is true for S; and if a human being believes that some proposition p is false, then p is false for S.

So, for example, if Henrietta believes that Epidauros is an amphitheater in Greece, then it is true for her that Epidauros is an amphitheater in Greece. Similarly, if Henrietta believes that the white race is superior to other races, then for her this too is true. Finally, given the unrestricted character of (MD$_T$) as stated, it will equally be true for her that squares have interior angles equaling 180 degrees, if this is what she believes. Here again the force of the doctrine, and in particular the locution "true-for-S," is a bit unclear and threatens in an analogous way to devolve into triviality.

However that may be, we have not yet seen a frontal assault on (MD), in any of its formulations.[26] This is what Plato delivers in the *Theaetetus*, where he concentrates mainly on (MD_T). The argument takes the form of a dilemmic *reductio* for the Protagorean Measure Doctrine (RMD). That is, it assumes (MD_T) as a hypothesis, and shows how, on the basis of an exhaustive dilemma, it reduces itself to absurdity.

1 (MD_T).
2 Some person S believes (MD_T) is false.
3 If S believes that (MD_T) is false, then what S believes is either true or false.
4 If what S believes is true, then (MD_T) is false for S.
5 If (MD_T) is false for anyone, then (MD_T) is not true.
6 If, on the other hand, what S believes is false, then (MD_T) is not true.
7 So, if (MD_T), then (MD_T) is not true.

If this is a sound argument, then Plato need not worry about general relativistic challenges to the theory of Forms.

The argument proceeds upon the assumption of (MD_T). The first premise is, then, wholly unobjectionable. (RMD-2) is a simple stipulation. Anyone, including Plato, is at liberty simply to assert that they reject the Measure Doctrine. Plato asserts this. (In fact, he thinks that almost everyone implicitly rejects it whenever they seek expert advice, by visiting a doctor, or contracting an engineer, or consulting a tax attorney.) So, it is hard to appreciate how the relativist might object to (RMD-2). Notice, however, that much of the work of the argument has already been done: Plato simply puts (MD) into its own scope and then observes what it entails as soon as it seems false to someone.

This is the business of the remaining premises. (RMD-3) may now seem objectionable to some, since it apparently appeals to a notion of truth which the relativist means to call into question, perhaps some notion of believer-independent truth. Plato will respond that neither Protagoras nor any other relativist has at this point given us any reason to suppose that any such notion is suspect. We all, after all, continue to suppose that it is true that squares have four sides and that it is true that Margaret Thatcher was the first female Prime Minister of Great Britain. (Only mean-spirited people will say that this is a matter of opinion.) What Plato seems to suppose is only that (MD) is the sort of thesis which we can evaluate before deciding whether we should accept or reject it; (MD), like other claims, is subject to rational scrutiny and consideration. If Protagoras now wants to deny that, then, Plato implies, he should not present it to us for our consideration and eventual acceptance.

If it is subject to evaluation in terms of its truth or falsity, then (MD) seems to fare rather poorly in the rest of the argument. (RMD-4) and (RMD-5) work together. The first of these premises simply points out that if someone believes that (MD_T) is false, and that person's belief is true, then, as (MD_T) itself requires, (MD_T) is false, for that person. Now, however, if

(MD$_T$) is false when applied to that person, then it is not true that each person is the measure of what is true or false for each person. So, in that case, what (MD$_T$) claims, namely that each person is the measure of what is true or false, cannot be correct. It seems, that is, to require its own falsity, so long as someone believes that it is false.

Finally, on the other hand, (RMD-6) entertains the possibility that its seeming to be false does not guarantee MD$_T$'s being false for the person who believes it to be false. Then, however, that person is not the measure of what is true or false for him- or herself. In that case, notes Plato, (MD$_T$) is incorrect. For it holds, after all, that each person is the measure of what is true or false for them. If we are now going to deny that (MD$_T$) is false for the person who believes it is false, then we are also implicated, directly, in denying (MD$_T$) itself.

Hence, concludes Plato, once (MD$_T$) is brought into its own scope, then as soon as someone thinks it is false, its obvious and self-undermining weaknesses become apparent. What holds for the special case of (MD$_T$) holds for the more general doctrine (MD) as well. This doctrine is self-refuting. In this sense, it is not only the case that if Plato is right about the existence of Forms, then Protagoras is wrong about the relativity of value. More to the point, as Plato sees things, if Protagoras is right then Protagoras is wrong.

There are, of course, various relativistic reactions to Plato's argument. Some of them are retreats which effectively eviscerate (MD) altogether. Others seek to remove it from the realm of rational scrutiny. More common still is an implicit restriction on (MD): it holds not for logical or mathematical or historical propositions, but for moral propositions only. Moreover, its proponents may now insist, it does not hold for regulative principles, the sort of principle which it is itself. This last suggestion attempts to remove (MD) from its own scope and so to make it immune to the sort of self-refutation argument to which Plato subjects it. There seems, however, to be little justification for restricting (MD) in just this way. If a human being is the measure of what is true, then we ought to be able to measure (MD) along with the other propositions we believe.

3.5   Three arguments for Forms

If this sort of argument against Protagoras is compelling, then it becomes open to Plato at least to attempt an argument for the existence of objective values which are neither created nor constituted by our attitudes or practices. His attempt consists in an argument for the existence of what he calls *Forms* (*eidē*), which he evidently understands as mind- and language-independent abstract entities which have all of their intrinsic properties essentially,[27] which are also, in some sense, perfect paradigms of the qualities they are. Thus, for example, Plato is willing to speak, using a distinctive and novel terminology, of "Beauty itself, taken by itself," or of "Justice itself by itself," or of "Wisdom itself, as it is in itself," or "the Good itself taken on its own terms"[28] – all ways of rendering Plato's epithet "*auto kath' hauto*," which he affixes to various terms in order to signify that he wants the things to which the terms refer to be considered as they are in themselves, on their own, according to their own natures, and not as they are manifested in various ways in the sensible world. Thus, for example, he will contrast the beauty that we see in Helen of Troy, a beautiful woman, with "Beauty itself, as it is in itself," an abstract entity to which Helen stands in some relation in virtue of which she qualifies as beautiful. This much should already be familiar from the *Euthyphro*, where the form of piety was something whose presence *made* individual pious actions pious.[29]

Given his pronounced tendency to reify qualities, to treat them as entities in their own right, indeed as entities which are explanatorily prior to their instances, Plato owes us an *existence argument* for Forms. This is an obligation he recognizes and accepts. In fact, he discharges it several times over in the dialogues, in some cases noting directly that certain sorts of people will be disposed to doubt the existence of Forms.[30] Some of his arguments have a primarily epistemological impetus; others are more directly metaphysical. In fact, however, one of the best approaches to the theory of Forms, one which derives initially from epistemological considerations, is offered not by Plato, but by Aristotle, on Plato's behalf. After reviewing that argument, we will follow with two of Plato's own arguments. None of these discussions is intended to show conclusively that Forms exist. Each is, however, intended to show how Plato conceives of Forms, and why he thinks a reasonable person should accept their existence. Certainly whether or not they are ultimately successful, Plato's arguments for the existence of Forms merit careful study.[31]

Aristotle's introduction to Platonic Forms

Aristotle provides an existence argument which serves as an especially useful introduction to the theory of Forms not only because of its structural perspicuity, but because it helps to identify one of Plato's central epistemological motivations for Forms, as it arose in the philosophical context of abiding concern to Plato himself.[32] As Aristotle stresses, Plato was influenced by the philosophy of Heracleitus,[33] evidently in a fairly extreme version owing to one of his adherents named Cratylus. According to Aristotle, once he familiarized himself with Heracleitean doctrines, Plato continued to endorse them, after a fashion, even as a mature philosopher. It is not that Plato was himself a thoroughgoing Heracleitean. Rather, he saw that Heracleitus had a point about the physical world. This is that a full range of qualities realized in the physical world are never stable, but instead are forever changing in time and context. Sensible entities are, to use Heracleitus' preferred terminology, everywhere in *flux*. This fact about flux is incompatible, supposes Plato, with our having knowledge of sensible things. Hence, if we have knowledge, its objects must not be sensible items at all: the objects of knowledge must be abstract, located in neither space nor time.

As a warm-up to Aristotle's presentation of Plato's argument, it is worth reflecting that Plato is at least initially justified in supposing that we do have some forms of knowledge. Paradigmatically, we do know that $2+2 = 4$; more importantly, we do know that this proposition is *necessary*. Moreover, its necessity is not an artifact of language, or a product of convention, or merely the result of some form of social practice or other. Plato wants us to reflect on the fact that *we grasp* the necessity of this and some other similar propositions when we fully understand their constituents. When we understand the plus function and the relation of numerical equality, we see directly not only that certain propositions are true, but that they are necessarily true. We are, moreover, in a certain sense passive in the face of their necessity. We do not make it the case that it is necessary that $2+2 = 4$; we simply appreciate that this is so. So too with some other paradigmatically necessary propositions, for example, that the sum of the angles of a triangle equals 180 degrees. Here too, thinks Plato, we have knowledge of necessity and we should admit that this knowledge is in no way conventional.

In allowing this much, we have not suggested that such claims are impervious to skeptical challenge. Rather, we should think of such propositions as *prima facie* secure, as privileged in comparison to some others, including, for example, the proposition that it is always right to prosecute one's own father when one believes him guilty of impiety.

Insofar as we see some necessary propositions as paradigmatic instances of secure knowledge, suggests Plato, we ought to be able to appreciate some facts about their objects which will have significant consequences for analogous objects in other domains. When we think about a right triangle, we use various sorts of representations as aides to our understanding, like line drawings in the sand or on the blackboard. These drawings are not, however, themselves actual triangles. A right triangle, for example, has one interior angle of exactly and perfectly 90 degrees. No drawing of a triangle has exactly that property. To begin, every drawing of a triangle has legs with breadth and depth, whereas a triangle has legs without breadth or depth. This fact about representations of triangles implies that they are only approximations, but not, so to speak, *real* triangles. Moreover, since every physical representation of a triangle will have imprecise features *insofar as they are physical*, it follows that real triangles are non-physical objects. Hence, the objects of knowledge in paradigmatic cases of knowledge are non-physical entities. Consequently, they are abstract; they are language-independent (it does not matter whether we call them "triangles," "*Dreiecke*," or "porcupines"); and they are perfectly and necessarily what they are (something with interior angles totaling 360 degrees would be a square and not a triangle).

Since, then, we have knowledge in such cases, we can extrapolate to determine what it would be to have knowledge in non-paradigmatic cases. It would be to have mental contact with abstract, mind- and language-independent entities which are perfectly and necessarily what they are. This is how Plato conceives of Forms. The Form of Justice, if there is a Form of Justice, is an abstract entity which is essentially what justice itself is, something whose nature is grasped by a discerning mind, something which is perfectly what it is and could not be otherwise. If I cannot by an act of will make a triangle be other than it is, then neither can I by an act of will make justice itself be something other than it is.

That is, I cannot will justice to be other than it is, *if* there is a Form of Justice. Aristotle's presentation of Plato's existence argument trades on these considerations by placing them in their Heracleitean context. Aristotle's Heracleitean-induced Argument for Forms (HAF) is:

1   Sensibles are in flux.
2   Whatever is in flux is unknowable.
3   Therefore, sensibles are unknowable.
4   There is some knowledge.
5   Therefore, there are non-sensible objects of knowledge, *viz.* Forms.

More modestly, (HAF-5) could conclude merely that there are non-sensible objects of knowledge available to human beings. Looked at this way, there would be a further question concerning the range of such objects of knowledge.

In any event, the first premise is in need of explication. It is most naturally taken to assert that physical objects change through time, that they suffer *diachronic succession of opposites*. That is, what is at t_1 a boy is at t_2 no longer a boy; what is at t_1 cold is at t_2 no longer cold; what is at t_1 beautiful is at t_2 withered and no longer beautiful. This much also ties in with the Heracleitean thought that one cannot step into the same river twice, because, having stepped into it once, it will have changed from one moment to the next, with the result that the refreshed river will be new and different.

Notice, however, that given Plato's appropriation of Heracleitus' notion of flux, it is necessary to become more fine-grained in our appraisal of this doctrine than we were in considering Heracleitus himself, who drew none of the consequences Plato draws from his own doctrine. For it now becomes relevant to our appraisal of (HAF) that the notion of a diachronic succession of opposites admits of an extreme and a mild formulation. According to *mild diachronic flux*, all physical objects change at all times in at least *some* respects. So much is defensible, provided that the change in question extends to relational change and is not restricted to intrinsic change. This mild interpretation can be contrasted with a notion of *extreme diachronic flux*, according to which all physical objects change at all times in *all* respects. This is the doctrine which, Aristotle reports, appealed to the most radical of the Heracleiteans, Cratylus, who "at the end of the day thought it necessary to say nothing, but only moved his finger," who even criticized Heracleitus for claiming that one cannot step into the same river twice, since, he thought, "one could not do this even once."[34] Cratylus evidently held the wildly extreme view that objects are at most instantaneous, so that any event requiring even a bit of time, like the action of stepping into a river, will be impossible, since things will have changed even before the event has been completed. This is why, presumably, he fell silent. He thought that before someone can successfully refer to an entity, it will have changed and become something other again.

If Cratylus were right about extreme diachronic flux, (HAF-2), the claim that sensibles are unknowable would also be correct. Surely Plato is right that knowledge requires at least some fixity: one cannot know what is forever changing in all respects. Unfortunately, however, the doctrine of radical diachronic flux is plainly false. At least some things remain the same through time in at least some respects. Although, for example, the reader of this book will have changed in countless ways during the course of reading it, there will be a myriad of other forms of stability. The reader will still be a human being, will still be alive, will still be, well, a reader. These forms of stability matter, since they show that the most the Heracleiteans, here including Plato, can hope for is mild diachronic flux, the view that everything changes all the time in some respects. This in turn matters because if this is all (HAF-1) comes to, then (HAF-2) is false: if some x remains F from one time to the next, then it ought to be possible to know that this is so. For example, if Jasper is a dog at t_1 and t_2, then it ought to be possible for someone to know that this is so. At any rate, nothing about flux precludes someone's having such knowledge.

Taken together, these remarks show that (HAF-1) may be interpreted as a mild or an extreme doctrine. The extreme interpretation yields a manifestly false premise, whereas the mild interpretation delivers something plausibly true. Unfortunately, the true reading of (HAF-1) renders (HAF-2) false. That premise is true only on the extreme reading of (HAF-1). Therefore, either (HAF-1) or (HAF-2) is false. Therefore, HAF so far appears unsound.

We should not, however, reject HAF at this juncture. For the line of evaluation which has led to its unsoundness is pursuant to only one interpretation of Heracleitean flux, one which is, admittedly, the most natural and accessible understanding of that doctrine, one given in terms of *diachronic* change. We have seen, however, that Heracleitus also intended to promulgate a second kind of "flux," one less natural, to be sure, but one which nonetheless commands some conceptual concern.[35] This is the notion of *synchronic* flux, that is, change at a time, relative to a context of specification. In this sense, Heracleitus wanted to call attention not only to the phenomenon of the succession of opposites, but to the *compresence of opposites* as well; and it is clear that Plato noticed this feature of Heracleitus' thought and used it himself in attempting to establish the existence of Forms.[36]

Heracleitus' idea here is worth considering. He notes, for example, that we are inclined to say that Helen is beautiful. When we speak this way, however, we are implicitly comparing her to some others, who are not so beautiful. Yet if we were to reflect on the matter we would appreciate that in making this sort of judgment we are implicitly restricting the comparison class by precluding considerations of some others, including the goddesses who are, we may presume, more beautiful still. (Heracleitus observes, in just this way, that humans are intelligent in comparison to the apes but not at all so in comparison with the gods.) So, there is a sense in which, relative to different contexts, Helen is both beautiful and not beautiful. So too with the Empire State Building: it is both large and not large. It is large in comparison with a normal suburban bungalow, but rather small in comparison with Mount Everest. In its turn, Mount Everest is large in comparison with the statue of the Admiral Nelson in Trafalgar Square, but positively puny relative to the Milky Way. In all of these cases, some x is both F and not-F at a single time. This, then, is Heracleitus' notion of synchronic flux, which Plato re-introduces as the compresence of opposites.

If we return to HAF armed with this initially peculiar notion of flux, things become more interesting, but also more complex. Now (HAF-1), the premise that sensibles are in flux, seems correct, but only for some range of properties. With regards to largeness, beauty and goodness, things really do suffer the compresence of opposites. Some things are both large and not large, both beautiful and not beautiful, and both good and not good – in each case specified to different contexts and in relation to different comparison classes. That said, some things plainly do not suffer the compresence of opposites. As Plato himself notes, my finger is not both a finger and not a finger. It is simply a finger.[37] Nor is any number both odd and not odd; rather, every number is either odd or not odd. The compresence of opposites extends only to evaluative or normative properties, to what we may call *contextually sensitive properties*. Now, although not all properties are contextually sensitive, it may be that there are far more such than we unreflectively suppose. In any case, however many contextually sensitive properties there may be, so far extends (HAF-1). So, if the argument turns out to be sound, it will have established Forms only for contextually sensitive properties.[38]

Its soundness is a complex matter, not least because (HAF-2) now becomes difficult to evaluate. According to that premise, we cannot know what is in flux, where that now amounts to the claim that we cannot know properties which are contextually sensitive, insofar as they are contextually sensitive. Presumably, Plato cannot mean that we cannot even be acquainted with such properties as they are manifested by sense particulars. After all, we do make the judgment that Helen is beautiful, or that Mount Everest is large. His thought here may instead be that we experience items in flux by sense perception, but that we cannot rely on sense perception alone when we seek explanations for the largeness or beauty in things. When things are in flux in the manner specified, they cannot be known by a faculty which experiences the sensible world directly. The idea would then be that if we know what largeness is, it must be in virtue of some non-sensory faculty.

This, at any rate, is what Plato suggests in the *Phaedo*, when he notes that we do not explain the largeness of a giant man by what we see in him.[39] If the man, Andre the Giant, is eight feet tall, then we explain his largeness by his being eight feet. This, however, cannot be an adequate explanation of largeness as such, since being eight feet tall in some other cases, for example in a giraffe, explains shortness, not tallness. Even so, we do know what largeness is, even if we cannot at present offer a completely satisfying analysis. That would be the purport of (HAF-4), the assertion that we do have some knowledge, even if our knowledge is not occurrent and conscious. (Perhaps, as Plato has suggested in the *Meno*, this knowledge may be available to us only by recollection or *a priori* reflection.) If we now must give up (HAF-4) by denying that we know what largeness is, then Plato will have a certain sort of victory, at least in the sense that we would need to claim something which ought to seem rather strange, that we do not even know what largeness is. What is more, our success in applying the property across a wide range of discrete contexts might tend to undermine any such admission. By contrast, if we affirm (HAF-4) by allowing that we do have some knowledge, then if we agree with (HAF-1) and (HAF-2) as we have been characterizing them, Plato has made at least some progress toward establishing the existence of Forms.

Plato's Heracleitean argument for Forms raises large and difficult issues. Our consideration of it has not established that it is obviously sound or unsound. Our interest has rather been to show how, as Aristotle suggests, someone enamored of Heracleitean themes, as Plato was, might well have a legitimate epistemologically based motivation for believing in the existence of abstract ideas, including even Forms.

Equality itself: an argument from the Phaedo

Aristotle's account of Plato's motivation for believing in Forms presents one kind of existence argument. That account is useful in part because it brings into especially sharp relief Plato's epistemological motivations for Forms by explaining his reaction to Heracleiteanism. Another existence argument, given directly by Plato himself, has a more metaphysical cast. It is a short argument, one which makes a central appeal to the compresence of opposites. It is a metaphysical argument because it is best understood as an attempt to thwart all efforts to *reduce* context-sensitive properties to sets of the sense particulars which manifest them. The argument, if sound, shows that no such reduction is forthcoming. If that is correct, then the properties themselves must be non-sensible, and so abstract. What is more, as abstract entities, Forms are assumed by this argument to have a special character: they never suffer the compresence of opposites. Instead, they are purely and essentially what they are, bereft of context-sensitivity, and so explanatorily basic relative to the particulars which, to use Plato's word, *participate* in them.

The argument occurs in the *Phaedo*, where Plato yokes together the doctrine of recollection and the theory of Forms by insisting that they are equally necessary and indeed that the entire notion of recollection would be futile if there were no Forms.[40] Minimally, his idea here is that there is no point in positing *a priori* knowledge if there are no abstract entities to serve as the objects of that knowledge. At any rate, he feels secure in asserting the existence of such objects, since he has just offered the following argument,[41] an argument which relies on the assertion that Forms never suffer the compresence of opposites (NCO):

1   Equal sticks and stones sometimes, staying the same, appear equal with respect to one thing and unequal to another. (They suffer the compresence of opposites.)
2   Equality itself [42] is never unequal (and so never suffers the compresence of opposites).
3   Therefore, Equality itself and equal things are not the same.

The argument is a simple appeal to Leibniz's Law.[43] Equality itself never suffers the compresence of opposites; that is, it lacks the property of suffering the compresence of opposites with respect to equality. Since all equal sense particulars suffer the compresence of opposites with respect to equality, Equality itself can never be identified with any sense particular or set of sense particulars. It follows, then, that Equality itself is an abstract entity.

The argument is plainly valid. Moreover, if the appeal to Leibniz's Law is legitimate, then as long as the premises are true, Plato has given us a good reason for accepting Equality as an abstract entity. Since he could easily have chosen any other context-sensitive property at random, the argument about Equality, if sound, also establishes that all such properties are abstract entities. This conclusion would not yet entail that there are Forms, abstract mind- and language-independent entities which have all of their intrinsic properties essentially; but it would take us a step closer to that conclusion, and would in fact provide additional evidence for accepting the existence of Forms for a full range of context-sensitive properties.

Again, (NCO) is best understood as an *anti-reductive* argument. That is, Plato is here envisaging an interlocutor who agrees that there is such a thing as Equality, but who denies that it is a Form or any other kind of abstract entity. Instead, the imaginary interlocutor insists that Equality is simply to be identified with all of the equal things there are. Plato thinks that facts about the compresence of opposites preclude any such identification. Since, then, all parties have agreed that there is such a thing as Equality, if (NCO) shows that it is not to be identified with any collection of sensible objects, Equality will have to be an abstract object.

(NCO-1) makes the point that equal sticks and stones, or any other randomly selected collection of equal things, will be both equal and not equal. Though the premise admits of a number of different interpretations, one simple and straightforward reading takes it to be suggesting merely, for example, that a stone and a stick may be equal in weight while not being equal in length. In some respects they will be equal and in others not. Now, suggests Plato, contrast this situation with what obtains for Equality itself. According to (NCO-2), Equality itself is never unequal; so, it never suffers the compresence of opposites. This might be for either one of two reasons: (1) Equality itself is equal, but never not equal; or (2) Equality itself is neither equal nor not equal. On the second approach, Equality itself would not be the sort of thing which could be equal or not. It would then be a category mistake to say of Equality itself that it is equal, akin to the mistake committed by someone who says that the plus function either snores or does not snore. Here it seems reasonable to point out that the plus function is not the sort of thing which can snore. In the same way, there might be some point in saying that Equality itself is not the sort of thing which can be either equal or not. On the first approach, one which much of Plato's language suggests,[44] and one also accepted by Aristotle,[45] Equality itself is equal, but never not equal. If this is his view, then Plato accepts a form of *self-predication*, a commitment which may cause him difficulty.[46] Minimally, the idea here would be that Equality itself is equal, where this might mean as much as its having the property it is and as little as its being the essence of equality. In either case, though, Equality would never be not-equal. If not, it would never suffer the compresence of opposites. Since collections of sense particulars always do, Equality cannot be identified with them. It must therefore be an abstract entity, like a Form.

It is tempting to complain at this juncture that Plato simply begs the question in favor of Forms in (NCO). After all, (NCO-2) uses "Equality" as if it were a singular term, a referring expression which picks out some one definite entity. That, however, seems to be the question at issue.

In response, Plato may fairly and appropriately appeal to the dialectical context of the argument. It had been agreed by all parties that there is such a thing as equality. Perhaps, though, this admission is dubious. In fact, an admission of this sort is a familiar and defensible strategy of Plato's. He will often pose the question: Is *the F* something or nothing?[47] Is, e.g., justice something or nothing? Is equality something or nothing? In each case, Plato's interlocutors assent. Although this may retroactively strike them as rash, this sort of concession is really rather modest. They are not conceding that justice or equality is something of any particular character or category. They are not even conceding that justice is a quality or property. Instead, they are merely allowing that justice is not nothing, that it exists. It is here important to recognize that if they later recant their earlier concession, they cannot lament that they had wrongly, if implicitly, accepted some form of realism about justice. Plato's ultimate strategy is to get them to appreciate that *if* justice is something, then it will turn out to have features which require it to be a Form. The denial of the antecedent of this conditional is not itself an affirmation of nominalism or of relativism. It is instead an avowal of nihilism, the view that really there is no such thing as justice. However coherent this position may be, it is not one which Plato's interlocutors have been willing to entertain; nor is it one which has the attractions of various types of nominalism about the qualities whose nature Plato investigates. Plato's strategy is thus best regarded as an attempt to force either realism or nihilism by showing that some moderate-sounding intermediate positions cannot be defended.

This can be appreciated by focusing again on the strategy of (NCO). The argument merely attempts to block one reductive analysis of equality, without trying to establish from unassailable first principles that there must be such a thing as Equality itself alone and by itself. In the dialectical context, it is rather as if a police detective when asked about the identity of a murderer had conjectured the butler. When it is pointed out to her on the basis of sound forensic evidence that the murderer, *whoever that is*, weighs over 200 pounds, but that the butler weighs only 145, she will be right to conclude, on the basis of Leibniz's Law, that the proposed identification fails. Similarly, Plato can now insist that Equality, *whatever it turns out to be*, cannot be identified with any collection of sense particulars. That blocked reduction, however, also yields some positive information about Equality, that it must be some sort of abstract entity. Of course, it is open to someone to opt out at this point by reneging on the admission that Equality exists, which in the context would be akin to denying that there was a murderer to be sought, since the death must have been accidental or a suicide. While there might, of course, be good reason to conclude this, it does not seem to be recommended by the mere fact that the butler did not do it. By analogy, suggests Plato, we should not immediately endorse nihilism when nominalist reductions fail.

If in view of these considerations we agree with Plato that Largeness cannot be reduced to any collection of sense particulars, then we will also be interested in seeing how he extends his observations about compresence of opposites in order to show that Forms cannot be reduced to another sort of more familiar entity. For he equally thinks that Forms cannot be identified even with some more familiar sorts of abstract entities, *sensible properties*, the kinds of properties whose instances are immediately accessible to sense experience. (So, *being green* is a sensible property; *being just* is not.) In seeking to extend his argument this way, Plato relies upon the explanatory role of Forms, as he conceives it. According to Plato, the presence of a Form *explains* why a given action qualifies as manifesting this or that property.[48] If Euthyphro's prosecution of his father really is an instance of piety, then what makes it so is its participating in Piety itself. If participation in a Form F-ness explains why some sense particular is F, then we can conclude more than that a reduction of F-ness to a collection of sense *"particulars"* is impossible. In addition, Plato urges, a reduction of Forms to sensible *"properties"* will be no less implausible. For example, if a stick and a stone are both large, perhaps because each weighs ten kilos, then we might be tempted to analyze

Largeness as *weighing ten kilos*. Plato counters that that same property, weighing ten kilos, might equally explain, in a different context, why something qualifies as small. So, for example, weighing ten kilos would render a fully mature female lynx small rather than large. Similarly, dissonance in one context makes a concerto ugly, when Bach is played poorly, and makes another concerto beautiful, when Bartok is played well. So, in different contexts, the same sensible property explains why different things, sometimes of disparate sorts and sometimes of the same sort, have completely opposite properties. Hence, that sensible property cannot be identified with Largeness or with Beauty, whatever these turn out to be. In these cases, Plato's observation about context sensitivity among properties intersects with his views about the compresence of opposites to show why attempted reductions of Forms to more familiar sorts of sensory properties fail.

In each of these ways, Plato relies upon (putative) facts about the compresence of opposites to block the reduction of Forms to more familiar sorts of entities, sense particulars in one instance and sensible properties in the other. Each of these two non-reductive arguments tends in the same positive direction. As long as we agree that there is such a thing as Largeness or Beauty, and we also agree that Plato's anti-relativistic arguments have some force, then we will also agree that Forms are not sense particulars, and so are abstract, and that they are not even sensible properties, and so are not even graspable indirectly by the senses. They are, as Plato often suggests, objects of thought, rather than objects of sense. In the argument from the *Phaedo*, Plato relies especially clearly on facts about compresence of opposites ultimately rooted in Heracleitean doctrines about flux. It is in response to such doctrines that Plato comes to think of Forms as permanent, unchanging, abstract entities, graspable by discerning minds but unavailable to unabetted sense perception. Further, depending upon how one understands such claims as "Justice itself is just," Plato may have additional reason to regard Forms not only as abstract, but as perfect exemplars which sense particulars only approximate but never realize completely.[49]

Knowledge and belief: an existence argument from Republic v

Aristotle's presentation of Plato's argument for Forms is largely epistemological in orientation; Plato's own argument in the *Phaedo* is more narrowly metaphysical, although it too is continuous with arguments which rely upon Plato's conception of explanatory adequacy. An extended and important argument from the *Republic* relies on all of these different sorts of considerations; by braiding together these strands in his thought, Plato seeks to convert someone skeptical about the existence of Forms into a full-blown Platonic realist.

The argument melds together Plato's metaphysical and epistemological interests in Forms by correlating different mental states or faculties and different classes of objects. He maintains that: (1) knowledge is set over what is; (2) ignorance is set over what is not; and (3) if there is something which is and is not, and this is between what is and what is not, there must be something between knowledge and ignorance, which turns out to be opinion.[50] The division Plato offers here is a bit obscure, especially if we understand him to be using, as well we might, the same sense of "is" throughout. There are effectively three choices in interpreting these correlations: existential, predicative, or veridical. Taken as existential, (1) claims that knowledge is of what exists, that ignorance of what does not exist, while opinion deals with what exists and does not exist. Taken predicatively, (1) claims that knowledge is of what is F, (2) that ignorance is of what is not F; and (3) opinion is of what is both F and not F. Finally, taken veridically, (1) maintains that knowledge is of what is true, (2) that ignorance is of what is false, and (3) that opinion is of what is both true and false.

A brief reflection on these alternatives suggests that no one sense of "is" makes perfect sense in all cases. Thus, though it makes ready sense to assert that knowledge is of what is true, it is not immediately evident why ignorance should deal with the false (there are many true things I do not know). Similarly, while it is true that knowledge deals with what exists, it is hard to fathom what it means to say that opinion concerns what both exists and does not exist; indeed, it is difficult even to comprehend what could be meant by the claim that something both exists and does not exist. Existence seems to be an on/off notion, such that either something does or does not exist. Finally, if we reflect on Plato's preoccupation with the compresence of opposites, things may seem initially more hopeful. For it makes perfect sense to assert that opinion trades in what is F and not-F and that knowledge concerns what is purely F. Nonetheless, here too it is a bit hard to appreciate how ignorance concerns what is not-F. While it is true that as a result of ignorance I might make the false judgment that something which is not-F is F, perhaps that the mongoose is oviparous, it is hard to construe my ignorance in this or any other case as concerned exclusively with what is not-F.

Still, Plato clearly relies upon at least the predicative sense of "is" in his argument for Forms, even if he does not rely upon it exclusively. This is because he once again relies upon some facts about the compresence of opposites, where this undeniably employs a predicative sense of the verb.[51] It is, however, important to realize that Plato may in fact rely on several senses of "is" in his argument without falling into fallacy, so long as the various senses do not result in equivocations which render the argument unsound. Even so, it is worth formulating the existence argument of *Republic* v in different ways, by employing different senses of "is," as Platonic scholars have in fact done. The following formulation can then be viewed as a kind of template, which adheres to Plato's own presentation and which provides a framework for more fine-grained analyses.

The existence argument of *Republic* v is intended in part to buttress Plato's astonishing claim that cities will be forever beset with all manner of evils and bereft of happiness, public or private, until philosophers become kings. Plato expects this contention to be met with ignorant derision, but he thinks he can explain himself to a sympathetic audience.[52] Philosophers, after all, as lovers of wisdom (Greek: *philos*, love; *sophia*, wisdom) are naturally suited to know the Good and so are also suited to lead a city towards the Good. At least they will have the knowledge of what is best. In this, they contrast sharply with some others, including people of goodwill, the "sight-lovers" who love beautiful sights and sounds, but are unable, as only a very few are able, to "reach the Beautiful itself and see it by itself."[53] Those who can grasp Beauty (or Justice or Goodness) itself understand what Beauty is, and they see that some other things only participate in it. So, they will not mistake the things which merely participate in Beauty for Beauty itself or Beauty itself for its participants.[54] (Presumably, then, those who sought to reduce Equality to collections of equal things in the *Phaedo* were confused in just this way.)

If someone without knowledge grouses about this contention, because they mistake opinion for knowledge, Plato will seek to persuade them first of something which ought to be uncontroversial, that knowledge is not the same thing as opinion, and then of something altogether controversial, that knowledge requires Forms as its objects. The first phase of the existence argument of the *Republic* (EAR) proceeds as follows:[55]

1 Knowledge is set over F-ness itself, where F-ness is never not-F.
2 Opinion is set over what is F and not-F.
3 Capacities with different objects are distinct.
4 Hence, opinion is not the same as knowledge.

If we understand this much of the argument predicatively, its themes will be mostly familiar by now. (EAR-1) claims that knowledge concerns what is stable and so what cannot suffer the compresence of opposites; (EAR-2) adds that opinion's domain is precisely what suffers the compresence of opposites. New is (EAR-3), which suggests that each human capacity has a discrete set of objects in terms of which it is individuated from other capacities. Thus, as vision takes color as its objects and smell takes scent, with the result that vision and smell are distinct sensory capacities, so opinion and knowledge are different mental capacities, since their distinctive objects are necessarily discrete. It would follow, then, that opinion and knowledge are distinct. Note here that Plato seems to be speaking not of the states *having an opinion* and *knowing some proposition p*, but rather of the mental faculties in virtue of which we enter into these states.

The initial portions of the second phase of (EAR) are also familiar, though now Plato adds a modal twist. This phase of the argument, Plato says expressly, is directed to those who deny the existence of Forms:[56]

5 Each of the many Fs is both F and not-F.
6 The sight-lovers have intentional attitudes only towards the many Fs.

7 Hence, the sight-lovers have intentional attitudes only towards what is F and not-F.

8 Therefore, the sight-lovers have only opinion, and never knowledge.

9 Knowledge is possible.

10 Therefore, there must be potential objects of knowledge.

11 Therefore, there must be objects such as F-ness itself, where F-ness is never not-F.

12 Therefore, there are Forms, the objects of knowledge.

In differentiating true philosophers from sight-lovers and others who trade in opinion, Plato once again relies upon the compresence of opposites to distinguish objects of opinion from objects of genuine knowledge. Thus in (EAR-5) through (EAR-8), Plato seeks to establish that those who do not have intentional contact with the Forms lack knowledge. If we accept the results of the first phase of (EAR), we will conclude that the sight-lovers have only opinion.

Now, however, Plato points out that *there are some people who know some things*. These are philosophers. Again given the results of the first phase of (EAR), these figures must be able to see past what suffers the compresence of opposites. If, however, some people do have knowledge, and knowledge requires objects free from the compresence of opposites, then there must exist suitable objects of such knowledge, permanent and pure expressions of the qualities manifested imperfectly by objects of sense.

(EAR) raises a great many difficult issues. To begin, there will be those who simply deny that there are people who have knowledge. That may seem fair enough. Still, Plato evidently need rely only on the comparatively modest point, represented in (EAR-9), that knowledge is possible. This much is in any case already assumed in (EAR-1), where Plato relies upon the plausible thought that knowledge is not the same as opinion. If they are not the same, then there is something which differentiates them. What is more, given that we have already rejected Protagorean relativism, we have no reason to assert that knowledge is the same thing as opinion, a claim which seems on its face wildly untenable. If even that much is conceded, then on the assumption that the first phase of the argument is compelling, Plato may nevertheless have a point: if stable objects of knowledge are required even for the possibility of knowledge, and knowledge is possible, then there must be such objects. It is, Plato rightly assumes, easier to deny the existence of knowledge than to deny its bare possibility.

3.6   Plato's general characterizations of Forms

Like the other existence arguments, (EAR) raises many issues worth pursuing in significantly greater detail – issues both about the presuppositions of the existence arguments and about their proper formulations. The discussions to this point have been intended mainly to recapitulate Plato's philosophical motivations for maintaining his commitment to Forms by considering his existence arguments for them. If Plato is wrong about the existence of Forms, then the existence arguments he offers obviously fail. Even then, however, it would be instructive to uncover and explore their difficulties. In any case, it should not be assumed up front, before they are conducted, that these explorations are bound to turn up crushing objections. They may; but, then too, Plato may be right to be a Platonist. Moreover, insofar as we wish to discern whether *we* should become Platonists, it is necessary to consider the argumentative basis for accepting the theses which constitute the core of the theory of Forms.

Still, being a Platonist about Forms evidently embodies some commitments beyond just those generated by the existence arguments. At any rate, not everything Plato believes about the Forms comes to the surface immediately in his existence arguments. Sometimes Plato characterizes Forms in ways which are continuous with the results of his existence arguments, but which are not strictly entailed or implied by them. In some of these cases, it is easy to see how Plato might reasonably argue from the conclusions of the existence arguments to these further features. In other cases, the connections are not so obvious. In any case, if we reflect on Plato's dominant characterizations of them, we see that Platonic Forms:

1 are the objects of knowledge, the essences of qualities whose natures we seek in philosophical investigation;
2 never suffer the compresence of opposites, either because they are (a) self-predicative; or (b) categorically unsuited to have the qualities they are, or their opposites, predicated of them;
3 are stable, unchanging, abstract entities;
4 are perfect paradigms, or models which sensible entities copy but never equal;
5 are the sorts of beings in which sensible entities "participate," where this may be a primitive relationship, but seems akin to the instantiation or predication relation;
6 are separate.

The first three of these features played significant roles in the existence arguments. The remaining three require some explication, especially inasmuch as they seem to generate some tension within Plato's theory of Forms.

Plato often characterizes Forms as paradigms, as models copied by the physical entities named after them.[57] Thus, Justice itself is the very model of justice, so that those institutions or persons we call just are so called because of the likeness they bear to the Form of Justice. Now, in this sort of case, it is a bit difficult to know how to unpack Plato's suggestion. In the first instance, we expect a copy to resemble its model, at least to some degree, so that they will manifest many of the same properties. If so, then Justice itself will evidently be self-predicative,[58] since just things will be just by manifesting the property justice, by resembling the Form which manifests it perfectly. It is hard, however, to make literal sense of the claim that Justice itself is just, since Justice itself is an abstract entity, incapable of engaging in the sorts of activities required of just individuals or institutions. Perhaps, then, paradeigmatism should not be understood to require self-predication. Then, however, there will be a question as to how Forms will serve as models to be copied, since resemblance, in its most natural interpretation, seems to require shared properties of some sort. (This, of course, can be challenged.)

However that may be, sense particulars, according to Plato, not only resemble Forms, but *participate* in them. This is a term Plato admits he has trouble rendering literal.[59] Minimally, though, he seems to intend something akin to instantiation. On this approach, the relationship particulars bear to Forms will not be one of resemblance, but rather more like the relation a particular bears to a universal, when it betokens it. If Plato thinks this way about Forms, then he treats them as universals, rather than as perfect paradigms, as entities with instances rather than as entities with copies. Now, there is no contradiction in holding both that a Form is a universal and a paradigm; nor is there any incoherence in holding both that Forms are instantiated and copied. Still, these relations seem importantly different. Minimally, one would want from Plato an account of how they are to be understood in terms of their priority relations. Moreover, they seem to indicate different ontologies for Forms, paradeigmatism suggesting that Forms are particulars and participation suggesting that Forms are universals.[60] This is perhaps why Aristotle complained that, according to Plato, Forms were both universals and particulars, a situation he found intolerable.[61]

The last notion, that Forms are separate, also occasions a special reproach from Aristotle.[62] In claiming that Plato, but not Socrates, separated the Forms, Aristotle implies that according to Plato Forms are capable of existing without their ever being realized. That is, the Form of Justice exists alone and by itself, as an ideal, even if there is no justice in the world. In this sense, if Forms are universals, then separation amounts to nothing more than *ante rem* realism for Plato.[63] Now, given that Aristotle supposes that separation causes special difficulties for Plato, it is worth reflecting on the question of whether Plato in fact endorses the separation of Forms. Narrowly speaking, he does not: he never expressly characterizes Forms as separate or as capable of existing independently of sense particulars.[64] Still, three things Plato does say imply that he endorsed separation. First, Forms are perfect and unchanging, as paradigms, and in no way in flux. This suggests that they are what they are necessarily and essentially, in which case they seem indifferent to the comings and goings of contingent sense particulars. Second, they are objects of knowledge, which must be necessary and stable. Plato's Heracleiteanism requires him to hold that knowledge is never possible where impermanence pertains; so, here too, the demand seems to be that Forms are necessary and independent of sense particulars. Finally, if

Forms are not reducible to collections of sensibles, as the existence argument of the *Phaedo* requires, then Forms are abstract entities, a sort of entity normally thought to exist necessarily if at all, and not to suffer generation or corruption. If so, then Forms will in fact be separate, in just the way Aristotle says they are.

Aristotle presumes that separation causes special difficulties for Plato.[65] His arguments, however, are not always compelling. In general, if he is right to ascribe separation to Platonic Forms, Aristotle is not therefore right to presume that Plato as a consequence confronts insurmountable philosophical difficulties. On the contrary, Plato seems alive to modal data which Aristotle sometimes disregards. If justice is *possible* in this world, and if we have good independent reason to suppose that there is such a thing as Justice itself, something which serves as a paradigm towards which just individuals strive in their actions, then we also have good reason to suppose that something underwrites the very possibility of justice, something which exists even when nothing else succeeds in becoming just. In this way, if he is to be a realist about Forms, then *ante rem* realism may prove preferable to an *in rebus* realism endorsed later by Aristotle.[66]

3.7   Platonic analysis: a case study

Plato's existence arguments purport to show that there are such things as Forms. One benefit of the existence of Forms, if they exist, is that they provide a basis for stable, non-relativistic knowledge in domains where skeptics, even moderate skeptics, doubt knowledge is possible. Like Euthyphro, Plato is a realist about value; unlike Euthyphro, he doubts that values exist as a result of the legislative activities of the gods. Instead, they exist necessarily, as abstract mind- and language-independent entities. If we assume with Plato that there are Forms, then we ought to have them available to us as the standards and paradigms Plato asserts that they are. We ought, then, to be able to do what Socrates hoped Euthyphro could do for him: we ought to be able to look upon the Forms and use them as models to determine whether particular actions or institutions manifest the values of concern to us.

Thus, if we want to know whether communism is just, or whether *laissez-faire* capitalism is just, or whether monarchy is just, we should be able, if we are Plato's philosophers, to look upon the Form of Justice, grasp its nature, and then to determine on the basis of our experience of it, whether these sorts of social arrangements make the mark. That is, even if we agree that at least one of Plato's existence arguments is sound, that will do us little good unless we also come to be familiar with the content of a completed Platonic analysis. Because Plato does not shy away from the task of offering such analyses, we are in a position to evaluate his success. His most striking production in this regard is the analysis of justice offered in the *Republic*. This analysis will serve as a sort of case study.

Like other great works of literature and philosophy, Plato's *Republic* repays careful and repeated study. Our interest in it will be rather mono-dimensional, insofar as we will mainly set aside many of its areas of concern by focusing narrowly on the analysis of justice it offers. Still, this is clearly the dominant concern of the entire work, which is no doubt why it carried the subtitle *On Justice* in antiquity.

Plato offers this analysis by trying to meet a challenge, set by two characters, Glaucon and Adeimantus. They observe that there are three types of good things: (1) things welcome for their own sakes, like simple joys and harmless pleasures; (2) those welcomed for their own sakes as well as for what comes from them, such as health; and (3) the onerous, done only for the sake of what flows from them, but never chosen for their own sakes, such as physical training and medical treatment. They observe that most people treat justice as a type-3 good, chosen not for its own sake, but because they practice it only unwillingly, as necessary to join a society, where they are better off than they would be in a primitive state, overpowered by the strong and outwitted by the clever. Most people prudently judge that they are better off as members of a law-governed state than they would otherwise be. So, they act justly – but only to the extent that it is necessary for them to *seem* to be just, which is the real price of admission to civil society. They are in fact just only to the extent that they need to be in order to appear just to those with whom they have made agreements to be just. Their motivation for acting justly thus shows that they treat justice as a type-3 good, something not chosen for its own sake, but as a kind of medicine to be swallowed as an unpleasant and prudentially unavoidable imperative.[67]

They issue Plato a two-part challenge. First, he must offer an analysis of justice; second, he must show that it is the best form of good, a type-2 good, something chosen both for its own sake and for what flows from it. In order to make this challenge especially difficult for Plato, Glaucon defends the view adopted by the many, that justice is never chosen for itself, by means of a thought experiment, the first such in the history of Western philosophy. In this thought experiment, Glaucon disassociates two features of actions which normally accompany one another: their being just and their seeming just. The experiment involves imagining oneself to be in the position in which the ancestor of the Lydian Gyges, a shepherd,[68] found himself: he came into possession of a mysterious ring which made him invisible, thus freeing him from the normal requirement of having to be just in order to seem to be just. Before long, he used his special powers to seduce the queen, kill the king, and take over the kingdom. Glaucon suggests that all other people are like this shepherd: if given the chance to be unjust without fear of reprisal, they will inevitably become unjust, because it is in their interest to do so.[69]

Thus, the argument encoded in the tale of Gyges' ring (GR) is:

1   People are willingly just only if it is the case that, given the opportunity to act unjustly with impunity, they would nevertheless refrain

from unjust actions.

2   Given this opportunity, no one would refrain from unjust actions.

3   Hence, no one is willingly just.

4   Hence, insofar as people act justly, they do so only under compulsion.

5   Hence, justice is a type-3 good, done not for its own sake but for what flows from it.

No premise of this argument is silly or obviously incorrect; and both (GR-1) and (GR-2) strike a responsive chord in at least some of Plato's modern readers. (GR-1) plausibly suggests that it would be a fair indication of people's being just only unwillingly that they would not be just if they did not have to fear the reprisals of their being caught acting unjustly. (GR-2) is simply a naked claim, one left undefended by Glaucon. Some readers of Plato approve of it as obviously correct, because they believe that it captures some deep fact about human nature, however unpleasant that may be for us to acknowledge; others, unwilling to regard themselves as disposed towards injustice, prefer to deny it. Importantly, Plato feels its force, at least in the sense that he acknowledges that those without a proper understanding of the nature of justice, which he will argue is actually something beneficial to its possessor, might well carry on as Glaucon predicts they will. That is, Plato himself accepts Glaucon's egoistic presuppositions; but he will eventually want to deny that egoism gives anyone a reason to be unjust.

The edifice of the republic is Plato's response to this two-part challenge. He constructs an ideal state, he says, in order to discover the nature of justice writ large: if we can ascertain the nature of justice by observing it in the macrocosm of the ideal state, and can see that the individual is isomorphic with the state, in the sense of being identically structured, then it will be possible to transfer the account of justice in the republic to the individual. This strategy introduces the republic itself as a heuristic device whose ultimate aim is to discover the nature of justice in the individual, a task which is necessary if Plato is to meet the two-part challenge he sets for himself, to analyze justice and to show that justice is choiceworthy in itself.[70]

Plato conceives of a maximally just city as one in which each class of citizen – the rulers, the soldiering class, and the productive class – does its own work, never interfering with the natural and appropriate function of the others, and deferring whenever it is appropriate to do so. This conception develops partly from a more fundamental commitment to a principle of *natural suitability*, according to which different individuals are born with distinct sorts of gifts. Some are quick-witted, some physically strong and swift. Some are musically endowed; some have knacks for various crafts. "We are not," says Plato, "all born alike."[71] When natural endowments are cultivated by the appropriate forms of education, there results a society populated by citizens who are flourishing, at least in the sense that each citizen is doing best what he or she is naturally suited to do. (Plato, astonishingly for his period, insists that women no less than men should be educated as soldiers and rulers, since in fact natural aptitudes are distributed equally among both sexes. So, for the most part, he applies his principle of natural suitability evenhandedly.)[72] The picture of the just state, however illiberal it may be, is thus one of a state which is functioning smoothly, to the advantage of all of its citizens. The rulers rule with an eye on the good of the entire state, and not on their own narrowly conceived concerns; the soldiers defer to the rulers while conducting their affairs with courage and honor; and the productive classes carry out their function with a clear understanding of the contribution they make to the state while garnering such satisfaction as accompanies a job well done. Each class has its appropriate sphere and autonomy. Although the rulers rule, they would not meddle in the dimensions of a craft best left to the craftsperson; they would not, for example, instruct a baker how best to bake or an ironsmith how best to smelt.[73]

So, the account of justice in the ideal state is then really rather straightforward:

Justice in the city $=_{df}$ each of the three parts of the city (rulers, soldiers, productive classes) does its own work, deferring where appropriate and never meddling in the affairs of any other part.

Thus, any society which finds one of its classes meddling in the affairs of the other or failing to do its own appropriate work turns out to be unjust. In the first instance, for example, a state will be unjust if its soldiering class seizes control by a *coup d'état* even though its rulers had been just. Then again, a state will be unjust if its ruling class cares not about the good of the whole, but instead sets its sights on its own enrichment. In either case, the state as a whole has deviated from what is best for it and its various citizens and so no longer qualifies as just.

Plato's account of civic justice is, then, his final determination of the nature of justice in the macrocosm of the republic. Because this account was developed specifically for the purpose of illuminating justice in the individual, it will be wholly otiose unless we have reason to believe that it is transferable to individual citizens. This is something Plato clearly appreciates. He accordingly provides a principle of transference: every individual soul is isomorphic with the state. That is, every soul in fact has three parts, just as the state has three parts, and each of these parts has an analogue in the state. As the state has its rulers, soldiers, and productive classes, so the individual has a ruling faculty, a spirited faculty, and an appetitive faculty. It is obvious how the rulers are analogous to the ruling faculty of a human being; and it is also reasonably clear how the soldiering class, whose virtues are honor and courage, correspond to the spirited part of an individual, the function of which, though variegated, involves centrally one's self-conception in relation to the attitudes of others. It is a little less clear how the productive classes correspond to the appetites of a human being, beyond the fact that both are best advised to perform their functions in deference to a more far-sighted ruler. Perhaps Plato has in view the thought that as the productive classes of the state provide for its economic and commercial well-being, so in a human being the appetites have their appropriate function in maintaining the physical plant of the body.

However that may be, Plato is not content merely to assert isomorphism. Instead, by an ingenious argument, he seeks to establish that in fact every human being has the three psychic components mentioned. He is right to feel the need for a positive argument at this point, since otherwise his claims of isomorphism would ring hollow and *ad hoc*. The argument he offers relies upon a simple principle, a part-generating principle (PGP), according to which the same thing cannot do or undergo contraries with respect to the same element of itself. The status of (PGP) is debated, whether it is a substantive psychological principle or is intended to be a simple application of the principle of non-contradiction. It is hard to see how Plato can intend (PGP) to be a logical principle, since the examples he uses to illustrate its applications are not contradictories; but if it is not an instance of a logical principle, Plato will need to argue for it in its own right.

In either case, he uses it to show that the soul has at least two parts, reason and appetite, at least if this argument for psychic division (PD) is sound:

1   (PGP).
2   Acceptance and pursuit are contraries of rejection and avoidance.
3   So, if we find an instance of someone both having an appetite for x and refusing x, we will have an instance of someone undergoing contraries with respect to x.
4   In fact, our souls sometimes both have an appetite to drink and refuse to drink.
5   So, we have an instance in which our souls undergo contraries with respect to x.
6   Since, by (1), nothing can undergo contraries with respect to the same element of itself, whenever any soul is in the condition described in (PD-5), it must be with respect to different parts in the soul.
7   Hence, our souls have distinct parts.

We can give some content to (PD-7) by noticing that when we have the sorts of internal conflicts mentioned in (PD-4), often one part is concerned with our long-term well-being while the other focuses on immediate gratification only. The first part, which calculates about our long-term good, is plausibly thought of as Reason, the faculty with which we engage in conceptually rich long-term strategizing. The second part is easily recognized as Appetite, especially if we emphasize those sorts of bodily impulses which are primitive and urgent. Plato mentions thirst; other such desires would include hunger and sexual appetite. These sorts of appetites, considered in themselves, are mainly good—indifferent. They seek their own satisfaction without recourse to reflection on whether such satisfaction is really in the agent's long-term interest. In fact, sometimes it is and sometimes it is not. When, as we say, these sorts of appetites are checked or squashed because of their being bad for us, then this is due to the activity of Reason, whose job it is to determine when it is appropriate to satisfy our carnal urges. Here, of course, Reason functions as the Ruler.

While there are many difficult matters pertaining to this argument, at least the following can be said on its behalf. The psychological phenomenon to which Plato appeals in (PD-4) is a real one. Anyone who has ever dieted will instantly recognize what Plato has in mind. When we are hungry, but judge that it is best not to eat, we very often experience an inner turmoil, one which is easy to characterize in terms of warring factions. A desire to eat pushes against Reason's resolve; Reason pushes right back. Similarly, if less dramatically, the beginning of an exercise program will often involve internal conflict, especially if the exercise itself is difficult or painful. In these cases, if we persist, that is due to a commitment to doing what is best for us in the long term. Whether or not we do persist, however, that initial experience of internal conflict is palpable.

In this sense, Plato is surely right to appeal to the phenomenon of internal discord in (PD-4). What he makes of this experience is, however, a further matter. As we have seen, Socrates too recognized the data of conflict; but he resisted explaining our failure in terms of weakness of will or *akrasia*.[74] Plato's immediate goal is not to reinstate the phenomenon of *akrasia*, although he is understandably taken to introduce psychic division in part to make room for the sort of weakness ruled out by Socratic cognitivism.[75] Instead, his immediate argumentative goal is psychic division, and it is for this purpose that he harnesses the phenomenon of psychic conflict. For if conflicts involve tensions between opposites, then if (PGP) is defensible, we in fact have the two parts Plato mentions, though, of course, it will be a further question how these parts are to be understood: as proper parts, in the way that a leg is a part of a table, or as more attenuated conceptual parts, in the way a plaintiff's testimony is only one part of the story. In either case, though, individual psyches will have as distinct components both Reason and Appetite.

That will suffice to establish a partial isomorphism between state and soul. Still, the state has three parts, not only two. Plato addresses this worry by introducing two sorts of cases, each of which appeals to Leibniz's Law. He first considers the case of Leontius, who has a lurid and macabre desire to look upon some freshly executed corpses. (His desire seems akin to the fascination people unreflectively manifest when they slow down to observe a potentially grisly accident site across the median of a freeway.) His desire is plain to him; but he is disgusted with himself. When he rebukes himself, suggests Plato, it is not Reason which originates the self-reproach, which in its intensity borders on a form of self-loathing. Rather, Leontius has a faculty which opposes Appetite, and so cannot be Appetite, but which is not readily identified with Reason.[76] This third faculty Plato names *Spirit*. Plato also notes a second kind of case on behalf of Spirit: even children and non-human animals manifest Spirit, but neither has Reason, where this is understood as the capacity to calculate about one's long-term good.[77] These sorts of cases show again that Spirit cannot be reduced to Reason; but neither is Spirit the same as Appetite, since Spirit concerns itself with an agent's self-conception in relation to the attitudes of others. (If I care about courage in part because I wish to enjoy a reputation as especially courageous, then my concern is at least partly framed in terms of how others regard me.) Hence, there are, Plato concludes, three parts of the soul. With this phase of the argument complete, Plato can assert the isomorphism of the tri-partite soul and the republic in view of its three classes.

More importantly, he can, after wading "through a sea of argument,"[78] at long last meet the first part of Glaucon's challenge: he can now define justice. Given the strategy upon which he has relied, Plato regards himself as at liberty to transfer the account of justice writ large, in the republic, to the microcosm of the individual soul.[79] Since justice in the city consisted in the harmonious interaction of its three dominant parts, with each doing its own and never meddling with the work of another, we have the following account of justice in the individual:

> Justice in a person $=_{df}$ each of a person's three parts (Reason, Spirit, and Appetite) does its own work, deferring when appropriate and never meddling in the affairs of any other part.

Abstracting what is common to civic and psychic justice, we have as Plato's analysis of justice in the *Republic*:

> Justice $=_{df}$ the virtue whereby each essential component of a complex entity executes its appropriate function, while never interfering in the functions of any other component of that unity.

In short, justice is internal harmony: psychic harmony in an individual person and civic harmony in a state.

Various objections to this analysis immediately suggest themselves, some jejune and some not. It might in the first instance be objected that according to this analysis, my car's engine is just whenever it has been recently tuned. For then each of its components is discharging its function without interfering with the work of the others. This objection misses that the analysis places justice into the genus of virtue, which implicitly restricts its potential range of bearers. So, Plato need not worry about having gotten the extension of justice wrong, at least not for the reason given.

Importantly, the insistence that justice is a virtue is more than a definitional expedient. For some of Plato's interlocutors, including Thrasymachus in the early stages of the *Republic*, had gone so far as to deny that justice is a virtue.[80] Thrasymachus had argued that since injustice benefits its possessor, while justice harms the just, then since virtue is always in the interest of the agent, injustice and not justice is the real virtue. Plato is not here merely gainsaying Thrasymachus. For he takes the analysis to reveal that justice is after all in the interest of the just agent; a just person manifests an important kind of mental health, something we all rightly desire. The analysis is thus supposed to have revealed something about justice which Thrasymachus had missed. If he is now to remain consistent by maintaining his belief that virtues benefit those who have them, he will need to agree that injustice cannot be a virtue at all.

Thrasymachus will have to make this concession, that is, *if* Plato's analysis of justice is both correct *and* reveals justice to be a type-2 good, the type of good which is choiceworthy both for itself and for what flows from it. For recall that Plato had had two demands placed upon him: to define justice and to show, against the common conception, that justice benefits the just person. Now, there has been a fair bit of discussion about this second constraint. Is the state Plato analyses actually a state which is choiceworthy for itself? Do I, given the nature of justice, have a reason to be just?

It is important in the face of these sorts of questions to realize that the two constraints on Plato's account of justice are related. Neither is wholly independent of the other. If the correct analysis of justice turned out to show that justice was not in fact a type-2 good, then the constraint that it be shown to be so would not, and could not, be met. That would not, however, impugn the analysis itself. It would show only that the condition set on the analysis was unmotivated and unacceptable.[81] On the contrary, if the second constraint is a reasonable one, that can only be due to the fact that the correct analysis of justice will reveal it to be something choiceworthy in itself.

Indeed, when people come to assess Plato's success or failure, there is often a bit of an interplay in their reactions to the two constraints under which he is operating. There is a tendency to suppose that if the condition of psychic harmony characterized by Plato is choiceworthy in itself, then it is not really justice (that the analysis itself fails), or that if he has really captured the essence of justice, he has failed to demonstrate that it is choiceworthy (that the second demand has not been met). Thus, since individual justice is described as a sort of psychic harmony, and that is after all a kind of mental health, then perhaps what Plato describes is indeed a type-2 good. In that case, though, as some infer, there is little reason to suppose that the condition described is justice. After all, justice concerns essentially and ineliminably my other-regarding attitudes and activities. The sorts of unjust acts mentioned by Glaucon and Adeimantus include such ordinary violations of public morality as robbery and murder. If the condition Plato analyses is compatible with committing these sorts of heinous deeds, then it is hardly justice. On the other hand, if Plato's account is supposed to preclude our engaging in such crimes, it is unclear how this is so; moreover, if it really does have these results, then it again becomes unclear why the condition characterized is choiceworthy for itself. If he has not shown that much, then Plato has not given us a reason to be just, as opposed to merely seeming to be just. In sum, we are justified in wanting to know why, in light of Plato's analysis of justice, it should be a matter of complete indifference to us whether or not we wear Gyges' ring when it falls into our possession.

Plato is perfectly aware of these sorts of worries. His response comes in two parts, one brief and unvarnished, the other long and complex. First, he acknowledges forthrightly that justice as he describes it is self-regarding, not primarily other-regarding.[82] Even so, he insists, unjust actions tend to eventuate in psychic discord, while just actions promote psychic harmony. So, the just person, who has an interest in psychic harmony, will prefer those actions which are just to those which are unjust. Importantly, it turns out then that Plato's account of just actions is second-order: it says that x is just when, and only when, it promotes psychic harmony. So, actions of the same type of state might, on different occasions, qualify as sometimes just and sometimes unjust. That is, on one occasion lying might be unjust but on another just, depending upon whether the particular instance of lying promotes psychic harmony. This, however, does nothing to undermine the Platonic univocity assumption, since the account, though second-order, is perfectly univocal.

The second phase of Plato's response is best appreciated by considering an objection to the first part. Imagine a coolly dispassionate diamond thief, who, to all outward appearances, is psychically harmonious. She does not let her desires overwhelm her reason; nor does she deny her appetites. Moreover, she is brave, at least in the sense of having nerves of steel. All the while, she is a master thief. She will tell you that stealing brings her great equanimity. So, by the second-order analysis of justice, stealing should qualify as just. Now, while it is certainly true that some stealing could be in principle compatible with the second-order account of justice, it is hard to imagine how grand-scale theft of the sort under description could be described as just. Let it be the case that the jewels to be stolen are the property of an otherwise poor person, who scrimped and saved through a life of menial labor to purchase them. Their being stolen would be a significant harm and a grievous wrongdoing to their owner. If Plato's account of justice as a kind of psychic harmony turns this act of theft into an instance of justice, then he clearly has got the extension of justice wrong. As that has been a necessary condition on successful analysis since Socrates first asked his what-is-F-ness question, Plato's account of justice fails. So, at any rate, the detractor now concludes.

The second and more comprehensive response brings out what is left unfinished in the first. Plato does not allow that any old psychic harmony is sufficient for justice. Instead, he has taken pains to say that only the sort of psychic harmony which results from each part's doing its proper function qualifies as justice; it does not suffice that no part interferes with the others. Thus, the analysis is not merely formal. Instead, it carries with it some material implications regarding the requirements for psychic harmony. In particular, no soul is psychically harmonious in the requisite sense unless its Reason is functioning correctly, a result which for Plato has profound implications. To begin, it is the function of Reason to deliberate about the agent's long-term good. A properly functioning Reason, then, will have grasped this good, where this in turn involves its having knowledge and not merely true belief. So, minimally, the psychically harmonious soul is a knowledgeable soul, and so a soul which has come to appreciate that knowledge has as its primary object the Forms. In such a soul, Reason plays the role played by the rulers in the state: it grasps what is in fact good, and prefers it in every instance to what merely seems to be good. Consequently, a soul will be just only if it is drawn towards what is really good.

Taken together, these implications are as follows: (1) a soul is psychically harmonious only if it has knowledge; (2) no one has a knowledgeable soul without having come to know the Forms; (3) anyone who knows the Forms will also know the Good, and prefer it in every instance over what seems to be good but is not; (4) anyone who prefers real goodness over what is only apparently good will be sufficiently other-regarding that they will not seek to harm others or perpetrate crimes against them. So, anyone who realizes Plato's conception of justice will avoid manifestly unjust actions. Hence, Plato's analysis of justice is not extensionally inadequate. The fastidious master thief is not a counterexample, because she is not in a state of psychic harmony. She lacks knowledge of the Good, and she proves that she lacks this knowledge by living a life devoted to money, which is only an apparent good. She mistakes what is merely instrumental for something good in itself; and she is in fact wrong to do so.

Fairly clearly, each of the links in this chain of inferences is open to challenge. Taken together, they result in an ambitious but exceedingly fragile defense of Platonic justice. Plato's metaphysics of morality should help secure some of these inferences, even though, it must be said at the outset, some of his commitments are bound to seem extraordinary. Most extraordinary of all, even as Plato himself allows, is his conception of the Form of the Good.

3.8 The special role of the Form of the Good

So far Plato has argued that the person with a knowledgeably harmonious soul will be just. As Plato notes, this conception of justice departs in some ways from our pre-theoretic conception of justice as something which is essentially other-regarding. Still, there is no immediate reason to suppose that Plato has been unduly revisionary about justice. For the analysis offered, he maintains, will have consequences for action which will result in the just person's avoiding actions commonly and rightly viewed as unjust, including thievery and other forms of harm. He has also argued that once the true nature of justice is understood, it becomes clear that justice is itself a type-2 good, something good in itself as well as for what it contributes to forms of goodness beyond itself. It is, in the end, a kind of health, psychic health. Just as physical health is desirable in itself and because the most desirable form of life includes such health as a constitutive good, so justice is desirable in itself and because practicing it contributes to the best form of life available to humans. In all of this Plato assumes, reasonably enough, that we all seek the best form of life we can structure for ourselves.

Given the role of Reason as the ruling component of the soul, it is clear that one crucial component of Plato's overall project is highly and unapologetically rationalist. The best form of life includes knowledge of the Forms, not only because knowledge succeeds where belief fails but also because human beings are essentially rational creatures whose highest good involves the exercise of reason. In expecting the most highly developed individuals to rule the state, Plato also expects them to be philosophers who love knowledge in general, and knowledge of the Form of the Good in particular. This is because he thinks that the Form of the Good is pre-eminent among Forms. Indeed, he claims that the Form of the Good is more important than even Justice itself,[83] and that knowledge of other things is of no benefit to us if we do not know the Good.[84] It follows that no ruler will have a full appreciation of just and fine things without knowing why they are good, and so will never be an adequate ruler without knowledge of the Form of the Good; by contrast, the ruler with such knowledge will order the state's constitution perfectly.[85] So, knowledge of the Forms, including knowledge of the Good, is both necessary and sufficient for ruling the ideally just state. Further, assuming the isomorphism which Plato takes himself to have established, a maximally just individual will be one with knowledge, including knowledge of the Form of the Good. It follows then that the ideally just person will also be a philosopher, someone who loves wisdom.

When prodded to characterize the Form of the Good directly, Plato demurs. He says that it is clear that most people are wrong to think that pleasure is the same thing as the Good, for the simple reason that there are bad as well as good pleasures. Pleasures are sometimes good, to be sure. But some pleasures only seem to be good, and nobody wants what is only apparently good for themselves. As anyone will tell you upon reflection, what they seek for themselves is what is genuinely good, not merely what seems good to them at the moment.[86] "Every soul," claims Plato, "pursues the Good and does whatever it does for its sake."[87] So, nobody should pursue pleasure as their ultimate good. What is Plato's alternative? He says that he cannot characterize the Good directly, both because the topic is too large for the occasion and for fear that he will embarrass and disgrace himself even by trying.[88]

Instead, Plato reverts to a stunning analogy. In drawing this analogy, he feels at liberty to rely upon features of the theory of Forms already introduced and defended: the Forms are intelligible, but not visible, while the objects of sensation are visible but not intelligible.[89] The analogy he develops likens the role played by the Good in the intelligible realm, the realm of Forms, to the role played by the sun in the sensible realm, the world of ordinary sense experience. He highlights especially two features of this analogy. First, just as the sun provides illumination to the world, thus making its objects visible, so the Form of the Good provides illumination to the other Forms, thus making them knowable. Second, as the sun gives existence to the objects of sense, since without the sun there would be no visible world, so the Form of the Good gives existence to the remaining Forms. This second point of comparison is striking, and suggested to some later Platonists in antiquity that Plato intended the Form of the Good to be understood as a generative or causal principle which actually created the other Forms, a consequence we should probably resist, if we are to continue thinking of Forms as necessarily existing abstract entities.[90] Moreover, cautions Plato, we should not think of the Form of the Good as existence as such. In his ultimate and extraordinary observation about it, Plato insists that the Form of the Good is not the same thing as Existence, but "surpasses Existence in dignity and power," a remark which understandably sent Plato's interlocutor into an astonished giggle.[91]

Plato's characterization is not comical; but it is hard to fathom. Presumably Plato means to indicate at least that no Form could exist as a Form if it were not perfectly what it is. This same perfection is also what makes each individual Form intelligible: as perfectly what it is, no Form suffers the compresence of opposites and so cannot be reduced to any set of sense particulars or to any sensible quality. His point would then include the thought that the Form of the Good differs from Existence as such, since although it is true that all Forms exist, and so must, so to speak, participate in the Form of Existence, their doing so does not yet explain how they are perfect exemplars. So, we have first a point familiar from the *Euthyphro*,[92] that necessary co-extension is not sufficient for identity. Necessarily, every Form exists. Necessarily, every Form is perfect, and so superlatively good. Still, Plato cautions, it is not the case that what it is for them to be good is the same as it is for them to exist. To be good, Forms must participate in the Form of Goodness. In this sense, Plato may well be relying on a familiar point, though now at a higher level of abstraction: the Form of the Good is *explanatorily prior* to the other Forms, in that its presence makes them perfectly good. For this reason, the Form of the Good will be distinct from and prior even to existence, since though all Forms of necessity exist, what makes them Forms is not merely their existence but rather their surpassing goodness.

This point about priority relations among Forms carries with it a kind of epistemological corollary. Knowledge as such requires knowledge of the Form of the Good, because without such knowledge, full appreciation of the other Forms, as Forms, will be impossible. If it is not known for any given Form F-ness that F-ness is perfect F-ness, then a potential knower's cognitive relation to F-ness will be incomplete. If that is correct, knowledge of any Form implicates the knower in knowledge of the Form of the Good, which would be why, again, Plato insists that knowledge of other things is knowledge to no advantage unless it is accompanied by knowledge of the Form of the Good.

If we are willing to follow Plato this far, we will appreciate why he thinks that the just soul requires not only knowledge, because justice is psychic harmony and psychic harmony requires the full functioning of Reason, but also knowledge of the Form of the Good, because full knowledge of other Forms is not possible with knowing how they are good. It turns out, therefore, that a Platonically just person must have a fair bit of material knowledge to qualify as such. Since that knowledge includes knowledge of the Good, and every soul seeks the Good, it will follow that the Platonically just person, the person of maximal psychic harmony, will never do what is in fact bad. Hence, Plato has gone a long way toward meeting both of the main challenges set to him: to analyze justice and to show that its possession is good for the just person. It turns out that some common conceptions of justice were incorrect, but not therefore wholly misguided. Justice does have an other-regarding property; but it is not, in its essence, exhaustively other-regarding. Instead, Plato maintains, it pertains to a person's inner psychic condition, to a person's harmonized implementation of the knowledge of Goodness itself in the conduct of a human life.

3.9   Plato's line and cave: our epistemic prospects

We have seen that though knowledge of the form of the Good is central to Plato's program in the *Republic*, he feels constrained to approach the question of our acquaintance with it gingerly, by analogy. It is "the greatest thing to be learnt,"[93] but not something readily grasped without years of training and hard work. Indeed, he thinks that philosophers need some 50 years of training before they can approach it. They receive early education in music and gymnastics as children, followed by 10 years of advanced study, including the study of abstract mathematics, 5 years of dialectic, and a final 15 years learning statecraft by serving in the city's lower offices.[94] Only such highly prepared philosophers, suitably educated and habituated by such extensive groundwork, can grasp the nature of goodness. Even then, however, Plato rather oddly thinks that those on the verge of coming to know goodness must be compelled to do so:

Then, at the age of fifty, one must lead those who have survived, who have excelled in all matters and manners, in both their deeds and their studies, to their immediate goal; and one must compel them to throw open the soul's shining eye, to focus on that very thing which provides light to all, and once they have seen the Good itself, to use it as their paradigm when ordering the city, the citizens, and themselves.[95]

Compulsion seems out of place here. It is unclear why philosophers who have prepared themselves so diligently would not propel themselves eagerly towards the goal they have been striving so long to attain. Plato portrays the visage of the good as something formidably awesome.

However that may be, Plato describes the philosopher's grasp of the Form of the Good in quasi-perceptual terms. A philosopher on the verge of grasping the Good must "throw open the soul's shining eye" and "focus" upon the Form of the Good, and thereafter she must use it as a paradigm in conducting all her affairs, whether public or private. On their surface at least, these terms imply that the philosopher who comes to know the good does so by some form of acquaintance – that is, that the mind grasps this form in a direct and unmediated way. Perhaps Plato is implying that without such acquaintance knowledge of the Form of the Good is unattainable, just as one comes to know the taste of lemons only by tasting them and in no other way. Someone who has never tasted a lemon, but who knows *that lemons taste sour* because a reliable authority has reported that this is so, still seems to be somehow deficient knowledgewise with respect to lemons. Such a person could believe lots of true things about lemons (that they are sour, that they are acidic, that they are the star ingredients of lemonade); but they will still have something to gain epistemically by actually tasting a real lemon. What is wanted to address the lack in their second-hand knowledge is simple experience. So, by parity of reasoning, what is wanted with respect to goodness is an unmediated experience of the Form of the Good itself.

If Plato's perceptual analogy is understood in this way, then he seems to be implicated in a striking and controversial thesis in moral epistemology, namely that we are so mentally equipped that we can have a direct apprehension of goodness, that we have a faculty for knowing goodness as surely as we have a faculty for tasting lemons or seeing red.

Here it is crucial to distinguish sharply the metaphysics of Platonic *ante rem* realism from its attendant epistemology. So far, we have been considering arguments for the existence of Forms without giving much thought to the sorts of access we might have to them if they do indeed exist in the way in which Plato contends, namely as abstract, mind- and language-independent entities which are invariably and essentially what they are and nothing else. This is how he characterizes beauty, and presumably how he equally thinks of other forms: "Beauty itself, taken by itself, within itself, one in Form, and existing always."[96] So too, then, for Justice itself and Goodness itself. This is to say, then, that moral properties, like other properties, exist independently of our beliefs, desires, hopes, and aspirations. This is Plato's metaphysical realism about Forms.

The question then arises as to how we come into intellectual contact with such Forms. They are abstract, it seems, and avowedly non-perceptual. So, our contact with them, if any, is not through any normal form of sense perception. In this sense, when describing our access to Forms in quasi-perceptual terms, Plato is simultaneously giving guidance and postponing at least one ultimate question about our access to them. He is giving guidance by characterizing our interaction as perception-like, suggesting that we have direct experiences of them in a way analogous to the way we have direct experiences of objects in our visual field; yet he is postponing another question, since however perception-like our experiences of them may be, Forms are not objects of perception. In fact, Forms *cannot* be perceived. So how do we interact with them? If the state we are in when we grasp Forms is perception-like but not perception, then what state is it?

Plato addresses this question in his striking image of a divided line, which, like another image to follow, the cave, has rich implications for his moral epistemology. As his line indicates, Plato's moral epistemology turns out to be a special case of his epistemology for all of our interaction with Forms, including those not implicated in our moral conduct. He thinks that knowledge of Forms is a kind of direct, non-inferential, non-perceptual, and unmediated intellectual apprehension. Further, Plato maintains, we are endowed with a faculty for such apprehension: our minds. As our sensory faculties bring us into contact with perceptibles, so our minds bring us into contact with intelligibles.

Although both the line and cave have rich implications heading in a number of different directions, we will focus in the present context on their ramifications for Plato's epistemology of Forms, and so, more narrowly, for his moral epistemology.

Let us begin, then, with a visualization of the line, which he describes as unevenly divided (Figure 3.1). The line represents a hierarchy of cognition, ranging from the lowliest use of muddled images to the pellucid grasp of pristine Forms. The higher a philosopher ascends up the line, the less she relies on images in her cognition. The line itself is effectively, then, an account of epistemic ascent, beginning in unthinking reliance on jumbled, unstable appearances and rising up to a secure apprehension of unwavering realities, the Forms.

Importantly, then, Plato conceives of this epistemic ascent as keyed to a correlative ascent of objects. So, in each quadrant of the line, we are given both epistemic states and their corresponding metaphysical objects. The left hand represents the features of Plato's metaphysics already introduced, namely perceptible and intelligible objects; the right side represents his epistemology, characterizing the sorts of psychological states we manifest as we perceive or know these objects. Those who dwell at the bottom of the line lead beastly lives; the philosopher, who attains its apex, touches the divine.

Plato's Line
Republic 509d–513e

Metaphysical   Epistemological

Forms   Understanding
                         (noêsis)

Intelligible Realm   Realm of Knowledge

Mathematical   Reasoning
Objects   *(dianoia)*

Sensible   Opinion
Objects   *(pistis)*

Sensible Realm   Realm of Belief

Images   Imagination
                         (eikasia)

Figure 3.1

At the bottom of the metaphysical side are images such as paintings or reflections in a pool, the sorts of thing only a dog or someone deeply deluded might mistake for something real. (Thus, one of Aesop's fables tells the story of a dog carrying a bone in its mouth which, upon seeing its reflection in a pool, decides to snatch the bone from the "other" dog's mouth, only to see its own bone sinking into the pool as it makes the attempt.) Ascending up one level, though still in the realm of perception, are regular objects of belief, objects which do not permit of knowledge. As we know from Plato's existence argument from the *Phaedo*,[97] with respect to at least some range of predicates such objects suffer the compresence of opposites and are never purely what they are. So, these objects cannot be objects of knowledge.

Crossing over into the intelligible realm we encounter objects of mathematics, which can be known, but which still, Plato suggests, involve the use of images, though now very abstractly. Finally, when the philosopher grasps the Forms, her awareness is direct and immediate: no image is involved at all. When the philosopher knows the Form of Justice or the Form of the Good, there seems to be nothing between that philosopher and the Form known. Understanding a Form thus involves an immediate apprehension of the Form itself, taken by itself, in its very nature.

Plato's quasi-perceptual characterization of the grasp of Forms grows strained as we cross into understanding. What one sees with the shining eye of the soul is nothing visible, but rather only something intelligible. One "sees" the Form of the Good in the way that one sees the solution to a difficult mathematical problem, by an intuitive and immediate grasp, by an exercise of the mind rather than of the senses.

The connection between mathematical and philosophical reasoning in the line is crucial to our understanding of Plato's moral epistemology. To begin, mathematical reasoning prepares the philosopher-in-training to move readily through abstract forms of reasoning:

> It occurs to me, now that the study of calculation has been mentioned, how very refined and multiply useful it is in relation to what we wish to accomplish – provided that one pursues it for the sake of discovery and not for commerce! ...This [*viz.* the study of calculation] draws the soul sharply upward and makes it reason about the numbers themselves, never permitting anyone to reason with it by putting forward as instances visible or tangible bodies as numbered.
>
> (*Republic* vii 525c9–d8)

The study of mathematics turns the soul towards the abstract realm. More importantly, though, the primary division in the line suggests that except for the use of images in mathematics, philosophical reasoning has features directly akin to mathematical reasoning. The implication is that knowing *that justice is internal harmony* is rather like knowing that *2 + 2 = 4*: when one grasps the plus function for the first time, it becomes obvious that this proposition is not only true but indeed necessary. One is not at liberty, having acquired this understanding, to suppose that two plus two might as easily have equaled five or, say, the color yellow. To one acquainted with the plus function such suggestions appear impossible and absurd.

In the same way, Plato implies, when we grasp Justice itself or Beauty itself, no further justification about the nature of either is necessary, or perhaps even possible.[98] The nature of each is manifest to the person who has adequately grasped them. This knowledge too carries with it some compulsion, again akin to the compulsion experienced in mathematical reasoning:

> In the intelligible realm, the Form of the Good is the final thing to be grasped, and it is seen only with difficulty; but once it is seen, it *must* be concluded that it is in all ways the cause of all that is right and beautiful.
>
> (*Republic* vii 517b8–c2)

Perhaps the necessity here will not seem as strong as the necessity involved in mathematics. Plato's contention is the opposite, however: when grasped, the Form of the Good impresses itself upon the subject of awareness and requires that subject to come to various conclusions first about the Good itself and then also about its relation to other things.[99] Plato speaks of knowledge of the Forms in much the way the great twentieth-century mathematician Kurt Gödel speaks of mathematical knowledge: "Despite their remoteness from sense experience, we do have also something like a perception of the objects of set theory, as is seen from the fact that the axioms force themselves on us as being true."[100] So Plato's line suggests something similar with respect to Forms: despite their remoteness from sense experience, we have something like perception of the Forms. When we encounter them, they force us to accept their natures as what they are; and they compel us to draw certain secure conclusions based upon our acquaintance with them.

The compulsion with regard to the philosopher's grasp of Forms does not end there. The *Republic* contains a final analogy, in addition to the sun and the line, which Plato suggests must be fitted together with the first two.[101] This is the cave, one of the most stunning and enduring of all of Plato's images.

Plato's cave is nothing less than the human condition. In the cave, prisoners are bound and constrained to look only at the cave's bottom back wall. What they see, what they take to be real, are shadows flickering on that wall. These are the shadows cast by puppets being manipulated between them and a fire behind the puppets, none of which they can see. They understandably think that the shadows they experience exhaust all there is to the world: they have no conception of the puppets behind them and still less of the world beyond the puppets, the world outside of the cave illuminated by the sun. In fact, if they are freed and turn around, they become perplexed and angry. Most prisoners prefer their comfortable, familiar ignorance to the difficult and destabilizing epistemic demands posed by the reality standing behind the manifest image of the world. Only a select few can bear to realize that the shadows are just that: shadows. To recognize this is to acknowledge that the world they inhabit is inauthentic, transitory, illusory.

Those with naturally strong minds may, however, begin a difficult journey out of the cave towards intellectual and personal liberation. These intrepid few proceed with difficulty, at first overwhelmed by the sun, because dazzled by its overpowering brightness. As they emerge from the cave, they cannot bear to gaze upon real objects directly, but in time, with effort, they learn to live in the light of the sun and then eventually even to look upon the sun itself.

Plato rather distressingly says of the prisoners that "they are like us."[102] This seems a bleak and depressing view of the human condition. Most of us, Plato insinuates, live unaware that our lives are illusory, even to the point of lashing out violently when someone dares to upset our blinkered insistence that the manifest image of the world *is* the world. If Plato's benighted cave-dwellers are "like us," then few of us have any sense of truth beyond appearance: for the prisoners, "would absolutely think the truth to be nothing other than the shadows of the puppets."[103] If someone dares to point out the prisoners' ignorance to them, they grow agitated and menacing. Indeed, if someone having seen the light of day returns to the cave with tales of the reality beyond, says Plato, the prisoners will immediately ridicule and demean him because his sight has been diminished when first forsaking light for darkness. If such a person persists in trying to liberate them by freeing them from their epistemic bonds, trying in vain to drag them up into the light of day, the prisoners will eventually rise up against him and would do what Athens did to Socrates: they will kill him.[104]

Even so, the philosopher who came to know the Form of the Good would be compelled by that very knowledge to return to the cave. This philosopher might well prefer to remain in the light of day, contemplating the Forms and engaging in philosophy. Still, insists Plato, the philosopher must be compelled to return to the cave in order to undertake the needful work of realizing justice in the world. He insists that this would be no injustice to the philosopher, since the role of the philosopher all along had been to foster justice in the state, just as it has been the role of reason within the soul to guide and direct the other parts of the soul to the heightened harmony which constitutes justice in the individual.[105]

In a different way, then, Plato's cave is a marvelously hopeful image of epistemic optimism. While we begin our lives deluded, thinking that the manifest image of the world *is* the world, we can with unrelenting effort come to know the world as it is in itself, including the moral world as it is in itself, and not merely as it appears to those who have not reflected upon the question of whether what appears to be the case is indeed the case. The moral world lies before the gaze of the well-trained mind, which, as all of Plato's images imply in complementary ways, acquires this ability only through sustained acculturation and education. Goodness grasped in turn commends its own inculcation for the benefit of those not privileged to apprehend it directly.

3.10   Problems about Forms

As should be plain, Plato's account of Forms places strong epistemic and metaphysical demands on his readers. His theory is fully *ante rem*: Forms exist of necessity and prior to their being known or instantiated. Still, they can be known, he argues, by an intuitive grasp, in much the manner the objects of mathematics can be known in perception-like intellectual awareness. We should therefore not be surprised when we find him relying on the *a priori* knowledge he claims to have attained when discussing such Forms as Equality or Justice or even Goodness itself. Even as he proceeds with due humility, as he does most markedly with respect to the Form of the Good, Plato is not shy about putting his knowledge to work in the *Republic* and beyond.[106] He no doubt expects to encounter some detractors; and it is fair to assume that he would welcome intelligent challenges of all sorts, though he takes himself to have set aside sophomoric relativism as a legitimate source of criticism.[107] One form of reasonably motivated criticism will be epistemological in character. How, one may want to know, is knowledge of the Forms possible? Plato surely thinks that it is possible, that it will be *a priori* in character, and that someone with the right form of education can reasonably expect to progress towards such knowledge. Indeed, as we have seen, he goes so far as to prescribe the path of education which will lead to knowledge of the Forms.[108] His success in plotting out this educational course will depend in part, of course, first, upon the defensibility of *a priori* knowledge as such, and second, upon the appropriateness of Plato's attempt to deploy it in the philosophical arena in just the way he does.

A second form of criticism is more metaphysical in character. This form takes on a special significance, since Plato himself was greatly concerned with its consequences for the tenability of the theory of Forms. It is, indeed, a great testament to Plato's deep philosophical integrity that he saw fit to advance searing criticism of his own theory, presumably in an effort, first, to determine whether it ought in the end to be accepted and, second, if so, to recommend a formulation immune to the sorts of criticisms he considers. If these criticisms prove compelling, then the entire edifice of the *Republic*, including centrally its analysis of Justice, will have to be set aside as misguided.

In the opening portions of his dialogue *Parmenides*, the eminent Presocratic philosopher Parmenides, accompanied by his protégé Zeno, the originator of Zeno's paradoxes,[109] quizzes Socrates, here portrayed as a budding teenager teeming with profound if ill-formed ideas about the nature of reality. In this dramatic context, Parmenides grills Socrates about the nature of Forms and their relation to the particulars which are held to participate in them. Parmenides poses a question for Socrates in characteristically Platonic language: "Is there a Form, itself by itself,[110] of the Just, the Beautiful and the Good?" There are, Socrates replies, and other things are named after them, so that large things are called large because they have a share of Largeness, and just things are called just because they have a share of Justice.[111] In fact, whenever there are a number of F things, there is some one Form, F-ness, over them. Armed with this much, Parmenides sets out six distinct arguments, all intended to play up difficulties with Plato's theory. Some purport to show that there are insurmountable epistemological obstacles to knowing the Forms, so that even if we were to grant one of Plato's existence arguments, Forms would be useless because unknowable.[112] Others attack the theory of Forms directly, by showing that the theory has absurd consequences and so must be abandoned.

The most notorious of these arguments, both in antiquity and in the contemporary scholarship on Plato's metaphysics, is the so-called Third-Man Argument (TMA), which purports to use Plato's own characterizations of Forms to generate an infinite number of Forms corresponding to every group of F-things. So, if sound, the (TMA) will generate an infinite number of Forms of Beauty, an infinite number of Forms of Largeness, and so on for each case where Plato recognizes a Form. Beyond being intuitively absurd and extravagant, any such result would vitiate the explanatory role of Forms envisaged by Plato. If we wanted to explain the beauty in beautiful things by appealing to the Form of Beauty, but then in turn had to appeal to some prior beauty, Beauty$_1$, to explain the Form of Beauty itself, and so on *ad infinitem*, we would never get around to discharging the explanatory role of the Form for which it was initially introduced. When Plato speaks of the Form of F-ness as "itself by itself," or "itself in its own terms," he means, at least in part, that F-ness is self-explanatory, and not in need of anything beyond itself to explain its F-ness. It is essentially F itself.

This last thought, though, carries an important presupposition about Forms which we have encountered from the beginning, but which seems now to create some difficulty for Plato. In his existence argument for Forms in the *Phaedo*,[113] Plato relied crucially on an appeal to Leibniz's Law, because he wanted to show that Forms could not be reduced to collections of sense particulars. F-ness itself could never suffer the compresence of opposites; so, it could not be identified with the particulars which do. Now, as we have seen, there are at least two ways in which Forms could fail to suffer the compresence of opposites, by being F but not not-F, or by being neither F nor not-F.[114] The first alternative suggests that Forms themselves are F, so that Beauty itself is beautiful. Plato himself evidently embraces this first alternative, since he speaks as if Forms were *self-predicative* in a host of passages.[115] It also seems implicit in, although not strictly entailed by, his treatment of Forms as *perfect paradigms*, as exemplars which are copied by likenesses which resemble them.

The problem with self-predication is two-fold. First, taken in its own terms and as a literal doctrine, it creates intolerable results for Plato. What is more, it forms part of the premise set of the (TMA) of the *Parmenides*; hence, even if the first set of problems could be addressed, that argument would be looming.

The first problem first. If we understand Forms to be universal properties, then the doctrine of self-predication (SP) holds that every Form F-ness *has* the property that it *is*. For every case of F-ness, F-ness is F. Assuming a broad range of Forms for purposes of illustration, we can see that this result is exactly right for some Forms, not especially problematic for some others, and utterly disastrous for still others. In some cases, (SP) is not only true, but necessarily true. The Form of Abstractness is abstract, and necessarily so. The Form of Beauty might well be beautiful, though this is open to question. At any rate, there is no immediate problem for this case, as there is when we turn to the Forms of Being Concrete, or Being a Magnitude, or Being Human. If Forms are abstract entities, then no Form could be concrete or have magnitude. Necessarily, such Forms, if there are such Forms, would be abstract and so not concrete magnitudes at all. Similarly, the Form of Being Human could not itself be human: humans exist in space and time, walking around here and there, perceiving and causing things to happen. No abstract entity could do any of these things. It is as if we expected the number 7 to weld one piece of steel to another. So, (SP), if applied to a full range of Forms, seems to yield gibberish.

These criticisms of (SP) thus construed assume some things we might want to regard as only inauthentically Platonic. Still, they are useful because they put pressure on Plato to explain what is meant by saying that F-ness is F, where this surely sounds as if he is expressing the view that a given form F-ness has the property it is. Some possible Platonic responses involve accepting literal self-exemplification, where Forms are universals which have the properties they are, but delimiting the range of Forms in some principled way that precludes (SP) from being applied where it is not wanted. Another is to deny self-*predication*, by supposing that Plato is not claiming, e.g., that Justice has the quality of being just, but rather means only to be asserting that Justice is essentially what Justice is. Strategies of this sort are periphrastic, in that they require taking Plato's plain language and re-interpreting it in some way or another. Their being periphrastic, of course, does not render them unacceptable. (When I say that the average German family has 1.4 children, I say something true but in need of paraphrase.) Still, it places a burden on the promoter of paraphrase to justify one particular paraphrase over another, as well as against other non-periphrastic strategies. One such non-periphrastic strategy would be to query not the notion of predication, but rather the assumption that Forms are *self*-predicative, by denying that Forms are the kinds of things that can be predicated. Perhaps a Form is a perfect particular, and so not something which can be predicated at all. In that case, when Plato says, e.g., that Justice is just, he means that Justice, the perfect paradigm of justice, has the quality of being just. How promising this strategy will be turns in part on the ontology of Forms as perfect paradigms, a conception which invites some difficulties of its own.

All of these responses envision ways of deflecting criticism of (SP), taken as a literal doctrine. However one is to proceed, it seems clear enough that Plato relies upon a fairly pedestrian notion in mounting the Third-Man Argument (TMA) against the theory of Forms in the *Parmenides*. To be explicit, it accepts the following assumptions, all stated by Plato or at least suggested by some of his characterizations of Forms.

(SP): The Form F-ness is itself F.

(OM): For any set of F things, there is a form F over that set of F things.

(NI): The form over any set is not a member of that set.

(U): There is just one unique form, F-ness, corresponding to F things.

With these assumptions in place, the (TMA) proceeds as follows, expanded somewhat from the text for expository convenience:

1   There are some large sensible particulars $\{L_1, L_2, L_3 \dots\}$.
2   (OM).

3   Hence, there is a Form, L-ness, over that set of L things.
4   (SP).
5   Hence, L-ness is itself large.
6   (NI).
7   Hence, L-ness is not a member of $\{L_1, L_2, L_3 \ldots\}$.
8   But now there is a set $\{L_1, L_2, L_3, L\text{-ness} \ldots\}$.
9   Hence, there is also a Form, L-ness$_1$, over that set of L things (by a new application of (OM)).
10 Hence, not (U): it is not the case that there is just one Form corresponding to F things.
11 Indeed, by repeated applications of (OM) and (NI), an infinite number of Forms will be generated corresponding to each set of L things.
12 So, there are an infinite number of Forms corresponding to each set of L things.

As Parmenides concludes, each Form "will no longer be one, but unlimited in multitude."[116]

Bearing in mind that it is not Parmenides who wrote the *Parmenides*, but that it is rather Plato himself who advances the anti-Platonic conclusion of the (TMA), scholars have adopted an astonishingly broad range of responses. On the one end are those who regard the (TMA) as utterly devastating to the theory of Forms, so that with it Plato announces his abandonment of that theory, or at least any version of it which commits him to all of the premises of the (TMA). Some others regard the argument as forceful, but deny that Plato ever accepted the assumptions which lead to it, at least not in the versions employed in the argument. Still others have regarded the argument as a total failure (in this or another version), preferring to believe that it is merely Plato's way of instructing us how not to think about his theory of Forms.

How we regard these responses will depend on a series of intersecting exegetical and philosophical matters, some of them rather delicate. Prominent among them are our assessment of the argument's soundness, our view about whether or not its premises are genuinely Platonic, and our conception of the assumptions which lead to its formulation. Of course, our attitude towards these matters is extremely important for our eventual assessment of Plato's theory of Forms. Here, though, we are mainly concerned with the narrower topic of the success or failure of the argument as formulated.

The argument does generate a problem for Plato, if he accepts all of its presuppositions, since it forces him to abandon (U), the doctrine that there is one unique Form corresponding to each set of unique things. That takes us through (TMA-10). That problem is not, however, the problem articulated by Parmenides, who asserts not just a plurality of Forms but a countless number of them. For that conclusion we need repeated applications of (OM) and (NI) in a way which may become problematic. For one may be able to apply them in such a way that no *new* Form F-ness needs to be generated, since it may be possible to use a Form already generated to stand over a newly generated set without violating (NI) simply by removing an already generated Form and setting it over the new set of F things. Still, (NI) could be reformulated in a way which blocks this maneuver, so that we really do end up with Parmenides' extreme conclusion. That conclusion would seem to yield a genuinely unacceptable consequence for Plato's theory of Forms and so would constitute a formidable refutation. Any such refutation would seriously undermine the edifice of Plato's metaphysics, and with it, his metaphysics of morality.

3.11 Conclusions

All of this commends a closer look at Plato's ontology of Forms; at the question of whether he has *a* theory of Forms or several, each a refinement and an improvement over its predecessor; at competing ways of rendering his sometimes metaphorical language about Forms literal and precise; and at the competing conceptions of Forms embodied in Plato's treating them in different contexts as perfect paradigms, which particulars copy only imperfectly, and as abstract entities, evidently universals, in which particulars participate. It would be premature at this stage to regard as decisive the sorts of criticisms considered by Plato himself in the *Parmenides*. Nor, by the same token, is it appropriate at this juncture to endorse any one of Plato's existence arguments as conclusive. It is hoped here instead only that this introduction to Plato has provided some incentive to pursue these matters in significantly greater philosophical depth and detail. Plato's philosophy pays rich dividends to those who approach it with the serious intellectual effort it demands.

Notes

1 A.N. Whitehead, *Process and Reality* (New York: Macmillan, 1929), p. 39.
2 On the distinction between *a priori* and *a posteriori* knowledge, see note 4 to Chapter 1.
3 See *Metaphysics* 978b1–2.
4 Aristotle was a student and an intimate associate of Plato's, as well as the first systematic historian of philosophy. He was a member of Plato's school for approximately twenty years. It is therefore hard to disregard his characterization of the differences between Plato and Socrates.
5 In dating the Platonic dialogues, scholars have relied upon the following criteria: (1) the ancient testimony (including external reports, e.g. Aristotle's remarks at *Metaphysics* i 6, xiii 4 and 9; and *Politics* 1264b24–30, as well as internal cross-references among Plato's own works; (2) stylometric analysis (focusing on features of Plato's diction and syntax); (3) broadly literary features (depth of characterization, concern for dramatic setting and detail); (4) philosophical and doctrinal matters (e.g. whether they are aporetic or dogmatic, whether they are restricted to moral matters, whether they adhere to the (a) theory of Forms).

Using these criteria, we can hypothesize the following coarse dating of the principal works most commonly read by students:

1 Socratic: *Euthyphro, Apology, Crito, Alcibiades, Charmides, Laches, Lysis, Euthydemus, Hippias Major* and *Hippias Minor, Ion, *Protagoras*, and **Gorgias* (* = probably transitional, in the sense that they incorporate some features of early Platonic dialogues).

2 Platonic: A. Earlier: *Meno, Phaedo, Cratylus, Symposium, Republic, Phaedrus*, and *Parmenides*; B. Later: *Theaetetus, Timaeus, Philebus, Critias, Sophist, Statesman*, and *Laws*.

6 The principal distinguishing features of the Socratic dialogues are these: they are short, dramatically lively, elenchtic, concerned almost exclusively with moral matters, and ultimately aporetic.

7 *Apology* 40c–e.

8 See 2.2 for a discussion of the elenchus which opens the *Meno*.

9 *Meno* 79e, 81d.

10 On Xenophanes, see 1.2.

11 Meno's paradox of inquiry and Plato's initial response: *Meno* 80d–81a.

12 So, for example, if ABCD has sides of two feet, it will have an area of four square feet. Then the square with sides twice as long, four feet, will have an area of sixteen square feet and the square with sides half again as long, three feet, will have an area of nine square feet. In fact, the square with an area of eight feet, the one twice the area of ABCD, will be the one based upon the diagonal of ABCD, the line which stretches from corner to corner on the original square.

13 The slave passage: *Meno* 82a–86c. The slave speaks Greek (82b), but was not taught geometry (85e).

14 It does not matter whether we call the process discovery, since what matters is whether it is teachable: *Meno* 87b–c. Significantly, Plato later identifies recollection with the process of providing a rational justification (*Meno* 98a).

15 Moving from true belief to knowledge: *Meno* 85c–d.

16 Knowledge equals true opinion plus a rational account: *Meno* 98a.

17 Recall that *a priori* knowledge is knowledge whose *justification* does not reside in any ultimate appeal to sense perception. It is not a thesis about the genesis of knowledge. On the distinction between *a priori* and *a posteriori* knowledge, see Chapter 1 note 4.

18 On Protagorean relativism, see 1.6.

19 On Protagorean relativism, see 1.6.

20 *Theaetetus* 151e2–3. Here and throughout the locution "$=_{df}$" is to be understood as specifying the essential or defining features of the thing defined. So, the schema means: "an essence specifying definition of something's being an instance of knowledge is that it be an instance of perception." The point of this sort of locution is just that it makes plain that Plato is after accounts which do more than merely capture the extension of the qualities investigated; he wants to know what they are essentially, in their own natures.

21 *Theaetetus* 187b5–6, 187c5.

22 *Theaetetus* 201c9–d1.

23 The identification of the first definition with Protagoreanism occurs at *Theaetetus* 152a.

24 On Heracleitus, see 1.3. The affiliation of Protagoreanism and Heracleiteanism occurs at *Theaetetus* 152e1; cf. 179d–e.

25 On positive and negative formulations of Protagorean relativism, see 1.6.

26 *Theaetetus* 169d–171d and 177c–179b.

27 An *intrinsic* property is a property had by some subject without reference to anything outside of itself. Intrinsic properties may be contrasted with relational properties, properties subjects have only with reference to other subjects. If Harold is taller than Maude, than he stands in the relation of *being taller than* with respect to her. So, *being taller than* is a relational property. By contrast, if Maude is content, then she has the property of *being content*. This is a property she has without reference to any other subject. So, *being content* is an intrinsic property. A property is *essential* only if the subject which has it could not lose it and continue to exist. So, *being content* is not an essential property of Maude's; she might one day grow dissatisfied with her life. Plausibly, *being human* is an essential property of Maude's, since she could not lose that property while continuing to exist. If there

are Forms, then they are unlike Maude or other material particulars in that they have all of their intrinsic properties essentially. Evidently, every material particular has at least some intrinsic properties non-essentially.

28 *Phaedo* 100a; *Euthydemus* 281e3–4.

29 Aristotle claims that both Plato and Socrates accepted the existence of Forms, but that Plato took things further than Socrates by *separating* them: *Metaphysics* 1040b26–30, 1078b31, 1086a32–b13. On separation, see 3.5. I note the difference between Socratic and Platonic approaches by capitalizing Platonic Forms, but not Socratic forms.

30 For example, in *Republic* v, Plato notes that there are many such people and sets out to persuade them. See especially 475d–480a, esp. 479a.

31 In addition to the passages regarding Forms discussed in the text, some important passages include: *Phaedrus* 247c; *Republic* 477a–480e; *Symposium* 210e–211e; *Timaeus* 27d–28a, 38a, 52a–b; *Philebus* 59c.

32 *Metaphysics*, 987a29–b13. Aristotle's argument may draw in part on Plato's *Timaeus* 51b–52b.

33 On Heracleitus, see 1.3.

34 *Metaphysics* 101a10–15.

35 On Heracleitus' notion of synchronic versus diachronic flux, see 1.3.

36 Each of the next two existence arguments in this section appeals to the compresence of opposites as a premise.

37 *Republic* 523d.

38 This is a result which Plato expressly embraces in some passages (e.g. *Republic* 523a–e), but implicitly rejects in some others (e.g. *Republic* 597d). This is not by itself a contradiction, if we assume that (HAF) establishes Forms for some range of properties, but that other arguments do so for others. There would, however, be an incompatibility if Plato maintained that the range of Forms were restricted to those generated by (HAF). Relevant passages in this regard include *Republic* 523a–b and *Parmenides* 130b–d.

39 See *Phaedo* 76d–77b.

40 *Phaedo* 76d–e, Plato mentions the Good and the Beautiful, and "all that sort of reality."

41 *Phaedo* 74b–d.

42 In fact, Plato speaks rather perplexingly here of "the equals themselves" (*ta isa auta*) and not simply of Equality itself. I have adapted the argument slightly for simplicity's sake; nothing in terms of its philosophical purport is lost in this adaptation.

43 In its simplest formulation, Leibniz's Law holds that for any two things x and y, $x = y$ if, and only if, x and y share all of the same properties.

44 Passages suggesting self-predication: *Phaedo* 74e–75a; *Protagoras* 330c–d; *Symposium* 211a–b.

45 *Metaphysics* 1038b35–1039a3; *Topics* 178b36–179a10.

46 See below 3.10 for self-predication and difficulty about Forms.

47 A typical example: *Republic* 476e.

48 *Euthyphro* 7d; *Phaedo* 100b.

49 Plato often treats Forms as perfect paradigms: *Parmenides* 132d; *Euthyphro* 6e; *Timaeus* 28a–b; *Republic* 452d–e, 500c, 596b; *Symposium* 211d; *Sophist* 240a.

50 *Republic* 477a–b, 478d.

51 *Republic* 479a.

52 *Republic* 473c–474c.

53 *Republic* 476b.

54 *Republic* 475d–476d.

55 *Republic* 476e–478e.

56 *Republic* 479a–480a.

57 See note 49 above.

58 On self-predication and the problems it makes for Plato, see 3.10 below.

59   See *Phaedo* 100c–e; cf. *Parmenides* 130e–131e; Aristotle faults Plato on just this score, *Metaphysics* 991a20–23.

60   For a discussion of some tensions in Plato's theory of Forms, see 3.10 below.

61   *Metaphysics* 1086a35–b14.

62   *Metaphysics* 991b1.

63   Realists about universals can be: (1) *ante rem*, by holding that universals exist *prior* to their instances and can exist without being instantiated; or (2) *in rebus*, by insisting that though universals exist they do so only when instantiated. Although equally realist, these positions differ on the question of the *ontological dependence* conditions of universals.

64   He comes close, however, at *Timaeus* 52d, where he insists that being, where this seems to indicate the Forms, existed *before* the sensible universe was generated. See also *Parmenides* 130b, a difficult context; and *Republic* 484c–d and 501b–c, where Plato evidently presupposes that Forms exist uninstantiated, and so separately.

65   *Metaphysics* 1079b35–1080b1.

66   On Aristotle's *in rebus* realism, see 4.2.

67   *Republic* 357b–359c.

68   Although Plato does not say so, it is customary to call Gyges' ancestor Gyges as well, on the assumption, which seems to have been corroborated in antiquity, that they have the same name. At any rate, I will follow that custom in what follows.

69   *Republic* 359c–360d.

70   *Republic* 368c–369a; cf. 434d–435e.

71   *Republic* 370a.

72   *Republic* 455d–e; cf. 456a, 563b.

73   *Republic* 434b–c.

74   On Socrates' denial of *akrasia*, see 2.3.

75   Indeed, it seems to many that *Republic* 338a alludes unfavorably to Socrates' denial of *akrasia*.

76   Leontius: *Republic* 339e–440b. On the basis of an inconclusive fragment of ancient comedy, Leontius' desire is often thought to be sexual or quasi-sexual in nature. Plato's presentation does not obviously presuppose this; nor is this supposition necessary to understand the force of Plato's example. At the same time, such a supposition, if legitimate, would provide another dimension to Plato's point.

77   *Republic* 441a–b.

78   *Republic* 441c.

79   Plato is explicit about this part of his strategy: *Republic* 441c–4, 442d.

80   *Republic* 343a–c. In denying something which most people accept as obvious, that justice, whatever else it is, is a virtue, Thrasymachus implicitly points out a shortcoming of the Socratic elenchus. He shows that it is possible not to give up the proposition Socrates might have wished for him to give up in order to avoid internal inconsistency. On the Socratic elenchus, see 2.1.

81   As seems to be the case with a third demand set by Glaucon and Adeimnatus, that Plato show that justice is a type-2 good by showing that the just person is always and in every circumstance happier than the unjust person. See *Republic* 361b–362d. This is an unreasonable demand since one can show that F (say being healthy, which is Glaucon's own example) is a type-2 good without showing that the F person is always and in every instance happier than the not-F person.

82   *Republic* 443c–d.

83   *Republic* 504d.

84   *Republic* 505a.

85   *Republic* 506a.

86   *Republic* 505c–e.

87   *Republic* 505e.

88   *Republic* 506d–3.

89   *Republic* 507b.

90 Though cf. *Republic* 597c–d, where Plato may allow that Forms can be created. This contrasts sharply with his normal practice.

91 *Republic* 509b.

92 On the demands for successful analysis in the *Euthyphro*, see 2.2. Plato's remarks about the Form of the Good suggest that he continues to accept the constraints on successful analysis articulated in the *Euthyphro*.

93 *Republic* vi 504e4–5, 505a2.

94 *Republic* vii 540a2–c2.

95 *Republic* vii 540a4–b1.

96 *Symposium* 211b1.

97 See 3.5 for a discussion of this argument.

98 It is important to stress in this connection that Plato does *not* contend that an experience of the Forms yields infallible knowledge. Here his quasi-perceptual metaphor is apposite. If someone tastes a lemon in normal circumstances, that person will have exceedingly good grounds for knowing what a lemon tastes like; it does not follow, however, that that person has become infallible with respect to lemons or even their taste.

99 For a sure-footed and accessible defense of a form of ethical intuitionism akin to Plato's approach, see Huemer, M., *Ethical Intuitionism* (Palgrave Macmillan, 2006). Huemer characterizes the notion of an ethical intuition: "An initial, *intellectual* appearance is an 'intuition.' That is, an intuition that *p* is a state of its seeming to one that *p* that is not dependent on inference from other beliefs and that results from thinking about *p*, as opposed to perceiving, remembering, or introspecting" (2006, p. 112). Using this notion, he develops the perceptual analogy by recommending that an ethical intuitionist "should be a direct realist about ethics. He should not say that intuition functions as a kind of *evidence* from which we ... infer moral conclusions. He should say that for some moral truths, we need no evidence, since we are directly aware of them, and that awareness takes the form of intuitions; that is, intuitions just partly *constitute* our awareness of moral facts. Intuitions are not the objects of our awareness when we do moral philosophy; they are just the vehicles of our awareness, which we 'see through' to the moral reality" (2006, pp. 121–2).

100 Gödel (1964, p. 271).

101 *Republic* 517a.

102 *Republic* 515a.

103 *Republic* 515c.

104 On Socrates' trial and execution, see 2.5.

105 On psychic justice, see 3.7.

106 On Plato's existence arguments for Forms, see 3.5.

107 On Plato's refutation of relativism, see 3.4.

108 See *Republic* 492a, 540a–b.

109 On Zeno's paradoxes and their relation to Parmenides' attack on *a posteriori* knowledge, see 1.4.

110 On this language, see 3.3 above.

111 *Parmenides* 130a–131a.

112 *Parmenides* 133b–d, 135a–b.

113 For this existence argument, see 3.5 above.

114 On the role of the compresence of opposites in Plato's existence arguments, see 3.5 above, especially (NCO), where the relevance of Leibniz's Law to compresence is most clear.

115 Self-predication: *Protagoras* 330c, 330d; *Phaedo* 102d–e; *Hippias Major* 292e; *Symposium* 210e–211a; *Euthydemus* 301b; *Parmenides* 132a–133a; and *Sophist* 258b–c.

116 *Parmenides* 132b.

117 Numbers in brackets refer to the comprehensive Suggestions for Further Reading compiled at the end of this book.

Suggestions for additional readings

Primary text

There are many translations of Plato's dialogues, of varying quality. Some stress fidelity over naturalness of English while others subordinate accuracy to style. The best and most comprehensive set of translations is [22].[117] These translations for the most part strike an appropriate balance between fidelity and readability. Many of the dialogues published in that collection are also available individually from Hackett Publishers. For the works discussed in the text, these include, in addition to [23]:

Republic, trans. G. Grube and C. Reeve (Cambridge, MA: Hackett, 1992).
Phaedo, trans. G. Grube (Cambridge, MA: Hackett, 1980).
Meno, trans. G. Grube (Cambridge, MA: Hackett, 1980).
Parmenides, trans. M. Gill and P. Ryan (Cambridge, MA: Hackett, 1996).
Protagoras, trans. S. Lombardo and K. Bell (Cambridge, MA: Hackett, 1992).

Especially recommended for students who seek close and illuminating discussion of the dialogues are the volumes in the Clarendon Plato Series from Oxford University Press. As relating to the works discussed in the text, these include the following, each an accurate translation with commentary:

Phaedo, trans. D. Gallop with introduction and notes (Oxford: Oxford University Press, 1975).
Protagoras, trans. C. Taylor with introduction and notes (Oxford: Oxford University Press, 1991).
Gorgias, trans. T. Irwin with introduction and notes (Oxford: Oxford University Press, 1979).
Theaetetus, trans. J. McDowell with introduction and notes (Oxford: Oxford University Press, 1973).

Secondary literature

As is the case with Socrates, the secondary literature on Plato is vast. For general background, see [4] and [5]. An extremely useful set of introductory discussions can be found in [38], which also contains a helpful bibliography for further study, arranged by dialogue. Two very useful collections of high quality scholarly articles are:

Fine, G. (ed.) *Plato I: Metaphysics and Epistemology* (Oxford: Oxford University Press, 2000).
—— (ed.) *Plato II: Ethics, Politics, Religion, and the Soul* (Oxford: Oxford University Press, 2000).

Works [55] and [56] also offer well-organized bibliographies for further study.

4 Aristotle

"Every human being, by nature, desires to know." So Aristotle begins one of his greatest works, the *Metaphysics*, with a remark both arresting and theoretically motivated. In so speaking, Aristotle intends, first, to affirm that human beings have some sort of determinate nature and, second, to characterize that nature as essentially knowledge-seeking. Aristotle's remark is hardly an innocent observation. Instead, it follows from a carefully constructed technical framework featuring a theory of essential predication enmeshed in an articulated taxonomical system.

Despite its technical pedigree, Aristotle's conception of human nature seems also to have a personal implication. If he thinks that all humans by nature desire to know, then he trivially also thinks that he himself by nature desires to know. About that he is surely correct: Aristotle manifests in a pronounced and uncommon way the nature he ascribes to everyone. Indeed, so great is his thirst for human knowledge that it is tempting to assume that he bases his conception of human nature in large measure on his own self-conception. For Aristotle was a man almost maniacally engaged in the pursuit of human wisdom in all its forms.

His passion for learning led him into a variety of different fields, well beyond philosophy as we conceive it today. Evidence for his breadth of inquiry is reflected in a catalogue of Aristotle's writings compiled by an ancient bibliographer, Diogenes Laertius. Diogenes introduces his list, which runs to over 150 items, with the remark that Aristotle "wrote a large number of books which I have thought it appropriate to list because of the man's excellence in every field." The list which follows contains titles in a bewildering number of areas. A small sample of these titles suggests the multi-faceted character of his inquiries: *On Justice, On the Poets, On the Soul, On the Sciences, On Species and Genus, The Art of Rhetoric, Lectures on Political Theory, On Animals, On Plants, Dissections, On the River Nile*, and even one *On Drunkenness*. There are in addition treatises in logic, language, the arts, ethics, psychology and physiology, and, of course, metaphysics and the theory of knowledge. Unfortunately, we do not possess much on this list, probably less than one-fifth, though the surviving corpus contains a fair number of works not mentioned in the ancient bibliographies. Mainly lost are those works of Aristotle which indicate that he was capable of uncommon grace and elegance, an accomplishment praised by Cicero, someone certainly capable of judging expertly on matters of prose style, when he noted that if Plato's prose was silver, Aristotle's was gold.[1]

Anyone who approaches Aristotle for the first time will see immediately that Cicero could not have been talking about the works we read in the canonical Aristotelian corpus. What we have available to read today is hardly golden: it is instead more often than not crabbed, terse, and initially difficult to comprehend. Certainly it could not be compared favorably to prose of Plato's dialogues in terms of sweetness or suppleness of expression. It seems to follow that the extant works are not those which Cicero had before him, nor even those Aristotle prepared for public consumption. Most likely, the writings in the surviving Aristotelian corpus were composed as lecture notes, or as lecture records, for use mainly by those already familiar with the rudiments of Aristotle's methods and procedures.

This presents an impediment to novice readers of Aristotle, one most readily overcome first by appreciating the ways Aristotle's works engage the thought of Plato and his other predecessors and second by learning the basics of his pervasive technical terminology, beginning with the terminology used in articulating his preferred explanatory framework, the doctrine of the *four causes*. The first three sections of this chapter effect this sort of introduction to Aristotle. The remainder explores ways in which he employs his doctrine of the four causes in a variety of related subject areas, some forward- and some backward-looking. This is because, given the precepts of his philosophical methodology, Aristotle was inclined to consider the works of his predecessors before setting out on his own positive theoretical constructs.

4.1   From Plato to Aristotle

"For those who wish to solve problems," Aristotle suggests, "it is helpful to state the problems well."[2] He is right about that: in philosophy, stating the problems well is often half the battle. Fortunately, Aristotle regularly follows his own advice by setting out puzzles and conundrums at the beginnings of his investigations, in an effort to bring the utmost clarity to issues he wishes to engage. For the student of Aristotle, this means that in order to understand his views, it is essential first to appreciate how he conceives the problems of concern to him. This in turn requires coming to terms with a further feature of Aristotle's methodology, one concerning his attitudes towards his predecessors. For Aristotle, the injunction to state one's problems well carries with it an obligation to canvass the treatments of the issue already extant: he thinks, in fact, that to make progress on the problems of philosophy, it is in the first instance necessary to attend to the expression given them by the philosophical tradition. In Aristotle's terms, it is first of all necessary to set out the *phenomena*, the way things appear to the untutored eye, and to consider the *endoxa*, the reputable or entrenched opinions, which are those "accepted by everyone, or by the majority, or by the wise."[3] Aristotle here makes the reasonable suggestion that we should not begin every inquiry *de novo*, as if we were the first to take up a given topic of philosophical interest. Instead, we should look to our predecessors as sources of information and enlightenment. Of course, Aristotle did not regard himself as slavishly bound to opinions of his predecessors or even to their formulations of the problems. On the contrary, he is often critical not only of their opinions but also of their preferred methods of explanation.

Though he regularly looks backward through Plato, Socrates and the Sophists to the earliest Presocratics, Aristotle's immediate and most important source for philosophical stimulation is clearly Plato. Aristotle had come to study with Plato as a youth, probably at the age of 17, and remained with him in his Academy for twenty years, until Plato's death, when the headship of Plato's school passed not to Aristotle, but to one of Plato's nephews, Speusippus, at which time Aristotle left Athens for a period, before returning to set up his own school, the Lyceum. During their two decades of association, Aristotle would have had extended contact with Plato, whose views he repeatedly engages in his own works, very often critically, sometimes caustically, but more often than not with deference and affection. In any case, it is often helpful, as a first approach to Aristotle's gnarly prose, to read in it a response to a position espoused by Plato, since in very many cases, though not always, Aristotle proceeds in his own philosophy with a wary eye on Plato's positions.

4.2 Aristotle's introduction of category theory

Aristotle's anti-Platonism comes immediately to the fore in an early work, the *Categories*. Judged from a certain remove, this work seems delivered from on high: in it, Aristotle articulates a theory of the general categories of being, thereby offering a classificatory schema which is evidently intended to specify a complete and exhaustive list of the kinds of things which exist – or perhaps even of the kinds of things which *could possibly* exist. If he is right about the taxonomy he introduces, then Aristotle will have accomplished something whose very conceit came to be derided by some later, lesser philosophers: he will have limned the true and ultimate nature of reality.

Aristotle proceeds in outlining the categories of being in two stages, the first of which is immediate in its anti-Platonic impetus. He first observes that predication relations are much more complicated than Plato had imagined. He then goes on to articulate and explicate his theory of categories proper. Various questions arise regarding both parts of Aristotle's *Categories*; another, more immediate question pertains to the connection he envisages between these parts.

Although he had expressed some reservation about how best to conceive the relations between particulars and Forms, Plato was mainly content to suggest that particulars "participate" or "have a share" in Forms (Plato's word for this relation is *metechein*).[4] However this suggestion is ultimately to be unpacked, it seems clear that with this locution Plato understands only one main relation obtaining between Forms and the particulars named after them.

1   Socrates is pale.
2   Socrates is human.

Particulars (1) and (2) both say that some particular thing, Socrates, stands in the participation relation to a Form, in one instance to the Form of Pallor and in the other to the Form of Humanity. Presumably, unless he thinks there is more than one participation relation, Plato's analysis will postulate the same relation in both cases.

Aristotle contends that by doing so Plato is being unduly simple. Aristotle holds, by contrast, that the surface grammar of (1) and (2) obscures a deep and significant difference between them: (2), but not (1), expresses an essential predication relation; and (1), but not (2), expresses an accidental predication relation. That is, Socrates is a human in a way very different from the way in which he is pale: most immediately and importantly, Socrates could cease to be pale but continue to exist, whereas if he ceased to be human, Socrates would cease to exist altogether. If, that is, Socrates went to the beach and returned sporting a tan, he would still be Socrates. On the other hand, if he went to the beach and were dismembered and eaten by sharks, Socrates would cease to be a human being and so would cease to exist altogether. There are, then, some properties Socrates can afford to lose while remaining in existence and some properties whose loss would spell his demise.

In the *Categories*, Aristotle wants to distinguish between these two distinct kinds of predication by speaking of things as being "said-of" and being "in" other things. In his terminology, humanity is *said-of* this particular human, Socrates. When he focuses on Socrates' particular color or on a particular bit of his knowledge, an instance of his grammatical knowledge, for example, an instance of knowledge which will be distinct from Protagoras' particular knowledge of grammar, then Aristotle says the color or the knowledge is *in* Socrates. Taking these two distinctions together, Aristotle presents the possible permutations in Table 4.1.

So, some things are both said-of and in, others are said-of but not in, still others in but not said-of, and significantly, suggests Aristotle, some

Table 4.1 Types of predications/types of beings

Said-of	In	Type of being	Examples
Yes	Yes	Non-substance universals	White
Yes	No	Secondary substances	Human
No	Yes	Non-substance particulars	This knowledge of grammar
No	No	Primary substances	This human

things, this particular man or this particular horse, are neither said-of nor in.

Although he does little to characterize these relations in the abstract, Aristotle's examples do suggest a reasonably clear and important difference between essential and accidental predication. If we suppose that he is right about that, we perhaps also agree that Plato has failed to mark a distinction with profound consequences for scientific taxonomy and explanation. Aristotle maintains that adequate explanations are always essence-specifying. When we explain, for example, what it is to be a human being, it will not suffice to mention some accidental if universally held feature, that no human has ever been to Pluto, for example, or even some other features which are universal but not so obviously accidental, that humans are hirsute or are capable of laughter.

Instead, contends Aristotle, it is necessary to provide a definition which captures what it is to be a human being, and this in at least two ways. First, it is necessary to specify a property without which something could no longer be human. Second, it is necessary to specify a property which is explanatorily prior even to a human being's other necessary properties. So, for example, it might be universally true of all human beings that they are capable of mastering a finite grammar, which mastery in turn equips them with the ability to process and understand a potentially infinite number of novel sentences. Still, this fact about them, however central it may be, seems explained by another still more fundamental fact, that human beings are essentially rational. Moreover, there is an apparent explanatory asymmetry between being capable of grammar and being rational: we explain grammatical capacities in terms of rational faculties, but not the other way around. Hence, supposes Aristotle, in choosing between these two properties, rationality has the better claim to stating the essence of humanity.

However essences are to be determined, Aristotle supposes that certain kinds of beings, including human beings, do have essences. He further supposes, in a realist vein, that this fact calls for an explanation which Plato's unaugmented theory of Forms fails to provide. That said, it is not immediately difficult to see how Plato might develop his theory in order to capture a distinction between essence and accident. Indeed, Plato seems himself to be moving in just this direction in some later dialogues. Hence, it is difficult to conclude that Aristotle's categorial schema by itself convicts Plato of any damaging form of over-simplicity. At best, so far, it seems that the most damaging thing Aristotle has to say about Plato's theory of Forms in this connection is that it is underdeveloped or that as stated it obscures distinctions which ought to be drawn.

Another anti-Platonic impetus stands behind the second, and more important, stage of the *Categories*, in which Aristotle presents his categorial schema proper. Recall that in various contexts Plato invests Forms with a kind of necessary being which sense particulars lack.[5] In some cases, it is a bit difficult to make ready sense of Plato's contentions in this regard.

For example, when he seems to suggest that Forms alone are *really real*, or that Forms exist more than sense particulars, which occupy a shadowy halfway house of becoming, Plato invites paraphrase. Still, in some other contexts, his characterizations of Forms are easy to fathom. He thinks, for example, that Justice itself is perfect, whereas humans and their varied institutions are at best imperfectly just, forever striving towards a state of perfection which perpetually eludes them. Humans progress by viewing the Form of Justice and moving towards it, even if they recognize that perfection in terms of Justice will always be beyond their grasp. In these cases, Plato makes perfect sense, whether or not what he says is true: perfect justice exists, even though it is never, perhaps never can be, realized in the sensible world. Justice itself exists necessarily.

Aristotle thinks that his categorial scheme shows that Plato is wrong to believe that Justice (*inter alia*) can exist uninstantiated. For after having distinguished the said-of and in relations, Aristotle draws special attention to the fact that certain things, Socrates or the horse Secretariat, are neither said-of nor in anything. Socrates is, therefore, what Aristotle calls a *primary substance*. What makes him a primary substance is precisely that other things depend upon him for their existence, while he does not depend upon anything else.

In fact, Aristotle identifies ten categories of being, each presumably basic, ineliminable, and irreducible to any other kind. These ten are:

Category	*Example*
Substance	man, horse
Quantity	two feet long
Quality	white, grammatical
Relative	double, half
Place	in the Lyceum, in the market
Time	yesterday, a year ago
Position	lying, sitting
Having	has shoes on, has armor on
Acting upon	cutting, burning
Being affected	being cut, being burnt

Typically, Aristotle does not list all ten categories when referring to them. Indeed, he provides the whole list only twice in all his writings, and even then with some minor variations. Usually, he mentions only the most important categories: substance, quantity, and quality, while merely alluding to "the remaining delineated categories."

Two questions immediately present themselves regarding this list of categories. First, and most generally, how does Aristotle conceive of this schema? Is it an attempt to lay bare the foundations of human thought structures and patterns? Or is it, rather, an attempt to specify the ultimate kinds of things there are, such that any possible rational thought about the universe, if it is to be truth-tracking, would need to countenance just these ultimate kinds?

Aristotle does not say. He is clearly a realist about categories, in the sense that he takes himself not to be characterizing language usage or any form of pragmatically constrained human explanatory proclivity. Still, it must be allowed that he does not, within the *Categories* itself, move to justify in any overt way the categories he introduces. Nor, more fundamentally, does he characterize the aims or ambitions of category theory as such.

What he does concern himself with instead are the internal relations among the categories themselves. He argues in particular for the priority of substance; and his arguments in this regard have a clear anti-Platonic purport. The two stages of Aristotle's *Categories* come together when he distinguishes between two sub-kinds of the most important category, substance. He distinguishes between what he calls *primary* and *secondary* substance, by reminding us that some things, individual humans and individual horses, are neither said-of nor in anything else. This, he supposes, makes such entities *primary* relative to other substances, like the species man and the species horse. These substances, secondary substances, are said-of primary substances; they are, Aristotle rightly contends, predicated essentially of individual humans and individual horses. (Again, if Socrates ceased to be human, he would cease to exist.)

Moreover, primary substances are not primary relative only to secondary substances: in general, Aristotle is keen to insist that all things depend upon primary substances for their existence, a result Plato plainly rejects. Thus, contends Aristotle, if there were no healthy organisms, if every organism in the universe were somehow sick, there would be no health. Similarly, if the universe were to have all of its sources of light extinguished, there would be no light. It is not as if there is some great Form of Light, itself perfectly light and never not-light, imitated only imperfectly by all of the lights we see, which only strive to be light but never quite arrive at being perfectly light. On the contrary, insists Aristotle, if there were no lights, there would be no light. Plato, contends Aristotle, has gotten things not only wrong but completely backwards.

In the *Categories*,[6] Aristotle offers a brief argument intended to show how Plato has failed. This is his argument for the primacy of primary substance (PPS):

1   Everything which is not a primary substance is either said-of or in a primary substance.
2   If (1), then without primary substances, it would be impossible for anything else to exist.
3   So, without primary substances, it would be impossible for anything else to exist.

(PPS-1) is the premise which combines the two stages of Aristotle's *Categories*. According to this premise, there are things which are neither said-of nor in anything else, things, that is, which are not predicated of anything at all, which also enjoy a certain important status: everything else is ultimately predicated of them. We can say that tigers are animals, can predicate animality of tigers; but ultimately this is because we say that there is some individual tiger which is an animal. (PPS-2) adds an important further claim, that in virtue of this ultimate dependence on primary substances, nothing else could exist without there being primary substances in the first place. From there, its conclusion follows directly.

If true, the conclusion of (PPS) has direct and dire anti-Platonic consequences. Consider Justice itself, which Plato holds to exist necessarily, even if it is never realized by human beings. According to (PPS), not only is there no justice without there being just persons or just institutions, there *could be* no justice without there being such persons or institutions. Justice depends for its existence, of necessity, on there being instances of justice somewhere in the world. If that is so, if (PPS) is sound, then Aristotle's categorial scheme threatens to undermine a central tenet of Plato's theory of Forms.

Plato should not find this argument, stated thus baldly and directly, overly impressive. Having stated the argument, that is, Aristotle does little in the context of the *Categories* to defend its premises. We have in this argument an assertion of an anti-Platonic orientation; but an assertion by itself should hardly impress anyone not already persuaded of its conclusion on independent grounds. The most one can say without further development on either side is that Plato and Aristotle have reached a stalemate on this point. Indeed, Plato might well respond on his own behalf that if secondary substances really are said-of primary substances, as Aristotle himself contends, and so are essentially predicated of them, then primary substances depend upon secondary substances no less than secondary substances depend upon primary substances. At this juncture, Plato can legitimately demand additional reasons for regarding primary substances as primary in the first place.

This sort of stalemate is unfortunately common in the *Categories*. This is not because its arguments are especially weak or ineffectual. It is due, rather, to the fact that the *Categories* contains more assertion than argumentation. It is easy to find oneself wondering whether Aristotle takes himself to be reporting the conclusions of arguments he has developed elsewhere or whether this work is intended to be little more than the expression of a regimented common sense.

4.3   The four causes introduced

The sense that the principal claims of the *Categories* require foundations left unprovided in its chapters is enlarged by the discovery that Aristotle has a developed explanatory schema of great power which is conspicuously absent from that work. This is Aristotle's justly celebrated *four-causal explanatory schema*. Its absence from the *Categories* is surprising, since in the remainder of Aristotle's surviving metaphysical writings we find him making frequent appeal to this framework of explanation. He uses it both to display the short-comings of his predecessors, as he conceives them, and to articulate and defend his own positive alternatives. One easy explanation has it that the *Categories* is simply an early work, written before Aristotle developed the four-causal schema. Other, more complex explanations attempt to find the four causes standing behind Aristotle's categorial schema.

However we are to understand the ultimate underpinnings of Aristotle's *Categories*, this much is clear: it is impossible to understand the bulk of his philosophy without first understanding his doctrine of the four causes. We will explore this doctrine in two stages, first by focusing, as Aristotle himself does, on a simple example, and then by delving more deeply into his motivations for each of the four causes individually.

If we were walking across a town square one day and noticed a large piece of shaped metal in its center, we might well want an explanation of its being there. (Aristotle, of course, thinks it is in our natures to want such an expla-nation!) Is it a fallen meteor? Is it rubble from a construction site? Or is it, perchance, modern art?

When we ask these sorts of questions, we seek explanations; and when we seek explanations, we implicitly adopt standards for adequacy in explana-tion. If, that is, we were told that the metal in the town square simply materialized out of thin air, uncaused and uninvited, we would not be satis-fied. Instead, we would regard the explanation proffered as suspect, if not wholly unsatisfactory. In doing so, we would be relying on some conception, however unarticulated, of adequacy in explanation. Aristotle's doctrine of the four causes attempts to articulate and defend our expectations in this regard by specifying the components of a complete and fully adequate account of causal explanation. His doctrine of the four causes, that is, states and defends the adequacy conditions for successful explanation. In this way, for the first time, Aristotle offers a self-conscious theory of explanation. To be sure, his predecessors had relied upon principles of explanation and argu-mentation, some more and some less defensibly; but none had addressed the topic with anything approaching Aristotle's systematicity or overtness.

To appreciate this, we can begin by approaching our novel object from behind, from which vantage point we might ascertain that it is made of a certain metal, perhaps bronze. Still, knowing just that much would not tell us what the bronze was doing occupying pride of place in the town square. Upon a closer inspection, we might also discern that it is not rubble, but art, that it is a somewhat abstract sculpture of a human figure, a man whose form is cast into relief in the front of the bronze. It is, in fact, a statue. So, we infer that the metal is neither atmospheric rubble nor construction debris: a sculptor deliberately put a form into the metal. Still, we wonder *why* the monument was erected, at least until we come to appreciate that it is a representation of one of our town's early leading citizens, the man, in fact, whose name our town bears. So, finally, we know why the shape was put into the metal and why the metal thus shaped was placed in the town square: we have come upon a new monument erected in order to honor our town's founding father.

As we trace through these simple explanations, according to Aristotle, we more or less unself-consciously illustrate his doctrine of the four causes. What we have done in order to explain some novel experience is to specify, in turn, its material constitution, its form, its maker, and its function. We have specified its four causes:

1   *Material cause*: what x is made of or comes from, for example, the *bronze* in a bronze statue of Hermes.
2   *Formal cause*: the *shape* or *structure* of x, what x is essentially, for example the *Hermes-shape* of a bronze statue of Hermes.
3   *Efficient cause*: what puts the form in the matter, for example, the *sculpting* of the sculptor Praxiteles as he enformed the bronze with a Hermes-shape.
4   *Final cause*: the purpose or end of x, for example, the bronze statue of Hermes is *for honoring Hermes*.

Aristotle suggests two central theses regarding the four causes: (1) for a very broad range of phenomena, citing the four causes is necessary for adequacy in explanation; and (2) citing all four causes is in every case sufficient for adequacy in explanation.

These two theses permit him both to use the doctrine of the four causes to criticize his predecessors, even while praising them for their accomplishments, and to offer his own preferred alternative explanations in terms of the framework it provides.

On the critical side, Aristotle often notes that his predecessors have offered explanations made incomplete by their failures to cite all four causes. The earliest natural philosophers cited only material causes; Plato, who appreciated this shortcoming in the Presocratic philosophers, erred in the opposite direction by concentrating exclusively on the formal cause. So, for example, from Aristotle's point of view, even if Thales were right that everything is made of water, mentioning this much would hardly explain the variegated phenomena we experience in the macroscopic world. Knowing, for instance, that the hunk in the town square was ultimately suitably transmuted water, or suitably transmuted x, where x is any basic elemental stuff you like, would never, and could never, explain that the object in the town square is a monument placed in honor of a pre-eminent citizen. Plato saw this, and Aristotle credits him for his insight. Still, at least according to Aristotle, Plato neglects to specify the efficient cause of the statue's generation. He complains, in fact, that Plato's Forms, as necessarily existing causal agents, ought to be ceaselessly generating their own instances. Plainly, they do not. What caused the generation of the statue was not the Form of Statue itself, or the Form of Monument itself, but rather the gradual realization of a specific shape or form in a particular lump of bronze by the agency of an individual human sculptor. So, while Aristotle agrees with Plato, against the Presocratic naturalists, that complete explanations must cite formal causes, he denies that formal causation suffices, since efficient causes too must be indicated; and he certainly denies that the citation of formal causes implicates him or anyone else in the metaphysics of Forms as Plato conceived of them.

Taken together, Aristotle's criticisms of his predecessors illustrate, in different ways, how their explanations prove to be insufficient by failing to cite each of the requisite four causes. To the degree that his criticisms seem apt, then Aristotle's doctrine of the four causes receives some indirect support. For a more direct defense, it is necessary to turn to Aristotle's own introduction of the individual causes, which occurs most overtly in scattered passages of his *Physics*.

4.4 The four causes defended

Aristotle does not offer a developed argument for the contention that citing all four causes is sufficient for adequacy in explanation. Instead, he offers a sort of a challenge to his readers: if you can identify another kind of explanation, name it.[7] Now, in the face of this challenge, it should be made explicit that Aristotle's four causes are *types* of causes, and that consequently it will be possible to cite individual causes at higher or lower levels of generality. For example, it is clearly true that we have not said everything there is to say about the matter of the statue in the square when we have identified it as bronze, since we might well want, for some purposes, to investigate its micro-structure, perhaps because we wish to ascertain what makes it rust-resistant or to discover its specific density. Still, Aristotle's point about the necessity of the material cause should not be confused with the untenable suggestion that citing just any material cause suffices. Rather, his claim about the sufficiency of four-causal explanation operates one level up: any fine-grained specification of the material cause is ultimately just an instance of material causation and not some other kind of causation, as yet unnamed. Moreover, what holds for the material cause holds for the other causes as well. Although we can provide more or less fine-grained specifications of the four causes, we miss nothing explanatorily pertinent, contends Aristotle, when we have cited all four causes. That is, again, citing the four causes is sufficient for adequate explanation.

In contrast to his rather brief treatment of the sufficiency of the four causes taken corporately, Aristotle provides detailed and engaging arguments for their individual necessity. He argues for the introduction of form and matter simultaneously, as is appropriate, inasmuch as they are correlative notions. Arguing directly for one premise in Aristotle's argument for the existence of matter and form, *that there is change in the universe*, proves challenging, since this ultimately involves him in trying to establish something so foundational that it almost defies defense, namely that there is motion.

(Aristotle rightly identifies the main opposition here as Parmenides, whose argument against the possibility of change he first disarms and then undermines.)[8] Equally foundational in this regard is one premise in Aristotle's defense of efficient causation, the claim that *when something moves, something causes it to move*, a presupposition of any search for an efficient cause. Though less foundational, the most difficult task for Aristotle is certainly his defense of the final cause, whose existence has been roundly denied and for whose defense Aristotle has been reviled.

Aristotle's defense of matter and form

At the core of Aristotle's philosophy is his commitment to hylomorphism, where this is simply his commitment to the existence of matter and form as real features of objects which, accordingly, must be mentioned in full and accurate explanations of natural phenomena (Greek: *hulê* = matter; *morphê* = form). Aristotle's argument for their existence comes in two phases. He first argues that since there are, without a doubt, motion and change in the universe, and that since motion and change require the existence of form and matter, there are also form and matter. Set out schematically, Aristotle's initial argument for the existence of form and matter (EFM) is:

1   There is change in the universe.
2   A necessary condition of there being change is the existence of matter and form.
3   So, there are matter and form.

(EFM-1) barely needs defense, although, in the face of Parmenidean challenges to its truth, it nevertheless receives one from Aristotle. This defense turns out to be important and interesting in view of its general strategy. We will turn to this defense after considering Aristotle's treatment of (EFM-2) which, by contrast, quite obviously requires explication and defense.

Aristotle's principal defense of (EFM-2) begins with a simple observation, that there are two types of change: qualitative alteration and substantial generation. In cases of qualitative alteration, a particular substance, some man for example, continues to exist but loses or acquires some quality, perhaps by learning to play the piano or more passively by getting a sun tan. In these sorts of cases, we say that something continues (the man) but that he changes in terms of his accidental characteristics. In substantial generation, by contrast, a new being comes into existence, for instance a new table or a baby. In these cases, too, something persists: there is no generation *ex nihilo*. About that much, Parmenides was right.[9] In the case of the table, the wood persists, although it is fashioned into a something table-shaped. Similarly, if less obviously, something persists in the creation of a baby, which results when some raw materials mix and acquire some new structures.

Though distinct, both kinds of change have something in common: each involves a complex of something which persists and something which is gained or lost. Taken in their broadest terms, these two factors are form and matter. The matter is that which persists through change. The form is that which is acquired or lost by the matter. When a substance gains an accidental form, it changes accidentally; when some matter acquires a new substantial form, a new substance is generated. Crucially, both kinds of change involve a complex, which is simply a complex of form and matter. Hence, if there is change, there are form and matter.[10] Consequently, Aristotle takes himself as warranted in having established (EFM-3) – on the assumption, that is, that (EFM-1), the claim that there is change in the universe.

That premise finds its defense in Aristotle's reasons for refusing to take seriously those who deny the existence of change altogether. As indicated, it seems almost incredible to suppose that an argument for (EFM-1) is necessary. In fact, Aristotle seems in some ways disinclined to provide an argument for the claim that as a matter of fact some things sometimes do change. He regards it as a first principle of natural philosophy, the branch of philosophy which investigates puzzles regarding change, motion, time, and, in general, all of the properties that pertain to physical bodies.[11] Still, it has had its detractors, including most notably Parmenides. If some are impatient with the very idea of arguing that there is such a thing as change, that some things sometimes change, then they may nevertheless find Aristotle's defense of (EFM-1) instructive. Beyond its foundational character, Aristotle's argument for the existence of change is worth studying if only for the resourcefulness of argumentative strategy, a strategy, it will turn out, that can be deployed in other contexts as well.

After upbraiding those who demand an argument for the existence of change, Aristotle provides this one (AEC):

1 Suppose there is no change in the universe, that everything is always at rest.
2 If (1), then what the senses tell us about the world results in our forming false beliefs.
3 If it is possible for us to form false beliefs, then there is change.
4 So, if we suppose that there is no change in the universe, then there is change.
5 So, there is change in the universe.

(AEC) is a certain kind of refutation, one which begins by entertaining the hypothesis advanced by the opposition. The opposition say there is no change and try to induce us to understand that our beliefs to the contrary are false. So, they try to induce us to *change* our beliefs. If so, then they try to induce us to do what they say is impossible: to change. Now, they may back away at this point and try to suggest that we do not really have false beliefs about the natural world at all. It only seems to us that we believe that it changes. Aristotle's response to this retort is two-fold. First, he notes that the senses really do seem to record motion and change. When I turn the page of a book, it seems to change directly before my eyes. So, it is hard to take seriously the suggestion that things do not even seem to me to change. Second, Aristotle notes that the entire apparatus of forming beliefs, whether true or false, or of engaging in other forms of mental activity implicates us in changing: mental changes are changes no less than physical changes. If we imagine something, we change; in general, if we come to think anything at all, then we change from the state we were in before we were thinking it. So, insofar as our opponent wishes us to reject all forms of *a posteriori* justification, which is precisely what Parmenides had recommended, she wishes us to form a belief counter to what the senses enjoin us to believe. She wishes us, that is, to change our minds.[12]

The crux of Aristotle's argument is (AEC-3), the premise that even our belief formations count as changes. If this contention is correct, it forces Aristotle's opponents into an awkward position. For it forces them to appreciate that their point of view is self-undermining, that a necessary condition of the truth of their approach is its falsehood. The argumentative strategy proves to be quite a powerful tool for Aristotle when attempting to refute his opponents on foundational points which seem to defy direct argumentation. (He uses a similar strategy against those who deny the principle of non-contradiction, the principle that nothing can be both F and not-F at the same time in the same respect. He agrees that no one could argue directly for any such principle, since an argument for its truth would need to employ it and so, in that sense, make no progress. Still, if someone claims that this principle is false, then they claim something definite and not its opposite. If so, then even in issuing their claim, the denial of the principle of non-contradiction, they presuppose its truth. So, a condition of asserting the falsity of the principle of non-contradiction is an acquiescence in its truth. If someone, in response, then refrains from asserting the falsity of the principle of non-contradiction, Aristotle has nothing to say to them.)[13] However that may be, in the context of defending the claim that there is change, Aristotle need only encourage his opponent to reflect upon the necessary preconditions of their point of view. To the extent that their proposal presupposes the existence of the phenomenon whose defensibility they doubt, their point of view is self-undermining.

With this argument, Aristotle completes his defense of the material and formal causes.

The efficient cause

Aristotle does not argue for the existence of efficient, or moving, causes. Having established that there are motion and change, he assumes, as most of us do, that such motion and change is initiated and not simply indiscriminate or inexplicable. If we were to hear a loud explosion coming from the basement one evening, but were incapable of locating its source upon a cursory survey, we would hardly conclude straight away that the explosion must simply have been an uncaused, random event, that the explosion simply happened but was not caused to happen. Instead, we would assume that we had simply been unable to locate its cause and would, in the interests of our own safety, redouble our search. When things move or change, something is responsible for their moving or changing. This something Aristotle regards as the efficient cause.

That said, Aristotle does wish to offer some recommendations for the best way to specify or designate a particular instance of efficient causation. He notes that some ways of citing efficient causes may be more perspicuous than others; indeed, some ways may even be true but completely misleading. Suppose, for example, we identified the efficient cause of the plumbing in my house as my uncle. That may be true, but it hardly explains anything. Aristotle suggests that we should specify the efficient cause more exactly as the *activity* of my uncle, insofar as he is a plumber. It may sound initially trivial to cite as the efficient causal explanation of the installation of plumbing in my house "the plumber plumbing." So far, in fact, it is. The explanatory force, though, resides in the fact that the effect – the existence of plumbing in my house – is commensurate with the cause. Thus, for example, it may be true that I was electrocuted because of my touching a large object which was struck by lightning. Its being a large object, however, does nothing to explain my electrocution – until I learn that the large object is a flag pole, made of a highly conductive metal. In fact, had it been made of some non-conductive material, I would not have been electrocuted at all. So, it is necessary, concludes Aristotle, to specify the efficient cause in such a way that a law-like connection can be established between the cause and its effects. To illustrate this point in another way, suppose that my uncle the plumber is also a chess champion. It will be true, but surely misleading and explanatorily impotent, to identify the efficient cause of my plumbing as "the activity of this year's chess champion." So, efficient causal explanations are subject to fine-grained specification. If some x happens to be both F and G, its being F may or may not be relevant to its status as an efficient cause. What matters is that its being F actually explains the result whose efficient cause we seek.

The final cause

Virtually everyone will accept some version of Aristotle's contention that there are efficient causes, even if it is disputed – as indeed it has been vigorously disputed – how best to characterize the precise nature of efficient causation. Aristotle's arguments for the existence of such causes need not enter into these disputes. Rather, he contends that there is change, something only incredibly denied, and that there exist causes responsible for individual instances of change, a claim which, while not as secure as the foundational commitment to the bare existence of change, finds easy and appropriate acceptance from just about everyone who considers it.

Things are very different when we turn to Aristotle's commitment to final causation. Indeed, Aristotle's commitment to final causation has earned him a widespread derision by those who think that he somehow single-handedly managed to shackle scientific progress by insisting on the existence of explanatorily vacuous causes or on causes which require future states to affect past ones by reaching backward in time. (Evidently, his detractors seem to suggest, Aristotle foisted his views on those in the centuries following his death who agreed with him, and so is responsible for their accepting his false beliefs.) In any case, the final cause has, in many quarters, fallen into disrepute.

Given the unproblematic nature of Aristotle's other three causes, it is surely worth reflecting on his motivations for postulating final causality. Moreover, whatever its ultimate credentials, Aristotle's conception of final causation must be understood if his remaining philosophy is even to be approached; for his commitment to final causation informs virtually every facet of his philosophy.

Perhaps, then, it is best to start with an appeal to final causation which ought to appear at least *prima facie* plausible. Thinking back to our initial illustration of a statue, it seemed that something was left unexplained until we appreciated *what the statue was for*. In Aristotle's preferred way of speaking, we lacked a complete explanation of the statue before we grasped its function (*ergon*). His point can be further illustrated by considering another form of artifact, one not available to Aristotle himself. Suppose that one day we learn that life exists elsewhere in our solar system. We come to know this because an exploring spacecraft, unmanned, returns from a distant planet carrying objects whose intricacy of form provides clear evidence that they were fashioned by intelligent agents rather than by random processes in nature. Suppose, for example, the craft returned a device manifesting roughly the complexity of a G4 Macintosh computer. We could admit that it was remotely possible that the object was formed by natural processes; but that possibility would be neither credible nor interesting. Instead, when confronted with this device, scientists would want to figure out what it was. They might initially be able to ascertain its precise form, or configuration, as well as its exact material constitution; and they might reasonably accept as a working hypothesis that something or other had put the materials into the form displayed. That is, in Aristotle's terms, scientists might well and easily determine the material and formal causes of the device, and might also assume that it had an efficient cause of a particular sort, that the efficient cause was an intelligent designing agent. Nonetheless, it is fair to say, in these circumstances, that the scientists would still not know *what* the item in question was. Though they would know a good deal about it, its *nature* would be unknown, because its nature, as an artifact, is given by its function. If it turned out to be a digital processor capable of realizing sophisticated programming languages, then it would be reasonable to infer that the device was, after all, a computer, and that its designers had designed and built it for the same reason we design and build computers: to compute.

This make-believe story illustrates both an epistemological and a metaphysical point. First, since humans want to know what things are, contends Aristotle, they will also want to know, for some range of entities at least, what their function is. That is, when explaining some things, we want to know the final cause; and we do not think that we have adequate knowledge until we discover it. This epistemological point has a metaphysical underpinning: people want to know the function of things because they want to uncover essences, and function determines essence. That is, as Aristotle often suggests, what it is to be an F is to have the function of Fs; all and only things capable of doing what Fs do are genuine Fs. So, for example, what it is to be a knife is to be able to cut. Given that knives are *for cutting*, only certain sorts of shapes will do. So, the function determines the appropriate range of shapes. Moreover, the form in question, one designed for cutting, can be realized only in functionally suitable matters. If the shape of a knife were realized in marshmallow, then we would not have a knife at all. Or, to use Aristotle's preferred technical expression, we would have a knife only *homonymously*, that is, we would have something which we might call a knife, but which would not be a real knife, in the way in which a decoy duck is not a real duck at all.[14] So, taken together, Aristotle supposes that function is prior to both form and matter: function determines appropriateness in both form and matter. Put non-technically, his view is just that *what something is for* sets conditions on what kinds of form and matter that thing can have.

So much should seem unproblematic for artifacts. We know that artifacts have functions because we give them their functions. Moreover, when we design artifacts, function determines form and the selection of materials. If we need an implement for driving nails, we need something with a particular configuration, made of some suitably dense material. So, hammers are shaped as they are and are made of steel and not cotton.

Perhaps so far so good. Unfortunately, Aristotle's commitment to final causation takes on a more difficult caste when he insists that not only artifacts have final causes. Instead, natural entities – entities which, unlike artifacts, were not designed, were not given their function by designing agents like ourselves – nevertheless have functions. So, for example, a human being has a function, as does a tree and a mongoose. It should hardly be obvious how various natural organisms came to have functions when they were not designed to have those functions in the way that artifacts are. Aristotle owes us some sort of explanation and defense.

He does provide a defense; but it is first of all important to get clear about the character of the claim being defended. If we stipulate that the only things with functions are those which were designed by the conscious activities of designing agents, then, trivially, Aristotle will be wrong to hold that some things have functions even though they were not designed to have them. A surprising number of contemporary philosophers seem content with just this kind of shallow victory. Such a victory is shallow because it trades upon a simple linguistic stipulation, which is then taken to masquerade as a substantive principle. In fact, the view which Aristotle means to promote is this: natural organisms and their parts exhibit behavior which is best characterized as end-directed, because such a characterization best or uniquely explains the behavior in question. If we think that hearts are *for pumping blood*, or that kidneys are *for purifying blood*, but we deny that these organs were given these functions by the activities of a designing agent, then we have come at least part of the way towards accepting Aristotle's views regarding teleological explanation. These organs will then have functions, though they were never designed to have them. Instead, they will receive them from the role which they play in larger systems, in this case, living animals.

Still, many will not be satisfied with Aristotle's contention that the organs of animals have functions without having been designed by conscious agents. There are, in fact, two radically different ways to deny Aristotle's claim. At one end of the spectrum are those who will insist that there is a grand cosmic designer, who set things up just as they are so that, e.g., kidneys will filter blood; at the other end are those who think that all talk of kidneys as having a function is shorthand for a more precise kind of naturalistic talk which has no recourse to suspect teleological language, with the result that, at the end of the day, all such talk is sloppy talk and is to be eliminated in favor of more perspicuous language. This second sort of challenge, mounted from a broadly naturalistic framework which eschews all appeal to teleology, can be likened to the sort of response we would have to someone who insisted that since the average American family has 2.4 children, there must be, out there in America, a fair number of 0.4 children. While it is a shorthand convenience to speak of the average family, one which can be extremely useful for all sorts of purposes, including resource distribution and environmental planning, we do not really ever commit ourselves to the literal existence of individual families with the features we employ. Similarly, one might say, although it is convenient to talk of functions in the case of organs, we do not think in fact that they literally have such. When we are pressed, we have a way of paraphrasing away such talk.

For his part, Aristotle rejects both of these extremes: he allows that functions have a role in a mature biological science, even though it is inappropriate to understand them as being due to the work of designing agents of any kind.

The first thing to notice about these contentions is that if they are correct a human being is something more than Democritus thought: a person is more, that is, than atoms swirling in the void, because only those atoms subservient to the function of a human being will qualify as human atoms.[15]

Aristotle's teleology provides him with a way to identify just which atoms constitute a human being at any given moment in its history.

The second thing to notice about Aristotle's contention is that it is hard to defend. Aristotle's primary argument is problematic because it presents formidable difficulties of both interpretation and defense. In the *Physics*, when Aristotle overtly undertakes to defend final causation, he first notes that we might be inclined to treat everything as if it were purposeless, as if everything which occurs does so by dint of brute necessity. Sometimes, of course, this is just what we think: ground water is heated to the point of vaporizing; it is drawn up, cools, and forms clouds; eventually, it cools sufficiently until it liquefies and pours down as rain. The rain makes corn grow. Still, we do not say that it rains *in order* to make the corn grow. It rains, rather, of necessity. Perhaps, then, we should view all natural processes on the model of rain: everything happens of necessity, never for the sake of anything else.

In particular, why not treat the teeth, the heart, and all parts of humans, "where purpose seems to be present"[16] as occurring not for the sake of the benefits they bring to the organism whose parts they are? Aristotle responds strongly to this suggestion by insisting that "it is not possible that things should really be so." Unfortunately, the initial argument does not provide any strong support for this contention. He offers the following argument for the existence of the final cause in nature (AFC):

1   Natural phenomena exhibit regularity, occurring "always or for the most part."
2   Things happen either by chance or for the sake of something.
3   What happens by chance does not exhibit regularity; chance events do not occur "always or for the most part."
4   So, natural phenomena occur for the sake of something.

Hence, since natural phenomena occur for the sake of something, they have final causes whose omission would result in incomplete forms of explanation. To take an example from Aristotle, it happens always or for the most part that our teeth grow with incisors in the front, evidently for tearing and ripping food, and our molars grow in the back, for crushing and mashing. This pattern repeats with great regularity, if not in every human then in virtually every human. This regularity itself cries out for an explanation. Since it cannot be an oft-repeated accident, the shape and position of our teeth must be *for something*. What they are *for*, suggests Aristotle, is the benefit they bring us. So, citing this benefit explains something which would otherwise remain mysterious.

As stated, this argument is unpersuasive. The first and most obvious problem crops up in (AFC-2), the claim that things happen either by chance or for the sake of something. In order for this argument to have any force, this premise needs to be understood as an exclusive and exhaustive disjunction. So, there can be no room for regularities which are neither accidental nor purposeful. There are such, however. Even if we allow that it is not reasonable to suppose that accidents happen always or for the most part, it need not follow that all regularities are purposeful. It would, of course, be odd to believe that a man might just accidentally bump into a particular woman each day after work, regardless of where she traveled, to a tavern, to a shopping mall, or to a restaurant. The reasonable thing to believe in this case is that the meetings are not inadvertent, that one or the other of them is orchestrating things so that they meet. In this case, then, we rightly look for purposefulness. That said, there seem to be countless regularities which are neither purposeful nor merely accidental. Suppose that each time my phone rings, my parrot squawks. This is not accidental; but the phone does not ring in order to make the bird squawk. Every time a car is driven, fossil fuels pollute the atmosphere. Still, no one drives *in order* to pollute the atmosphere. On the contrary, although there is a perfectly predictable correlation between driving and polluting, we drive not in order to pollute, but in spite of the fact that we pollute. Nor is this an accident. The emission of carbon monoxide is a law-governed consequence of the combustion of distilled petroleum.

These sorts of examples, which could easily be multiplied, show that there are regularities which are not *for* anything. So, it is not the case, as (AFC-2) contends, that all non-accidents are for something. It should be stressed, however, that despite his advancing (AFC), this fact is hardly lost on Aristotle. For he himself recognizes countless instances of non-purposive regularity in his own biological writings. Thus, for example, my spleen produces bile which is yellow on a regular basis. Even if bile is good for something or other, its being yellow is neither here nor there; this is a non-purposeful regularity, perfectly predictable and explicable in wholly non-teleological terms. Similarly, the hearts of mammals produce noise as they pump blood. Even if we allow that hearts are for pumping blood, we have another kind of regularity, one which is non-purposeful but non-accidental, namely, that hearts make noise. Certainly, at any rate, they do not pump blood in order to make noise. Aristotle's awareness of these sorts of cases suggests that he cannot regard (AFC-2) as perfectly general or correct as stated. Of course, in some cases, he will allow, we have regularities which are epiphenomenal upon genuinely purposeful regularities. Presumably, he will think of the noise produced by the heart on this model. The heart is for pumping blood; its pumping necessitates its making some noise, hence, although it does not pump blood in order to make noise, its making noise is nevertheless explained by its executing its function. Its making noise is a regular epiphenomenon, or by-product, of its executing its characteristic function.

That concession, however, tends to undercut (AFC-2) itself, since it implicitly recognizes non-accidental, non-purposive regularities. So, a defender of (AFC) would minimally need to restructure the argument in some non-question-begging way, a task which turns out to be difficult and complex. More important, at the moment, however, is the question of motivation. Why, after all, should one want to defend (AFC)? There seem to be two reasons present in Aristotle's writings. The first is an implicit appeal to the explanatory power or success of teleological causation. The second has a more metaphysical character. We will consider each in turn.

Aristotle's own explanations of biological phenomena are replete with appeals to teleology. Why, he wants to know, do humans, birds and quadrupeds, whether viviparous or oviparous, have eyelids? The reason, he suggests, is that the eyes are fluid in their tissue consistency. So, they need to be protected from ambient objects of all sorts. He concedes that this could have been avoided had all such animals developed hard skin for eyes, rather than soft tissue. Then, however, keenness in vision would have been sacrificed, since subtle discriminations require subtle tissue. So, we have eyelids ultimately so that we might have keen vision, where, it is assumed, our having keen vision benefits us. So, in all of these ways, suggests Aristotle, we appeal to the *benefit* offered to the animal by the configuration of its eyes and lids when we want to explain those very configurations.[17] This, though, is straightforwardly teleological. Presumably, the justifications for these sorts of explanations can in this context only be that they — unlike competing forms of explanation — are explanatorily efficacious.

Now, it should be noted that despite the severe reservations expressed about this style of explanation, it remains a plain fact that many contemporary biologists make ready appeal to *benefits offered* when seeking to explain the occurrence of a given trait. One need only look to any introductory text in the biological sciences to see that this is so. (Plumage is *for* attracting mates; hearts are *for* pumping blood; rods and cones are *for* detecting light and color; the pancreas is *for* regulating blood sugar.) Philosophers, and indeed biologists themselves, sometimes insist that all such talk should be understood as shorthand for the more defensible descriptions (i.e. those free of appeal to final causation) into which they can be translated; but then the postulated translations may take one of two forms, eliminativist or reductivist. The first sort, which has proven notoriously inadequate, has wanted to show that we should eschew talk of final causation because in point of fact there are no final causes. Final causes are like witches: we can talk about them, for convenience's sake, if we wish ("The judges in Salem sought to rid the community of witches through aggressive legal action"), though we know there never really were any witches. The second, reductivist sort has enjoyed more success: there are final causes, but they are actually co-extensive with efficient causes. It is not clear why Aristotle would object to reductive approaches to final causation, especially given that he himself insisted that in some instances at least final, formal, and efficient causes coincide. What he wants to insist upon is that there are final causes, and that we cannot adequately describe the workings of nature and its organisms without appeal to them.

We can see his line of reasoning especially clearly when we focus on the fact, as Aristotle did, that human beings are part of nature. We characterize the intentional behavior of human beings as goal-directed. That is, we describe their behavior by appeal to their own reasons as causes. (Belle went to the store in order to buy milk. This was her purpose in acting; and her purpose explains her gross bodily movements.) Here appeals to final causes are natural; and claims that all such appeals need to be squashed have been ill-motivated, even to the point of engendering research programs which have resulted in palpable failure. If we think that we will not be able to eliminate appeals to teleology in psychology, then it is not immediately clear what is to be gained in terms of parsimony by eliminating them in the biological sciences. Now, if we admit the general form of explanation as acceptable, we do not thereby license it in every domain in which it might be applied. At the same time, we deny ourselves any reason to be suspect of teleological explanation as such. If we then want to regard such explanation as inadmissible in a certain domain, special reasons will have to be given.

Aristotle doubts that such reasons will be forthcoming in at least some domains of biological explanation, and not only because of its (putative) explanatory efficaciousness. In addition, he thinks, there are general metaphysical reasons for supposing that at least some biological facts will ultimately, at least implicitly, rely on teleological principles. That is because he regards it as a non-conventional fact that some living organisms, substances like this particular woman or this particular horse, exhibit both synchronic and diachronic unity. That is, when we individuate an organism at a time or through time, we implicitly appeal to some principle of unity. Whereas it is conventional that the border between Germany and Poland is conventionally determined, even if it is established by violent conquest, it is in no way a matter of convention that my body ends before the sofa on which I sit begins. Similarly, though it is conventional, and perhaps indeterminate, whether the members of the Heritage Club today in New York City are members of the same club founded in London in the nineteenth century, which ceased to exist during the Second World War and then was reconstituted in the new world after the war's end, it is not a matter of convention, and it is in no way arbitrary, that the body I have today is an older version of the same body I had a decade ago. Despite its gaining and losing matter, there is one body, my body, which existed before and exists now. Now, Aristotle supposes that this non-conventional fact requires some explanation; and he doubts that it can be given in anything other than teleological terms. If a man and a woman are in an office hugging, what makes half of the organs in that region of space his and the other half hers is just that it is a unique fact about one collection of them that they are subordinate in their activities to one organized living system, and of the other to another. What organizes one life system into one life system, suggests Aristotle, is the presence of its final cause. In a similar way, what makes one body one body through time, despite its suffering material replenishment, is its being organized around one life directionality, again explicated in terms of the presence of a final cause. No explanation in terms of mere chemical processes will do, in either case, since there will always be myriad chemical interactions in and around the region of any given living system, only some of which will qualify as processes of the living system in question.[18]

Taken together, then, Aristotle's metaphysical argument for teleological causation (MTC) is this:

1   It is a non-conventional and non-arbitrary fact that individual organisms are synchronic and diachronic unities.
2   The only possible unifying factor in either case is the presence of a final cause.
3   Hence, there are final causes.

If we accept as a datum (MTC-1), as seems reasonable, then the only premise to discuss is (MTC-2), which identifies final causation as the only possible explanation of unity.

There might be two styles of argument for (MTC-2). First, one can argue, as some contemporary philosophers have for similar conclusions, *by exhaustion*. That is, it is possible simply to list all of the possible or plausible competitors, show that each in turn fails, and then default to teleological causation, which, it is suggested, explains unity by subordinating diversity in process and material constitution to a single end. Aristotle offers no such general argument, though he does at least consider some competitors. Another defense looks instead to a categorical basis, by attempting to situate organisms into a recognizable category of being, in this case *substance*, by showing that all and only members of that category are unified by the presence of a non-derived final cause. Some of Aristotle's arguments also tend in this direction.

As for the first style of argument, it is worth reflecting on the sort of challenge Aristotle puts to the atomists, who thought that everything could be explained by postulating atoms and the void, or more strongly, that atoms and the void alone exist.[19] Taken one way, atomism is a form of eliminativism, according to which nothing exists beyond atoms and the void. In that case, taken strictly, not even Democritus, the main proponent of atomism, existed; Democritus is supposed to be a person and not an atom. (We shall assume that he is not the void.) Taken another way, atomism allows that Democritus exists, in a derivative way, by being identical with some configuration of atoms. (MTC-2) now asks Democritus to specify just which collection of atoms he is to be identified with, without, of course, appealing to any state or condition beyond atoms and their positions in the void. The claim is that it cannot be done: no answer given in terms of physical proximity or chemical association will succeed. By contrast, if he were an atomist at all, Aristotle would have at least this answer: just those atoms which serve the interests of this living system – this system, that is, with an intrinsic end. These atoms jointly constitute the body of a human being. His answer, though, appeals ineliminably to final causation.

So, in at least this way, Aristotle defends his appeals to teleological causation. Interestingly, in this, he comes to an important sort of agreement with Plato. In the *Phaedo*, Socrates had recounted his own search for adequacy in explanation. There, he notes wryly that simple material explanation is never enough. Something, he says, explains his remaining in prison when he has the chance to escape. After all, if it were up to his bones and sinews, he would long since have bolted out of Athens. What bids him to stay, he implies, are his *principles and reasons*. But what room is there, in a world admitting only material causes couched in the language of an objective third-person naturalistic science, for such things as principles and reasons? If citing such causes is really only a manner of speaking, in principles eliminable in favor of a preferred idiom, how do they direct Socrates as they do? Aristotle takes a step towards a position which Plato also seems inclined to make but never quite does make, at any rate not with Aristotle's self-conscious methodology and terminology: he affirms the existence of teleological causes as ineliminable explanatory features of the world.

With that affirmation, Aristotle completes his defense of all four of his causes: the material, formal, efficient, and final. Once he has defended their status as required for adequate explanation, Aristotle puts the four causes to work in a series of philosophical contexts, ranging from philosophy of mind, to metaphysics, to ethics and politics. We turn now to some representative samples of the four causes at work. It will be appreciated that these samples are hardly comprehensive; it is hoped, however, that a study of them will equip a reader of Aristotle to proceed to self-guided explorations of other facets of his philosophy.

4.5   The four causes applied: soul and body

Armed with the doctrine of the four causes, Aristotle thinks he can make progress on some important issues whose resolution had eluded Plato and his other predecessors. Prominent among them is a question regarding the relation of the human soul to the human body. If we agree with Aristotle's reasonable injunction that those who wish to make philosophical progress had better take care to state their problems well, it is worth reflecting on just what problem or problems we have in view when we investigate the relation between soul and body. This is especially so since there are in fact various distinct problems in play in this arena. (Is the soul an immaterial entity, separable and capable of a *post-mortem* existence? Or is the soul, by contrast, identical with the body? Is the soul itself a substance? Or is it rather a collection of dispositions realized by certain sophisticated bodies? Is there such a thing as a soul at all? Or is this already a misleading way of speaking?) Aristotle seems most concerned to determine whether we should think of the soul as a material entity, or should rather side with Plato in regarding it as somehow immaterial, as non-identical to the body and capable of existing without it. In the *Phaedo*, Plato had argued at length for a strident form of dualism, according to which death brings not the end of existence, but the mere separation of an immaterial soul from the body. The soul, with which we are evidently identified, continues to exist in a disembodied state, with the result that we turn out to be immortal, a sentiment which later, Christian Platonists found highly congenial. This is the reason why Socrates in the *Phaedo* jokes that he does not care what is done with his body after death: he will himself be gone, and his body might as well be thrown on a rubbish heap like a discarded threadbare suit. Put this way, Plato's view is a far cry from the Presocratic materialist monists and atomists. If I am really a collection of atoms swirling in the void, then when my atoms scatter to the wind I do not continue to exist. I end. These stark alternatives presented themselves to Aristotle, who understandably wanted to know whose camp to join.

Aristotle presents himself as a moderate in this debate between materialism and dualism. He sees the virtues of both sides. He thinks that Plato has a point against the forms of materialism endorsed by the monists and atomists; and at the same time, he thinks that Plato's response is an overreaction, because the remedies to the defects of reductive materialism do not warrant a commitment to Platonic dualism, with its endorsement of the reality of *post-mortem* existence.

In general, Aristotle first wants to know what a soul (a *psuchê*) is. He notes that it is that in virtue of which living beings are alive. So, for Aristotle, every living thing is ensouled. Now, this observation does not commit him to any sort of occult view, that plants are spiritual beings endowed with special plant consciousness. On the contrary, he regards it as a sober biological fact that some things are alive and some are not: a rose bush is alive, but a cell phone is not. Among living things, some display more abilities than others, with the result that souls form a kind of hierarchy. All living things have *nutritive souls*, because they take on nutrition and use it for their own ends; some living things, non-human animals, have *perceptual souls* which are also implicitly nutritive souls, since they are endowed with a sensory apparatus which they use to further their ends, including securing the nutrition required for life and reproduction; and, finally, human animals have not only nutritive and perceptual abilities, but *rational souls*, which permit them to engage in higher-order cognitive activities, including scientific and philosophical inquiry and explanation. All living things, as we have observed, are teleonomic systems, that is, systems whose organizations and behaviors are best explained by regarding them as engaging in end-subordinated activity. Just as a rose bush engages in photosynthesis in order to flourish, so a human being thinks, strategizes, and acts in order to procure the best form of life available to it, given the kind of being it is.

Unsurprisingly, on Aristotle's approach, all souls lend themselves to a *hylomorphic* analysis, that is, to an analysis in terms of the material and formal causes. In fact, Aristotle regards soul–body relations simply as a special case of form–matter relations, an attitude which, he thinks, allows him to position himself as a moderate between what he regards as the excesses of Presocratic materialism and Platonic dualism. Just as a statue is analyzable into a complex of form and matter, so a human being has both a form, its soul, and some matter, its body. Thus, we have the following governing analogy:

form : matter :: soul : body

In just these terms, Aristotle likens the relation of soul to body to the relation between the shape of a candle and its wax. Although a soul is not a static shape, it is nevertheless akin to a shape: it structures the body, makes the matter of a body into a living body by its presence, and explains why just this matter qualifies as the matter for this body. When we hold hands, our matter is intertwined, but there is a fact of the matter as to where your matter ends and mine begins. Aristotle thinks that this fact is determined by another fact, that the matter in your hand is ultimately the matter structured by your soul, and not mine. Similarly, if a box of birthday candles contains twenty-four candles, what explains their being twenty-four is the presence of twenty-four individually shaped bits of wax. If that same wax had been molded into a single candle shape, with one wick, there would have been one candle and not two dozen. In the same way, the presence of an individual soul explains why just these molecules, and not those nearby, nor even those intermingling, are parts of a human body. If a spear punctures a body, it is not part of that body, even if it is partly inside the body. This is because the form of the body is not also the form of the spear, in whole or in part.

So, Aristotle's attitude towards his predecessors will be familiar from his more general attitude towards them vis-à-vis their relations to the four causes. The Presocratic naturalists discovered and dwelt exclusively upon the material cause. So, their explanations were at best misleadingly incomplete, or positively false if they thought they had explained everything in need of explanation. They talked only about the body and its constituents, and could not explain even why just these atoms qualified as being this distinct human body, as opposed to another, or in distinction to the other atoms with which they were contiguous. Consequently, Aristotle reasons, Plato was right to criticize them, and right to stress against them the role of the formal cause. But then he went too far in the other direction in his reaction. Plato stressed the formal cause to the exclusion of the material cause, thereby neglecting something centrally important in any explanation of a human being: namely, that every human being has a body which realizes its psychic functions.

In slightly more detail, Aristotle will regard an attempt to identify a human being (or an octopus or a rhododendron) with some atoms swirling in the void as hopelessly inadequate. It is a non-conventional fact about human beings that they, for example, engage in higher-order cognitive activities. If we are to say why just these particular atoms are arrayed so as to engage in such activities, we are already implicitly invoking formal causation, since there is in principle no way even to select the relevant atoms without first identifying them as the atoms belonging to this human body: that is, to this enformed matter. On the other side, though right to insist on the formal cause in any explanation of a human being, Plato is nevertheless wrong, contends Aristotle, to suppose that the mere appeal to formal causation provides any reason at all to postulate the separability of soul from body. Even if we allow that the soul, as form, is distinct from the body, this by itself gives us no reason at all to suppose that the soul is capable of an independent existence. Here it is worth stressing that soul–body hylomorphism is a special case of form–matter hylomorphism. If we think that a house is an enformed collection of brick and mortar, because just this brick and mortar might be a wall, and not a house, if otherwise enformed, then we accept a central point about hylomorphism, and reject any attempt to identify a house with its material constituents. Still, so much gives us no reason at all to suppose that the form of the house carries on after the destruction of the house. Where does the form of the house go when the house is razed? Aristotle thinks that it does not go anywhere. So, by parity of reasoning, we are to conclude that the formal causation does not guarantee separability in the case of the soul either. Plato was wrong about that.

Aristotle's reaction to his predecessors is thus also reflected in two inferences he derives from his hylomorphism. First, he concludes *that the soul is not separable from the body*. Second, he decides *that it is not necessary to ask whether the soul and body are one*. They are one in the way that some wax and its form are one: there is but one thing, a candle, which burns until it is gone.

Now, Aristotle's appeal to hylomorphism seems in these ways to have direct anti-Platonic consequences. Still, for better or worse, Aristotle does not draw them in quite so stark a fashion. In any case, a Platonist might well respond that he can jolly well ask all he wants whether the soul and body are one: the question is not Aristotle's to legislate. That is, even if Plato takes on board the hylomorphic framework, and concedes that the mere appeal to formal causation does not by itself guarantee separability or a capacity for independent existence, it may remain consistent with hylomorphism that *for other reasons* a soul may yet be separable. Moreover, it is often supposed that the reason it is not necessary to ask whether soul and body are one is precisely because *they are one*. But this does not seem to be right, or obviously right, even in Aristotle's own terms. Indeed, one would have thought that the wax of a candle was not the same thing as the candle's shape. After all, the wax is some material quantity while the shape is rather a quality of a precise sort. Hearkening back to Aristotle's own category theory, a quantity is not and could not be a quality. So, it hardly seems like the wax and its shape are one and the same thing. The best one could say is that they come together to constitute some one thing, a candle. This, though, is something even the most rabid Platonist could accept by allowing that the soul and body come together to create a human animal.

This is a point worth stressing, since Aristotle himself is rather guarded in his own statement of the results of his hylomorphic analysis of soul and body. In the first instance, he does not conclude that the whole soul is not separable, but insists instead that nothing prevents some parts of the soul from being separated, where this seems a rather significant concession to Platonism.[20] Second, the part of the soul which Aristotle intends to reserve for special treatment is the mind, which he ends up characterizing as "unmixed" with the body and something separate, in some fashion or other.[21] So, his attitude seems, in the end, subtle and complex. Although hylomorphism does not open the door to Platonism, neither does it close the door altogether. Aristotle's middle way, like some other philosophical compromises, is attractive in virtue of its attention to the phenomena on both sides of the divide, but also for that very reason in some ways elusive in terms of its own ultimate commitments.

4.6   The four causes applied: happiness and the human function

Whatever its ultimate ontological commitments, Aristotle's conception of the human soul informs much of his theorizing about human nature and human morality. Just as we see the four causes at work in Aristotle's hylomorphic conception of soul–body relations, so we see both the four causes and Aristotelian hylomorphism at work in his conception of human happiness. The result is an objectivist account of human happiness and goodness which receives most of its support from the explanatory framework in whose terms it is articulated.

Aristotle raises a simple question which ought to be considered by every reflective person: what is the ultimate good of human life? Unsurprisingly, this question has for Aristotle a teleological flavor. It is, in essence, the question of what we live for. That is, Aristotle points out, we do everything we do intentionally *for the sake of something*. We work in the evening in order to make money to continue our education. We try to educate ourselves for a variety of reasons, including, in many cases, because we wish to make ourselves fit for gainful employment. We seek employment so that we can maintain ourselves and perhaps get ahead in the world, materially speaking. All these things we do with some purpose in view.

Aristotle supposes, with some plausibility, that we do not carry on doing things forever in an effort to attain goals that are then subordinated to further end states. (Recall Plato's distinction in *Republic* ii between those things we do for their own sakes and those things we do only for the sake of other things.)[22] Instead, ultimately we have some dominant goal in mind, which is that for the sake of which we do all else. It would be odd if this goal were, for example, simply to make money, since money is an instrument and not an end: we want money for what it can do for us, not simply for the sake of having money. Instead, notes Aristotle, most people agree that our final goal is *happiness*. Still, that agreement does not amount to much, since people have different ideas about happiness. Consequently, when we say that we ultimately seek happiness, our agreement may be merely verbal. If you think happiness is the same as pleasure, if you are a *hedonist*, while your neighbor in the military thinks that happiness consists in receiving high honors and accolades, then you do not really agree about the nature of happiness. Indeed, you may be the sort of hedonist who cares only for bodily pleasures, while another sort of hedonist denies that bodily pleasures are the best sorts of pleasures, because she regards intellectual pleasures as incommensurably superior to bodily pleasures. So, we have a diversity of views falling under the same general term.

Aristotle's attitude towards this plurality of views is not terribly accommodating. First, he is no sort of *relativist* about happiness. He agrees with Plato, as against a Protagorean, that it is simply false to suppose that my happiness is simply whatever I think it is. Unless there are general reasons for being a relativist, then there seem to be no special reasons for being a relativist in this domain; as we have seen, Plato sought to show that relativism as a general doctrine seems at best marginally coherent, if not immediately self-undermining.[23] So, Aristotle supposes that a person can be wrong about what his or her happiness consists in. If that seems in any way surprising, then perhaps we need only reflect that there are a lot of unhappy people, including many who have accomplished their most central life goals. (Rock stars commonly whine about how gloomy their lives are, even though, as they will say, before they became rock stars they wanted nothing other than to be rock stars.) Moreover, Aristotle is not a *subjectivist* about happiness. That is, he denies that happiness consists in mere desire satisfaction, whatever those desires happen to be. At times, it turns out, we have desires which are perverse or silly, perhaps because they are occasioned in us by clever marketing campaigns or because of our own feelings of envy, revenge, or inadequacy. When such desires are satisfied, we end up feeling hollow, wondering why we had developed such desires in the first instance. We do not, then, regard ourselves as happy even though we have secured the objects of our desire. This suggests that mere desire satisfaction is not sufficient for happiness.

Instead, thinks Aristotle, we are happy when we have secured our real ends, those which flow from our essences as human beings. In a certain way, Aristotle is disinclined to quibble about what "happiness" means. (He is interested in the nature of *eudaimonia*, conventionally rendered as "happiness." This rendering is appropriate if we are willing at least to entertain – as indeed we really should be willing to entertain – the question of whether happiness is possibly objective and not subjective.) What Aristotle wants to know, and presumably what we want to know, is this: what is the best form of life available for human beings? What, more immediately, is the best form of life available *for me*? What is it, upon reflection, that I should pursue for its own sake, not for the sake of anything else, for which I should do other things (like earning money), and which, when secured, will make me a complete human being, lacking in nothing? Aristotle's answer: *eudaimonia*, properly understood.

The route, he thinks, to proper understanding involves an appeal to his doctrine of the four causes with a special emphasis on the role of final causation. In his *Nicomachean Ethics*, Aristotle understandably approaches the question of the best form of life for humans by appealing to final causes, since he thinks that if we want to know what constitutes goodness for a human being, then we need to uncover the function of a human being, in much the same way that we know what a good knife is by appreciating what a knife is *for*. Since a knife is for cutting, a good knife is one which cuts well. Just as there would be little point in criticizing a knife on the grounds that it does a poor job of computing π, and every point in assessing a knife's goodness in terms of its fulfilling its proper function by cutting well, so there is little point in expecting a human being to excel at something other than an essentially human activity, and every reason to determine the best form of human life by appealing to the final causes of human beings, their function or end.

Aristotle appreciates that some will be skeptical of any appeal to an objective human function. Still, he is confident that humans do have a function and that we can with reflection determine what it is:

> But perhaps saying that the highest good is happiness will appear to be a platitude and what is wanted is a much clearer expression of what this is. Perhaps this would come about if the function of a human being were identified. For just as the good, and doing well, for a flute player, a sculptor, and every sort of craftsman – and in general, for whatever has a function and a characteristic action – seems to depend upon function, so the same seems true for a human being, if indeed a human being has a function. Or do the carpenter and cobbler have their functions, while a human being has none and is rather naturally without a function? Or rather, just as there seems to be some particular function for the eye and the hand and in general for each of the parts of a human being, should one in the same way posit a particular function for the human being in addition to all these? Whatever might this be? For living is common even to plants, whereas something characteristic is wanted; so, one should set aside the life of nutrition and growth. Following that would be some sort of life of perception, yet this is also common, to the horse and the bull and to every animal. What remains, therefore, is a life of action belonging to the kind of soul that has reason.
>
> (*Nicomachean Ethics* 1097b22–1098a4)

In this passage, central to his entire ethical outlook, Aristotle shows himself sensitive to the worry voiced by many that human beings are naturally functionless, but then tries to meet this worry by demonstrating what that function might be.

There is first of all the worry already mooted that it may be inappropriate to speak of functions without also speaking of conscious designers. Now, we have seen that Aristotle does not share these reservations;[24] at this juncture, in any case, he takes himself to be at liberty at least to attempt to identify the human function, since he supposes that non-designed organisms have functions no less than artifacts or, indeed, no less than their own parts. He suggests that we should doubt that human beings have functions only if we are also prepared to doubt that, e.g., human eyes have a function. Since he takes it as obvious that they do, since eyes are *for seeing*, he attempts to identify the function of human beings as such. This attempt takes the form of his *function argument* (FA):

1 The function of any given kind x is determined by isolating x's unique and characteristic activity.
2 The unique and characteristic activity of human beings is reasoning.
3 Hence, the function of human beings is (or centrally involves) reasoning.
4 Exercising a function is an activity (where, in living beings, this will be the actualization of some capacity of the soul).
5 Hence, exercising the human function is an activity of the soul in accordance with reason.

This argument admits of a number of challenges. First, though, it should be clear that it does not by itself attempt to establish that it is possible for human organisms to have functions. Instead, this possibility is assumed as warranted by the four-causal explanatory schema and the role of teleological explanation within it.

That allowed, even if we are prepared to agree that, in principle, organisms can be teleological systems even though they are not designed, (FA) presents some formidable problems. (FA-1) may seem perverse: there may be a fair number of things which some x does uniquely, even though its doing so is hardly x's function. The function of a key is to open a lock (this we know, because we gave it this function). If it turns out that, by chance, a particular aluminum key, in virtue of its composition and configuration, does a uniquely excellent job of attracting lightning when worn on a chain around one's neck, we would be hard pressed to allow that the key's function is to electrocute by conducting lightning – and this even if it also turns out to be an exceedingly poor key, because it is inexpertly cut and so incapable of opening the lock we intended it to open.

Aristotle need not buckle before this objection. To begin, (FA-1) is a premise about *kinds* of things. If it turns out that some keys are freakish relative to the kind *being a key*, that gives us no reason to suppose that keys are for anything other than their intended functions. What is more, as we have seen, Aristotle will go so far as to deny that a key which cannot open a lock is really a key. As he prefers to say, again, such a key is a key only homonymously: we call it a key because it looks like a key, but it is a key no more than a statue of a woman is a real woman.

Moreover, it turns out that (FA-1), like much of Aristotle's function argument, is deceptively simple-sounding. In fact, Aristotle's point about *kind membership* finds support in a broad and far-reaching essentialist metaphysical thesis of his, the *functional determination thesis* (FD):

> An individual *a* is a member of a kind *K* just in case *a* manifests the capacities essential to members of *K*.
> (*Meteorologica* 390a10–15; cf. *Generation of Animals* 734b24–31, *Politics* 1253a19–25)

In so speaking, Aristotle offers a highly abstract principle of kind membership which has at least the following two defensible motivations. First, we are willing to treat as members of a single kind entities exhibiting a wide spectrum of different material constitutions and structural features: incandescent and fluorescent bulbs, halogen tubes, camp lanterns, fires, and the sun are all *lights*. There is not one material composition which all of these share. Instead, they are united by their ability to illuminate. (FD) explains why they all fall into the same category. Second, we are inclined to treat non-functioning copies of things as falling outside the class of real entities: a life-size model of the atomic bomb is not a bomb; and a decoy duck is not a duck. This too is as (FD) decrees. Something which has the outward shape of F things but cannot do what Fs do is not a real F, as Aristotle says, except homonymously, where this means that we call them "F" only by a certain kind of linguistic extension.

There is a serious question about whether (FD) is the perfectly general thesis Aristotle supposes it to be. If we assume, though, that it can in principle be generalized, then we have a theoretical reason for taking the first premise, (FA-1), of Aristotle's function argument seriously. Indeed, (FA-1) will simply be an application of the broader functional determination thesis. That then takes us to (FA-2), the substantive claim that the unique and characteristic activity of human beings is reasoning. As we have seen in our discussion of the *Categories* above,[25] Aristotle has an especially rich conception of essentialism, according to which this claim amounts to more than the mere modal commitment that without being rational, Socrates would not be human. It does entail that much, to be sure. Additionally, though, Aristotle's point is that Socrates' being rational grounds and explains, in an asymmetric way, many of his other features. So, for example, suppose we find Socrates laughing at a punning joke told by Prodicus. His laughter will be explained, ultimately, by the fact that he is a rational being. Because he is human, Socrates is able to engage in linguistic activities of a variety of sorts, and so can interpret complex syntax and grasp semantic value. When he finds some double meaning amusing, he laughs. Laughter is in this way a complex human ability, one not shared with cows or rosebushes. It is also one explained in an asymmetric way by Socrates' rationality: he has the ability to laugh because of his being rational, though we would not say he has rational faculties in virtue of his being able to laugh.

These points about Aristotle's approaches to essentialism and kind membership bear on our understanding of (FA), his function argument. They show that Aristotle is not, in (FA), merely in some superficial way noticing that humans are somehow uniquely rational and then jumping to the conclusion that rationality is the human function. Instead, he is drawing upon broader non-ethical principles he has developed and defended elsewhere. Consequently, his first important conclusion, (FA-3), that the function of human beings is (or centrally involves) reasoning, draws such support as it has from these broader principles. Accordingly, if they are defensible, so too is (FA-3). This is significant, since the remaining premise of the argument is much less controversial. (FA-4) simply observes that the exercise of reason involves *activities* of various sorts. Taken broadly, as Aristotle evidently takes it, rational activity encompasses not only thinking in the narrow sense of calculating, but also reasoning, including practical reasoning and planning, and producing, including the creation of art and literature. In some sense, the activities of the mind are all of the things we do insofar as we are human beings, the full constellation of science and speculation, of creating and sustaining friendships, business enterprises, governments, and cultural institutions. In all these ways, we exercise our specifically human function; and when we do these things well, we are happy.

Aristotle's claim, to be precise, is not that engaging in rational activity, thus construed, *makes* us happy. Instead, engaging in this sort of activity *is* what it is to be happy. This claim may jar against some natural and normal ways in which we might speak of being happy. The winner of the Tour de France naturally *feels* tired but happy, even though he is doing nothing but resting and relaxing after a month's hard work. Aristotle does not deny, of course, that such feelings of satisfaction are pleasurable. He does deny, however, that happiness – understood as the best state available to human beings – can be identified with just that state.

His reasons are three. First, and most centrally, he observes that it is incompatible with the function argument that pleasure, or warm self-regard, should be identical with happiness. Given that pleasure is common to all animals, human and non-human alike, it cannot be what is distinctively the *human* good. Pleasure does follow upon happiness, but it is not therefore identical with it. Second, feelings of warm self-regard are largely passive.

If Aristotle is right that happiness requires a life of activity in accordance with reason, then it will not do simply to regard passive states of any kind as our final good. Finally, Aristotle makes the observation that we should accept Solon's advice and "look to the end" in order to determine whether someone's life is happy. By this he means not just that we judge happiness as summed over an entire lifetime, since a life which is initially happy might be made wretched by some grievous misfortune. In addition, Aristotle means that it is inappropriate to consider only a tiny fragment of a life when we are wondering whether the person living that life is leading the best form of life available to humans. Happiness is in this way a bit like vegetarianism. I cannot determine that someone is a vegetarian merely by noticing that they have eaten no meat between breakfast and lunch. Rather, I need to determine longer-term patterns of settled behavior in order for my judgment to carry any weight. So too with happiness: fleeting feelings do not suffice for happiness.

Now, it must be said that sometimes we do refer to fleeting feelings as times of happiness. Not much really turns on whether we are prepared to use the word "happiness" to translate what Aristotle calls *eudaimonia*. What matters, substantively, is whether we are prepared to agree that the condition, characterized as it is by Aristotle, really does constitute the best form of life available to human beings. If he is right, and on the assumption that we all want what is best for ourselves, we should be prepared to follow Aristotle's prescription for attaining our final good, however we name it. As we have seen, Aristotle has himself noted that we all say we want happiness, but then go on to specify very different things when we explain what we mean, with the result that our initial agreement was merely verbal. What is wanted, he thinks, is an objective account of the human good so that we might pursue it with clear vision.

4.7   The virtues of a happy person

By introducing reason as the human function, Aristotle identifies the best form of human life as one centrally involving the expression of reason. He does not suppose, however, that just any expression of reason suffices for living well. Instead, he understandably restricts happiness to those who reason well. "The human good," he says, "turns out to be an activity of the soul expressing virtue (*aretê*)" (*EN* 1098a16–17). The activity in question is rational activity, whether narrowly theoretical or more broadly practical, and the "virtue" in question will be the form of excellence associated with the expression of either sort of reasoning.

Aristotle's speaking of "virtue" here is apt to sound a bit odd or even tendentious. Nowhere have we so far been given reason to believe that only virtuous people can be happy. This natural worry is at least partly addressed by recalling a simple linguistic observation about Aristotle's Greek that we have already encountered in connection with Plato's *Meno*.[26] The Greek word *aretê* overlaps with the English word "virtue," but is also a bit broader in its ordinary use. Indeed, if we are thinking of virtue as limited to *moral* virtue, then we miss the force of Aristotle's point. For him, virtue includes moral virtue but extends as well to other forms of human excellence. So, one might reasonably translate his contention about the human good by saying that it is "an activity of the soul expressing excellence (*aretê*)." This captures his thought that not just any kind of reasoning makes for happiness. It is rather only excellent reasoning which suffices, whether practical or theoretical. That said, the English word "virtue" suits the context, at least insofar as our conception of virtue is in fact not restricted to moral virtue: we are equally willing to assign virtues in the non-moral sphere ("One of his surpassing virtues as team captain was his ability to inspire everyone to play to their fullest potential, even when the odds looked long"). It is this broader use that equates with Aristotle's notion of *aretê*. It encompasses moral virtue narrowly conceived but embraces other forms of human excellence as well. His view, then, is that the human good consists in excellent forms of rational activity, that is, in rational activity expressing virtue.

Aristotle thus owes his readers an account of virtue. After all, since we wish to be happy, and since we are told that happiness will require rational activity of a virtuous sort, then without knowing what virtue is we will not have any reliable sense of how to attain our good.

Much of Aristotle's *Nicomachean Ethics* discharges this obligation. In fact, as already indicated, he distinguishes rational virtue into two dominant types, theoretical and practical. The theoretical sphere reflects that part of our rational activity dedicated to understanding rather than doing: when we understand mathematics or paleontology or the chord structure of a Brahms piano sonata, we are not aiming at action. Of course, the knowledge gained in this sphere may be put to use, but then we are engaged in a different sort of intellectual enterprise, namely, determining the best way to act in a given situation. Hence, Aristotle concludes: "Virtue is of two sorts, intellectual and moral" (*EN* 1103a14–16).

If we focus on the moral virtues, those pertaining to the sphere of human action, we learn how Aristotle proposes to implement the demands of his function argument (FA) in daily life. After all, he observes, the point of engaging in ethical theory is to help us become good (*EN* 1103b26–34). Although this observation may sound obvious or trivial, in fact it is contentful and crucial for our understanding of Aristotle's enterprise in ethics. He is not trying to offer a taxonomy of good and bad action, or trying to characterize in the abstract which sorts of actions are permissible, impermissible, or obligatory. He is instead trying to focus our attention on what *makes someone a good person* by describing those virtues someone must exemplify in order to be good. His is an ethics of virtue, then, where virtue ethics investigates the stable features of character exemplified by the good person, as well as the route required for their development.

Aristotle begins with a simple thought, one which will prove consequential for his entire ethical theory. If we wish to see how goodness is exemplified in a broadly functional context, he suggests, we may usefully look first to the kinds of excellence we indisputably observe in a master craftsman. When we see a beautifully crafted piece of furniture, we recognize that it not only does what it was designed and built to do, but that it does so in a manner which achieves a perfect balance: it lacks nothing it needs and is encumbered with nothing superfluous. If this is so, then adding or subtracting anything would detract from its goodness (*EN* 1106b8–16). The virtues of character, suggests Aristotle, follow suit: they achieve a mean between excess and deficiency.

Armed with this sort of conception, Aristotle is able to state his general account of the virtues of character as follows:

> Virtue is a state of the sort which issues decisions, consisting in the mean relative to us, determined by reasoning of the right sort, that is the reason in terms of which a practically wise person would determine it. It is a mean between two vices, one of excess and one of deficiency.
>
> (*EN* 1106b36–1107a6; cf. 1138b18–20)

Aristotle's doctrine of the mean specifies that in order to reach a state of virtue, a practically virtuous person needs to develop into someone who acts in a moderate and appropriate way in any given circumstance, neither shying away from what the situation requires nor overreacting by ignoring the fact that too much salt spoils the soup no less than too little.

To illustrate first with a case favorable to Aristotle's point of view, we may consider the virtue of courage.[27] What is courage? Who qualifies as courageous? First, no one is courageous unless he is in a certain kind of settled state. An habitual coward does not qualify as a courageous person simply because she manages to do a brave thing on one occasion, any more than an habitual drunkard qualifies as a sober sort of man by refraining from drink one day a year, on his mother's birthday. The particular settled state in courage is one which yields action of the right sort when circumstances demand it. If a soldier must expose herself to danger in order to achieve a noble end, then courage is required. Note, however, that courage is never foolish: courage falls on a mean between cowardice and rashness. Engaging in rash behavior is a vice no less than cowardice; it shows a lack of virtue to disregard the normal and reasonable canons of military protocol, especially to the point of endangering one's colleagues in arms. This a practically wise person would never do. So, courage is a sort of mean, falling between two vices, one of deficiency, cowardice, and one of excess, rashness.

Aristotle supposes that courage is typical of all virtuous states of character, and notes that we can consequently define the individual virtues using this same framework.[28] In general, all virtues, according to Aristotle, should answer to this basic framework. Two of its features are thus worth highlighting.

First, a virtue, as we have seen, is a settled state, a stable feature of a virtuous person's character. Since virtue ethics aims to determine what sorts of people we should wish to become, and not merely to specify whether this or that act on this or that occasion is permissible or required, this is hardly surprising. Even so, it serves to reinforce Aristotle's general approach to happiness, which is equally a theory about the best sort of life for human beings. Just as his account of happiness is not an account of what feels good from a subjective point of view at any given moment in time, but concerns rather what makes life as a whole, over time, worthwhile, so his theory of virtue deals not with the description of actions in a given moment, but focuses rather on the features of character which make a person good over the long haul.[29]

Second, when Aristotle speaks of virtue as being the sort of state determined by reason, and indeed, by the sort of reason a practically wise person would use to determine it, he is *not* saying that what makes virtue virtue is that it be chosen by the practically wise person. If he were, he might well become liable to a dilemma of the sort Euthyphro encountered when he claimed that the pious is what is loved by the gods.[30] Socrates wanted to know whether the pious is pious because it is loved by the gods or do the gods love it because it is pious. Either answer seemed to lead to difficulties. Similarly, one might be inclined to ask whether the prudentially wise chooses this particular mean because it is virtuous or is this mean virtuous because the prudentially wise person selects it? In fact, however, Aristotle is not liable to this criticism. The sense in which the practically wise person *determines* the mean is rather paradigmatic. A prudentially wise person reasons well and appropriately, and may thus be held up as a model or guide for others who are still trying to become habituated in virtue.

Here we may revert to the analogy deployed by Aristotle to launch his theory of virtue: we might say that the balance to be achieved in furniture making is the balance determined by the master craftsman. But the craftsman determines the balance because it is the balance: because he is able to recognize balance he sets the standard for the craft. In the case of craft and virtue, "determines" functions as it does in "He determined the quickest way home, given the traffic jam on the freeway." Consequently, as the craftsman serves as a model to the apprentice, so the practically wise person serves as the model to the one learning to be virtuous.

Taking that all together, Aristotle argues that happiness requires the excellent, or virtuous, expression of reason, including practical reason. To express practical reason virtuously requires the inculcation of stable traits of character capable of issuing in appropriate action in a great range of circumstances. Of course, we cannot pretend to enumerate all possible circumstances of action. Instead, suggests Aristotle, we can offer a basic framework, the doctrine of the mean, which specifies in a general way how we are to achieve virtuous characters, and then also, in keeping with our characters thus developed, to act virtuously in the conduct of our daily lives.

4.8 Aristotle's treatment of a Socratic paradox: *akrasia*

Another feature of Aristotle's theory of virtue comes to light in the context of his treatment of a Socratic paradox concerning *akrasia*, or weakness of will. As we have seen, Socrates offers an argument intended to show the impossibility of *akrasia* (IA),[31] the conclusion of which suggests, at least for hedonists, that it is never possible for a subject S to determine that some course of action A is more pleasurable than B, but to do B (knowingly and willingly) because of being overcome by pleasure. Often this conclusion is generalized to the thesis that "no one does wrong willingly" and is then reasonably regarded as paradoxical. It is a datum of our lives, distressing but a datum all the same, that we often choose some course of action, declare ourselves determined to pursue it, but then swerve at the last moment, only to feel remorse and regret thereafter. Socrates' denial of *akrasia* is paradoxical because it seems to fly in the face of this unfortunate but obvious fact.

Aristotle opens his own discussion of *akrasia* by admonishing Socrates by name, on the grounds that he "contradicts the manifest appearances" (*EN* 1145b27–28). He then attempts to address these manifest appearances by offering an account of how *akrasia* actually occurs. Surprisingly, though, he concludes his own discussion by offering a more favorable view of Socrates, even allowing that his own account in a certain way agrees with the very thing Socrates had wanted to show, namely that knowledge cannot be dragged about like a slave by the passions (*EN* 1145b324–25, 1147b15).

In the end, both Aristotle and Socrates seem to agree that for a person with secure knowledge *akrasia* is impossible or at least altogether inexplicable. Importantly, though, for Aristotle this knowledge extends to *practical knowledge*, the sort which the practically wise person manifests.

Aristotle casts his view within the context of a device he uses when thinking about human action, the practical syllogism. Although we do not need to suppose that each time we perform an intentional action we rehearse a little syllogism in our heads, Aristotle suggests that our actions at least admit of a rational reconstruction in syllogistic form. So, for example, if Edgar is getting a bit pudgy, he might come to think that sweet things are bad for his health. So, when presented with a piece of cake after an otherwise healthy dinner he will decline. His practical syllogism is the *healthy practical syllogism* (HS):

1 Unhealthy food is to be avoided.
2 This piece of cake is unhealthy.
3 Therefore, this piece of cake is to be avoided.

Again, even if he has not overtly run through this practical syllogism in his head before declining, it captures and explains his decision to refuse the offer of cake.

Of course, Edgar, like other people, is sometimes weak. Sometimes, despite his acceptance of (HS-1), he finds himself indulging in the unhealthy treat.

What has happened? One thought is that a second syllogism interposes, the *indulgent practical syllogism* (IS):

1 Sweet foods are to be enjoyed.
2 This piece of cake is sweet.
3 Therefore, this piece of cake is to be enjoyed.

Edgar then indulges and enjoys the cake, even though earlier he had embraced (HS-1) and had earnestly pledged to himself to adhere to the path of health.

What has gone wrong? Aristotle suggests that *akrasia* occurs insofar as a subject like Edgar can be described as both "knowing and not knowing" how to act (*EN* 1147b17–18). Perhaps he has knowledge but fails to use it. Or perhaps he knows something only insecurely and so has his knowledge pre-empted at the moment of action.

We may profitably think of Edgar as subject to dueling syllogisms, so to speak, one healthy and the other indulgent. It is noteworthy that the second premise of each syllogism is true, or at least plausibly taken to be true by Edgar: the piece of cake is unhealthy and the piece of cake is sweet. So, Edgar may struggle to determine which description he ought to apply to the cake at the moment it is presented to him. One description becomes salient and brings the cake under the more general premise related to that particular description; then the more general premise directs him to act in one way or another, either to avoid or to indulge. If he focuses on the unhealthy character of the cake, Edgar declines the offer. If he focuses on the sweetness of the cake, and thinks that sweet things are to be enjoyed, he sets aside the healthy syllogism. Or, perhaps, if he does nothing overtly or actively by way of setting it aside, the healthy syllogism simply remains dormant and so has no role to play in directing his action.[32] To this extent, then, Socrates was right: *akrasia* involves a knowledge failure, even if it is a more complicated sort of failure than Socrates had envisaged (*EN* 1147a14–19).

Given that virtuous action requires knowledge, and given that knowledge can be both active or inactive and both securely or insecurely developed, we can come to see how knowledge failures explain, or at least help to explain, the phenomenon of weakness of will. This is welcome, since Socrates was surely right to insist that the phenomenon is puzzling. Minimally, it seems to involve odd forms of psychic fracturing. When we experience remorse for failing to do something that we had resolved to do, the person blaming and the person being blamed are one and the same.

Socrates and Aristotle dealt with this odd phenomenon in different but related ways. Both suggest that genuinely secure knowledge renders *akrasia* impossible or at least inexplicable. This appeal to moral knowledge and epistemic security, importantly, helps us to appreciate another feature of Aristotle's theory of virtue, one that is otherwise easily missed. So far, we have been speaking as if the virtuous person is the one who does not succumb to *akrasia*, because the virtuous person does not permit his practical knowledge to be knocked aside by a desire for pleasure or gain. That is correct, but it obscures an important distinction which Aristotle is keen to draw. One might avoid *akrasia* in two ways, by being fully virtuous or by being merely continent. In our illustration, a continent person is subject to dueling syllogisms and is tempted to eat the cake even while knowing in some way that the cake is to be avoided. The continent person does the right thing. Yet, according to Aristotle, the continent person does not qualify as virtuous. Unlike the merely continent person, the virtuous person never struggles. Instead, the virtuous person performs the virtuous action easily and gladly, because it is the virtuous thing to do, and never even feels the pull of vice.

So, in Aristotle's hierarchy of character, from top to bottom we find: (i) the virtuous person; (ii) the continent person; (iii) the incontinent person; and, finally, (iv) the vicious person. The lowest on the scale is like the virtuous person in never suffering any internal strife. It is just that the virtuous person always does what is right without needing to struggle with temptation while the vicious person is wholly bestial and so simply follows his appetite for pleasure without ever reflecting on what else might be done instead. Between are two further ways of going wrong: by being incontinent, or *akratic*, or by being continent, or *enkratic*. Although it is better to be continent than *akratic*, neither qualifies as virtuous in Aristotle's account.

Aristotle's hierarchy thus serves to reinforce a central feature of his virtue ethics. Ultimately his theory of virtue is developed in service of his functionally driven approach to happiness, or *eudaimonia*. Consequently, the primary question he is asking does not concern the criteria for determining rightness or wrongness in action – though, to be sure, the virtuous person will act rightly and will do the good thing at each moment. Rather, Aristotle is primarily concerned with the prior question of what makes a good person good, how the good person expresses practical rationality virtuously, or excellently. To do so, as Aristotle's approach to *akrasia* underscores, it is necessary to act from a firmness of character developed through long habituation and training. A virtuous person is like a skilled violinist. After having learnt the scales of virtue by acting at first hesitantly and insecurely, looking to the practically wise person as a model and guide, the fully virtuous person acts with a glad ease, without hesitation, without internal struggle, and with every cause for confidence.

4.9   Aristotle on philosophical analysis: homonymy

In thinking about Aristotle's ethical theory, we have made free use of such terms as *good, virtue*, and *courage*. If we think back to Socrates' discussions with Euthyphro and Meno, as we have had occasion to do in connection with Aristotle's conception of the practically wise person, we will recall that the Socratic impulse for analysis manifested itself in the demand that virtue terms be defined univocally, that is, that each virtue term be given some one essence-specifying non-disjunctive account.[33] Thus, when Meno offered a whole variety of different virtues – one for men, one for women, one for children, one for slaves, and so on – Socrates was displeased. He responded that he was seeking the single feature that all instances of virtue had in common, that feature which made all the types of virtue virtuous. In return, Meno offered no resistance. He simply acquiesced and tried to offer Socrates what he demanded, namely a univocal account of virtue.

Strikingly, Aristotle has some sympathy for Meno's initial point of view. He does not think that we should presuppose that there is a single, non-disjunctive definition available for each core philosophical notion we might wish to investigate. On the contrary, he frequently assails the Socratic univocity assumption, by contending that various terms are "meant in many ways" or, more technically, are "homonymous." We have already encountered an instance in which Aristotle was prepared to call non-real instances of a kind F only "homonymously" F. His language in this regard is fairly technical in the sense that it appropriates a common word and then partially extends and renders precise its meaning by stipulation. (In juridical contexts "person" functions in this way, as when a tort lawyer speaks of corporations as "legal persons".) Aristotle's appropriation of this particular word, which means simply "having the same name as" has a special significance, since it reflects a deeply held and interesting attitude towards philosophical analysis which is deeply at variance with the approaches assumed by both Socrates and Plato. Aristotle speaks, in his technical way, of two things being homonymous when they have the same names but differ in their accounts. This can happen in some obvious ways, but also in some surprising ways as well.

It is obvious that we call a statue of a man and man "man" in different senses. One, the living human being, is a man because it manifests the essential qualities of humanity. The other, the statue, does not manifest these qualities. A statue cannot think or emote or perceive or do any of the things living systems do. So, a statue is not strictly or literally "a man." In these sorts of cases, Aristotle says, the statue is a man *only homonymously*. For the most part, though, his interest in homonymy becomes philosophically interesting only when we notice that in some important analytical contexts, Aristotle appeals to homonymy in an effort to undercut the very possibility of Platonic or Socratic definitions. We saw from the very beginning of the Socratic impulse for analysis that Socrates expected adequate responses to the *What is F-ness?* question to be univocal, epistemically serviceable, and more than extensionally adequate.[34] Of special relevance to Aristotelian homonymy is the first of these conditions, the univocity assumption, that philosophical definitions must be both fully general and unified. So, when Socrates had asked Meno to provide an account of *aretê* (virtue or excellence), and Meno responded that he could recount all of the different kinds of *aretê*, those belonging to men, to women, to the elderly, to children, and to slaves, Socrates remarked that he felt overrun by a plethora of virtues, as by a swarm of bees. What he wanted from Meno was the single form of virtue, as from Euthyphro he had wanted the single form of piety, that in virtue of which we call all virtuous or pious actions virtuous or pious. While both Euthyphro and Meno acceded to the request, evidently because upon reflection they too shared in the univocity assumption, Aristotle is not so sanguine. Indeed, Aristotle thinks that in very many contexts, Meno's initial inclination was actually preferable. This is because for a great many philosophical concepts, including some of central importance from antiquity to the present, the univocity assumption is misguided.

Aristotle will press his point first by appealing to some ordinary linguistic data. Now, Aristotle most certainly does not think that this sort of appeal wins the day, since he rightly insists we have a genuine instance of homonymy only when we have established a genuine difference in account. Put slightly more formally, Aristotle holds the *principle of homonymy*:

> *x* and *y* are homonymously F if, and only if, (1) *x* is F; (2) *y* is F; and the accounts of F-ness in '*x* is F' and '*y* is F' do not completely overlap.

In order to provide an account in the relevant sense, it is necessary to do more than appeal to mere lexical meaning. Instead, in order to make an appeal to homonymy stick, it will be necessary to do a good bit of philosophical analysis, in order to show that Socrates cannot have what he wants because in fact, for example, there is not one account of *aretê* available.

That said, Aristotle quite appropriately begins with some appeals to linguistic intuition, since these same intuitions may also reflect some deeper, less easily discernible differences. To take one of Aristotle's most famous and engaging examples, we may consider his attitude towards Plato's celebrated appeal to the Form of the Good in the *Republic*,[35] which Form is presumed to be the very essence of Goodness, that in virtue of which all good things are good, because of their participating in it. Now, though, consider the variety of things people call good in the following sentences, which could be multiplied several times over with no difficulty:

1 God is good.
2 My burrito is especially good.
3 The film was predictable, though the ending was good.
4 What that boy needs is a good talking to.
5 She means well; she has a good heart.
6 No good will come of it.
7 Good effort!
8 If you want a good time, try bungee jumping.
9 No good deed goes unpunished.
10 A sound investment guarantees a good rate of return.

If we survey even briefly the variety of good things mentioned in this list, suggests Aristotle, we will soon see that there is no lone thing, Goodness, which they all share. So, the univocity assumption is implausible. Hence, if philosophers persist in assuming it, their efforts are bound to be a fruitless waste of time.

Now, these distinct varieties of goodness create a presumption of non-univocity. It is hard to appreciate what it is that God, burritos, and rates of return are supposed to have in common. The case seems rather to be that God's goodness is a divine attribute of some sort, that goodness in a burrito consists in its being tasty or nutritious, while goodness in a rate of return involves a relatively favorable profit margin. Surely, profit margins, flavors, and divine attributes are different sorts of things. With this in mind, Aristotle suggests a kind of *paraphrase test* for determining homonymy: if it is possible to substitute paraphrases of some predicate *F* across a range of its applications while retaining both truth and good sense, then we will likely not have a case of homonymy; but otherwise we will. To illustrate using the case at hand, focusing on just a subset of our examples:

Original	*Paraphrase*
God is good.	God is supremely virtuous.
My burrito is good.	My burrito is tasty and nutritious.
The investment is a good one.	The investment is profitable.

Clearly enough, these paraphrases are non-equivalent. This becomes clearer still if we try to substitute one paraphrase for another. Any such attempt yields sentences that are obviously false or straightforwardly nonsensical ("My burrito is supremely virtuous," "The investment is tasty and nutritious"). Given that the paraphrases of instances of the predicate "good" are diverse and cannot be inter-substituted, suggests Aristotle, the meanings of "good" in the original cases must in fact also be distinct. If so, then, we may conclude, there is no one thing, Goodness, in virtue of which all of these good things are good. If that in turn is right, then the Socratic and Platonic univocity assumption will prove unsustainable.

This would be quite an important result for Aristotle: it threatens to render pointless a central feature of the Socratic mission, and with it, a governing assumption of a great deal of philosophical investigation since Socrates. The impulse for analysis, for better or worse, is endemic to philosophy. That said, in determining whether Socrates and Plato are ultimately vulnerable to Aristotle's objection, it will not suffice merely to rest with this sort of appeal to linguistic intuition, even when it is done up into Aristotle's paraphrase test. For at this juncture Plato may legitimately respond that there is yet possibly a *higher-order* notion of goodness which all good things share, the general form of goodness which is captured in the Form of the Good. The case may be analogous, that is, to the condition of *being an animal*, something which Aristotle himself regards as perfectly univocal. It is true, Plato may concede, that tigers, snakes, and human beings are all different kinds of animals, even though, he may plausibly insist, what it is for them to be animals is the same in each case. If being an animal is in the relevant way comparable to being good, then Plato will have a response to Aristotle's appeal to homonymy in this context. Of course, to make good on this comparison, Plato will have to provide the actual analysis in plain terms, something he found himself incapable of doing when he approached the subject in the *Republic*.

The matter does not end there, though. Importantly, Aristotle thinks he has a more abstract and compelling argument for the non-univocity of goodness than his simple paraphrase test. Just before advancing his function argument in the *Nicomachean Ethics*, Aristotle pauses to consider Plato's appeal to the Form of the Good, in an effort to determine whether there is some one notion of Goodness common to everything which is good. His reasons for doing so are appropriate: he is in this work seeking to uncover the nature of happiness, the highest good for human beings; if it turns out that there is a general all-encompassing notion of goodness, then it will turn out that the human good is simply a special case of it. Hence, an inquiry into human happiness will perforce cross over into an analysis of goodness as such, just as, in fact, transpires in Plato's *Republic*.

Aristotle thinks he can show that there is not a single form of goodness common to all good things. Even among things good for humans, such as pleasure, intelligence, and honor, he finds differences in account, and so non-univocity. His point is not just that the accounts of honor, intelligence, and pleasure diverge, but that what it is for these states to be good, the ways in which they are good for us, differs from case to case. Strikingly, in assailing the univocity of goodness, Aristotle makes a high-level appeal to his own doctrine of categories.[36] He claims, in his preferred terminology, that "goodness is spoken of in as many ways as being is." He means that goodness marches in step with being: just as what it is to be a substance differs from what it is to be a quantity, quality, relative, and so forth, so goodness differs in these various categories. In the category of time, for example, being opportune (or "timely", as we say) is good; in the category of substance, being God is good; in the category of quality, being virtuous is good. Since these are all distinct, it will also turn out that goodness is discrete across the categories. So, contrary to Plato's assumption, goodness is non-univocal.

Put schematically, Aristotle's argument for the homonymy of goodness (HG) is simple and intriguing, but controversial:

1   Goodness is spoken of in as many ways as being is.
2   Being is non-univocal.
3   So, goodness is non-univocal.

The argument relies on just two premises. (HG-1) tries to force a parallel between being and goodness, in the sense that each is a very high-level and general term. (HG-2) then appeals to the doctrine of the categories, a doctrine which is here assumed without argumentation, by pointing out that the highest-level taxonomical kinds, the category heads themselves, have nothing in common. There is no further genus which unites them, in the way that the genus *animal* unites horses, fish, tigers, and humans. If that is correct, then if the parallel asserted in (HG-1) obtains, Aristotle will have a formidable argument against a Platonic assumption of univocity.

Now, to determine whether Plato should accede to both (HG-1) and (HG-2) is a daunting matter. It will involve not only an inquiry into the doctrine of categories as such, an inquiry which already involves extraordinarily complex metaphysical questions, but also an inquiry into the parallels Aristotle sees between being and goodness as taxonomical terms. Here too the matter turns enormously abstract extremely quickly. Still, (HG) at least provides a framework of inquiry, one which a neutral third party can embrace when investigating Aristotle's anti-Platonism about goodness. It is also a framework which takes us well beyond Aristotle's paraphrase test, which, though attractive in its simplicity, could never deliver a final determination in one direction or the other.

Wherever that inquiry ultimately leads, it is important not to pursue it in such a way as to neglect a second feature of Aristotelian homonymy, one whose neglect would totally undermine an adequate understanding of his general approach to philosophical analysis. So far, we have seen that homonymy is sufficient for non-univocity. To this extent, it is primarily a negative and destructive notion. Plato or Socrates, or anyone given to the Socratic impulse for analysis, assumes univocity of F-ness; Aristotle deploys an argument to show that F-ness is actually homonymous and so non-univocal; if he is right, there is no point in engaging in Socratic- or Platonic-style inquiry. Now, significantly, Aristotle does not suppose that success in establishing non-univocity signals the end of analysis altogether. That is, he thinks that in some cases, even if F-ness is homonymous, there may nevertheless be room for constructive analysis. In this respect, his views need to be sharply distinguished from some twentieth-century philosophers who, following Wittgenstein's lead, thought that non-univocity by itself sufficed to undermine philosophical analysis. According to these philosophers, the most we ever really discover when we look hard at core philosophical concepts is a kind of "family resemblance," that is, the sort of resemblance the members of a family bear to one another. We notice, for example, that all the Wilson children resemble one another, even though there is no one feature which all and only the Wilsons display. In this sort of case, we see a series of criss-crossing resemblances which mark them as members of the same family, even though we cannot point to some single distinguishing mark. Using this model, Wittgenstein suggested that the property of *being a game* exhibited only family resemblance: there are no necessary and sufficient conditions for qualifying as a game, though we can still recognize all the activities we call games as games. After all, for instance, chess and rugby are both games; but it is difficult to see what they have in common which other rule-governed forms of organized activities which are not games do not. (The philatelic society meets in accordance with their rules, but their meetings are not games.) That perhaps is to be expected, since games are in every case conventionally determined. Matters become more interesting when a claim of family resemblance is exported to the sorts of concepts whose essence Socrates and Plato sought to capture. If we say that *goodness* or *beauty* or *piety* are mere family resemblance concepts, then we explicitly reject the univocity assumption and accuse Socrates and Plato of wasting their time and ours when they assume it.

Aristotle does not himself adopt this sort of arch attitude, because he does not regard homonymy as purely destructive, as Wittgensteineans regard appeals to family resemblance. Rather, if we place univocity at one end of the spectrum and family resemblance at the other, then we can find Aristotle as positioning himself in the middle when he claims that some instances of homonymy exhibit a special feature of *core-dependence*. Typically, Aristotle illustrates his notion of core-dependent homonymy by appealing to what should be an uncontroversial instance of the phenomenon. Consider the following sentences:

1   Socrates is healthy.
2   Socrates' complexion is healthy.
3   Socrates' exercise regimen is healthy.
4   Socrates' dinner is healthy.

Aristotle supposes that two things should be clear about these sentences: (a) the predicate "is healthy" is non-univocal in these applications; but nevertheless (b) the predicates in these applications are systematically related to one another.

That health is homonymous seems to follow from the fact that the account of health in the case of complexions is distinct from the account in the other cases. A complexion's being healthy consists in its being indicative of health; a regimen's being healthy is rather its being productive of health; and Socrates' being healthy is his being well and illness-free. If we are willing to grant that much, we have concluded that health is homonymous and so non-univocal. Now comes Aristotle's distinctive positive suggestion, that health is a *core-dependent homonym*. This constructive thought seems to follow from the fact that the accounts of *being healthy*, as it occurs in (2)–(4), all make an ineliminable appeal to the notion of health in (1), which Aristotle regards as the core instance. So, for example, a dinner is healthy because it is *productive or preservative* of health: that is, of the state which (1) holds Socrates to enjoy. So too a healthy complexion is one which is *indicative of health*, that same state (1) ascribes to Socrates. Moreover, in order to provide an account of (1), we do not need to appeal in any way, implicitly or explicitly, to the notions of health as they appear in (2)–(4). Taken together, these observations suggest that (2)–(4) asymmetrically depend on (1) for their analyses. So, they are non-core instances clustered around the core instance of health. Hence, *health* is a core-dependent homonym.

Now, just as an observation about the nature of games has little philosophical relevance until it is generalized, so Aristotle's appeal to health as a core-dependent homonym will hold little interest until we find him suggesting that core philosophical concepts often behave as health does. Strikingly, Aristotle makes just such a claim in the case of a host of concepts, including *justice*, *cause*, *necessity*, *friendship*, and even the highly abstract notions of *goodness* and *being* itself. His remarks in these regards become relevant not only to our eventual appraisal of Plato's commitment to philosophical analysis, but to a great many contemporary inquiries, ranging over a host of topics, including the nature of mind, causation, consciousness, justice, identity, and knowledge. For many contemporary philosophers assume univocity no less than Plato did; the very impulse for analysis which originated with Socrates continues to animate philosophical inquiry today. Aristotle's appeal to core-dependent homonymy is partly critical of this impulse, but ultimately accommodating. Though central philosophical concepts may display more heterogeneity than supporters of univocity would like to allow, they may nonetheless exhibit more unity, order and structure than permitted by the friends of family resemblance. Core-dependent homonymy provides for a form of positive philosophical theorizing even in the face of challenges to the sort of philosophical unity Socrates sought.

4.10   Conclusions

By the time we find Aristotle appealing to the phenomenon of core-dependent homonymy, we have traveled an impressive distance from the earliest natural philosophers, the materialist monists, who were content to postulate explanations which may now seem simple to the point of being simple-minded: that everything is water, for example. Even those earliest philosophers, however, responded to perplexing features within the manifest image of the world by advancing theories which, however quaint they may now seem, are also arrestingly modern in their implicit endorsements of parsimony, naturalism, and rational explanatory coherence. Socrates, Plato, and Aristotle all, in different ways, share in their early optimism: philosophical progress is possible – though, given the abstract and demanding nature of the enterprise, never easy. But the prize beckons. "Human beings began to do philosophy," says Aristotle, "even as they do now, because of wonder, at first because they wondered about the strange things right in front of them, and later, advancing little by little, because they came to find greater things puzzling." Indeed, "Someone who wonders thinks he is ignorant ... and engages in philosophy to escape ignorance." Eventually, though, we come out of our ignorance and into a contrary state, a state almost divine, as Socrates had thought, a state of knowledge which, Aristotle observes rather unassumingly, "is better."[37]

Notes

1 Cicero, *Academica* 38.119; cf. *Topica* 1.3; *De Oratore* 1.2.49. Aristotle mentions "exoteric" writings (intended for a popular audience), presumably of his own composition, at *Politics* 1278b30, and *Eudemian Ethics* 1217b22, 1218b34.
2 *Metaphysics* 995a27.
3 *Topics* 100b21–2.
4 For Plato's conception of the relations between Forms and particulars, see 3.5 and 3.6.
5 Plato's conception of Forms as necessarily existing emerges, for example, in his existence argument of *Republic* v. On this argument, see 3.5.
6 See *Categories* 5, especially 2b5–7.
7 *Physics* ii 4.
8 On Parmenides' arguments for the impossibility of motion, see 1.4.
9 See *Physics* 190b2 on the impossibility of generation *ex nihilo*.
10 It is worth noting that Aristotle also uses the apparatus of form and matter to reject Parmenides' argument for the non-existence of change. As we have seen, Aristotle thinks that Parmenides is right to question the possibility of generation *ex nihilo*. Still, Parmenides was wrong when he tried to infer from this fact that all change was impossible. For it is compatible with the truth of the claim that there is no generation *ex nihilo* that things nevertheless change by the loss and acquisition of forms. In effect, Aristotle shows how the apparatus of matter and form undermines Parmenides' argument against change and generation, and in particular premises (AAC-2) and (AAC-4) in the argument presented in 1.4. We can think of generation without thinking of generation *ex nihilo*, since generation involves the persistence of some matter. And we are wrong to attempt a reduction of qualitative change to generation, since not all form acquisition results in the generation of a new entity.
11 See, e.g., *Physics* 254a30, where Aristotle claims that it is an exercise in judgment to demand an argument for the claim that some things are in motion. It does not follow from his attitude towards those with bad judgment that he thinks no such argument can be given. On the contrary, he himself provides one.
12 Aristotle provides this sort of argument against Parmenides at *Physics* 254a23–31. Cf. *Physics* 253a32–b6.
13 See *Metaphysics* iv 4 for Aristotle's dialectical defense of the principle of non-contradiction.
14 For Aristotle's conception of homonymy and its role in philosophical argumentation, see 4.9.
15 On Democritean atomism, see 1.5.
16 *Physics* ii 8.
17 *Parts of Animals* 657a25–657b4.
18 These considerations combine discussions from *Metaphysics* vii 17 and *De Generatione et Corruptione* i 5.
19 On atomism, see 1.5.
20 See *De Anima* 413a3–10.
21 See *De Anima* 429a13–28, 429b22–4 as well as the whole of *De Anima* iii 5.
22 Plato's distinction is in fact threefold. See 3.7 above for a discussion.
23 On Plato's treatment of Protagorean relativism, see 3.4. Aristotle adopts a similar posture in *Metaphysics* 1007b19–1008a7.
24 See 4.4 for a discussion of Aristotle's conception of designerless final causes in nature.
25 On the *Categories*, see 4.2 above.
26 See 2.2 for a discussion of *aretê* in connection with Meno and the Platonic univocity assumption.
27 Aristotle discusses the virtue of courage in *Nicomachean Ethics* iii 6.
28 For a clear discussion of the individual virtues expressed in terms of their relative excesses and deficiencies, see Miller, Fred D., "Aristotle's Ethics and Politics," in C. Shields, ed., *The Blackwell Guide to Ancient Philosophy* (Blackwell, 2002), pp. 184–210.

29 On Aristotle's account of happiness (*eudaimonia*), see 4.6.
30 On Euthyphro's dilemma, see 2.2.
31 For (IA), together with a discussion of Socrates' denial of *akrasia*, see 2.4.
32 Aristotle suggests that the particular premise, the second in our two opposing syllogisms, "controls the action" (*EN* 1147b10–11).
33 On the Socratic univocity assumption, see 2.2.
34 On Socrates' conception of adequacy in definition, see 2.2. On Plato's maintenance of Socrates' strictures, see 3.7.
35 For Plato's treatment of the Form of the Good in the analogy of the sun, see 3.8.
36 On Aristotle's introduction of categories, see 4.2 above.
37 *Metaphysics* 982b12–20, 982b29–983a12, 983a19.
38 Numbers in brackets refer to the comprehensive Suggestions for Further Reading compiled at the end of this book.

Suggestions for additional readings

Primary text

Aristotle's complete works are available in a convenient two-volume set:

Barnes, J. (ed.) *The Complete Works of Aristotle: The Revised Oxford Translation*, 2 vols (Princeton: Princeton University Press, 1984).

Two very reliable collections of selected works, including all of those most read by students are:

Ackrill, J. (ed.) *A New Aristotle Reader* (Oxford: Oxford University Press, 1987).
Irwin, T. and Fine, G. (trans.) *Aristotle: Selections*, with introduction, notes, and glossary (Cambridge, MA: Hackett, 1995).

The glossary of Aristotelian vocabulary in [75][38] is excellent: well informed, usefully precise, and pedagogically alert. Students will find it especially helpful when conducting primary research in Aristotle's philosophy.

The Clarendon Aristotle Series from Oxford University Press is an excellent series of translations with commentaries and notes for students interested in pursuing Aristotle's philosophy. Some volumes related to themes discussed in the text are:

Metaphysics Z and H, trans. D. Bostock with commentary (Oxford: Oxford University Press, 1994).
Physics I and II, trans. W. Charlton with introduction and notes (Oxford: Oxford University Press, 1984).
De Anima, trans. D. Hamlyn with notes (Oxford: Oxford University Press, 1995).
Categories and De Interpretatione, trans. J. Ackrill with notes (Oxford: Oxford University Press, 1962).
De Generatione et Corruptione, trans. C. Williams with notes (Oxford: Oxford University Press, 1982).

Other volumes in the same series are usefully consulted for topics not covered in the text.

Many students have their first extended exposure to Aristotle by reading his *Nicomachean Ethics*. The best translation, which also includes an extremely helpful glossary together with a set of explanatory notes is:

Irwin, T., *Aristotle, The Nicomachean Ethics* (Cambridge, MA: Hackett, 1985).

Secondary literature

As with Socrates and Plato, the contemporary literature on Aristotle runs into thousands of books and articles. Much of this literature is technical and unsuited for all but advanced students. There are, however, a number of clear and accessible introductions. The best are:

Ackrill, J., *Aristotle the Philosopher* (Oxford: Oxford University Press, 1981).
Barnes, J., *Aristotle* (Oxford: Oxford University Press, 1982).
Lear, J., *Aristotle: The Desire to Understand* (Cambridge: Cambridge University Press, 1988).
Ross, W., *Aristotle* (London: Methuen, 1923).
Shields, C., *Aristotle* (London and New York: Routledge, 2007).

A classic on the question of Aristotle's development as a thinker is:

Jaeger, W., *Aristotle: Fundamentals of the History of His Development*, trans. by R. Robinson, with author's corrections and additions (Oxford: Oxford University Press, 1948).

Some useful anthologies include:

Barnes, J., *The Cambridge Companion to Aristotle* (Cambridge: Cambridge University Press, 1995).
This volume is especially useful for students on some topics and contains a full bibliography for further study.
Barnes, J., Schofield, M., and Sorabji, R. (eds) *Articles on Aristotle. 1: Science* (London: Duckworth, 1975).
Barnes, J., Schofield, M., and Sorabji, R. (eds) *Articles on Aristotle. 2: Ethics and Politics* (London: Duckworth, 1976).
Barnes, J., Schofield, M., and Sorabji, R. (eds) *Articles on Aristotle. 3: Metaphysics* (London: Duckworth, 1979).
Barnes, J., Schofield, M., and Sorabji, R. (eds) *Articles on Aristotle. 4: Psychology and Aesthetics* (London: Duckworth, 1975).

5 Hellenistic philosophy

5.1 The Hellenistic period

Earlier generations found it easy to suppose that Aristotle's death in 322 BC marked the beginning of a long-lasting philosophical decline. So, for instance, even despite his own searing criticisms of Aristotle, Bertrand Russell contended that "after his death it was two thousand years before the world produced any philosopher who could be regarded as approximately his equal."[1] While not mentioning the philosopher equal to Aristotle by name, Russell intentionally overlooks *all* of the towering figures of medieval philosophy as well as those of the highly sophisticated and permanently influential schools which flourished in the ancient world after the end of the Classical period. These were the schools of the Hellenistic period whose names worked their way into our own present-day popular vocabulary: the Epicureans, the Stoics, and the Skeptics.

It is true that Aristotle's death coincided with significant shifts in the Greek world, shifts eventuating in both development and decline. When Alexander the Great died in 321 BC, the year before Aristotle's own death, pan-Hellenic relations altered in a variety of ways. Notably, the Athenian dominance that had already begun to ebb before the rise of Macedonian power under Alexander further dissipated after his death. More generally, the power and pre-eminence of long-established city-states throughout the Greek world diminished in consequential ways in this period. These shifts in political relations mark the end of the Classical period, which had attained a philosophical high point in the towering figures of Socrates, Plato, and Aristotle.

Although it has been tempting for historians of philosophy to suppose otherwise, the political and social reconfigurations following the end of the Classical period did not issue in any general decline in philosophy. The first thing to appreciate about Hellenistic philosophy is that the tart dismissal of the philosophical work of the period offered by Russell and his ilk are impossible to sustain and difficult even to take seriously any longer. To some extent, perhaps, deprecation of Hellenistic philosophy was more understandable a few generations ago than it is today. To the extent that this is so, however, it is only because until fairly recently all but the most serious and well-equipped historians of philosophy were largely ignorant of what the Hellenistic philosophers actually held, and even, to a certain degree, who they were. Many figures of this period – including Zeno of Citium, Chysippus, Carneades, and Arcesilaus – were obscure or unknown; and indeed even today these philosophers are hardly the sorts of household names that Socrates, Plato, and Aristotle have become.

The relative obscurity of the philosophers of the Hellenistic period derives in part from the unhappy history of their writings. In contrast to Plato, whose works, uniquely for a major author of antiquity, survived in their entirety, and also to Aristotle, whose works survived incompletely but extensively,[2] no author of the Hellenistic period enjoys an enviable fate with respect to the survival of his writings. Unfortunately, we have almost no complete works surviving from this period. Instead we have for the most part only fragments quoted by later authors, paraphrases of principal doctrines preserved by doxographers (that is, authors who took it upon themselves simply to report the views of early writers), and discussions by later thinkers, as often as not philosophers unsympathetic to the views they were recounting. In quite a few instances, in fact, later philosophers deigned to reproduce the views of the Hellenistic thinkers only in polemical tracts composed solely for the purpose of refuting their views, so that we find their reports laced with ridicule. While we can nevertheless learn a great deal from such sources, a fair bit of cautious and deliberate intellectual archeology must be undertaken before serious philosophical appraisal can begin.

Fortunately, although research remains ongoing, much of this work has now been completed to an impressive standard. Consequently, we currently find ourselves in an exciting time regarding Hellenistic philosophy.[3] As odd as it may sound, we are in fact probably better placed at present to assess the views of the Hellenistic philosophers than at any time since their first formulations. Only within the last generation or two have we been in a position to come to reasonably firm judgments about the principal doctrines and developments of the individual schools, though of course questions of detail and judgments of ultimate purport remain subjects of lively debate. In the current presentation, we will recapitulate some of the most distinctive views of the Hellenistic philosophers, highlighting what is striking and challenging about them, and, where fruitful, contrasting them with the philosophers of the Classical period so far encountered.

As we approach the philosophy of the Hellenistic period, a cautious orienting generalization is apposite, whether or not we presume that the political instabilities and transitions of the period help to explain the developments in philosophy we observe: philosophy in the Hellenistic period takes an inward-looking, practical turn. Although Plato and Aristotle most definitely engage in practical philosophy in very serious ways – Plato's *Republic* concerns the question of why we should wish to be just,[4] while Aristotle's *Nicomachean Ethics* investigates human happiness with an eye towards characterizing the best form of life available to us[5] – both authors also pursue other forms of knowledge for their own sakes. Indeed, having divided branches of knowledge into the theoretical, practical, and productive, Aristotle states plainly that the highest form of human knowledge is theoretical rather than practical or productive.[6] By contrast, each of the principal schools of the Hellenistic period treats the point of philosophy as something overwhelmingly practical: we engage in philosophy, ultimately, so that we might live well, with the result that theory, however technical it may need to become, is expressly subordinated to this end and always serves this goal.

That said, two points of caution are immediately crucial, lest any misleading inference be drawn from this generalization. First, it should not be thought that the various schools of thought in this period self-consciously agree with one another about the pre-eminence of practical philosophy or, still less, that they endorse a single view about the best way to achieve success in life through philosophy. On the contrary, as we shall see, they diverge sharply on this topic, not only with the philosophers who came before them, but also with one another. Second, and more importantly, neither should it be supposed that the philosophy of this period becomes less technical or less demanding than it was in the hands of Plato and Aristotle. For, on the contrary, it becomes in many ways more technical and in equally many ways still more demanding. So, to the extent that this orienting generalization is true, it masks one of the significant and exciting intellectual aspects of this period: precisely because their recommendations for living well diverge so sharply, some of the philosophers of the Hellenistic period found it necessary to develop sophisticated systems of logic, and all three principal schools did strikingly original work in epistemology and philosophy of mind.

This is best appreciated by distinguishing the distinctive routes through which each of these schools recommends that human happiness be attained: (i) the Epicureans, followers of Epicurus (341–270); (ii) the Stoics, the most extensive and far-reaching school of the Hellenistic period; and (iii) the Skeptics, a loosely connected but persistent band of inquirers dedicated to the contention that happiness follows upon the suspension of all intellectual commitment.[7] Although none of these three schools is at all monolithic, each admits of a contentful core characterization in terms of its conception of the most secure path to happiness.

The Epicureans are hedonists who contend that happiness consists in pleasure; that pleasure consists in the absence of pain; and that a good deal of pain is caused by wholly avoidable mental disturbance. One key to human happiness, according to the Epicureans, consists in our coming to a proper understanding of the nature of the physical universe and humanity's place within it. As Epicurus sees things, the physical universe *is* the universe: beyond the ultimate atomic physical constituents and what they compose, there is nothing.

So, already we find the Epicureans sharply rejecting two central doctrines advanced in the Classical period, namely Plato's theory of Forms[8] and Aristotle's anti-hedonistic conception of happiness.[9] The Epicureans deny the existence of perception-transcendent entities of the sort Plato's Forms are alleged to be; and they think that happiness has more to do with the internal states of individual perceivers than with any objectively given framework of the sort underwriting Aristotle's function argument.[10] Instead, the Epicurean recipe for human happiness involves our coming to minimize pain and maximize pleasure – but this manifestly does *not* mean, as we shall see, that we should seek to lead sumptuous lives, as the contemporary eponymous adjective "epicurean" would have it. On the contrary, Epicureanism eschews rather than extols opulent pleasure.

Epicurus counsels us to seek only those pleasures least likely to elude us, simple pleasures which flow from satisfying desires which are both natural and necessary. We should, he urges, set aside our many very real but entirely unnecessary desires; such desires – desires for fame, immortality, conspicuous consumption – are artificially induced and can be seen to be, upon even a moment's reflection, entirely optional. Such desires prove to be nothing more than psychological dead weight, useless baggage weighing us down on our journey to happiness and best jettisoned once identified. The chore of determining which desires are necessary and which optional thus proves to be one of the first tasks of Epicureanism.

The Stoics do not approve of Epicurean-style hedonism, no matter how austere that hedonism may prove. Rather, and surprisingly, they hold that the sole human good is *virtue*, echoing Socrates, and thereby discounting all of the other sorts of things normally counted as good and desirable – pleasure, material comfort, money, family, reputation and even health. Although they will agree that many such items might be on occasion preferred or selected by the fully committed Stoic, strictly the mature Stoic will remain indifferent to all such attractions, because they have no share in human goodness. Human goodness resides in virtue alone.

To complicate matters, the Stoic account of virtue appears initially idiosyncratic, even odd: virtue consists in living in accordance with nature, or, more fully, in assenting only to what is given by nature, in accepting the universe as it is, rather than by striving fruitlessly to alter the way things are. Only unhappiness awaits those who rage against the inevitable; those discontent with their lot permit themselves to become foolishly angered or saddened by developments beyond their control. Thus, the goal of human life, its end, is virtue – and virtue consists in accommodating oneself to what is. To some extent, then, the eponymous adjectives "stoic" and "stoical," as they are used today, do derive from authentically Stoic positions; but these words are misleading if they are taken to imply that to attain happiness the Stoics require a grim or fatalistic acceptance of what one cannot alter.

Partly because of their drive to live in accordance with nature, the Stoics developed highly technical theories of logic and epistemology. For, naturally enough, successful accommodation with the world requires that one first determine how the world in fact is, which in turn requires differentiating how it appears from how it lies behind its appearances: things are not always as they seem. The manifest image of the world is not the world.

The Hellenistic Skeptics seized upon this latter fact and used it to bedevil especially the Stoics, but also all others they regarded as *dogmatists*. According to the Skeptics, a dogmatist is anyone who thinks she has a sufficient grasp of the world that she can say with confidence how things really are in distinction to how they appear. As the Skeptics observed, even according to the dogmatists' own contentions, living well requires being able to distinguish appearance from reality. After all, the Epicureans need to be able to distinguish false pleasures from true pleasures; and the Stoics, if they are to be able to assent to the world as it is, must first be able to distinguish what is real from what merely appears to be the case. The Skeptics contend that we are never in a position to make these sorts of determinations.

Happily, though, according to the Skeptics, there is an upside to our inability: once we realize that humans are never in a position to know how the world is in itself, we stop striving; we suspend all claims to knowledge and even to belief, and begin to live guided by appearances alone. When we do so, a great serenity descends upon us (they use the same word that the Epicureans use for this welcome state: *ataraxia*, that is, tranquility or freedom from strife). Life offers us perfect tranquility if only we relinquish our vain and ineffectual pretensions to dogmatism.

To this extent, then, the Hellenistic schools do become inward looking and practical, but only in an expansive sort of way. Each school in its own way counsels that we reflect upon the suitability of our desires, beliefs, hopes, and emotions; and each recommends that we come to a form of accommodation with the world. Each then also theorizes about the nature of desire and emotion, and, more generally, about appearance and reality. As we have started to appreciate already, however, their approaches to these topics, along with their routes to world-accommodation, diverge in fundamental ways. For more specificity about how their individual programs develop, we may now turn to the three principal schools in turn.

5.2   The Epicureans

More than the other two primary movements of the Hellenistic period, the Epicureans deserve to be called a school. This is because Epicurus owned property, the Garden, where he gathered together with his followers to philosophize along highly developed and systematic lines. His followers, unusually for a school in antiquity, included not only women and slaves, but also courtesans and other individuals of low social standing. This policy bespeaks a remarkable human openness on the part of Epicurus and reflects his admirable ability to harmonize theory and practice. Because Epicurean doctrine permits no invidious distinctions between humans and their capacities for experiencing pleasure, whatever their gender or class, Epicurus welcomed every human being into his fold regardless of background. Once admitted, his adherents sought to implement the principles of his philosophy fully into the conduct of their daily lives. They thus became intimately familiar with the highly developed set of doctrines Epicurus preached, and he in consequence achieved a remarkable degree of uniformity and consistency across his adherents, far more, in fact, than we find in either Stoicism or Skepticism.

The sources and core theses of Epicureanism

Our situation regarding our access to the views of Epicurus is in different ways both unfortunate and fortunate. Although he wrote a great deal,[11] almost all of his own work is lost, including his great treatise *On Nature*.[12] There remain, however, three highly instructive letters written by Epicurus, intended as basic guides for his followers: one, written to Herodotus, concerns Epicurus' physical theory, one, to Menoeceus, concerns his ethical doctrine, and a final one, to Pythocles, details features of his astronomy and meteorology. The authenticity of this last letter is sometimes disputed, but it is probably genuine; the first two, which are the main sources for the views considered here, may be accepted as genuine with confidence.

In addition to these letters, we have two overlapping collections of his doctrines, each of which offers a précis of Epicurus' fundamental principles, the *Principal Beliefs* (sometimes referred to as the *Principal Doctrines*, or simply by its Greek title, *Kuriai Doxai*) and the *Vatican Sayings*, preserved, as its name suggests, in a manuscript in the Vatican. Both are extracted from Epicurus' writings and assembled with the aim of instructing novices in the principles of Epicureanism. So, in this sense, we are most fortunate. We have the fundamental elements of Epicurus' system set out in a manner thought by him highly suited to those approaching his philosophy for the first time.

In addition to the writings of Epicurus himself, we have a valuable source of Epicurean doctrine in the Latin poet Lucretius, who wrote a long didactic poem intended to convert its readers to Epicureanism. Although Lucretius wrote in the first century AD, so some 300 years after Epicurus lived and died, and although scholars dispute his level of originality and independence as an Epicurean philosopher, it is reasonable to accept his poem *On the Nature of Things* (*De Rerum Natura*, also sometimes referred to as *On the Nature of the Universe*) as an authentic source of Epicurean doctrine. Certainly Lucretius presents himself as an apostle of Epicureanism, and in this he is not mistaken.[13]

Lucretius focuses repeatedly on an important fundamental feature of Epicurean philosophy, and we may follow him through the portal it offers into the world of Epicurean thought: we are enjoined by Epicurus to let go of our irrational and debilitating fear of death. As Epicurus says, "Death is nothing to us, since when death is, we are not, and when we are, death is not."[14] Although the fear of death pervades all ages and ranks, so that the old and the young and the high and the low tremble equally at its ever encroaching approach, this fear, says Epicurus, accomplishes less than nothing and so should be banished from human life. First, our fear of death certainly does not alter the fact that death lies before us: we are going to die. Second, and more importantly, this fear, though utterly pointless given the inevitability of our deaths, actively and acutely undermines our well-being. It causes all manner of disquiet and mental distress, and engenders in us pointless and painful trepidation. Instead of harboring this irrational, debilitating fear, we should release ourselves from its grip and turn our attention to the only good this world actually offers: pleasure. Pleasure, according to Epicurus, resides in our mental and physical composure; the fear of death undermines this composure. It follows, then, that the disquieting fear of death is deleterious to our well-being.

Epicurus' counsel regarding death encapsulates several of the core facets of his philosophy. To begin, people fear death for a variety of reasons. Some, mainly theists, fear what is to become of them after death. Will they be punished for their misdeeds? Will they suffer at the hands of spiteful gods? If they have sinned (and they have), will they be subjected to the torments of hell? Others have a different source of disquiet: the bare prospect of nothingness horrifies them. Thus, for example, the Spanish existentialist philosopher and essayist Miguel de Unamuno recounts his striking childhood dread of nothingness, a dread not of post-mortem punishment but of post-mortem oblivion: "For myself I can say that as a youth, and even as a child, I remained unmoved when shown the most moving pictures of hell, for even then nothing appeared to me quite so horrible as nothingness itself."[15] Unamuno fears not divine punishment or *post mortem* suffering, but recoils rather at the prospect of non-being itself.

Epicurus contends that these different sorts of negative reactions to death betray importantly different sorts of mistakes. Accordingly, they require different forms of therapy. To appreciate how he recommends that we proceed, we may move through three phases of Epicurean acculturation. First, we must understand that the universe and all its parts are material: just as Democritus had argued many centuries prior to Epicurus,[16] nothing exists beyond atoms and the void and whatever they compose. Second, consequently, we are ourselves material beings composed of atoms. As a result, when we die, we end. Our atoms scatter to the winds, and we no more survive our deaths than a glass of red wine survives being poured into the Atlantic Ocean. Finally, third, given the fact of our own personal mortality, our fear of death is irrational. There is no point in fearing something we cannot experience: non-being is painless.

Epicurean hedonism

We will start with the root source of Epicurus' conviction that death is unproblematic: hedonism. Epicurus is a hedonist,[17] and thus flatly rejects the Aristotelian picture of human flourishing as given in objective, eudaimonistic terms.[18] While Epicurus does not overtly address Aristotle's arguments for eudaimonism (since indeed there is reason to believe that he never read Aristotle's works), the contours of his reaction to an Aristotelian account are clear. Pleasure consists in bodily sensation, and we are so constituted physically that we seek pleasure as a perfectly natural matter of course.[19] We do not, and certainly according to Epicurus *should* not, seek just any passing pleasure. On the contrary, experience teaches that by indulging in certain pleasures we merely set ourselves up to experience long-term pain.[20] So, we should decide which pleasures are to be indulged when and why. Epicurus is explicit on this point, and maintains overtly that the variety of hedonism he proposes has nothing in common with the kinds of indulgence or opulence now associated with "epicureanism." So, the common meaning this term has come to have is misleading yet rooted in something real: Epicurus was a dedicated hedonist, but not the kind of hedonist dedicated to the pursuit of opulent or conspicuous or refined pleasure.

On the contrary, Epicureanism espouses a markedly austere brand of hedonism:

> We believe that self-sufficiency is a great good, not in order that we might always make do with little, but rather so that we can make do with a little when we do not have much, because we are altogether persuaded that those least in need of extravagances enjoy them most, and also because everything natural is easy to obtain, while vapid things are hard to obtain. Moreover, simple flavors provide pleasure equal to the pleasures of an extravagant lifestyle, when the pain of wanting is expunged: barley cakes and water provide the pinnacle of pleasure when someone who wants them takes them. Therefore, becoming accustomed to simple rather than extravagant ways of life is healthy … So when we say that pleasure is the goal we do not mean the pleasures of the profligate or the pleasure of consumption … but rather the lack of pain in the body and disturbance in the soul.
>
> (*Letter to Menoeceus* 130–132 = LS 21 B)

Pleasure is to be sought, then, but not pursued willy-nilly. Pleasure is to be maximized in a deliberate, constrained, and rationally governed manner.

To maximize pleasure, contends Epicurus, we must reflect on our desires. Notice that he implicitly characterizes certain desires as *natural* when he says that "everything natural is easy to obtain." He is here relying on his division of desires into two main types, the natural and the non-natural, where the contrast seems to differentiate desires by their objects. Those arrayed over artificial objects are non-natural, while those directed to natural objects are natural. A desire for food is natural; a desire to own the largest domestic swimming pool in Hollywood is not. Moreover, even among the natural desires some are necessary and some are not. A desire for food is perfectly natural, but even food comes in simple, readily available forms, like barley cake and water, and in highly rich and rare forms, like caviar and fine champagne. If we care about pleasure maximization, Epicurus suggests, then it behooves us to constrain our desires to those objects that are both natural and necessary. To begin, barley cake and water offer no less pleasure than caviar and champagne: these provide intense pleasure to those who want them intensely – and since pleasure is nothing more than a pleasurable bodily sensation, the pleasure provided by barley cakes to the hungry will be as good or better than the pleasure of splashing around in the largest domestic swimming pool in Hollywood.

What is more, natural and necessary pleasures are more likely to be secured than other forms of pleasure, because they are more likely to lie within our grasp. If I desire to own the largest swimming pool in Hollywood, then I must direct a fair bit of my energy towards attaining this goal. First, I will need a great deal of money; then I will need to rely on others to build and maintain the pool. I will also, it turns out, need the co-operation of other like-minded people. That is, if I manage to satisfy my desire to own the biggest pool in Hollywood, only to discover the following week that you harbor the same desire, and then also that you have managed to outdo me by building a still larger pool, I will end my week in frustration rather than satisfaction. At the end of the week, I am *disappointed* in my pool. My pool is inferior and so no longer satisfies my non-natural, non-necessary desire to own the biggest pool in town.

Perhaps, as I learn, you even turn out to be a contemptuous and spiteful sort who takes delicious pleasure in my ignoble defeat in the biggest-pool race. So, even though you do not much care for swimming, you build your pool just a bit bigger than mine so that you can lord your superiority over me at neighborhood cocktail parties. Then I am doubly frustrated and annoyed. Consequently, if I want to satisfy my original desire, I must begin the cycle anew, whereupon, assuming that I am successful, you are at liberty to outdo me yet again, leaving me forever antagonized and in a state of inner turmoil. By allowing myself such desires in the first instance, I make myself hostage to forces utterly beyond my control. I willingly make myself vulnerable to states of affairs that upon even a moment's reflection I see I cannot govern.

Once I have gone down this road, however, I am no longer master of my own pleasure: my pleasure becomes contingent upon your actions and the co-operation of others who may be at best indifferent to me – and, sadly, you and others like you prove unwilling to assist me in my quest for desire satisfaction and its attendant pleasures. Consequently, since my pleasure is also my happiness, I thus also allow my own happiness to become vulnerable to the vicissitudes of matters well beyond my control. My happiness, then, is no longer up to me. Yet my good, my happiness, is readily attainable to me all the while.[21] All I need do is curb my desire: if I restrict my desires to what is natural and necessary, to what lies easily within my own grasp, then my own happiness becomes largely, if not in every particular, up to me.

Fearing death: for the uninitiated

How do we achieve this obviously advantageous end? We submit ourselves to the first phase of therapy. We begin by asking ourselves *why* we have the sorts of desires we have when we spend our days striving to have the most lavish, conspicuous forms of consumer goods we can afford. Even here, implies Epicurus, lurks the gnawing fear of death. Among other things, when we act in these ways, we are looking for esteem or validation or the envy of others; we want other people to notice us, to feel inferior to us, to remember us, to take account of us. How, though, can this make us happy? Happiness consists in pleasure, and pleasure in bodily sensation. So, we are behaving irrationally, perhaps because we surreptitiously wish to appear godlike in the eyes of our neighbors or because we are confusedly seeking some simulacrum of immortality by trying to lodge ourselves in the permanent collective consciousness of humankind. Somewhere within we all realize that we are to die, but we hope to defeat death by fame, or, failing that, by infamy. If so, and even if not, what we desire in these cases ignores the simple fact that the universe is material in all its parts, and that we, as parts of this material universe, are ourselves material in all our parts as well. We are but congeries of atoms. Accordingly, even if we achieve the greatest fame of all, we will not be around after our deaths to enjoy this marvelous feat.

This is why Epicurus enjoins us to study nature. We may move ourselves closer towards self-sufficiency in the first instance by developing a realistic conception of the universe and our place within it:

> If we did not suspect that celestial phenomena and death might matter to us, that they somehow are of concern to us, and if we did not fail to understand the limits of our pains and desires, then we would not need to study nature. It is, however, not possible, to relieve the fears regarding such significant matters for someone who does not know the nature of the universe but rather retains some of the fears drawn from mythology. Consequently, there is no way to secure pure pleasure without studying nature.
>
> (*Principal Beliefs* 11–12 = LS 25 B)

Our baseless fears mainly stem from a lack of understanding. Superstition is really nothing more than the direct result of failing to come to appreciate how things really are; superstition is a belief, a false belief, in a magical universe which does not in fact exist. By studying nature, we learn the truth of atomism, and so of materialism. We learn too that we are material beings – beings composed of atoms swirling in the void.

If we persist in believing that we are not ourselves simply part of the vast web of atoms, that we are exceptions, that we have souls of the sort that Plato taught us to believe that we have,[22] then the Epicureans offer us a simple remedy. They usher us into the first phase of therapy by way of a crisp argument, put plainly by Lucretius:

> This same reason proves the material nature of both mind and spirit. For they are seen to propel the limbs, to rouse the body from sleep, to change facial expressions and to both rule and steer the whole man – none of which would be possible without touch, nor touch in turn without matter. How then can we deny the material nature of the mind and spirit?
>
> (Lucretius, *De Rerum Natura* iii 161–167 = LS 14 B)

As Lucretius notes, the mind affects the body and the body affects the mind. None of this would be possible if mind and body did not come into contact with one another; but they come into contact with one another only if they touch, but obviously touch is impossible unless both mind and body are material.

This argument is directed to the uninitiated, to those who have yet to accept the material nature of our minds, or souls, those who persist in thinking that we are somehow exceptional in the realm of nature. So, for those uninitiated to materialism (FUM):

1 Minds (or souls) and bodies causally interact only if minds (or souls) are material.
2 Minds (or souls) and bodies do causally interact.
3 So, minds (or souls) are material.

For those who have studied modern philosophy, this argument may appear remarkably similar to an argument deployed a millennium and a half later, in the seventeenth century, by various critics seeking to undermine the soul–body dualism advanced by René Descartes in his *Meditations*. This is because it is the same argument.

Epicureans accept as unassailable (FUM-2), the claim that mind (or souls) causally interact. They think of it, in fact, as an obvious empirical truth. Even casual observation shows that causal interaction between the mind and the body takes place, heading in both directions. As Lucretius notes, it is simply a fact that when a warrior has a spear run through his sternum, he bleeds, grows faint, and loses consciousness. Since being conscious is a state of the mind, this, a manifestly physical act of a spear piercing his sternum, causes that, a mental effect, namely the loss of consciousness. Heading in the other direction, as Lucretius notes, the mind is seen to change the body. A student is working hard trying to solve a difficult quadratic equation. She fails repeatedly and grimaces in frustration. At last she grasps the solution in an instant, and smiles with relief and satisfaction. This, the mental event of grasping the solution, causes that, a physical effect, a change in facial expression. She decides to reward herself by going to the café to buy a caramel latte. Just as Lucretius says, her decision "is to propel her limbs" as she walks down the stairs, out of her flat, and down the street towards her local coffee shop.

Obviously these illustrations could be multiplied thousand-fold without effort. So, let (FUM-2) stand: there is two-way causal interaction between the mind (or soul) and the body. That leaves only (FUM-1) for the uninitiated to grasp: minds (or souls) and bodies causally interact only if minds (or souls) are material. Lucretius provides only an abbreviated argument for (FUM-2). He says that such interaction requires touch, but that touch requires matter. In fact he says that such interaction would *not be possible* without touch, which suggests that he regards (FUM-2) as a necessary truth. His suggestion thus seems to be that it is conceptually or metaphysically impossible for a non-physical something to enter into a causal interaction with a physical something, for instance, for a non-physical something to cause a billiard ball to move across a table. The initiation of motion requires force, but force is physical; without the exercise of something physical, then, no motion will result. What holds for billiard balls, Lucretius implies, holds for all physical change. Billiard balls are, like everything else, collections of atoms. So, he concludes, minds (or souls) no less than billiard balls and bodies, are physical. Again, bodies, minds, and billiard balls are all and equally composed of atoms swirling in the void.

A Platonist will not let Lucretius' defense of (FUM-2) rest there; but if we are persuaded, then we have become initiated. We now accept the truth of materialism. By studying nature, we see that there is nothing to fear in death, since when death is, we are not. Nothingness gives us nothing to fear.

Fearing death: for the initiated

Or does it? Epicurus takes his campaign against the fear of death to a second phase because he recognizes that so deeply ingrained is this fear in our psyches that it might exercise its pull on us even after we have come to appreciate that the prospects of post-mortem punishment are non-existent, even after, that is, we have come to learn that death is the end of sensation. Epicurus argues his case more fully as follows:

> Accustom yourself to thinking that death is nothing to us, since every good and every evil resides in sensation, and death is the absence of sensation. Hence, a correct understanding of the fact that death is nothing to us makes the mortality of life enjoyable – not by adding infinite time, but by taking away our yearning for immortality. For there is nothing fearful in living for one who truly concludes that there is nothing fearful in not living. Consequently, he speaks idly who says that he fears death not because of its being painful when present but because it is painful when coming. For if something does not cause pain when present, it is pointless to be pained by the anticipation of it. Therefore, death, the most horrible of evils, is nothing to us, since while we exist death is not present, and whenever death is present, we do not exist. Therefore, death is nothing to the living or the dead: it does not exist for the former, and the latter no longer exist.
>
> (Epicurus, *Letter to Menoeceus* 124–5 = LS 24 A)

He addresses the passage to the initiated by insisting that it is idle for someone who has accepted the truth of materialism to continue fearing death.

Epicurus' argument trades upon the fact that pain, like pleasure, consists in bodily sensation. He fully allows that it is perfectly rational to fear certain sorts of unavoidable pains. If we have in view an impending, inescapably painful death, then we might well fear that prospect. This, however, amounts to fearing *dying*, not fearing death. In this case, we have before us an anticipated, unavoidable pain, and pain is indeed an evil. It is thus rational to fear an inescapable pain. By the same token, Epicurus urges, it is wholly irrational to fear a pain which is *known* not to exist. He thus offers the following argument *for those initiated to materialism* (FIM):

1   A subject S can rationally fear at t_1 some state of affairs at t_2 only if S will exist at t_2.
2   So, if t_2 is later than the time of S's death, S can fear some state of affairs at t_2 only if S exists after death.
3   S does not exist after S's death.
4   So, S cannot rationally fear any state of affairs after S's death.

In effect, Epicurus begins by reminding the initiated that pleasure consists in bodily sensation and that there is no bodily sensation after death. He also implicitly notes that even the initiated may continue to be plagued by utterly illicit fears. Plainly, anyone initiated to the truths of materialism, by (FUM) or some other means, will accept (FIM-3), the claim that for any subject S, S does not exist after S's death. Since (FIM-2) follows directly from (FIM-1), all that remains for the initiated is the first premise, that S can rationally fear at t_1 some state of affairs at t_2 only if S will exist at t_2.

One can perhaps illustrate Epicurus' attitude towards (FIM-1) as follows. Imagine that you have long harbored a secret crush on someone, and that you have finally worked up the courage to ask that person to join you for a date, let us say on a picnic two weeks from the time of asking. To your surprise, the object of your affection agrees enthusiastically. You begin to plan your outing with meticulous care and delight. Even the planning itself affords you great pleasure. Then, alas, you learn from a severe medical authority that you are slated to die a swift, painless, but certain death in one week. Will it be rational for you to continue anticipating the picnic with pleasure? It seems not.

By parity of reasoning, if instead of a picnic you were scheduled to undergo a painful root canal in two weeks, you would, in the same medical scenario, be irrational to continue dreading the pain you were expecting to experience in your dental appointment. The dental appointment will not be kept. (We are assuming that you are not the fastidious sort who will ask your dentist to move it forward so that you can have your root canal completed before you die.) What holds for these individual anticipated pleasures or pains holds quite generally. There is no reason to anticipate the pleasure of your picnic if it is not to be, and there is no reason to fear the pain of your root canal, for precisely the same reason. The pain is not to be. You will not be there to experience either – or indeed anything else. So, if you are initiated to the truths of materialism, you are enjoined to expunge your irrational fears, and concentrate on satisfying your natural and necessary desires.

Even now, though, having come this far, someone might dread the onset of nothingness, in the manner of Miguel de Unamuno. That is, one might accept the truth of materialism, agree that is it irrational to fear what one cannot experience, and yet still recoil at the horror of sheer nothingness. Surely somethingness is preferable to nothingness. In the first place, there is a point derived from Epicurus himself. Let us grant, even as Epicurus insists, that we can experience pleasure when and only when we exist; and let us further allow that pleasure is a good, in fact it is *the* good. If so, however, then when we die, we will be *deprived* of our sole form of goodness, and that is surely to be lamented, if not exactly feared.

In response to this sort of worry, Lucretius moves engagingly to the final phase of Epicurean therapy. He suggests that when we die we are not really *deprived* of anything at all. He urges us to reflect upon the following simple fact: each of us was born on some specific date, before which we were not. Before the date of our birth, whenever that may be, we were not. In fact, before we were born, we were nothing at all for the period spanning the entire of the history of the universe. Yet at no point during that vast stretch of time were we *deprived* of anything. We simply were not:

> Therefore, death is nothing to us and is of no concern at all, once it is granted that the nature of mind is mortal. Just as in the past we had no sensation of discomfort [i.e. before we were born] ... so also when we no longer exist, when the soul is severed from the body, from whose union we are constituted, nothing will be able to excite us or move our senses.
> (Lucretius, *De Rerum Natura* iii 830–840 = LS 24 E)

Our attitudes to our future non-existence should match our attitudes to our past non-existence. Since we do not lament our pre-mortem non-existence, neither should we lament our post-mortem non-existence.

Lucretius thus offers to the initiated an argument from *symmetry of the future and past* (SFP):

1   Our pre-natal and post-mortem non-existences are directly symmetrical.
2   If (1), then it is rational for us to lament our post-mortem non-existence only if it is rational for us to lament our pre-natal non-existence.
3   Hence, it is rational for us to lament our post-mortem non-existence only if it is rational for us to lament our pre-natal non-existence.
4   It is not rational to lament our pre-natal non-existence.
5   Hence, it is not rational for us to lament our post-mortem non-existence.

What holds for lamentation holds also, and more manifestly, for fear. Just as we have no reason to fear our pre-natal non-existence, so we have no reason to fear our post-mortem non-existence.

(SFP) is again addressed to the initiated. Such a person will have accepted the truth of materialism, and will even have acknowledged that there is no point in fearing pains which will not be. Still, like Miguel de Unamuno, this initiate is horrified by the prospect of sheer nothingness. Such a person experiences *non-existential dread*.

The most tendentious premise in the argument addressed to this wobbly initiate is (SFP-1), the claim that that our pre-natal and post-mortem non-existences are directly symmetrical. In some sense, if we are initiated, then we will already have accepted this. They are symmetrical at least from the standpoint of sensation. Exactly as we failed to experience painful and unwanted sensations before we were born, so we will fail to experience painful and unwanted sensations after we die. So far, the symmetry holds.

In other ways, though, one may doubt whether our past and future non-existences are perfectly symmetrical. There is first the fact that all planning and intention are forward-looking, directed of necessity towards the future and never towards the past. So, there is this difference about our relation to the past and future: while we certainly cannot hope or intend to make something happen in the period before we were born, we can intend or at least hope to make something happen in the period after our deaths. Thus, Antonio Gaudí, the great Catalonian architect, might reasonably have hoped that the Sagrada Família, the cathedral he designed in Barcelona, be completed after his death. Indeed he might have intended that its construction move forward along a determinate schedule, even while knowing that he would not be present to oversee its implementation. By contrast, in 1925 Gaudí could not have intended for it to have been completed before World War I broke out.

In general, the past is closed: the world is not such as to be altered in its past. So, although we can surely experience regret, we cannot in the present hope or intend to alter the past. The past cannot be undone. The future, in shining contrast, remains open, even after our deaths. We can accordingly hope and intend for all manner of outcomes to take place after our deaths. Indeed, some martyrs sacrifice themselves because they believe that their doing so is the only route to some highly desirable state of affairs. If a sergeant in a military platoon – an Epicurean initiate let us stipulate – throws himself on a grenade believing that otherwise all in his platoon will die, he envisions some worthy good obtaining after his death and intends to bring it about by his actions. So, the open future can be affected in ways the past cannot. Is this not an asymmetry?

The question merits further reflection, as does (SFP-4), the claim that it is not rational to lament our pre-natal non-existence. Both claims invite similar sorts of scrutiny. We may grant, again, that it would be irrational to *fear* a painful experience pertaining to the time when were not. One might wonder, however, about how we should view the past. Counterfactually, for example, we might believe that if only we had existed at some time gone by we could have prevented some great tragedy; and this thought alone might give us grounds to lament our pre-natal non-existence. Such judgments are inherently unstable, of course, but to the extent that we feel justified in forming them, we might think it rational to have negative attitudes about the past. If those are appropriate, then the very parity Epicurus seeks to exploit might be turned back against him. That is, by the very parity that (SFP-1) demands, just as we might lament our past non-existence we might come to lament the fact that we will not be here in the future, that we will lose the goodness of our lives, and this lamentation may take hold as dread or some other form of psychic distress. In general, if we think that life itself is a good, then its loss is something to be disvalued.

Responses to (SFP) of this form are ultimately challenges to the kind of hedonism embraced by Epicureanism. If we think that there is some locus of value in addition to pleasure, then we will have grounds for lamenting the loss of that value, even if we might not ourselves experience its loss personally. We might well agree, of course, that subjective pleasure is *a* good without agreeing that it is *the* good. Accordingly, we might think that life itself is a good, but not (only) because we think of life as something pleasurable. If we have reason to favor this more comprehensive sort of value schema, then we also have reason to attach value to some things beyond subjective pleasure, and so also to challenge Epicurus at a fundamental level of his philosophy. If Epicurean hedonism fails, then so too does Epicureanism.

Questions about the tenability of Epicureanism therefore lead us directly back to questions about what constitutes our final good.

5.3   The Stoics

The Stoics advance a starkly non-Epicurean conception of our final good. They are, however, like the Epicureans in being *value monists*: they think that only one sort of thing is good.[23] Unlike the Epicureans, however, they do not suppose that the sole value in life is pleasure. They argue, instead, that *virtue* and virtue *alone* is good; virtue is the one and only supreme good.

The sources and core theses of Stoicism

As we go forward to understand the Stoics' motivation for this sort of monism, we need to be aware that we are setting aside many fascinating and intricate questions about the development of Stoic thought. When we speak of "*the* Stoics," we are not in fact referring to a monolithic group of tightly knit authors united by their adherence to an undisputed master, as we are in the case of the Epicureans, and still less are we dealing with a single author whose works span no more than several decades, as we are in the cases of Plato and Aristotle. We are referring, instead, to a set of doctrines developed across a broad range of works written in several different genres, composed by many different authors, and spanning not decades but centuries.

The earliest Stoics were in Athens, active not long after the death of Aristotle, where the school was founded by Zeno of Citium in roughly 300 BC. Zeno was succeeded by Cleanthes (c. 331–230) and he in turn by Chrysippus (c. 280–204). Even talk of "founding a school" here is misleading, if by this we are understanding the modern practice of the setting up of an institution of higher learning by design on a specific date, in the way, for instance, that Edward and Lavinia Talbot founded Lady Margaret Hall, the first women's college in Oxford, in 1878, and named it after Lady Margaret Beaufort, the mother of Henry VIII, who was a patron of learning and the arts. That all happened in a dateable time and place, with the specific intention of establishing a college with a particular character and remit. By contrast, the inception of the Stoic school, or movement, was much more informal. The school came about not by design or decree but rather simply emerged in Athens at the time of Zeno, who began the practice of expounding distinctive doctrines while lecturing and strolling along the painted porch or colonnade (in Greek *hê poikilê stoa*) which runs along the north side of the Agora in Athens. The Stoics derive their name from this *stoa*, or colonnade. The first three leaders, Zeno of Citium, Cleanthes, and Chrysippus, constitute the Early Stoa, as the movement came to be called, and among them Chrysippus is generally regarded as the most significant driving force. Indeed, since antiquity it has been said "but for Chrysippus there would have been no Stoa."[24] Unfortunately, although Chrysippus wrote voluminously, we have almost nothing of his first hand. Nor do we have anything extensive of the other two early heads, Zeno and Cleanthes. Instead, regrettably, we need to rely on the reports of later sources for coming to know the doctrines of the Early Stoa.[25]

Thereafter, matters improve but also become more complicated. They improve, because for later periods of Stoicism we come to have complete works authored by self-proclaimed Stoics; they become more complicated, because these self-proclaimed Stoics lived and worked in a wide variety of times, places, and social milieux. To name just a few, the Stoics count among their number: Epictetus (50–130 AD), a slave whose lectures were taken down and preserved by the historian Arrian; Seneca (1 BC–65 AD), the tutor of the Roman emperor Nero, who wrote both essays and literary epistles in Latin; and Marcus Aurelius (121–180 AD), a Roman emperor who wrote in Greek. Other sources for Stoicism are not even Stoics, but critics of the Stoics, who recounted Stoic views primarily in an effort to discredit them. These include Galen (c. 129–210 AD), the physician of Marcus Aurelius, and Plutarch (45–125 AD), an Academic philosopher who left us such works as *On the Self-contradictions of the Stoics* (*De stoicorum repugnantiis*) and *On Common Views Opposed to the Stoics* (*De communibus notitiis*). These last sources are often manifestly hostile.

By working with these sources, and holding in abeyance some difficult questions concerning internal divisions among the Stoics, we can reconstruct their core beliefs, many of which, for better or worse (they will say for the better) run counter to common sense, just as the hostile Plutarch alleges.

First among their core commitments is their variety of value monism. Virtue, not pleasure, is the sole human good, and is indeed, according to Zeno, in common with all Stoics who came after him, the goal or end (*telos*) of human life:

> Therefore Zeno in his book *On the nature of man* was the first to say that living in agreement with nature is the end (*telos*), which is living in accordance with virtue. For nature leads us to virtue ... Further, living in accordance with virtue is equivalent to living in accordance with experience of what happens by nature, as Chrysippus says in *On ends* I: for our natures are parts of the nature of the whole. Therefore, living in agreement with nature comes to be the end, which is in accordance with the nature of oneself and that of the whole, engaging in no activity wont to be forbidden by the universal law, which is the right reason (*orthos logos*) pervading everything and identical to Zeus, who is the director of the administration of existing things. And the virtue of the happy man and his good flow of life are just this: always doing everything on the basis of the concordance of each man's guardian spirit with the will of the administrator of the whole.
>
> (DL VII 87–88)

This is a complex characterization which usefully situates the Stoic conception of the good in its broader context. The Stoics not only think of virtue as the human good, but also have a highly distinctive view of that in which virtue consists: virtue is living in accordance with nature. Living in accordance with nature, in turn, requires coming to terms with what nature requires: nature itself is pervaded with *right reason* (*orthos logos*), which we must ascertain if we are to mold ourselves to nature's direction. This we wish to do, say the Stoics, because it is good for us; and they take it as beyond controversy that we all want what is good for us.

If we can understand three central points made in this important passage, we will arrive at a reasonable first approximation of the richness of Stoic philosophy. These are: (i) the Stoics offer a distinctively teleological account of human virtue, which carries with it a clear prescription for leading a good life; (ii) that teleological account of human virtue is situated within a broader, and prior, teleological conception of the universe at large, which they regard at once as both end-directed and highly deterministic; and (iii) in order to understand the character of this universe and our place within it, we must adopt a highly systematic way of thinking about the world. According to the Stoics, an optimal system of thought will comprise three main branches: logic, physics, and ethics.

The Stoics offer several comparisons to bring out the interconnectedness of these three components of their system:

> Philosophy, they say, is like an animal: logic corresponds to the bones and sinews, ethics to the fleshy parts, and physics to the soul. Another simile

they use is an egg: logic is the shell, then comes ethics, the egg white, and at the center is physics, the yolk.

(DL VII 40 = LS 26 B)

While it is natural to wonder whether these similes are intended to portray some priority relations of the branches of the Stoic system, the Stoics in fact seem much more interested in highlighting a different aspect of their comparisons: interconnectedness. An egg is not an egg without all three contributing components, and an animal is an organic unity, composed essentially of all the parts listed, each of which makes an indispensible contribution to the whole. So too with Stoic philosophy: we can enter where we wish because each branch makes an ineliminable contribution to the whole of their system. Although we must eventually pass through all parts of philosophy, our single end in doing so never varies: we wish to understand nature so that we may live in accordance with it. Our good resides in our doing so.

Stoic virtue: oikeiôsis and living in accordance with nature

Let us enter the Stoic conception of living in accordance with nature via Zeno's highly loaded claim that "nature leads us to virtue" (DL VII 87). We might think that studying nature involves us in the value-neutral job of describing the fundamental features of the physical universe in terms of particles, forces, and laws. When we learn, for instance, the second law of thermodynamics, we come to understand something about the ways in which temperatures, pressures, and chemical potentials interact with one another within a closed physical system. The second law of thermodynamics seems to tell us nothing at all, however, about how we should lead our lives; it seems, on the contrary, that it *could not* give us any such instruction, because this law, like every other physical law, is value-neutral, while every question about the good life is inevitably value-laden. We cannot seem to derive statements of value from statements of empirical fact. As those following the Scottish philosopher David Hume like to say: one cannot derive an *ought* from an *is*. So, in particular, one cannot determine how one *ought* to live merely by determining how things *are*.[26]

Looked at one way, the Stoics simply concede this point. They do not think that we can derive an *ought* from an *is*. They think, rather, so to speak, that *ought* goes all the way down. That is, they disagree with the contention that the universe is value-neutral. This is what they mean when they speak anthropomorphically of Zeus as being identical with 'the right reason (*orthos logos*) pervading everything' (DL vii 88). Their repeated suggestion is that nature presents itself to us as an ordered whole, a structured teleological system, whose terms we must simply grasp if we are to live good lives. The second head of the Early Stoa, Cleanthes, even composed a hymn to Zeus, who is treated as the rational pulse of the universe:

Most majestic of immortals, many-named, ever all-powerful Zeus, nature's source, steering all with your law: Hail! ... The entire cosmos spinning about the earth obeys you, willingly submitting to your rule wheresoever you should lead. Such is the double-edged ever-living thunderbolt of fire which you hold in your unconquered hands. For beneath its blows are all works of nature accomplished. With it you direct the universal reason (*koinos logos*) which runs through all things, mixing with celestial lights both great and small ... Scatter all feebleness from our soul, Father. Give to us the power of judgment, in whose trust you steer all with justice, so that by gaining honor we may repay you with honor, ever singing the praises of your works, as is meet for mortals. For neither men nor gods have any greater privilege than this: to sing forever in justice the praises of your universal law (*koinos nomos*).

(Stobaeus 1.25, 3–27, 4 = LS 54 I)

Scholars debate the degree to which Cleanthes and the other Stoics understand Zeus to be a literally living, thinking, divine being who orders the universe as a law-giver and to whom humans must submit in common with the rest of nature. In this passage, as in many others, Zeus is portrayed in just this way, as a supreme being to be obeyed; in other, more naturalistic passages, Zeus seems closer to an anthropomorphized natural universe as a whole. So, Cicero represents Chrysippus: "The world is wise, and hence is god."[27] In either case, the universe pulses with rationality, directionality, normativity. How things ought to be is given by the natural universe itself; it falls to imperfect rational agents such as we are to discern the direction of the perfectly rational universe to the best of our ability and then to mold ourselves to its order.

An appreciation of nature's direction forms the basis of the distinctive Stoic doctrine of *oikeiôsis* – the process of moral development from its inception to maturation, a process of coming to recognize and accept what belongs to one and what befits one. No single English word captures the full sweep of *oikeiôsis*; so, we will leave it transliterated. Its root involves the Greek word for home or household (*oikos*), the overtones of which signify for the Stoics the process of finding one's proper place, finding what is authentically dear to one, finding, in short, one's home in the world.

Cicero describes the process compactly:

The first appropriate act is to preserve oneself in one's natural constitution; the next is to retain those things which are in accordance with nature and to repel those that are contrary; then when this principle of choice and also rejection has been discovered, there follows next in order choice conditioned by appropriate action; then, such choices become a fixed habit; and finally, choice fully rationalized and in harmony with nature. It is at this final stage that Good properly so-called first emerges and comes to be understood in its true nature.

(*De Finibus* iii 5–6)

Diogenes Laertius reports the process of *oikeiôsis* somewhat more fully in this way:

> They say that the first inclination (i.e. impulse) which an animal has is to protect itself, as nature brings itself to take an interest in it from the beginning, as Chrysippus affirms in the first book of his treatise on ends, where he says that the first and dearest (*oikeion*) object to every animal is its own existence, and its consciousness of that existence. For that it is not natural for any animal to be alienated from itself, or even to be brought into such a state as to be indifferent to itself, being neither alienated from nor interested in itself. It remains, therefore, that we must assert that nature has bound the animal to itself by the greatest unanimity and affection for the means by which it repels all that is injurious, and attracts all that is akin to it and desirable. But as for what some people say, that the first inclination of animals is for pleasure, what they say is false. For they say that pleasure, if there be any such thing at all, is an accessory only, which, nature, having sought it out by itself, as well as these things which are adapted to its constitution, receives incidentally in the same manner as animals are pleased, and plants made to flourish.
>
> (DL VII 85 = LS 57 A)

Many centuries later, writing in 1685, the Dutch political philosopher Grotius endorses this doctrine, which he characterizes succinctly as follows:

> But among the traits characteristic of man is an impelling desire for society – that is, for social life – not of any and every sort, but a peaceful life, organized according to the measure of his intelligence with those who are of his own kind. This desire the Stoics called *oikeiôsis*.
>
> (*De iure belli ac pacis*, Prol. 6)

Although he misdescribes the desire for *oikeiôsis* as *oikeiôsis* itself, Grotius captures an important element of the Stoic doctrine with his suggestion that every person has an untutored impulse to live "with those who are of his own kind." As it will emerge, the Stoics suggest that nature teaches us that in the final analysis we are all of the same kind.

This, though, is at the end of the process. Both Cicero and Diogenes appropriately highlight a salient fact about its beginning: every infant has a natural, in-born, unlearned impulse for its own self-preservation. In repeatedly calling this fact "natural," both authors bring out that for the Stoics this value-laden impulse is no less natural than the second law of thermodynamics. What untutored infants seek is nothing less than their own good. It is not that they conceive of their good *as* good. On the contrary, infants lack reason, are at best proto-rational, and lack the conceptual repertoire necessary to conceive of the good as good. Even so, they lunge towards their good, reliably, predictably, and in ways which cannot be explained in terms of random chance.

Nature has infused them with a drive, an impulse towards something of value to them. The Stoics here imply, then, first, that the universal impulse for self-preservation is in no way artificial, since it is inborn and unlearned, and, second, that it is value-laden, since the impulse for self-preservation is an impulse to attain one's own good.

These sorts of arguments, so-called "cradle arguments," used equally by the Epicureans who think that we all have an immediate impulse for pleasure, are only, for the Stoics, the first steps on a long road home. The process of *oikeiôsis* involves a gradual expansion of a maturing agent's appreciation of the locus of natural value. Hierocles, a little known Stoic of the second century AD, describes the process attractively in terms of ever-expanding concentric circles.[28] The value grasped by the infant is simply her own good, and at this stage in her development she is only dimly aware of the small circle of her own value. Soon, and with equal naturalness, the infant understands that her own circle is contained within the larger circle of her family, whose value she also comes to recognize and appreciate; thereafter, the developing human comes also to recognize and appreciate, if properly attuned and developing as nature intends, that even this circle is enclosed in a whole series of ever expanding circles. Surrounding her immediate family is next her extended family, then those in her local neighborhood, her town, her country, and so finally the whole of humanity. Crucially each expansion is in effect a kind of *recognition*: the recognition that the value residing in the smaller circle equally resides in the next concentric circle in succession. At the end of the process, the Stoic is a true cosmopolitan – that is, literally, a citizen (*politês*) of the universe (*kosmos*). The fully mature Stoic, the Stoic sage, is at home in the universe.

The true Stoic sage manages to complete the process of *oikeiôsis*. The sage can thus accurately be described as fully mature, fully virtuous, and fully rational. If the description of this process of moral maturation is to have any prescriptive force however – if, that is, it is to count as something more than an instance of the Stoics valorizing the heroes of their movement – *oikeiôsis* must be shown to be a process to which each of us *should* aspire. We should wish to undertake this journey. This the Stoics emphatically maintain: for each of us, the process of *oikeiôsis* is at the same time the process of attaining our highest good.

To come to understand the Stoic approach, we can reflect upon a sort of overarching prescriptive argument, lying behind, in a general way, Stoic depictions of *oikeiôsis*. Although no individual Stoic puts the matter this way, the general sense of their prescriptions may be captured in terms of an *Oikeiôsis Argument* (OA):

1   It is in the interest of every human being S to maximize S's own good.
2   In order to maximize S's own good, S must progress through a process of *oikeiôsis*.
3   So, it is in the interest of every human being S to progress through a process of *oikeiôsis*.

4   To progress through a process of *oikeiôsis*, S must recognize and appreciate the features of nature, including its value-laden features, and live in accordance with them.

5   In order to recognize and appreciate the features of nature, including its value-laden features and to live in accordance with them, S must assent to all and only true propositions.

6   So, to progress through a process of *oikeiôsis*, S must assent to all and only true propositions.

7   So, it is in the interest of every human being S to assent to all and only true propositions.

8   In order to assent to all and only true propositions, S must come to recognize and appreciate rationality as the only good.

9   So, every human being must come to recognize and appreciate rationality as the only good.

By the time we arrive at (OA-9), we can see the point of Cicero's remark that at the top end of the process of *oikeiôsis*, the sage lives a life "fully rationalized and in harmony with nature" and that it is "at this final stage that good properly so called first emerges and comes to be understood in its true nature" (*De Finibus* iii 6). The good properly understood is the very rationality that permits the developing Stoic to recognize and appreciate the value-laden features of nature in all their complexity, where these extend to her own value-laden features – and thus include the goodness of her own rationality, a rationality fully attuned to the more encompassing rational structure of the universe as a whole and pulsing in common with the right reason of the cosmos, the will of Zeus.

This argument is a sketch of a large Stoic program, a program which has many demanding and engaging sub-components. The cradle argument already considered undergirds (OA-1), the claim that it is in the interest of every human being S to maximize S's own good. The untutored impulse evident in the infant already provides evidence that this is so, suggest the Stoics. More broadly, they imply that (OA-1) is more or less patently clear in any event. Of course, the Stoics fully realize, as did Plato and Aristotle before them, that many people, sadly, will fail to pursue their own good. More like Socrates, however, they locate the genesis of this failure in a shortcoming of rationality.[29] When people fail to pursue what is in fact good for them, this is only because they are insufficiently rational. So, it behooves all humans to value reason and its power to deliver what is best for them, its unique ability to bring them to the highest human good.

Two propositions of (OA) command special attention, in part because they are by far the most distinctively Stoic: (OA-4), the claim that to progress through a process of *oikeiôsis*, S must recognize and appreciate the features of nature, including its value-laden features, and live in accordance with them; and then also the final conclusion (OA-9), the claim that every human being must come to recognize and appreciate rationality as the *only* good. Each of these claims is counterintuitive, and each embroiled the Stoics in severe controversies with their philosophical opponents in the Hellenistic period and beyond.

(OA-4) is striking not least because it contends that every human *must* recognize and appreciate the features of nature and *must* live in accordance with them. This sort of contention suggests what is true if misleading about the linguistic appropriation reflected in the contemporary adjective "stoic" or "stoical," where these are taken to be characterizations, often with positive overtones, of people able to bear adversity with strength or resignation. If the world is in fact a certain way, and if one judges that this is so, then assenting to the proposition with equanimity seems perfectly rational. This is the true part of the semantic appropriation. The misleading part, which reflects a perplexing feature of the Stoic system, is this: the Stoic sage will not bear adversity with *resignation* – at least not if this means that the Stoic sage will judge that the world must be tolerated because its fundamental way of being is unavoidably bad. The universe is something rational and good, not something wicked and stupid. Accordingly, it is not something to be tolerated or borne with resignation, but rather grasped and revered.

Let us begin with an example initially favorable to the Stoics, though it will also eventually bring to light some of the more challenging aspects of their way of thinking. Suppose that you have a plane to catch, because you have an important meeting, perhaps a job interview in a foreign city. You plan well and leave your flat sufficiently early, so that you can arrive at the airport, check in, and clear security in good time. Unfortunately, en route your train suddenly grinds to a halt and fails to start up again. The conductor reports that there has been a signal failure and that the train cannot proceed until it is fixed. As time wears on and your train sits unmoving, you grow apprehensive about your flight until, in the end, you come to realize that you will miss your plane, and so miss your interview, and so, you fear, will miss your chance for an attractive position. So, the signal failure has put your job prospects in jeopardy. How are you to react? The world is now a certain way, and you have grasped and assented to the proposition that you will miss your plane. You can grow angry and agitated; you can lash out at the train's conductor, and you can complain bitterly and loudly on your mobile phone to your partner back home. Or you can accept things as they are: the world is such that you will not catch your scheduled plane.

The Stoic recommendation is clear. It is your power to choose one course or the other; and the Stoic sage will clearly exercise that power in the direction of happiness. As Cicero reports:

> It is indeed an easy conclusion for the Stoics, since they have conceived the final good as agreement with nature and as living consistently with nature, and this is not only the proper function of the wise man but also something in his power alone. It necessarily follows that anyone who

has the highest good in his power equally has in his power a happy life.
So the wise man's life is always happy.

(Cicero, *Tusculan Disputations* 5.82 = LS 63 M)

You decide. It is up to you. The world has not said to you: be angry, be upset,
be unhappy. Rather, it has said: this train will not deliver you to the airport
at thus and such a time. If you additionally judge that this result is somehow
bad, that it is *frustrating*, and that generally speaking the direction of the
universe is not to your liking, then this is both because you have located value
somewhere it does not belong, outside the sphere of rationality, and because
you have emotionally clouded your own judgment-making faculty to your
detriment. You have relinquished control over your happiness by failing to
conform your judgments to the world as it is, preferring instead to rage
against fact and to demand with uninformed impotence that the world follow
a course other than the one it is set to follow, the optimal course ordained
by Zeus.

From one perspective there is something eminently, well, *reasonable*, even
anodyne, about the Stoic prescription. When nothing can be done to alter
some state of affairs that we have not preferred, then the available choices may
seem limited to two: whine ineffectually or acquiesce gracefully. The Stoics
note that when we acquiesce, we exercise our power to be happy. The matter
is wholly up to us. This is why the "wise man's life is always happy" (Cicero,
Tusculan Disputations 5.82 = LS 63 M).

So far, then, the Stoics seem to be prescribing wholesome medicine. Still,
two features of this Stoic attitude have occasioned criticism. First, it seems to
many that the Stoics are at variance with themselves, insisting both that the
optimally rational person *must* assent to the world as it is and yet also that that
same person is somehow free. Second, Stoic assaults on emotional engagement
with adversity seem to many somehow inhuman: is it not appropriate, because
fully human, to become angry when, despite one's own rational planning, the
universe thwarts one's intentions, hopes, and expectations? Especially when
the relevant quadrant of the universe is brought on by human ineptness and
culpable inattention? Is it not in fact simply bad that things go awry? To take
an example less favorable to the Stoics: if a child dies a miserable, avoidable
death, is it not right and appropriate that her parent should lament and grieve?
Is it not *human* to lament and grieve? It seems harsh and alien to adopt the
posture that the parent should simply assent to the proposition "My child was
mortal" and carry on with the day's set activities.[30] Of course the Stoic knew
that his child was mortal before her untimely death; but it does not follow
that his knowledge precludes or should preclude his feeling searing pain and
bewildering grief. Should he not call the sadness of the universe by its rightful
name and respond accordingly?

To appreciate the Stoic reaction to these sorts of questions, we must
investigate their accounts of human freedom and human emotion.

Stoic freedom

First, then, is the problem of freedom. If the universe is fully determined, if it has its own directionality, and if, as the Stoics repeatedly insist, we are but parts of the universe and so fully governed by its right reason (*orthos logos*), how can we be in any sense free? We are no less determined than any other part of nature. In fact, the Stoics repeatedly insist that the universe is determined, that every event is caused, and that we are but parts of its great causal nexus. As we have been describing their view so far, though, they maintain that even so we have the power to assent or not to assent: therein lies our freedom. But we may ask how we come to have this power. Is not this very act, this act of assent, itself part of the fabric of the universe, and so also governed by its immutable laws? If so, our own assent is governed by the will of Zeus. Yet if that is so, how can we regard our lives as anything other than fated?

Cicero presents one form of this sort of worry for the Stoics, but it is one that they can easily meet:

> If it is your fate to recover from this illness, you will recover whether or not you call the doctor. If it is your fate not to recover from this illness, you will not recover, whether or not you call the doctor. And one of these outcomes is fated. Therefore, calling a doctor achieves nothing at all.
>
> (Cicero, *On Fate* 28 = LS 55 S)

Only one of two outcomes will accrue when you are sick: either you are going to return to health or you are not. One of these outcomes is *determined*. So, why bother calling the doctor? It will only prove to be either a needless expense or a waste of money.

This argument is exactly parallel to another argument, the lazy man, which the Stoics consider only to reject. Let us update it slightly and introduce it as the Lazy Student (LS):

1   Necessarily, either I will receive top marks on my final examination or I will not receive top marks on my final examination.
2   If I am in fact to receive top marks, then studying is pointless, because unnecessary and so a waste of time.
3   If I am not in fact to receive top marks, then studying is pointless, because ineffectual and so a waste of time.
4   So, studying for my final examination is a waste of time.

A lazy student might find this argument congenial, and so head to the pub this evening rather than to the library for revision. Unfortunately for her, the Stoics are quick to point out, in so acting she deludes only herself.

The argument is *lazy*, says Cicero, because it encourages indolence: "If we gave in to it we would do nothing whatever in life."[31] It is also lazy because it relies upon slovenly and inept reasoning. Of course, (LS-1) is plausibly true:

there are only two outcomes for a student's final examination. Either she will receive top marks or she will not. Those are the only possibilities. The problem begins thereafter: both (LS-2) and (LS-3) are false. It may be true that she is to receive top marks on her examination; but this may be true *only if* she studies. Of course, she may fail to receive top marks even if she studies, but that does nothing to challenge the truth of the conditional *she will receive top marks only if she studies*. Compare: necessarily, either Stanislaw will arrive in Paris before noon or he will not. If he is to arrive there before noon, then there is no point in his buying an expensive rail ticket. If he is not, then, again, there is no point in his buying an expensive rail ticket. So, he should save his money and avoid buying an expensive rail ticket. Plainly, however, this argument is fallacious. If it is the case that Stanislaw is to arrive in Paris before noon, then this will be so *only if* he arranges some mode of transport.

More generally, the Lazy Student Argument conflates two radically distinct theses, which need to be kept scrupulously separated in discussions of human freedom:

- *Determinism*: every event has a cause.
- *Fatalism*: the world will turn out how it will turn out, no matter what I do.

The Stoics endorse determinism,[32] but they do not thereby, as the Lazy Student Argument pretends, embrace fatalism. Some things may turn out the way they do precisely and only because I cause them to happen. So far, then, the Stoics have nothing to fear from their commitment to determinism.

That allowed, there is another, deeper sort of worry about human freedom which the Lazy Student Argument fails to capture. This is a problem about freedom which does not trade upon a conflation between determinism and fatalism. Happiness is up to us, according to the Stoics, because with respect to any given proposition we might be entertaining it is within our power either to assent or to withhold assent. To revert to our example of the frustrated traveler: the rail passenger can assent to the proposition *that this train will not arrive at the airport in time to catch my scheduled flight*, without also assenting to the further propositions *that this is a horrible turn of events* or *that these incompetent rail employees are forever irksome in their incompetence*. It is only by assenting to these latter sorts of propositions that the passenger becomes angry. The first proposition, taken by itself, need have no such consequences. So, by choosing to withhold assent to these latter, value-laden sorts of propositions, the Stoic sage avoids all engagement with anger.

One may wonder, however, how this very choice between assenting or withholding assent is really anything but an illusion. One event will occur. It is determined – not fated in the sense specified by the fatalist, but determined all the same. This means, it seems, that there is an antecedent sufficient condition for its occurrence. If that is so, then even before I decide, whether I will assent or withhold assent is something readily known by the all-seeing

Zeus. This result, indeed, the Stoics consciously embrace, as becomes clear when they undertake to defend the practice of divination:

> Since all occurs by fate ... if there were some human being who could see with his mind the interconnection of all causes, he would certainly never be deceived. For whoever grasps the causes of future things must necessarily grasp what the future will be. But since no one other than god can do this, it is left to man that he comes to know what will be by means of various signs which indicate what will occur in the future. For the things which will be in the future do not spring up suddenly. For the passage of time is as the unwinding of a rope, bringing about nothing new and reproducing what was first there with each turn.
>
> (Cicero, *On Divination* i 127 = LS 55 O)

If a bystander does not know whether the sage will or will not assent to a given proposition, then that is only because he does not know all the relevant facts. An all-knowing god, by contrast, will grasp all the pertinent causes and will know the effects set to accrue from them. It may seem, then, that the facts are already in, that they are already there to be known, and that, consequently, the "choice" to assent or withhold is already determined, and so not really open to the agent. Determinism itself seems incompatible with freedom.

In this vein, one might argue *Against Stoic Freedom* (ASF) as follows:

1   If S's decision to assent or to withhold assent to a proposition is causally determined, then S makes no causal contribution to the direction of S's own action.
2   If S makes no causal contribution to the direction of S's own action, then S is impotent and could not have done otherwise with respect to any given action a.
3   If S is impotent and could not have done otherwise with respect to any given action a, then S is not free.
4   So, if S's decision to assent or to withhold assent to a proposition is causally determined, then S is not free.
5   If (4), then determinism and human freedom are incompatible.
6   So, determinism and human freedom are incompatible.

In sum, if every event is causally determined, then we are but dominoes in a long line, each being toppled by the one in the line before us. We may feel as if we are making choices, but our claims in this direction are about as credible as those of a domino which says, "Maybe I will hurl myself to the ground in a moment, or maybe I won't," but which then, just as it feels the force of the push from behind, says, "Yes, upon reflection, I think I will."

This argument, together with many variations upon it, has a long history in debates about human freedom. There are, consequently, a variety of different strategies open to those who wish to maintain the compatibility of determinism and freedom of the will. These are to be distinguished from those strategies which accept the incompatibility of freedom and determinism, but still then proceed to affirm freedom by denying determinism. Since they are thoroughgoing determinists, the Stoics have no interest in these sorts of incompatibilist strategies. Instead, they endorse a variety of compatibilism.

The Stoic Chrysippus in particular responds to the sort of challenge reflected in (ASF) with an engaging but difficult simile intended to help explicate his form of compatibilism. As Cicero reports:

> [When pressed,] Chrysippus resorts to his cylinder and spinning-top examples. These cannot begin to move without being pushed, but once that has happened, he thinks that it is through their own natures that the cylinder rolls and the top spins. "Hence," he says, "just as the person who pushed the cylinder gave it its beginning of motion but did not give it its ability to roll, in the same way, although an object when seen imprints something and as it were inscribes its appearance on the mind, assent will be in our power: assent, just as with the case of the cylinder, although instigated from the outside, will thereafter move through its own force and nature.
>
> (*De Fato* 42–3 = LS 62 C)

Chrysippus evidently means to call into question the linear picture of causation presupposed in (ASF-1). The situation is not, implies Chrysippus, that an agent makes no causal contribution by assenting or withholding assent. On the contrary, although assent must be prompted, whether it is finally offered or not depends upon the agent. So while it may be allowed that no action relies entirely upon the contributions of the human agent, it hardly follows that the human agent makes *no* contribution at all to the direction of his own behavior. A full explanation of a cylinder's rolling makes ineliminable mention of the cylinder's being cylindrical. This explanation refers, therefore, to a feature of its own nature. After all, if the cylinder were a block and not a cylinder, it would fail to roll even when pushed.

Crucial to this Stoic response is a distinction between several different kinds of causes. Some causes are sufficient by themselves, while others are causes which contribute to an effect without being themselves sufficient. Consider a car which has run out of gasoline. It might be towed to the station by a tow-truck, which would then be the sufficient or principal cause of its motion in that direction; or it might be pushed by three of the car's four passengers, no two of whom are strong enough to push the car by themselves. The individual passengers are then the *co-causes* of the car's motion.[33] So, the first Stoic observation is that when we speak of *the* cause of an event, we need also to specify the kind of cause in question, since different causal discriminations will yield different ascriptions of responsibility.

Chrysippus' cylinder example focuses attention on yet another kind of contributing cause: the car itself. A car has, after all, round wheels suited for rolling; without them the car could neither be pushed by its passengers nor pulled by a tow-truck. If, for instance, one or more of its wheels had been stolen by neighborhood hoodlums, then neither the current principal cause nor the current co-causes working in tandem would have sufficed for the car's motion. In the same way, the cylinder makes a causal contribution to its own motion in virtue of its own nature; it provides something without which the effect would not have accrued. So, one might infer, we are not passive in matters of assent: we contribute something by dint of our very ability to assent or withhold assent. Our own rational natures thus play a key, indispensible role.

Of course, there is *some* sense in which the sage is constrained to assent to what is in fact true; he is constrained to assent to what is true precisely because his surpassing virtue requires him to assent to the truth that the universe presents him. Surely, however, given that the sage is a rational being, and in fact strives to be maximally rational – not least because his happiness depends upon his being so – this is something the sage will only be too pleased to do: the sage positively wants to assent to every true proposition presented to him, while, of course, withholding assent from all the false ones. This is what it means for the sage to be rational, to have completed the full process of *oikeiôsis*.

A critic will want to press Chrysippus further on the purport of his cylinder analogy, however. For instance, is the cylinder free to roll or not roll once pushed? By analogy, then, is the sage really free to assent or to withhold assent once presented a true proposition? Which premise, precisely, does the cylinder example mean to undermine? It seemed at first that it was deployed to falsify (ASF-1), the claim that if S's decision to assent or to withhold assent to a proposition is causally determined, then S makes no causal contribution to the direction of S's own action. Upon reflection, however, it is not clear precisely how this might be thought to be so, since it does not immediately address the question of whether the assent itself is causally determined or not. Looked at another way, then, the example may be taken as an attempt to sidestep (ASF-2), the claim that if S makes no causal contribution to the direction of S's own action, then S is impotent and could not have done otherwise. It might be thought to *sidestep* rather than falsify (ASF-2) because the point would be that the sage *does* make a causal contribution, but that the contribution made is not by itself a principal or sufficient cause. This would in turn refocus interest on the conception of causation presupposed by the detractor, who has been maintaining against the Stoics that determinism and freedom are incompatible. This proves to be, then, just one of many instances in which the Stoics introduce necessary technical complexity into their approach to human happiness – and then rightly demand the same level of rigor from their opponents.

Naturally enough, this single Stoic rejoinder to worries about the compatibility between human freedom and determinism hardly settles the matter. On the contrary, Stoic discussions of freedom and determinism inaugurated a conversation about compatibilism which continues down to the present day. When we wonder about human freedom today, we reflect upon the nature of causation, on the sense in which we might have done otherwise if determinism is true, and we refrain, if we are suitably schooled, from conflating determinism and fatalism. In all these ways, we owe to the Stoics the terms of our debates.

Value monism: Stoic emotions and preferred indifferents

Let us grant provisionally that the Stoic sage is free, that he contributes to the direction of his own action by assenting to all and only true propositions, and that in this way he proves to be consummately rational. Moreover, the sage is unflappable in the face of adversity, because he never assents to any proposition which is inappropriate. As the Stoic Epictetus contends:

> It is not things themselves that disturb men, but their convictions about things. For example, death is nothing terrible – for if it were, it would have seemed so to Socrates. What is terrible is rather a conviction about death, namely the conviction that death is terrible. So, whenever we are impeded or disturbed or distressed, let us blame no one but ourselves, that is, let us blame nothing but our own convictions.
>
> (*Meditations* 5 = LS 65 U)

There is nothing inherently terrible about death. Death simply is. If death seems terrible to you, that is only because you are thinking that death is somehow bad or wrong. What is wrong – in the sense of being false – is rather the thought that death is good or bad: the judgment *that my child's death is a bad thing* is false, as is the judgment *that my child's death is a good thing*. Each of these judgments locates a value in a circumstance bereft of normativity, beyond, of course, the normativity it may inherit by being one small component of the rationally ordered, good-directed universe. As regards the sage considered locally, what has value is virtue. The Stoic sage, of course, strictly avoids false judgment and so would never assent to either of these false propositions, locating as they do value where it does not reside. Doing so is simply incompatible with the sage's virtue.

It may in consequence seem that the Stoic sage is a moral monster. Such a person may well appear inhuman, an insentient stone unwilling to grieve even for the tragic death of his own child. Would not such a man be devoid of something deeply human, namely the sort of compassion we expect of morally mature members of our communities? One might easily think, against the Stoics, that the capacity for appropriate emotional response is something noble and decent rather than something unfortunate and shameful.

The Stoics reject this sort of criticism. Their response has two flanks, one regarding the character and suitability of emotion and the other, again, regarding the proper locus of value. They portray the sage as a model to us all precisely because he lacks emotions; and they argue that the sage is a model as emotion-free because he alone appropriately tracks value. The sage alone sees matters aright and so avoids ascribing value to valueless items; the sage alone does not mistake items without value for items with value. By contrast, emotional responses arise in others because they locate value, positive or negative, where in fact there is none. The non-sage has emotions, then, because he has false judgments about value. In fact, strikingly, an emotion *is* a false value judgment.

To characterize their view in a manner initially favorable to the Stoics, let us return to our mundane example of the delayed train. The value judgments associated with the delay are not in the least unavoidable. On the contrary, you become agitated when, and only when, you decide that the circumstance in which you find yourself is insufferable, and this you do by assenting to such propositions as *this delay is a disaster for my future* or *these egregiously incompetent railroad employees are hopeless*. Just as Epictetus says, if the employees annoy you, then that is because *you* judge them to be annoying. Further, your future will be as it will be. If you judge the direction of your future to be disastrous, then that is only because you had false views about how it was to be, and consequently now also have false views about its value-laden features. Zeus never thought that things would be other than they are. You, for some reason, are intent upon ascribing a negative value to the direction of your life. This your life in fact lacks. Absent such false judgments, you will find yourself sitting composedly in the train assenting to the true proposition *that this train will not deliver me to the airport in time for my flight*. Beyond that, you will assent to nothing, unless it is the proposition *that this delay forms a small part of the rational order of the universe and is fully in accord with its right reason*. Taken by itself, your assent to the true, value-free proposition occasions no further response. Certainly your assenting to this proposition by itself provides no occasion for growing agitated.

Still, the Stoic conception of the emotions is bound to seem peculiar, because highly revisionary. Although there is some tension and unclarity in their view as it develops, the orthodox Stoic position is this: an emotion is actually neither more nor less than a belief of a certain sort. As the Stoics see things, emotions are simply wayward movements in the rational soul, where a wayward movement is a false belief, one perhaps accompanied by some bodily concomitants, but the bodily motions do not constitute the emotions properly considered:

> [The Stoics] say that an emotion is an excessive impulse and is disobedient to rational decision, or that it is a movement of the soul contrary to nature; and they say that all passions belong to the soul's commanding faculty ... The four primary genera are: appetite and fear ... [and] pleasure and distress ... By "contrary to nature" in their outline of emotion they mean something that happens contrary to right reason (*orthos logos*) and against natural reason. Anyone in an emotional state turns away from reason, but

not in a way comparable to those who have been deceived in some way (for instance, those who have been deceived into believing that atoms are first principles ...), but rather in a peculiar way. For those in an emotional state, even if they learn or are taught to realize that they should not feel distress or fear or should not in general be in an emotional state of soul, they nevertheless do not give them up, but are brought by their emotional states to a place where they are controlled by tyranny.

(Stobaeus 2.88, 8–90, 6 = LS 65 A)

Fear is the belief that something future is evil and so to be avoided; desire the belief that something future is good and to be pursued; pleasure the belief that something present is good and to be cherished; and pain the belief that something present is bad and a source of distress. Other species of passion are all subordinate to these four.[34] All these emotions have in common that they are false beliefs, each incorporating a time-index and a value judgment. Unlike a garden-variety false belief, the agitation and bad feeling associated with an emotional state tends to linger even after the false belief has been uncovered and corrected. Examples favorable to the Stoics might include jealousy and mourning, which are both species of pain. Even if a husband were persuaded that his wife's having sexual relations with other men were not really a bad thing, his churning feelings of jealousy might well linger.

On its face, the revisionary character of the Stoic theory of the emotions seems an affront to common sense. This, indeed, is just what some of the Stoics' ancient critics contended. From a common conception, emotions are, or at least centrally involve, affective dimensions: emotions *feel* a certain way. Indeed, some theories of the emotions, along with some uncomplicated common-sense conceptions, treat the emotions as exhausted by feelings. On this, the *purely affective approach*, an emotion simply is a feeling of a certain sort, a feeling which might well be opposed to reason, or, short of that, will at least exist apart from reason. In either case, on the purely affective approach, an emotion is not itself a species of reason, contrary to what the Stoics contend. On the purely affective approach, to experience joy, for instance, is to feel a certain way; this feeling is not at all, as the Stoics contend, a judgment to the effect that something has or lacks a value-property. The Stoics deny this altogether – and that is apt to seem perverse. This is why the Stoic theory of the emotions has met with incredulity since antiquity.

In response, the Stoics may fairly point out that emotions encompass value judgments in all sorts of intimate ways. If Sally hates Pauline, then presumably she judges Pauline to be contemptible; minimally she assents to the proposition *that Pauline is a bad sort* or *that Pauline is a horrible person* – else she could hardly be said to hate her. To this extent, the Stoics seem perfectly justified in insisting that emotions *involve* judgments in central, even crucial ways. Yet it is a further, more demanding and much less intuitive step to claim that emotions *are* judgments. If we progress along a continuum from purely affective or feeling theories of the emotions, through moderate, mixed theories according to which emotions have both affective and cognitive components, then we arrive at last at purely cognitive theories of the Stoic variety. On their approach, an emotion has no intrinsic affective component whatsoever; an emotion is exhausted by being the judgment that it is.

Importantly, for the Stoics, emotions are not just judgments, but *false* judgments. This is why, after all, the Stoic sage is emotion-free: he assents to nothing false but always lives by judging in accordance with nature. This is equally why, then, the Stoics derogate the emotions and urge their extirpation. Here, however, great care must be taken if we are to understand the Stoics on their own terms. A familiar sort of rationalist disvalues emotions and treats them as impediments to reason. Emotions cloud sound judgment, this rationalist insists; or, worse, she continues, emotions too often combat and overwhelm reason, causing people to behave in ways that occasion regret.

The Stoics do not endorse this sort of rationalist view: the emotions cannot cloud judgment or combat reason, because they are not alien non-rational episodes gurgling up in some quadrant of the soul secluded from reason. When they contend that "all emotions belong to the commanding faculty,"[35] the Stoics mean not just that emotion is subordinate to reason but that each emotion *is* an instance of reasoning. Further, because they are judgments, emotions run contrary to nature not by being ungovernable contentless feelings of one sort or another, but rather, and more simply, by being false. While not every false judgment is an emotion, every emotion is a false judgment. Living in accordance with nature requires assenting to all and only true propositions; emotions implicate an agent in assenting to false propositions; so, emotions are contrary to nature.

However one may come to regard the revisionary character of the Stoic analysis of emotions, it seems plain that the final plausibility of their approach rests in part on the second flank of their response to the charge of moral monstrosity. This second flank concerns the proper locus of value. If we come to agree with the Stoics that an emotion is a false judgment, then this is at least in part because we have also accepted a highly distinctive, even idiosyncratic theory of value. This is the value monism of the Stoics, according to which virtue alone has value. Nothing else – not wealth, not health, not food, not friendship, not love – has any value whatsoever. The sage is indifferent to all such matters.

It is instructive in this connection to appreciate that one might not be persuaded by the Stoic analysis of emotion, according to which an emotion is neither more nor less than a false judgment, and yet come to view the world in largely Stoic terms by nonetheless accepting their value monism. Suppose, for instance, that you have been persuaded by the Stoics to abandon as feeble the purely affective theory of the emotions, the common-sense understanding according to which they are nothing more than feelings. Instead, you have come to realize in the face of Stoic prodding that the emotions centrally involve judgments of various sorts. You have been moved, then, to embrace a moderate mixed theory of the emotions, according to which an emotion is a complex of an affective state and a judgment. This seems plausible for many emotions, including, as we have seen, hatred. It is easy to extend this same thought to all four primary Stoic emotions: fear, desire, pleasure, and pain. From this, it will be a small step to extend it to species of these basic types. For example, jealousy will be the familiar feeling of uncomfortable suspicion coupled with the judgments that one's partner is entertaining other lovers *and* that this is a very bad thing. Love will be the familiar warm fuzzy feeling of longing coupled with the judgment that the object of love has all manner of fine and estimable qualities.

To be clear, this is not the strict Stoic theory, but it accords with their view that the emotions centrally involve value judgments. On this mixed, moderate theory, emotions partially consist in judgments of value, negative or positive. Even allowing this much, one might fall in line with the Stoic sage – but only on the assumption that Stoic value monism is defensible. One can appreciate this by focusing on an argument about the Emotions of the Sage (ES):

1   The sage lives in accordance with nature.
2   If he lives in accordance with nature, then the sage assents to all and only true propositions.
3   So, the sage assents to all and only true propositions.
4   Nothing has value other than virtue.
5   So, if a proposition p ascribes a value ϕ to a subject lacking virtue, then p is false.
6   So, for any proposition p ascribing a value ϕ to a subject lacking virtue, the sage will not assent to p.
7   Every emotion is a false judgment, ascribing a value ϕ to a subject lacking virtue.
8   So, the sage will never assent to a proposition constituting an emotion.
9   So, the sage will be free of all emotion.

So far we have in effect been concentrating on (ES-7), the claim that every emotion is a false judgment, involving assent to a false value-ascribing proposition. This premise reflects the Stoic *analysis* of emotion.

Note now, however, that one could reasonably reject (ES-7), by adopting a moderate theory, according to which emotions incorporate value judgments without being exhausted by them, or by allowing more weakly still that emotions are value-responsive and so vary with judgments of value. By adopting one of these more moderate theories of the emotions, one could, and presumably would, continue to act in the manner of the sage. In particular, one might do this by embracing (ES-4), the claim that nothing has value other than virtue. For if one accepts (ES-4), and allows that the emotions are at least value-responsive, then it will follow that no emotional states will arise in the subject who withholds assent from propositions which wrongly attach value to value-less states of affairs. So, in this way, although one would certainly not become a sage without endorsing (ES-7) (for then one would assent to the false proposition that the Stoic theory of emotions is false), one might nevertheless become moderately sagacious, and live a life of emotional intelligence. All that is required is that one endorse (ES-4) from the perspective of one who also accepts the moderate view that the emotions are value-responsive.

That allowed, (ES-4) is a surprising claim in its own right. The worry here is not that the Stoics are value monists, for many others have been value monists as well. The Epicureans are value monists, for example, but think, more in line with common conception, that only pleasure has ultimate intrinsic value. What is striking in the Stoic approach is that they contend that virtue is the sole value. Nothing else. Not wealth. Not health. Not even pleasure.

Again, although our sources are mixed on this point, let us put the Stoic view in its most extreme formulation, which is nicely captured by Cicero, who has the Stoic Cato represent their view in a tidy syllogism:

> Everything which is good is praiseworthy. However, everything praiseworthy is virtuous (*honestum*). Therefore, that which is good is virtuous. Does this conclusion follow? Certainly. You see that it follows from the two premises laid down. Now, of the two premises from which this conclusion follows, it is customary to deny the first premise, by saying that not everything good is praiseworthy. For it is taken for granted that the praiseworthy is virtuous [= the second premise]. But it is thoroughly absurd to claim that the good is not something to be desired, or that what is to be desired is not pleasing, or if pleasing that it is not also to be valued (*diligendum*), and therefore that it is also to be approved of – and so also praiseworthy; but the praiseworthy is honourable. So, it follows that what is good (*bonum*) is also virtuous (*honestum*).
>
> (Cicero, *On Ends* iii 27 = LS 60 N)[36]

Importantly, this passage follows Cato's recapitulation of the process of *oikeiôsis*, which, as we have seen, eventuates in the emergence of the fully rational and virtuous sage. Cato stresses in this connection that virtue (*honestum*) is living in accordance with nature, and that this *honestum* is the *only* good (*solum bonum*; Cicero, *On Ends* iii 17 = LS 59 D).

As stated, Cato's argument that virtue is the only good (VOG) is entirely perspicuous:

1   Everything good (*bonum*) is praiseworthy (*laudabile*).
2   Everything praiseworthy (*laudabile*) is virtuous (*honestum*).
3   So, everything good (*bonum*) is virtuous (*honestum*).

Cato occupies himself with defending (VOG-1), by offering an ancillary argument on its behalf: everything good is something to be desired and whatever is desired is pleasing; yet everything pleasing is to be valued and thus worthy of receiving our approval; if something is worthy of receiving our approval then, of course, it is praiseworthy. Thus, just as (VOG-1) asserts, everything good is praiseworthy.

One might wish to take issue with one or another of the links in this chain, but let us set that aside. For there is a deeper problem with (VOG). If it is meant to be an argument that virtue (*honestum*) is the *only* good (*solum bonum*), then the argument is a *non sequitur*. One might happily grant (VOG-3), the claim that everything good (*bonum*) is virtuous (*honestum*), without also concluding that virtue is the only good. One might be quite willing, that is, to concede that virtue is *a* good, or indeed even that it is *highest* good, without also concluding that it is *the* good in the sense of its being the *only* good. One might think, as for instance, Aristotle does,[37] that happiness is the highest good, while allowing that there are all manner of other goods, including health and pleasure, which are good because they lead to happiness or even partly constitute happiness. Though good, such good things are not the highest good; typically, though not necessarily, their goodness derives from their being subordinate to the highest good. So, for Aristotle, the highest good is not the only good.

Taken in this extreme way – and this is the way in which the Stoic Cato evidently intends it to be taken – (VOG) is an uncompelling argument. Of course, the Stoics may yet accept a conclusion stronger than (VOG) warrants on other grounds. Such grounds might, perhaps, derive from the *oikeiôsis* argument (OA) discussed in section 5.3. Recall the final conclusion of that argument, (OA-9), that every human being must come to recognize and appreciate rationality as the only good. As his progression towards fully mature rationality proceeds, the Stoic grows ever keener in insight and so sees not only that the cosmos as a whole is rationally structured, but that he himself has some role to play within that whole. Crucially, he realizes self-reflexively that his understanding of that role is itself an expression of his own rationality, that *by understanding he is doing something good*, that, in short, his share of goodness resides in his own rationality.[38] Ultimately, it is precisely this general rationality – manifested locally as the sage himself understanding the cosmically expressed godly order of all – that the Stoic comes to recognize as the sole locus of value in the universe. The sage thus also comes to appreciate that his own local value relative to the value of the universe consists in nothing more than molding himself to nature's direction. This is what it means, finally, for the Stoic always to live in accordance with nature.

Once again, however, the Stoic view is at least initially highly counter-intuitive. The Stoics seem blithely to ignore many other instances of goodness available to us in life, as Diogenes Laertius reports:

[The Stoics] say that among existing things some are good, others are bad, and others are neither of these. The virtues (courage, moderation and the rest) are good; the opposites of these (foolishness, injustice and the rest) are bad. Everything which neither benefits nor harms one is neither of these: for instance, life, health, pleasure, beauty, strength, wealth, reputation, noble birth, and their opposites, death, disease, pain, ugliness, weakness, poverty, low repute, ignoble birth and the like ... These things are not good or bad but are indifferent, though of the preferred sort ... Benefitting, not harming, is the peculiar characteristic of what is good. But wealth and health no more do benefit than they harm. Therefore, wealth and health are not something good. Further, they say, that which can be used well and badly is not something good. But wealth and health can be used well and badly. Therefore, wealth and health are not something good.

> (DL vii 101–103 = LS 58 A; cf. Alexander,
> *On Fate* 199.14–22 = LS 61 N)

On the Stoic view, then, we should not regard health as something good. Virtue is good and nothing else. Nor should we judge pain to be bad; pain is not bad, but rather neither good nor bad. Indeed, as we have seen, to judge pain to be bad is not only a false judgment but the sort of false judgment that qualifies as an emotion. If we wish to be sages, then, we should avoid all such emotional entanglements.

As is their custom, the Stoics offer a series of arguments for their position; and if these arguments are compelling, then the initially counterintuitive character of their view must simply be set aside. As a Stoic could well observe, the history of science is littered with discarded theses whose replacements struck all but their earliest adherents as so wildly counterintuitive and patently false as to merit not the slightest consideration. For one example among many, a fair number of perfectly intelligent, well-educated people found Darwin's theory of evolution so outlandish as to be quite literally incredible; and so they simply recoiled from it in ridicule without considering his presentation of the data. These detractors were not sages.

What, then, can be said on behalf of Stoic value monism? First, there are the sorts of arguments we have just seen recounted by Diogenes Laertius. Second, there follow a series of softening accommodations. Despite their value monism, the Stoics recognize a category of things Diogenes mentions in passing as "indifferents ... of the preferred sort."

As for the positive arguments, Diogenes presents two, though the Stoics offer many more, some rather involved, like the *oikeiôsis* argument, and others rather terse, like Cato's syllogism. Let us consider the second of Diogenes' arguments, an argument from *use of goodness* (UG):

1   If x can be used well or badly, then x is not good.
2   Everything other than virtue can be used well or badly.
3   So, nothing other than virtue is good.
4   Virtue is, however, good.
5   So, virtue is the only good.

Once again, we find the Stoics arguing succinctly and forcefully for an initially surprising contention.

We are granting (UG-4), the claim that virtue is something good. (UG-2), the claim that everything other than virtue can be used well or badly, seems initially plausible. Wealth, for instance, is something neutral: one might use it for good or ill. It places no constraints on its use by dint of its own nature. Perhaps other examples of putative neutral states are not so easily dismissed on this score, but we may set them aside at present. If we do, we are left with only (UG-1), the claim if *x* can be used well or badly, then *x* is not good. This claim is problematic. To begin, it sets the bar for something's qualifying as good rather high. It might be thought a reasonable standard for something's qualifying as *the* good or the *highest* good, but it seems to rule out a vast category of apparently good things from the category in which they would otherwise naturally be placed. Thus, even if we grant that health, and eyesight, and intelligence, and strength, and so on for a long list of putative goods, can be used for good or ill, we might none the less be inclined to count them among things rightly regarded not only as good but as intrinsically good.

The Stoics will wish to address this sort of worry too, but in the present context we may move to their second sort of response, one which seems somehow to qualify their strident value monism: Diogenes mentions a category of non-good things which are "indifferents ... of the preferred sort." According to the Stoics, properly speaking none of the things in the long list of customary goods mentioned by Diogenes – life, health, pleasure, beauty, strength, wealth, reputation, noble birth – in fact qualifies as anything good. If these things are not regarded as good, then they should have no value at all for the Stoic, positive or negative.

To illustrate, suppose Hildegund does not really care at all about opera. She neither likes it nor dislikes it. In fact, she simply does not give much thought to the genre. If someone were to offer her a pair of free tickets to see Wagner's *Parsifal*, we would accordingly expect her to be indifferent to the prospect. By contrast, if Wolfgang thinks that opera is one of the world's great goods and regards Wagner's operas as the surpassing instance of the genre, then other things being equal we would expect him to respond warmly to the offer of free tickets to *Parsifal*. She is indifferent to the tickets; he values them. They have a neighbor who detests opera and especially loathes Wagner. He likes to repeat Mark Twain's remark that "Wagner's music is not as bad as it sounds." "No," he then adds, "It's even *worse*." The neighbor, we may presume, will heap scorn on the offer of free tickets. He too, like Wolfgang, places a value on opera, but in his case it is a disvalue. Only Hildegund is indifferent.

By analogy, then, we should expect the Stoic sage to be perfectly indifferent to life, health, beauty, wealth and the rest, and instead to value virtue alone. For some Stoics, at least, the analogy is perfect. One early, fairly extreme and ultimately rather unorthodox Stoic, Aristo, affirms just that: we are to "live in perfect indifference to all those things that are of an intermediate character between virtue and vice, making not the slightest difference between them, but regarding them all on a footing of equality" (DL vii 160).

Aristo is like Hildegund. He adopts neither pro- nor con-attitudes towards anything other than virtue. Mainstream Stoics disagree – or, at least, in one manner of speaking they disagree. Chrysippus, the most important early Stoic, in fact criticizes Aristo by name,[39] insisting that life would be impossible if we were to maintain a *perfect* indifference to all matters neither virtuous nor vicious. To see how he proceeds, let us call items on Diogenes' long list of goods *customary goods*. To these, he says, the Stoic is indeed indifferent. Still, among the customary goods to which the Stoic is indifferent some may be *preferred* or *promoted* or *selected*. (The Greek word is *proêgmenon*, which might fairly be translated in any of these ways.) These preferred indifferents are contrasted with dispreferred or demoted or deselected items on the indifferent list of customary goods (*apoproêgmenon*). Again, Cicero puts the matters plainly, commenting on Zeno, the founder of Stoicism:

> To Zeno, all other things are neither good nor bad, but nevertheless some of them are in accordance with nature and others contrary to nature, as well as another class between them, namely intermediate things. He taught that things in accordance with nature are to be esteemed and that they have a certain value, and their opposites, the opposite; things which were neither in accord with nature nor contrary to it he left in the intermediate class. These latter he declared to have no motive force whatsoever, while among the others relevant to choice, the more valuable he termed "preferred" and the less valuable he termed "non-preferred."
>
> (Cicero, *Academica* i 36–37)

As represented here, Zeno recognizes Aristo's category of truly indifferent things, but shrinks it considerably so that other indifferents may yet be preferred and others dispreferred.

Aristo's view has a certain sort of welcome if relentless clarity. He treats the class of good things and the class of things to be preferred as perfectly co-extensive. All and only good things are to be preferred. So, the items on the list of customary goods are in fact neither good nor to be preferred. Nothing has positive value unless it is good, and only virtue is good; indifferent things like life and health fall outside the sphere of virtue, and consequently have no value. So, for Aristo, all and only virtuous things are to be preferred. Conversely, vice is co-extensive with what is bad, and so all and only vicious things are to be shunned. To the rest he is simply indifferent.

When they reject this extreme view, mainstream Stoics have a harder time explaining what they mean by "indifferent." There are, says Zeno, like Chrysippus after him, a class of *preferred indifferents*. Initially, this seems oxymoronic: the notion of "preferred indifferents" calls to mind the revised maxim of Orwell's *Animal Farm* that "All animals are equal, but some animals are more equal than others." After all, if Wolfgang prefers something, then it is manifestly *not* a matter of indifference for him, while if Hildegund is indifferent to something, then she will neither prefer nor disprefer it.

Instead, all things in this class of indifferents will be for her a matter of, well, indifference.

As Cicero represents the orthodox Stoics, they break out of this worry by denying that value and goodness are completely coextensive: they *value* some indifferent things, but in doing so they do not come to regard the things they value as good. In responding in this way, the Stoics incurred the disdainful dismissal of their critics in antiquity – and the stream of invective has never really abated. Plutarch derided them as indulging in double-speak and obfuscation:[40] they pretend to be indifferent to health and wealth, and to sickness and poverty, but then they discriminate among them, preferring some over others and according a value to those they favor while denying value to those they discount.

Plutarch finds a critical colleague in Antiochus, a member of the descendant of Plato's Academy. Antiochus charged the Stoics with officially denying but then surreptitiously affirming the goodness of health and wealth.[41] After all, he notes, if I say that x is to be preferred over y, or that x is to be selected rather than y, then am I not saying that x is *better* than y in my estimation? Yet surely "better" is the comparative of "good"? If so, then I am saying both that x has more goodness than y and that x has no share of goodness. To illustrate, if Mordechai prefers health to sickness, then he thinks that health is *better* than sickness. Yet if he thinks that health is better than sickness, then he also thinks that health has some measure of goodness – more of a measure of goodness, in fact, than he thinks sickness has. So, it is hard to see how Mordechai could also be a Stoic who believes that health is something indifferent and utterly bereft of goodness. When pressed, Mordechai the Stoic insists that health has a sort of value which is not at all good. Antiochus will surely ask him for amplification. What sort of value is not good? For his part, Antiochus urges the Stoics to give up on the pretense that virtue is the *only* good, even if they persist in maintaining that virtue is the pre-eminent or highest good.

This is, of course, only the beginning of a dispute and not its resolution. It is noteworthy that this difficulty about preferred indifferents in Stoicism brings us around to the very place where we left our discussion of the Epicureans: in a dispute about the locus of value.[42] Each school espouses a form of value monism, the Epicureans as hedonists and the Stoics as champions of virtue, and each school is called to task for some of the consequences, or alleged consequences, of their commitments in these directions. Although we have not sought to advance conclusive refutations of either of their approaches, we have seen that the routes towards equanimity espoused by these schools encounter formidable roadblocks before arriving at their shared destination. So far, at least, neither school demonstrably delivers the imperturbable tranquility it promises.

5.4   Skepticism

The Hellenistic Skeptics seize upon the very existence of these sorts of roadblocks to forge yet another route to tranquility. In fact, they undertake to construct additional impediments in the pathways of the other Hellenistic schools, because they regard their dogmatic pretensions as wholly misguided: according to the Skeptics, the dogmatism of schools like the Stoics and the Epicureans, and equally of schools like the Platonists and Aristotelians, positively impedes any pathway to tranquility.

The Skeptics thus wish to suggest that the disagreements and the (alleged) failures we have been witnessing so far are consequential in a surprising way. What is sole good? Is it pleasure? Virtue? Happiness? Is there a *sole* good or does the world hold a plurality of goods? Is there really such a thing as goodness? If so, is it something objective or something subjective? Different schools promulgate different responses to these and like questions. Consider as a case in point the difficulties regarding Stoic and Epicurean value monism we have just been exploring: the Epicureans are hedonists who think that the good is pleasure; the Stoics counter that so far from being *the* good, pleasure is not even *a* good. These divergences, the Skeptics urge, are symptomatic of an initially uncomfortable fact about us: we know much less than we would like to think we know, even about some of the most familiar and fundamental features of our existence.

Still more troubling is the admission that if we are willing to put aside our unthinking prejudices and give the proponents of these various schools a fair hearing, then it is easy to find ourselves growing attracted in turn to each of the different and incompatible views they espouse. Especially when confronted with a confident, superior dialectician, we may find ourselves coming to be persuaded by views we first found implausible and counterintuitive. First we regarded death as something to be feared; then we were persuaded that perhaps, since it is nothing, death is not so bad after all. First we thought it natural and appropriate to emote in the face of loss; then we were persuaded that loss has no negative value, since it does not affect our virtue. Along the way, we first accepted and then rejected hedonism and then also changed our minds about the character of virtue and the locus of value.

Even if we have not made this journey ourselves, we might easily take a step back from the intra-scholastic and inter-scholastic debates of the philosophers we have been reviewing and wonder whether it is at all likely that one side or the other will ever emerge as holding the golden key to understanding. If we do step back in this way, we are likely to be given pause. We see various perfectly intelligent, indisputably capable thinkers being persuaded this way and that about even such fundamental questions as whether pleasure is or is not something good, about whether the good is something subjective or objective, about whether the good is one thing or several – or is indeed rather nothing at all. We should then wonder in a more general way, the Skeptics suggest, about whether anyone has any *real* grounds for endorsing one answer to these sorts of questions over any other. Perhaps we should simply admit that we do not – that we cannot – know such matters and so simply stop trying to figure them out. We cannot fathom the depths of the deepest questions of human existence. It is better that we should stop pretending otherwise.

This Skeptical suggestion may seem a defeatist attitude of despair. Perhaps, we are apt to counter, if only we try harder we will uncover the deep natures of such matters. Then, having earned the answers to our questions, we will be satisfied and find our repose in the tranquility of truth. The Skeptics of the Hellenistic period recommend quite the opposite tack: we should come to embrace our failure and accept that knowledge of how things really are is simply beyond our ken. Happily, they contend, our doing so turns out to be far from a miserable admission of defeat. On the contrary, the moment we acknowledge our limitations turns out also to be the moment of our liberation. When we relinquish our prideful and self-deceptive pretensions to knowledge, a great release descends upon us, and it is the very release the Stoics and Epicureans were chasing, but chasing in vain:

> A person who takes no position as to what is by nature good or bad neither avoids nor pursues intensely. Indeed, what happened to the Skeptic is just like what is told of Apelles the painter. Once, they say, when he was painting a horse and wished to represent in the painting the horse's foam, he was so unsuccessful that he gave up the attempt and flung at the picture the sponge which he used to wipe the paints off his brush, and the mark of the sponge produced the effect of a horse's foam. So, too, the Skeptics were hoping to achieve tranquility (*ataraxia*) by resolving the anomaly of the way things appear (*phainomena*) and the way things are thought to be (*nooumena*), and, being unable to do this, they suspended judgment. But then, as if by chance, when they were suspending judgment, tranquility (*ataraxia*) followed, as a shadow follows a body.
>
> (Sextus, *Outlines of Pyrrhonism* i 27–28)

By their own account, the Skeptics made a wholly fortuitous but happy discovery. Like other philosophers, they were striving to determine how things stand in the world. They wanted to know what *really* has value, not what merely seems to have value; they wanted to know whether death is *really* something to be feared or merely seems terrifying; they wanted to know whether the universe is *really* organized along rational principles in accordance with the will of Zeus or merely seems that way to us because our tropism for order bids us to etch upon the unstructured universe the pattern we hope to uncover there.

At some point in their intellectual struggles, the Skeptics gave up and simply suspended all belief – and then something wonderful happened: the tranquility they had sought in the elusive security of knowledge was visited upon them. Like Apelles the painter, the prize that had eluded them in their ineffectual labors was gifted them in the frustrated moment of their presumed defeat.

A moral for us all lies near. If we really seek tranquility, say the Skeptics, the route is not through dogmatism, but through its polar opposite, suspension of all belief. When we relinquish our pretensions to knowledge, we win the prize we had sought but could not attain in our earnest but ultimately futile inquiries.

Sources of Skepticism and core approaches

When we speak of the Hellenestic Skeptics, the caution regarding sources we have entered regarding the Stoics and Epicureans is once more apposite. Indeed, it is still more in order. Although Epicurus established a reasonably secure set of doctrines defining the contours of his school and the Stoics adhered to a set of core theses even while refining them in successive waves, the situation with Skepticism is far more complex and fractured. We have first the early figure of Pyrrho, evidently an active Skeptic who lived from about 365 to 270 BC, but who left behind not a school or a movement but at most a loose cadre of followers. More than a century after his death, Aenesidemus founded a movement bearing Pyrrho's name, the Pyrrhonists, who remained active for several centuries more. Aenesidemus founded this movement evidently in a pique of dissatisfaction with the members of the Academy with which he had been associated. This Academy is the same Academy that Plato had founded, though some while after his death it had taken a decidedly Skeptical turn under the headship of Arcesilaus, who ran it from around 273 to 242 BC. It may seem odd to think of the school founded by the author of *Republic* as a bastion of Skepticism, but the members of the Academy in this period saw matters very differently. Highlighting Socrates' frequent disavowals of knowledge, they saw themselves as taking up mantel of the true Academy, and began a long and entrenched practice of assailing Stoic claims to knowledge. We may do them a service by viewing them as they viewed themselves, as doing no more than Socrates had done in practicing his elenchus on figures such as Euthyphro and Meno.[43] Like Socrates, the Skeptics saw themselves as upending the unwarranted pretensions to knowledge displayed by their own contemporary Menos and Euthyphros, namely the Stoics, Epicureans, and Aristotelians – dogmatists one and all.

The fact that Aenesidemus broke with those in the Skeptical Academy by deriding them as "Stoics fighting with Stoics" already suggests the internal complexity of Hellenistic Skepticism.[44] Given that their credo, so to speak, involved them in disavowing all claims to knowledge and even belief, it is impossible to identify any set of propositions endorsed by them all, or indeed, properly speaking, even by any one of them taken individually. Still, the Skeptics did manage to find sources of both agreement and disagreement with one another, so that they may be regarded if not as a school then at least as a band of fellow travelers.

Even so, disagreements within this band were fairly pronounced. One form of disagreement pertained to the methods and ultimate aims of the Skeptical posture in philosophy. Sextus Empiricus, a Skeptic of the second century AD, an avowed Pyrrhonist, offers a brief characterization of the types of Skepticism to be encountered in the ancient world:

When people search for something, the likely outcome is that either they find it or, if they do not find it, they either accept that it cannot be found or they continue to search. So also in the case of what is sought in philosophy, I think, some people have claimed to have found the truth, others have asserted that it cannot be apprehended, and others are still searching. Those who think that they have found it are the Dogmatists, properly so called – for example, the followers of Aristotle and Epicurus, the Stoics, and certain others. The followers of Clitomachus and Carneades, as well as other Academics, have asserted that it cannot be apprehended. The Skeptics (*skeptikoi*) continue to search.

(Outlines of Pyrrhonism i 1–3)

Sextus draws two distinctions, the first of which is inter-scholastic and the second of which is intra-scholastic. The Aristotelians, Epicureans, and Stoics are all dogmatists, philosophers issuing positive views about all manner of subjects. All Skeptics deny the success of the claims of the dogmatists and ridicule their pretensions to knowledge. Even so, among the Skeptics, some are, so to speak, *dogmatically skeptical* while others are *provisionally skeptical*. The dogmatic Skeptics, including according to Sextus the Academics, claim to know that things cannot be known and so recommend the *permanent* suspension of all beliefs. Other Skeptics, the Pyrrhonists, deny even this: they are non-dogmatic Skeptics, who provisionally suspend judgment but carry on seeking. These are sometimes referred to as *zetetic Skeptics*, since they do not give up on the process of inquiry (inquiry = *zetêsis* in Greek). As they view their own situation, they have no grounds for claiming – dogmatically, as they would contend – that inquiry will be forever futile.

We will investigate the presentation of Pyrrhonian Skepticism as we have it from Sextus Empiricus, both because he is a rich source of data and because he is himself a practicing Pyrrhonist. In so doing, we will largely set aside the intricate and interesting intra-sholastic disputes to which he alludes, and we will mean by "Skepticism" the sort of Pyrrhonian Skepticism practiced by Sextus. As we do so, however, we should bear in mind that we are mining but one vein of ancient Skepticism.

Let us enter into the spirit of the Pyrrohnian enterprise as Sextus himself introduces it:

Concerning the Skeptic Way we shall now give an outline and account, stating in advance that as regards none of the things that we are about to say do we firmly maintain that matters are absolutely as stated, but in each instance we are simply reporting, like a chronicler, what now appears to us to be the case.

(Outlines of Pyrrhonism i 4)

We are to avoid dogmatism, according to Sextus, even about our own Skepticism. We report how things appear to us, and we acknowledge, in all humility, that we may well be misguided. The world is a dark, mysterious place – so dark that we do not even know how light it is not.

The character of Pyrrhonism

Sextus presents the zetetic Skeptic as someone who shares a goal in common with other philosophers:

> Skepticism has as its inception and cause, we say, the hope of attaining tranquility (*ataraxia*). Men of noble nature had been disturbed by the irregularity of things, and puzzled as to where they should place their belief. Thus they were led on to investigate both truth and falsity in things, in order that, when truth and falsity were determined, they might attain tranquility of mind. Now, the principle fundamental to the existence of Skepticism is the proposition, "To every argument an equal argument is opposed." For we believe that it is in consequence of this principle that we are brought to a point where we cease to dogmatize.
>
> (*Outlines of Pyrrhonism* i 7)

The Skeptics began like other philosophers, puzzled by what they saw before their own eyes. Sextus' view here echoes an observation of Aristotle's: "Human beings began to do philosophy even as they do now, because of wonder, at first because they wondered about the strange things right in front of them, and later, advancing little by little, because they came to find greater things puzzling."[45] The difference is that Aristotle, dogmatist *par excellence*, thought progress possible and even actual. The Skeptic notices that many of Aristotle's dogmatic contentions are earnestly denied by other philosophers, who trot out equally compelling arguments firmly opposed to his conclusions. To take but one example, Aristotle argued that pleasure could not be the highest good;[46] starting just a few years after his death, the Epicureans affirmed exactly the opposite.

Sextus suggests that this sort of fundamental philosophical disagreement is really quite a general phenomenon. In fact, he introduces its generality as a fundamental precept of Skepticism: "To every argument an equal argument is opposed." For any given argument on behalf of p, there is an equally compelling argument on behalf of *not-p*. When faced with these *equipollent arguments*, equally powerful arguments for and against a given proposition p, we have no recourse but to suspend judgment about p. Sextus is suggesting that in the face of equipollent arguments it is not merely prudent or intellectually responsible to suspend judgment. Rather, once we have seen that the grounds for and against any given proposition p perfectly balance against one another, we have no real alternative to suspension.

To start with a trivial example, suppose that you are wondering about some simple fact, for instance, whether the prime minister has been hit by a bus while riding his bicycle this morning. A perfectly credible witness has informed you that that he had seen this very event occur earlier today; unfortunately, another equally credible witness claims that no such thing ever happened, that she has been with the prime minister later in the day and that she can attest that he had not been hit by a bus. You can hardly believe them both, and, assuming that they really are equally credible, you can hardly prefer one report to the other. In this circumstance, you should, and presumably would, withhold judgment until you found out some additional information one way or the other. You would in fact in all likelihood suspend judgment in this matter and go on seeking. You would thus be acting exactly like a zetetic Skeptic.

Of course, in this trivial case we are inclined to say that the issue is decidable, that one of the reports must be false and that with just a bit of further investigation we will able to determine which. Sextus doubts that, but we may set that aside for the present. What matters in this humble example is something revealing about the character of ancient Skepticism. Presumably in the case imagined we would not merely fail to *know* whether or not the prime minister had been hit by a bus while riding his bicycle: we would further have no grounds for *belief*. We would suspend not merely any claim to knowledge. We would suspend also all claims to belief as well. If *p* is the proposition *that the prime minister was hit by a bus*, should we believe *p* or not-*p*?

The answer seems to be: neither. We should withhold judgment.

This further fact brings out a striking feature of ancient Skepticism, pertaining to two types of doubt we might come to manifest:

- Epistemic Doubt: we might come to doubt that we have grounds to *know* anything – and so give up all our claims to knowledge.
- Doxastic Doubt: we might come to doubt that we have grounds to *believe* anything – and so give up all our claims to belief.

Epistemic doubt is the sort of doubt Descartes seeks to induce in the first of his *Meditations*. Possibly, he insists by a variety of mechanisms, you do not really know the things you think you know. Possibly you are dreaming, or perhaps an evil genius is deceiving you by feeding you false information. Perhaps, to update the mechanism a bit, you are a brain in a vat being fed neural stimulations by mad, evil cognitive scientists who delight in making you believe that you are currently skiing in Sweden, carving elegant tracks in freshly fallen snow, even though you are in fact but a brain in a jar in their laboratory in Reading. These sorts of scenarios may provide you reason to doubt your claims to knowledge or your pretensions to certainty. Perhaps, despite their vividness, your current perceptions are wholly non-veridical. These sorts of arguments, then, are attempts to induce epistemic doubt in you. Note, however, that none of these scenarios gives you any reason at all to doubt that you *believe* what you seem to be perceiving. On the contrary, these Skeptical scenarios presuppose belief and then attack the issue of whether belief is suitably justified so as to qualify as knowledge. It is perfectly consistent with your admitting a lack of knowledge that you believe, even wholeheartedly, that you are currently enjoying a descent through powdery snow. You simply concede that your belief lacks the requisite justification. Whatever their final purport, then, these sorts of Skeptical scenarios give you no grounds for doxastic doubt.

Immediately striking – and eventually challenging – is this arresting difference between Pyrrhonist and Cartesian Skepticism: Sextus is a doxastic rather than epistemic Skeptic. That is, Sextus intends the kinds of Skeptical arguments he deploys to induce his readers to give up not only all claims to knowledge, but also all claims to belief. He thus understands his arguments to be so deep and searing that anyone who grasps their force will thereafter look at the world and allow only that it *appears* a certain way without ever forming a belief that it *is* as it appears. On the contrary, the Skeptic will never assert that the world is as it appears; instead, conceding that appearances are what they are, he will be content to stop and thus to live by appearances alone, to the extent that this is possible. Sextus is, in fact, explicit on the point of accepting appearances:

> Those who claim that the Skeptics deny appearances (*phainomena*) seem to me not to have heard what we say. For, as we stated above, we do not reject the things that lead us involuntarily to assent in accord with a passively received impression (*phantasia*) and these are appearances. And when we question whether the external object is such as it appears, we grant that it does appear, and we are not raising a question about the appearance but rather about what is said about the appearance; this is different from raising a question about the appearance itself.
>
> (*Outlines of Pyrrhonism* i 7)

He claims that the Skeptic cannot avoid assenting to propositions of the form "It appears to me that *p*." Even so, in assenting to this sort of proposition, which we may call *phenomenal propositions*, the Skeptic forms no belief about whether *p* is true, or accurately describes the world, or, generally speaking, obtains.[47] A Skeptic standing in a swollen river in the spring can assent to the phenomenal proposition "It appears to me that this river is cold." Indeed, Sextus contends that if things so appear to him, the Skeptic cannot but assent. A phenomenal proposition commands assent, but only to the phenomena, the appearances; no non-phenomenal proposition merits assent, because every non-phenomenal proposition takes us beyond the phenomena to the way things really are. Since belief requires assent to a non-phenomenal proposition, the Skeptic forms no beliefs.

Some might counter that the Skeptic will then at least form beliefs about the phenomenal propositions which command his assent. So, from "It seems to me that this river is cold" the Skeptic can allow "I believe that it seems to me that this river is cold." So, the critic presses, the Skeptic does in fact assent to some non-phenomenal propositions.

One sort of response is to grant the objection only to denounce it as a hollow victory. The Skeptic's point about suspending belief is really a point about non-phenomenal belief, that is, belief about the external world. Sextus makes this perfectly clear when allowing that "when we question whether the external object is such as it appears, we grant that it does appear."

A more strident Skeptical response queries even the move from the phenomenal proposition:

- "It seems to me that *p*."

to the non-phenomenal proposition

- "I believe that it seems to me that *p*."

on the grounds that the second but not the first ascribes an actual belief to an existing subject, namely the bearer of the belief in question. Perhaps all that the Skeptic needs to allow by way of inference at this juncture from

- "It seems to me that *p*."

is

- "It seems to me that I believe *p*."

In this way, the Skeptic will keep the circle of appearance unbroken.

Such challenges highlight an important feature of Hellenistic Skepticism: by embracing an extreme, doxastic Skepticism, the Skeptic lays himself open to all manner of table-turning arguments. As we shall see, the Skeptic will face a series of related charges to the effect that his Skepticism is self-refuting or at least pragmatically self-undermining. One pragmatic formulation of these sorts of criticisms alleges that the Skeptic cannot really live his Skepticism. If we can assent to no non-phenomenal proposition, and so can believe nothing at all about the world, how can we manage to navigate our way through even our immediate neighborhood? Suppose, for instance, that the Skeptic sees a large truck rumbling down the street in his direction. Does not his reluctance to step in front of it betray his unacknowledged belief that it will flatten him if he walks in its way?

So far, however, these sorts of challenges to Skepticism are mainly pre-emptory. At this point, we have not yet been given any reason by the Skeptic to conclude that belief is never warranted. For instance, the Stoic who has committed to assenting to all and only true propositions will be little moved to engage with the Skeptic unless he is given some manner of argumentative prompting. Let us now, then, present some typical tropes from the Skeptic's argumentative arsenal.

Skeptical tropes

Why should the Stoic, or anyone else, take doxastic Skepticism seriously? Sextus begins his campaign against dogmatism by reaching back to one of the earliest philosophers, the Presocratic atomist Democritus. Recall that Democritus had conceded that atomism has an unexpected epistemic consequence.[48] Sextus highlights this feature of atomism by quoting Democritus appreciatively: "It has been demonstrated over and over again that in reality we do not grasp what each thing is or is not … It is necessary to realize that by this measure, we humans are cut off from reality" (Sextus, *Against the Professors* vii 136). Democritus had reached this conclusion by suggesting everything beyond atoms exists by convention (by *nomos*). If you are standing in the river and finding the water cold directly next to your partner who is at the same time finding the water warm, and you are both sincerely reporting how things seem to you, then whose judgment is to be deemed superior? Which of you is to say how the water *really* is? Sextus contends neither: the water appears one way to you and another to your partner and that is all one can say with confidence about the question of whether the river is cold or warm.

Note, however, that Democritus himself had been perfectly prepared to allow that other things do not exist merely by convention. Atoms and the void exist not by convention but by nature (by *phusis*). Although we cannot experience them in sense perception, we can infer their existence, and, having done so, we can see that they exist independently of our interactions with them. Roughly, and recalling the context of the emergence of atomism in the wake of Parmenidean monism,[49] because we know that there is motion and that motion requires the existence of atoms and the void, we can justifiably infer that there are atoms and the void.

Here, however, Sextus parts company with Democritus and others of his ilk. The first thing the Skeptic will point out is that the atomist has reached his commitment to the existence of atoms by means of an argument. This argument will turn out upon inspection to be like every other argument: neutralized by another argument on the opposite side, an argument which, if we are honest, we will admit to be equally good. So, for example, one might counter that the very notion of an *atom* is incoherent. An atom is supposed to be something indivisible. After all, in Greek the word *atomon* just means "not divisible" or "not cuttable." Yet atoms have magnitude. So, they are supposed to be indivisible magnitudes. Plainly, though, every magnitude, no matter how small, could in principle be divided by a blade of an even smaller magnitude. So, atoms must be divisible after all – which is to say that an atom is not really something *atomon* after all. So, one argument tells us there must be atoms; another argument tells us that there cannot be atoms.

This circumstance is really quite general. In fact, contends Sextus, for any non-phenomenal proposition *p* there are *equipollent* arguments on both sides. That is, there exist arguments of equal force and persuasiveness for and against every non-phenomenal proposition. This is the phenomenon Sextus has identified as "the fundamental principle" of Skepticism: "to every argument an equal argument is opposed" (*Outlines of Pyrrhonism* i 7). Let us call this the *Equipollence Principle* and the argument to which it gives rise the *fundamental argument for suspension of belief* (FSB).

1   For any arbitrary non-phenomenal proposition *p*, if the reasons for assenting to *p* are no better or worse than those for assenting to not-*p*, then one has an epistemic duty to suspend judgment with respect to *p*.

2   In fact, for any arbitrary non-phenomenal proposition *p*, the reasons for assenting to *p* are no better or worse than those for assenting to not-*p*.

3   Hence, for any arbitrary non-phenomenal proposition *p*, one has an epistemic duty to suspend judgment with respect to *p*.

The conclusion of (FSB) is an entirely general statement of doxastic Skepticism. If (FSB-3) is correct, we should suspend judgment about everything and merely report our appearances. Speaking of "epistemic duties" in this connection relies on language not deployed by the Skeptics themselves, but is meant to capture Sextus' repeated contention that in view of the existence of equipollent arguments, one *should* or one *must* suspend judgment, that in view of our actual epistemic context it is incumbent upon us to do so. Of course, the Skeptic will also point out that, happily, for those following the Skeptical way a great benefit accrues: tranquility (*ataraxia*) will descend upon them.

As regards our epistemic circumstance, Sextus encourages us first to admit and then to bring to full awareness the inescapable fact that equipollent arguments are available for any random non-phenomenal proposition we might care to consider. (FSB-1) merely encodes the Skeptic's plausible thought that in the face of truly equipollent arguments with respect to *p*, we should – and presumably automatically will – suspend judgment about *p*.

Imagine, for instance, that you are ill and that to regain health you will need to submit yourself to some course of therapy or other. One physician recommends course A, but you gain a second opinion from another physician who counsels against course A as ineffective and outmoded and suggests instead course B. As far as you can ascertain, both physicians are fully accredited and qualified. So, you do some further research of your own. It emerges that some excellent studies show, or seem to show, that the A-course is efficacious; others, equally excellent, show, or seem to show, that the A-course effectively confers no benefits at all. Alas, the same state of affairs obtains for the B-course. You learn also that there is another, much more comprehensive, more fully funded study underway at present and that its results are soon to be published. Fortunately, your illness is not debilitating and you can afford to wait until the results of the new study are published. In this circumstance, it seems that you should simply suspend judgment, and that in fact you probably *will* suspend judgment more or less automatically. Surely, to begin, it would be imprudent of you to do anything else. More to the point, it would be irrational of you to conclude that the A-course is clearly preferable to the B-course or vice versa. It is better to suspend judgment and, in the manner of a zetetic, to carry on seeking. That is to say, then, that (FSB-1) is a perfectly plausible and reasonable premise for the Skeptics to advance. Of course, if you are already a Skeptic, you will hardly assent to the proposition that "(FSB-1) is true." Still, you will find it hard to refrain from assenting to the phenomenal proposition that "It seems to me that (FSB-1)."

Matters become much more complicated and contentious when we return to the only remaining premise, (FSB-2), the surprising claim that, in fact, for any arbitrary non-phenomenal proposition *p*, the reasons for assenting to *p* are no better or worse than those for assenting to not-*p*. While we might be willing to grant this for various sorts of evaluative and obscure claims, surely we have no reason to suspend judgment about such basic propositions as *I see words before me right now as I read* or *2 + 2 = 4*. The mathematical proposition is necessary and the perceptual proposition is patent. In this connection, it bears recalling that we are in the context of doxastic rather than epistemic Skepticism. Sextus is not merely trying to show that we cannot *know* such propositions or that we cannot know them *with certainty*. Instead, he is contending that each of these non-phenomenal propositions falls prey to a pair of equipollent arguments, such that we have no reason even to *believe* either. So, his view is really rather radical.

Sextus offers argument after argument that equipollence in fact obtains for every non-phenomenal proposition. In fact, he thinks that by recounting the many types of these sorts of arguments, suspension is bound to follow. As a good Skeptic, however, he does not claim to believe that these arguments are actually sound. It is just that they seem so:

> But in order that we may more accurately understand these oppositions, I shall set down the modes or arguments by means of which suspension of judgment is brought about, without, however, maintaining anything about their number or force. For they may well be unsound, and there may be more than the ones I shall mention.
>
> (*Outlines of Pyrrhonism* i 35 = LS 72 A)

Sextus provides a series of *modes*, or ways of arguing for equipollence or, more generally, for achieving suspension.[50] Of these series, two command special attention, one group of five derived from Agrippa, an otherwise obscure figure in the history of ancient Skepticism, and another group of ten, probably derived from Aenesidemus,[51] the Skeptic who broke away from the Skeptical Academy in disgust with the allegation that the Academics were closet dogmatists, unwilling to take the full measure of their Skeptical stance.

Sextus characterizes the ten modes in his typically non-dogmatic fashion:

> The older Skeptics [*scil.* Aenesidemus; *M* vii 345], according to the usual account, have handed down some modes (*tropoi*), ten in number, through which it seems that suspension of judgment is brought about, and which they also synonymously call "arguments" (*logoi*) or "points" (*topoi*). And these modes are as follows: first, there is one based on the variety of animals; second, the one based on the differences among human beings; third, based on the differences in constitution of the sense organs; fourth, on the circumstances; fifth, on positions, distances and locations; sixth, on admixtures; seventh, on the quantity and constitution of the external objects; eighth, on relativity; ninth, on the frequency or infrequency of occurrences; and tenth, on the ways of life, customs and laws, mythic beliefs and dogmatic opinions. We adopt this order without prejudice.
>
> (*Outlines of Pyrrhonism* i 36–38 = LS 72 A)

Some of these modes trade upon the differences in perceivers and their constitutions, others on differences in doxastic contexts, and still others on differences in the objects perceived.[52]

The modes in fact overlap in various ways, and their presentation is far from tidy. That is, however, not a problem as far as Sextus is concerned. What he wishes is merely to offer them with sufficient clarity that his readers may apprehend their force and so suspend judgment. Let us take just the first mode as an illustration of how the modes proceed.

Sextus draws attention to the evident differences among the constitutions of different animals. As he rightly urges, different kinds of animals are outfitted with different manner of sense organs, with the result that they will interact with the world in markedly different ways:

> If the same things do appear differently because of differences in animals, then we shall be in a position to say how the external object looks *to us*, but we shall suspend judgment on how it is in nature. For we shall not be able to decide between our impressions (*phantasiai*) and those of the other animals, since we are part of the dispute and thus are in need of someone to make the decision, rather than being competent to pass judgment ourselves.
>
> (*Outlines of Pyrrhonism* i 59–60 = LS 72 B)

Sextus makes two sorts of points in this passage. The first pertains to differences in the constitutions of various perceivers; the second pertains to the way in which a dogmatist might attempt to defuse the problem to which this circumstance gives rise.

Altogether, then, he offers a sort of *enhanced argument from phenomenal variation* (EPV), the more rudimentary version of which is already familiar from the ancient atomists:[53]

1   If sensory faculties are variously constituted, it is reasonable to assume phenomenal variation across the species.
2   If there is phenomenal variation across the species, we are able to say how external objects are by nature only if we can appeal to an *objective arbiter*.
3   Surely we are ourselves not objective arbiters; indeed, no subject of appearance has any better or worse claim to being an objective arbiter than we have.
4   If (3), we cannot appeal to any objective arbiter in the face of phenomenal variation.
5   Hence, we are unable to say how external objects are by nature.

(EPV-5) yields wanted Skeptical result.

The first premise seems reasonable. If different species have different sorts of sensory detectors, then we can expect them to detect phenomenally different features of the world. To take an example unkown to Sextus but which perfectly illustrates his point, certain sea anemones (*anthopleura xanthogrammica*) have specialized cells for photo-reception and so can detect light waves in the ultraviolet range indetectable to humans. Accordingly, when they perceive an object *o* reflecting waves in that region, their color experiences will differ markedly from those a human perceives. The human will see no color in that range at all. Let the color the sea anemones perceive be Φ. Should we say that *o* is Φ or not-Φ? Of course, we can say that *o* is not-Φ *for us*. We can also say, as marine biologists do say, that *o* appears Φ *to the sea anemone*.

Now, then, is *o* Φ or not-Φ? Sextus does not adopt the relativistic expedient of saying that *o* is Φ-to-S_1 (the sea anemone) but not-Φ-to-S_2 (the human being). Looked at one way, the relativist merely postpones the question we want to answer: is *o* *really* Φ or not-Φ? Looked at another way, she answers the question in a dogmatic fashion: *in itself*, says the relativist, *o* is neither Φ nor not-Φ.

How, though, does the relativist come by that belief? She might be inferring it from the bare fact of perceptual variation. In that case, her relativism is just that: an inference. Then the normal worry arises: why should we trust her inference? Maybe the sea anemone has it right after all. In a certain way, even the relativist seems to have set herself up as some sort of *objective arbiter*. She regards herself as being in the privileged position of having good reason to believe that *o* is neither Φ nor not-Φ in itself. Here, however, she seems precisely as dogmatic as the parochial human who insists that *o* is really not-Φ or as, if you will, the dogmatic sea anemone who insists that *o* most definitely is Φ, that he can simply *see* that it is Φ. The relativist merely adopts a different dogmatic point of view. It is this sort of dogmatism, whether relativist in orientation or not, that Sextus derides.

This is the point of (EPV-2), the claim that if there is phenomenal variation across the species, we are able to say how external objects are by nature only if we can appeal to an *objective arbiter*. Given perceptual variation, in order to settle the matter of how things really are, we would need some court of appeal. We would need, that is, an *objective arbiter* to settle the matter for us. An objective arbiter would be someone capable of judging things from an objective perspective, which is to say, then:

- *S* is an *Objective Arbiter* only if for any object *o* and for any phenomenal property Φ, when *S* judges "*o* is Φ," *S*'s attitude in judging does not even partially constitute Φ.

Of course, Sextus does not dogmatically claim that there could not be any such arbiter. He does, however, indicate that it certainly *appears* that there is no such creature. That is, from his own perfectly mundane human perspective it appears that an objective arbiter would be viewing things from a perspectiveless perspective. This contention understandably strikes Sextus as somehow desperate and ludicrous.

Further, one might wish to mount an argument for or against the non-phenomenal proposition *that there is an objective arbiter*. Needless to say, this would implicate us in all manner of complicated and convoluted *proofs* – and so would open the door to equipollence:

> For in addition to the possibility of there being no such thing as a proof, as we shall point out, any purported proof will either be apparent or not apparent to us. And if, on the one hand, it is not apparent, then we shall not accept it with confidence. But if, on the other, it is apparent to us, then since what is apparent to animals is the very matter in question, and the proof is apparent to us, and we are animals, the proof itself will be in question as to whether, as something apparent, it is true. But it is absurd to try to settle the matter in question by means of the matter in question, since the same thing will be both credible and not credible, which is impossible ... If, therefore, the impressions (*phantasiai*) differ because of the difference in animals, and it is impossible to decide between them, then it is necessary to suspend judgment concerning the external objects.
> (*Outlines of Pyrrhonism* i 60–61 = LS 72 B)

When the dogmatists trot out their various proofs, we will either find these proofs evident or not. If we do not find them evident, then they will have no doxastic value. If we do, at least initially, find them evident, then we need only reflect that we are not ourselves objective arbiters, and thus are hardly in a position to assert the existence of any such a judge. Then we will again recognize that our appearances have no doxastic value. By endorsing them, we would only be validating the very thing we were wondering about, namely whether we might somehow bring ourselves into a position of being able to adjudicate phenomenal disagreements by transcending our perspectival constraints. This now looks hopelessly circular, since we are evidently trying to suggest that there might be an objective arbiter by appealing to the possible existence of an objective arbiter. In the end, we would be forced to admit that at most *it seems to us that there is or could be an objective arbiter*. When the dogmatist offers a proof to the effect that there *is in fact or could be* such an arbiter, we can only expect an equipollent proof on the other side.

Each proof will thus be met with a counter-proof, and our proofs will surely grow less secure in direct proportion to their ever-increasing abstractness. We were first wondering about simple color properties. Before long, we found ourselves entertaining proofs about the correct basis of knowledge or belief, about the very natures of knowledge and belief, about the possibility of transcending our subjective perspectives, or about the possibility of there being an objective arbiter to assist us in our woes. The proofs march on and on, forever met in battle by equipollent proofs. A rational being who witnesses this endless cascade of proofs and counter-proofs throws his brush at the slate of argumentation and suspends belief. Then, and only then, she follows the Skeptical Way.

Arguments of this sort populate the modes of Skepticism. Each time we try to transcend our inherent constraints – perceptual, cognitive, perspectival – we are pulled into neutrality by the counterpunch of an equipollent argument on the other side. We have, then, according to the Skeptic, no grounds for belief regarding any non-phenomenal proposition *p*. So, it behooves us to stop dallying with the dogmatists and to suspend judgment directly, by holding *all* non-phenomenal beliefs in abeyance. Like Apelles the frustrated painter, we will be delighted by what we discover: the very thing we sought but never attained in our endless squabbles will visit itself upon us like manna from heaven: we will at last achieve tranquility.

Skeptical challenges

The history of Hellenistic philosophy records fascinating interplay between the Skeptics and dogmatists, especially the Stoics. The Skeptics act as gadflies to Stoic pretensions to knowledge, which, as the Skeptics try to show, are wildly overblown. A Stoic will be inclined to declare: "The virtue of the happy man and the well-ordered life consist in this: that all actions are based on the principle of harmony between his own soul and the will of the director of the universe."[54] This is an engraved invitation to the Skeptic: "So you, Stoic, know about *virtue*, about *happiness*, about the *well-ordered life*, and about the *soul*? You, Stoic, are privy to the *will* of the *director of the universe*, whom you have personally encountered exactly where? You might as well ask me to acknowledge the existence of Platonic Forms." Under Skeptical pressure, various Stoics in fact developed and refined their increasingly technical and sophisticated system, comprising logic, action theory, metaphysics, epistemology, moral psychology, theories of perception, theories of meaning, and more. Much of this was developed as an arsenal for the purpose of rebuffing challenges put to them by the Skeptics.

All the same, turn-about is fair play. If the Skeptics are determined to press their anti-dogmatic challenges, then they must confront challenges of their own, and in particular challenges to the effect that they are guilty of double-dealing. This proves especially true of the form of non-dogmatic zetetic Skepticism professed by Sextus. How can he say and do so many things when he pretends to live a life free of belief?

Two challenges to Skepticism have special bite. The first charges the Skeptic with his own favorite charge: the Skeptic is a dogmatist – a closet dogmatist, but a dogmatist all the same. Second, the Skeptic, whether or not liable to the charge of dogmatism, is wholly disingenuous. The Skeptic seeks to deflate pretensions to knowledge and belief, but then cannot live his Skepticism. Life requires doing and not just being, but doing requires belief and not just appearance. So, if he is sincere and authentic, then the Skeptic is frozen into inaction. This second argument, known as the *Apraxia Objection* (*apraxia* in Greek = inaction), forces the Skeptic into some tight corners.

Let us consider first the charge of dogmatism. The Skeptics seem to make all manner of pronouncements about the need to suspend belief, about the inevitability of suspending belief, about the benefits of suspending belief. Thus, when advancing his modes of Skepticism, Sextus makes bold and proclaims: "it is *necessary* to suspend judgment concerning the external objects."[55] This sounds as if it were a perfectly universal conclusion, a projection about how we *must* conduct ourselves in the face of phenomenal divergence. Elsewhere, Sextus makes a point about how he expects things to be in the future: "I shall be forced ... to suspend judgment as to how it is by nature."[56] Again we find him using the language of compulsion, and speaking in perfectly general terms. In these cases, Sextus is evidently *projecting* his Skepticism in ways that make him sound more dogmatic than zetetic. In these sorts of cases, he seems far removed from his official self-portrait as a humble chronicler of present appearance. The Skeptics do not dogmatize, he says, because "in each instance we are simply reporting, like a chronicler, what now appears to us to be the case."[57]

Yet a chronicler merely reports what has happened thus far, what he has experienced; a dogmatist analyzes and conjectures, extends and projects. A dogmatist does so by using some manner of inductive step to project how things will be, even how they *must* be, on the basis of the local results encountered thus far. This dogmatist now seems to be none other than Sextus himself.

Sextus is well aware of this sort of charge, and offers a rejoinder:

Not even in uttering the Skeptical formulae about unclear matters – for example, "In no way more," or "I determine nothing," or one of the other formulae which we shall later discuss – do they dogmatize. For if you dogmatize, then you posit as real the things that you are said to dogmatize about; but Skeptics posit these formulae not as necessarily being real. For they suppose that, just as the formula "Everything is false" says that it too, along with everything else, is false (and similarly for "Nothing is true"), so also "No more so" (*ouden mallon*) says that it too, along with everything else, is no more so than not so, and hence cancels itself along with everything else. And we say the same of the other Skeptical formulae. Thus, if people who dogmatize posit as real the things they dogmatize about, while Skeptics utter their own phrases in such a way that they are implicitly canceled by themselves, then they cannot be said to dogmatize in uttering them. But the main point is this: in uttering these formulae they say what appears to themselves and report their own feelings without any belief (*adoxastōs*), affirming nothing about external objects.

(*Outlines of Pyrrhonism* i 14–15)

In suggesting that the Skeptic's slogans "are canceled by themselves" Sextus means that they are self-applying, so that they do not engender belief in those who utter them.

For example, the Skeptic will say, regarding any non-phenomenal proposition *p*, "No more so" (*ouden mallon*), meaning that *p* is no more worthy of being endorsed than not-*p*. The critic now accuses the Skeptic of *endorsing* the slogan "No more so," which the Skeptic in fact utters with alarming regularity for someone who allegedly does not believe it. The slogan "No more so" seems to be a non-phenomenal proposition, a proposition *about* other non-phenomenal propositions to the effect that no one of them is more likely to be correct than its opposite, that no one of them is any worthier an object of belief than its opposite. So, the critic pounces: you are *asserting* a non-phenomenal proposition, namely "No more so." If you are asserting it, you do so because you believe it; and since belief requires assent, you have assented to it as well. Hence, the critic concludes, the Skeptic wants to have it both ways. The Skeptic wants to insist that no non-phenomenal proposition is worthy of assent – but then in the process of defending himself assents to that very non-phenomenal proposition, *that no non-phenomenal proposition is worthy of assent.*

Sextus' response has two phases. First, the Skeptic slogan "No more so" applies to itself: *it* is no more so than its opposite. The critic rejoins that the Skeptic slogan cannot be deployed if not endorsed, that if its opposite is just as attractive, then the Skeptic will have to withhold assent even to it. Just so, says Sextus. Once again we achieve equipollence, and so we reassert the fundamental thesis of all Skepticism: "To every argument an equal argument is opposed." Consequently, even "No more so" is no more worthy of assent than its opposite. It applies perfectly to itself.

This is why, in the second phase of his response, Sextus feels at liberty to insist that the Skeptic is merely reporting how things seem to him; he is merely reporting his phenomenal beliefs, or, more strictly, merely reporting how things seem to him. His report is simply beliefless (*adoxastōs*) as regards external objects. In response, then, Sextus contends that the Skeptic merely reports his appearances in a way that falls short of implicating him in non-phenomenal belief. How credible is this riposte?

When we address this question, we inevitably move in the direction of the second anti-Skeptical argument, the *apraxia objection* (AO). This argument may be put directly:

1   If an agent *S* is to engage in an intentional action, then *S* must assent to a non-phenomenal proposition.
2   If *S* assents to a non-phenomenal proposition, then *S* has non-phenomenal beliefs.
3   If *S* has non-phenomenal beliefs, then *S* is not a doxastic Skeptic.
4   All self-proclaimed doxastic Skeptics engage in intentional actions.
5   So, the self-proclaimed doxastic Skeptics are not doxastic Skeptics.

Or, as one may prefer, the self-proclaimed doxastic Skeptics are not *really* doxastic Skeptics. In the end, doxastic Skepticism is a kind of parlor game which no one can play outside of the Skeptic's own parlor.

Again, Sextus is aware of a version of (AO) and seeks to turn it back. He notes, consistent with what he has said all along, that the Skeptic will, indeed *must*, assent to various appearances (*phainomena*). This forced assent does not, however, push him in the direction of belief about how things are:

> When we say that the Skeptic does not dogmatize, we are not using "dogma" in the more general sense in which some say it is dogma to accept anything (for the Skeptic does assent to the experiences forced upon him in virtue of this-or-that impression: for example, he would not say, when warmed or cooled, "I seem not to be warmed or cooled"). Rather, when we say he does not dogmatize, we mean "dogma" in the sense in which some say that dogma is assent to any of the non-evident matters investigated by the sciences. For the Pyrrhonist assents to nothing that is non-evident.
>
> (*Outlines of Pyrrhonism* i 13)

Sextus freely allows that the Skeptic "accepts" some things, namely those appearances forced upon him. This sort of acceptance, an assent to an appearance, is not an instance of dogmatism, because it makes no claims about external objects or about how the world really is. So, regarding the conclusion of (AO), the contention that those who claim to be doxastic Skeptics are not doxastic Skeptics all, Sextus offers a clear response. The doxastic Skeptic certainly is a Skeptic, he maintains. As regards any non-phenomenal matter, he lives belief-free.

Still, the critic will press for more detail. The Skeptic allows that it appears to him that a large truck is approaching at a high speed. Does he *believe* that the truck is approaching? To the non-Skeptic, he certainly seems to have such a belief. He certainly *acts* as if he believed the truck were approaching. He steps out of the way, in order to avoid being run over. If he were merely reporting that things *appear* a certain way, without the least conviction that they are as they appear, then why should his action take the direction it does?

In response, Sextus may distinguish two notions of appearance. One can look at the familiar Müller-Lyer lines and say sincerely that they *appear* to be of different lengths, even while believing that they are of the same length:

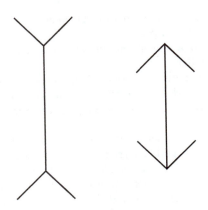

So there is, Sextus as rightly insists, a non-committal sense of "appearance." One can sincerely report that the lines *appear* to be different lengths while refraining from assenting to the non-phenomenal proposition *that the lines are different lengths*. So, in allowing that the truck appears to be approaching, the Skeptic does not thereby express any conviction about that appearance.

The dogmatic critic of the Skeptic will, however, press still further. The *apraxia* objection is not that there are no non-doxastic appearances, but rather that intentional *action* is utterly inexplicable without at least some modicum of conviction. To relate the problem to the Müller-Lyer lines: having said that they appear to be of different lengths (because they do), how much would you be willing to bet that this was in fact so? Presumably, nothing. This appearance, it would seem, is not action-implicating. Now, the Skeptic may seize upon your reluctance to bet by insisting that the world is not as it seems, so that suspension is warranted. This response, however, misses the point of (AO): it seems that even simple actions in the absence of conviction would be impossible or at least utterly inexplicable. Even a mental action is an action. The moment you decide to bet in one way or the other regarding the length of the lines, you assent to a non-phenomenal proposition, if only weakly. Moreover, the dogmatist insists, belief admits of degrees, and to believe something weakly rather than firmly is still to believe something. Action requires conviction, and is unfathomable in the absence of conviction-bearing assent.

Scholars have understood Sextus' response to (AO) differently. Some take him to be rejecting (AO-2), the claim that if S assents to a non-phenomenal proposition, then S has non-phenomenal beliefs. Their thought is that in this passage Sextus distinguishes two types of assent, one purely passive and one active. If there were such a distinction available, then (AO-2) might prove false for the fully passive sort of assent; one might assent passively, or, perhaps, simply *acquiesce in* an appearance without coming to believe anything non-phenomenal. The Skeptic might thus acquiesce in the appearance that a truck is rumbling towards him and so step out of its (seeming) way, but then deny all belief about this matter. This strategy is, however, unpersuasive. To begin, Sextus nowhere draws the alleged distinction between two types of assent. He certainly does think that assent is sometimes forced, involuntary, or beliefless (*adoxastôs*). These are not types of passive versus active assent, however, but rather claims about how assent is occasioned or how assent implicates itself in belief.[58] Moreover, it is not even clear what distinction is being offered Sextus. One type of assent is introduced as active and the other not. The notion of a *purely passive assent* is hard to fathom, bordering on the self-contradictory. To assent to something is to perform a definite mental act; to be passive is precisely *not* to act.

A more promising strategy for the doxastic Skeptic is to deny (AO-1), the claim that if an agent S is to engage in an intentional action, then S must assent to non-phenomenal propositions. Here one might legitimately appeal to Sextus' developed suggestion that the Skeptic merely "follows appearances."[59] In this way, one might suppose that S could indeed engage in an intentional action based solely on appearances, without ever assenting to any non-phenomenal proposition.

Consider a case favorable to the Skeptic's point of view. A captured soldier might develop an intrepid plan to escape a prison camp. He has a detailed appearance of how the escape is to go. His plan is intricate and highly improbable, so improbable, in fact, that he cannot bring himself sincerely to assent to the proposition *if I do series of actions $a_1 \ldots a_n$ I will escape and become a free man*. Yet, in his desperation, he acts *as if* the plan were a sound one, because he realizes that otherwise he will perish in the camp. Perhaps his intrepid plan works or perhaps, as he had feared, it fails. It does not matter. What matters in the present context is that he has been able to act *as if* it would work, holding in abeyance its vanishingly low probability of success and certainly not believing that he would prevail. Hope is not belief. So, he acts, following appearances, in the absence of belief.

If one can hold in abeyance belief and simply act by conforming to appearance, then (AO-1) is false. If we return to the Müller-Lyer lines one last time, we can now note something about our earlier betting behavior. We would not bet that the lines conformed to their appearance, but that was, upon reflection, because we already knew that the lines were in fact the same length. So, perhaps we were overly hasty in concluding that we cannot live by following appearances. We might, in cases where we genuinely have no conviction one way or the other, follow the appearances in a beliefless (*adoxastôs*) manner.

There remain several legitimate worries about this sort of response, including not least whether the prison-escape scenario could possibly generalize to the whole of life. There is further a worry about whether that scenario even adequately depicts a series of belief-free acts. Will not, for instance, the constituent acts in the plan require belief, e.g. that if this tunnel is to lead beyond the prison walls, it must be dug in this or that direction? These and other questions like them will pour forth from the dogmatist, who will rightly press the Skeptic to characterize and clarify the wellsprings of belief-free intentional action.

Needless to say, the dialectic between the Skeptics and their dogmatic opponents does not end there, and in fact played out along increasingly complex pathways throughout the Hellenistic period and beyond. Indeed, it is important to recall in this connection that we have so far been tracing just one form of ancient Skepticism, the sort marked by Sextus as zetetic and non-dogmatic. Other Skeptics of the period posed their own sorts of challenges to the dogmatists and faced in return their own sorts of counter-objections. At a very minimum, though, one can credit the Skeptics taken all together with the welcome effect of having forced those wishing to advance determinate claims about the nature of the universe – about its laws, about its sources of value, or about its ultimate constituents – to proceed with caution, clarity, and due humility.

5.5　Conclusions

The study of Hellenistic philosophy offers challenges unlike those met in the Classical period; but it equally offers different sorts of rewards. Because of the history of transmission of the writings of the period, we mainly lack the sorts of extended single-authored works that we have from Plato and Aristotle. Still, texts and views from the period have now been assembled by capable scholars, with the result that we are currently living in an exciting time regarding our knowledge of dominant philosophical schools from the Hellenistic period.

As we have seen, in their very different ways, the Epicureans, Stoics, and Skeptics seek the surest route to the best form of life available to human beings. In this sense, they are all practical philosophies, focused ultimately on providing concrete guidance to those wishing to live well.

This point of agreement, however, is doubly misleading unless interpreted with care. First, although they cohere at this very general level, the Hellenistic schools diverge sharply concerning the character of the best life for human beings, and more sharply still regarding the routes required to arrive at that destination. Second, no Hellenistic movement shies away from engaging in technical, sophisticated philosophy; inevitably the sorts of issues they engage lead them to develop and deploy highly nuanced, at times counterintuitive, and often challenging theories about the world and the forms of value that it may hold for us. This is partly a function of the fact that they are philosophers, willing to grapple with difficult and demanding questions, the sorts of questions which do not admit of simple-minded or formulaic resolutions. It is also, however, partly a function of the pressures these schools put on one another as they jockeyed for dialectical superiority. Because of this interscholastic pressure, although practical in orientation, the Hellenistic schools moved rapidly to develop quite technical innovations in philosophical theory.

For this same reason, the Epicureans, Stoics, and Skeptics in their different ways reached high points of sophistication in theory and method. It is, therefore, impossible to credit the once fashionable contention that philosophy became decadent and degraded after the death of Aristotle, that it went dormant until the Cartesian resurrection of the seventeenth century. Although we have only scratched the surface of the intricate intra- and inter-scholastic dialectic of the several centuries of philosophy after the death of Aristotle, it should be amply clear that the philosophers of the Hellenistic period richly reward the effort required to bring their views into sharp relief.

Notes

1   Russell, Bertrand., *A History of Western Philosophy* (London: Allen and Unwin, 1946), 159.
2   On the character of Aristotle's extant writings, see Shields, *Aristotle* (London and New York: Routledge: 2007), §1.4.
3   The single most valuable resource for English language students is the *The Hellenistic Philosophers* by A.A. Long and D. Sedley (Cambridge: Cambridge University Press, 1987). This two-volume source book collects texts for the Hellenistic philosophers from hundreds of different authors. The texts are topically arranged, expertly translated, and accompanied by astute introductory commentary. It should be the first port of call for students wishing to learn more about Hellenistic philosophy. In the text, I cross-reference this work, where possible, with the initials "LS." Thus, e.g., the first passage of Epicurus quoted below is cited as: "*Letter to Menoeceus* 130–132 = LS 21 B." This means that the quotation is excerpted from Epicurus' *Letter to Menoeceus*, lines 130–132, and that the relevant passage is reproduced in Long and Sedley, in their §21 as passage B.
4   For the account of justice in Plato's *Republic*, see 3.7 above.
5   For Aristotle's approach to happiness and human flourishing, see 4.6.
6   On Aristotle's division of the sciences, see Shields, *Aristotle* (London and New York: Routledge: 2007), §1.5.
7   On Socratic ignorance, see 2.3 above.
8   On Plato's theory of Forms, see 3.5–3.6 above.
9   On Aristotle's conception of human happiness, see 4.6 above.
10   On Aristotle's function argument, see 4.6 above.
11   The doxographer Diogenes Laertius, who wrote in the third century AD, and so long after Epicurus' death, devotes the tenth book of his *Lives of the Philosophers* to Epicurus. He lists over 40 works by him.
12   Some of this work has survived, in badly damaged condition, however, from a villa in Herculaneum, a town buried by the volcanic eruption of Mount Vesuvius in 79 AD. Restoration work is currently underway.
13   In what follows I will adopt the simplifying assumption that Lucretius speaks authoritatively for Epicurus.
14   *Letter to Menoeceus*, 122–25 = LS 25 A and 24 B.
15   Unamuno, Miguel de, *The Tragic Sense of Life*, trans. J.E. Crawford Flitch (New York: Doubleday, 1954), §1.
16   On Democritean atomism, see 1.5 above.
17   See Cicero, *De Finibus* I 29 (= LS 21 A):

> We are investigating what is the final and ultimate good, which all philosophers agree must be of such a kind that it is the end to which everything is the means, but it is

not itself the means to anything. Epicurus situates this in pleasure, which he wants to be the greatest good, while pain is the greatest bad. His doctrine begins this way: as soon as every animal is born, it seeks after pleasure and rejoices in it as the greatest good, while it rejects pain as the greatest bad and avoids it as far as possible.

18 On Aristotle's conception of happiness as objectively given, see 4.6 above. For a fuller treatment, see Shields, *Aristotle* (London and New York: Routledge, 2007), §§8.1–8.3.

19 In what follows I simplify Epicurus' account of pleasure somewhat for expositional purposes. His official view holds that pleasure resides in bodily sensation, though he allows a mental state akin to pleasure, which he calls joy (*chara*), which is strictly not pleasure (*Letter to Menoeceus* 128 = LS 21 B). He also distinguishes between static and kinetic pleasures. Kinetic pleasures involve movements from a state of lack to some manner of satiation, for example, from being hungry to being full; static pleasures are rather states accompanying well-being, and are superior to kinetic pleasures at least in the sense that they do not depend upon deprivation for their generation. According to Cicero, *De Finibus* I 35–38 (= LS 21 A): "We regard the greatest pleasure to be that which occurs which is perceived once all pain is removed. For when we are released from pain, we rejoice in this very freedom and voiding of all distress." The notion of perception to which Cicero alludes seems a broad one, perhaps akin to the sense of perception as "become aware of" in "She perceived there was a problem in her marriage when she noticed mysterious cash withdrawals from their joint savings account." If that is correct, then static pleasures arise in the mind when it becomes aware of its own well-being. Of course, since according to Epicurus the mind is itself bodily, because composed of atoms in the void, this perception is equally an awareness of bodily well-being.

20 See *Letter to Menoeceus* 129 (= LS 21 B).

21 Philodemus, *Against the Sophists* (= LS 25 J).

22 For Plato's conception of the soul see 3.7 above.

23 We will consider an important proviso to this claim below in 5.3.4. For now, however, let Stoic value monism be the claim that the only good is virtue.

24 DL vii 183.

25 On sources of Hellenistic philosophy, see 5.1.

26 Put slightly more formally, according to the Humeans, any argument with a conclusion of the form "*S ought* to do thus and such" (e.g. *S* ought to give 10 percent of his salary to the poor) will be fallacious unless somewhere in its premise set is a premise of the form "If *p*, then *S* ought to do thus and such" (e.g. "If *S* can alleviate suffering by donating 10 percent of his salary to the poor, then *S* ought to do so"). If the premise set contains only indicative claims ("*S* has more money than he needs." and "By donating 10 percent of his salary to the poor *S* will alleviate suffering"), a conclusion about what *S* ought to do will never be derivable. See Hume, *A Treatise of Human Nature* iii.1:

> In every system of morality, which I have hitherto met with, I have always remarked, that the author proceeds for some time in the ordinary ways of reasoning, and establishes the being of a God, or makes observations concerning human affairs; when all of a sudden I am surprised to find, that instead of the usual copulations of propositions, *is*, and *is not*, I meet with no proposition that is not connected with an *ought*, or an *ought not*. This change is imperceptible; but is however, of the last consequence. For as this *ought*, or *ought not*, expresses some new relation or affirmation, 'tis necessary that it should be observed and explained; and at the same time that a reason should be given; for what seems altogether inconceivable, how this new relation can be a deduction from others, which are entirely different from it.

27 Cicero, *On the Nature of the Gods* ii 39 = LS 54 H; cf. DL vii 147 = LS 54 A.

28 Stobaeus, *Florilegium*, 4.671 ff.

29 On Socrates thoughts about *akrasia*, see 2.4 above.

30 The quotation derives from the Presocratic philosopher, Anaxagoras, whose view is discussed as a prefiguring of the Stoic attitude by Cicero, *Tusculan Disputations* iii 24.

31 Cicero, *On Fate* 28 = LS 55 S.
32 See Plutarch, *De Fato* 574e: "Nothing comes about without a cause." The Stoics at times suggest that determinism follows directly the thesis that nothing comes to be from nothing (on which thesis see 1.4 above), but this inference is unstable (Cicero, *De Fato* 18).
33 See Sextus, *Outlines of Pyrrhonism* 3.15; cf. Clement of Alexandria, *Miscellanies* 8. 9. 33.
34 Stobaeus, 2.90, 29–91, 9 = LS 65 E.
35 Stobaeus 2.88, 8–90, 6 = LS 65 A.
36 Cicero is not himself endorsing this syllogism. On the contrary, he undertakes to criticize it at *De Finibus* iv 48. The syllogism itself seems to derive from the Early Stoa, where it was advanced by Chrysippus (Plutarch, *De stoicorum repugnantiis* 1039c).
37 On Aristotle's conception of happiness, see 4.6 above.
38 DL vii 85–86 = LS 57 A.
39 See Cicero, *On Ends* iv 25.
40 See Plutarch, *Stoic. rep.* 1042 c–d.
41 See Cicero, *On Ends* iv 25–28.
42 On objections to Epicurean Hedonism, see 5.2 above.
43 On Socrates' elenchus and his deflating refutations of Euthyphro and Meno, see 2.1 and 2.2 above.
44 See Photius, *Library* 169b18–170b3 = LS 71 C.
45 See Aristotle, *Metaphysics* i 2, 982b12.
46 On Aristotle's reasons for denying that pleasure is the highest good, see 4.6 above. For a fuller treatment, see Shields, *Aristotle* (London and New York: Routledge, 2007), §§8.1–8.3.
47 Some care is required here. In Greek, as in English, we can mark a distinction between two senses of "It appears that *p*." Consider (i) a woman who discovers a love letter in her husband's bureau and asserts, "It appears that Fernando is having an affair," and (ii) a woman standing on some railroad tracks saying, "It appears that the tracks converge." (i) carries conviction of some sort, while (ii) carries none; (i) but not (ii) may be corrected. That is, if she learns that the letter was planted there by a mischievous enemy of her husband, she stands corrected. By contrast, she does not stand corrected by the fact that the tracks do not converge. This is, after all, a fact she already acknowledges when she speaks of the appearance of convergence. Thus, (i) but not (ii) carries at least some modicum of conviction. For a Skeptic, a phenomenal proposition, like (ii), carries no conviction beyond the appearances. This distinction will become especially important when we come to assess challenges to Skepticism.
48 On Democritean atomism, see 1.5 above.
49 On Parmenidean monism, see 1.4 above.
50 He begins with some general modes (*Outlines of Pyrrhonism* i 31–35); adds ten further, the most often discussed of all, those presumably owing to Aenesidemus (*Outlines of Pyrrhonism* i 40–163); then five more, those perhaps owing to Agrippa (*Outlines of Pyrrhonism* i 178–179); and finally two further due to some more recent Skeptics, which are intended for those who presume to rely on causal explanations in forming beliefs (*Outlines of Pyrrhonism* i 180–186).
51 Sextus, *Against the Professors* vii 345.
52 Sextus, *Outlines of Pyrrhonism* i 39 = LS 72 A.
53 On phenomenal variation in ancient atomism, see 1.5 above.
54 DL vii 88 = 59 J.
55 *Outlines of Pyrrhonism* i 61 = LS 72 B.
56 *Outlines of Pyrrhonism* i 78.
57 *Outlines of Pyrrhonism* i 4.
58 For forced assent, see *Outlines of Pyrrhonism* i 23–24; involuntary assent *Outlines of Pyrrhonism* i 19; and beliefless (*adoxastôs*) assent *Outlines of Pyrrhonism* ii 102.
59 *Outlines of Pyrrhonism* i 21–24.

Suggestions for additional readings

Texts

The best single source for Hellenistic philosophy is:

Long, A.A. and Sedley, D.N., *The Hellenistic Philosophers* Vols. I and II (Cambridge: Cambridge University Press, 1987).

The first volume contains accurate translations of the principal sources of Hellenistic philosophy and is accompanied by incisive introductory commentary. The second volume provides the texts in the original Greek and Latin, and offers a useful bibliography, most of which caters to those who do not read Greek or Latin.

Other reliable translations, some covering the entire period, others dedicated to individual schools or authors, include:

Annas, J. and Barnes, J., ed. and trans., *Sextus Empiricus: Outlines of Scepticism*, second edition (Cambridge: Cambridge University Press, 2000).
Hallie, P., ed. and Etheridge S., trans., *Sextus Empiricus: Selections from the Major Writings on Skepticism, Man, and God* (Indianapolis: Hackett, 1985).
Inwood, B. and Gerson, L., ed. and trans., *Hellenistic Philosophy*, second edition (Indianapolis: Hackett, 1998).
Inwood, B. and Gerson, L., trans., *The Epicurus Reader* (Indianapolis: Hackett, 1994).
Inwood, B. and Gerson, L., trans. with intro., *The Stoics Reader: Selected Writings and Testimonia* (Indianapolis: Hackett, 2008).
Mates, B., trans. with notes and commentary, *The Skeptic Way: Sextus Empiricus's Outlines of Pyrrhonism* (Oxford: Oxford University Press, 1995).
White, N.P., trans., *Epictetus: The Handbook (The Encheiridion)* (Indianapolis: Hackett, 1983).

Secondary literature

There are a growing number of accessible monographs and student guides covering Hellenistic philosophy. Some useful places to begin are listed below, many of which contain bibliographies for more advanced study.

Two useful companions are:

Bett, R., ed., *The Cambridge Companion to Ancient Scepticism* (Cambridge: Cambridge University Press, 2010).
Inwood, B., ed., *The Cambridge Companion to the Stoics* (Cambridge: Cambridge University Press, 2003).

These monographs offer more extended discussion, mainly pitched to novices rather than scholars:

Long, A.A., *Hellenistic Philosophy: Stoics, Epicureans, Skeptics*, second edition (London: Duckworth, 1986).
O'Keefe, T., *Epicureanism* (Chesham, UK: Acumen, 2010).

Rist, J.M., *Stoic Philosophy*, (Cambridge: Cambridge University Press, 1969).

Sandbach, F.H., *The Stoics* (Indianapolis: Hackett, 1994).

Sellars, John, *Stoicism* (Berkeley: University of California Press, 2006).

Sharples, R.W., *Stoics, Epicureans and Skeptics* (London and New York: Routledge, 1996).

Thorsrud, H., *Ancient Scepticism* (Chesham, UK: Acumen, 2008).

Suggestions for further reading

Students wishing to investigate the topics discussed in this book in further detail would do well to consult the works listed below. This list is mainly restricted to studies in English and emphasizes works appropriate to students rather than to scholars. Many of the works listed also contain their own bibliographies; students looking to pursue the issues addressed in this work are encouraged to consult those bibliographies for the next stage of their research. In this regard, [8]–[11] are especially useful.

The presentation corresponds to the chapters in the text.

After a list of general works, there follow suggestions for philosophy before Socrates; Socrates; Plato; and Aristotle.

Recommended translations for the philosophers discussed in each chapter can be found in the relevant sections.

General

The best general overview of classical philosophy for students is:

1   Guthrie, W., *A History of Greek Philosophy: The Earlier Presocratics and the Pythagoreans* (Cambridge: Cambridge University Press, 1962).
2   —— *A History of Greek Philosophy: The Presocratic Tradition from Parmenides to Democritus* (Cambridge: Cambridge University Press, 1965).
3   —— *A History of Greek Philosophy: The Fifth-Century Enlightenment* (Cambridge: Cambridge University Press, 1969).
4   —— *A History of Greek Philosophy: Plato: the Man and his Dialogues: Earlier Period* (Cambridge: Cambridge University Press, 1975).
5   —— *A History of Greek Philosophy: The Later Plato and the Academy* (Cambridge: Cambridge University Press, 1978).
6   —— *A History of Greek Philosophy: Aristotle: An Encounter* (Cambridge: Cambridge University Press, 1981).

For an admirably succinct and philosophically adroit overview of the development of ancient philosophy, continuing down to the period after Aristotle, see:

7   Irwin, T., *Classical Thought* (Oxford: Oxford University Press, 1989).

Accessible topically arranged introductions with a primarily philosophical orientation can be found in:

8   Everson, S. (ed.) *Companion to Ancient Philosophy I: Epistemology* (Cambridge: Cambridge University Press, 1990).
9   —— (ed.) *Companion to Ancient Philosophy II: Psychology* (Cambridge: Cambridge University Press, 1991).

10   —— (ed.) *Companion to Ancient Philosophy III: Language* (Cambridge: Cambridge University Press, 1994).
11   —— (ed.) *Companion to Ancient Philosophy IV: Ethics* (Cambridge: Cambridge University Press, 1998).

Works [8]–[11] also contain extensive bibliographies.

For an engaging discussion of the conception of explanation and causation in classical philosophy and beyond, see:

12   Hankinson, R., *Cause and Explanation in Ancient Greek Thought* (Oxford: Oxford University Press, 1998).

Philosophy before Socrates

Primary text

For common reference to the Presocratics and some of the Sophists, scholars use the following collection of Greek fragments, most of which have accompanying German translations:

13   Diels, H., *Die Fragmente der Vorsokratiker*, sixth edition, revised by Walter Kranz (Berlin: Weidmann, 1952).

Students will find English translations in:

14   Sprague, R. (ed.) *The Older Sophists: A Complete Translation by Several Hands of the Fragments in Die Fragmente der Vorsokratiker*, edited by Diels–Kranz. With a new edition of Antiphon and of Euthydemus (Columbia, South Carolina: University of South Carolina Press, 1972).

For a selection of Presocratic fragments in Greek with English translations and helpful commentary, the best source is:

15   Kirk, G.S., Raven, J.E. and Schofield, M. *The Presocratic Philosophers*, second edition (Cambridge: Cambridge University Press, 1983).

Secondary literature

For clear and accessible introductions to the Presocratics consult:

16   McKirihan, R., *Philosophy before Socrates: An Introduction with Texts and Commentary* (Cambridge, MA: Hackett, 1994).
17   Hussey, E., *The Presocratics* (London: Duckworth, 1972).
18   Burnet, J., *Early Greek Philosophy* (London: A. and C. Black, 1932 [1892]).

A full and lively though somewhat less accessible treatment can be found in:

19   Barnes, J., *The Presocratic Philosophers* (London: Routledge, 1982).

Additionally, students will find a wealth of information about the Presocratics in [1], [2], and [3].

Two good collections of articles, mainly more advanced than what is offered in [16]–[19]:

20   Furley, D. and Allen, R. (eds) *Studies in Presocratic Philosophy* (London: Routledge, 1975).
21   Mourelatos, A., *The Presocratics* (London: Anchor Press, 1974).

Socrates

Primary text

The best collection of translations for Plato's presentation of Socrates is available in:

22   Cooper, J. (ed.) *Plato: Complete Works* (Cambridge, MA: Hackett, 1997).

All of the individual dialogues discussed in the text are also available in less expensive formats than [22]. A relevant selection of the texts regarding Socrates in [22] can also be found in:

23   Plato, *Five Dialogues* (*Euthyphro, Apology, Crito, Meno, Phaedo*) (Cambridge, MA: Hackett, 1981).

Secondary literature

Wading through the vast secondary literature on Socrates can be somewhat daunting. Good places to begin, in addition to [4], are:

24   Smith, N. and Brickhouse, T., *The Philosophy of Socrates* (Boulder, CO: Westview, 2000).
25   Vlastos, G., *Socrates: Ironist and Moral Philosopher* (Cambridge: Cambridge University Press, 1991).
26   Santas, G., *Socrates: Philosophy in Plato's Early Dialogues* (London: Routledge, 1979).

Also good are the following anthologies, which contain excellent articles on a variety of topics in Socratic philosophy:

27   Benson, H., *Essays on the Philosophy of Socrates* (Oxford: Oxford University Press, 1992).
28   Vlastos, G. (ed.) *The Philosophy of Socrates* (London: Doubleday, 1971).
29   —— *Socratic Studies* (Cambridge: Cambridge University Press, 1994).

Some more specialized books and articles include:

30   Benson, H., "The priority of definition and the Socratic elenchus," *Oxford Studies in Ancient Philosophy*, 1990, pp. 19–65.
31   Beversluis, J., "Socratic definition," *American Philosophical Quarterly*, 1974, pp. 331–6.
32   —— "Does Socrates commit the Socratic Fallacy?," *American Philosophical Quarterly*, 1987, pp. 211–33.
33   Brickhouse, T. and Smith, N., *Socrates on Trial* (Oxford: Oxford University Press, 1989).
34   —— "Socrates on goods, virtue, and happiness," *Oxford Studies in Ancient Philosophy*, 1987, pp. 1–27.
35   Geach, P., "Plato's *Euthyphro*: an analysis and commentary," *Monist*, 50, 1966, pp. 369–82.
36   Irwin, T., *Plato's Ethics* (Oxford: Oxford University Press, 1995).
37   Kraut, R., *Socrates and the State* (Princeton: Princeton University Press, 1983).
38   —— *The Cambridge Companion to Plato* (Cambridge: Cambridge University Press, 1992).

39 McPherran, M., *The Religion of Socrates* (Philadelphia: Pennsylvania State University, 1996).

40 Nehamas, A., "Meno's paradox and Socrates as a teacher," *Oxford Studies in Ancient Philosophy*, 1985, pp. 1–30.

41 Robinson, R., *Plato's Earlier Dialectic* (Oxford: Oxford University Press, 1953).

42 Rudebusch, G., *Socrates, Pleasure, and Value* (Oxford: Oxford University Press, 1999).

43 Santas, G., "The Socratic paradoxes," *The Philosophical Review*, 1964, pp. 147–64.

44 Woozley, A., *Law and Obedience: The Arguments of Plato's Crito* (Chapel Hill, NC: University of North Carolina Press, 1979).

45 Zeyl, D., "Socratic virtue and happiness," *Archiv für Geschichte der Philosophie*, 1982, pp. 225–38.

Plato

Primary text

There are many translations of Plato's dialogues, of varying quality. Some stress fidelity over naturalness of English while others subordinate accuracy to style. The best and most comprehensive set of translations is [22]. These translations for the most part strike an appropriate balance between fidelity and readability. Many of the dialogues published in that collection are also available individually from Hackett Publishers. For the works discussed in the text, these include, in addition to [23]:

46 *Republic*, trans. G. Grube and C. Reeve (Cambridge, MA: Hackett, 1992).

47 *Phaedo*, trans. G. Grube (Cambridge, MA: Hackett, 1980).

48 *Meno*, trans. G. Grube (Cambridge, MA: Hackett, 1980).

49 *Parmenides*, trans. M. Gill and P. Ryan (Cambridge, MA: Hackett, 1996).

50 *Protagoras*, trans. S. Lombardo and K. Bell (Cambridge, MA: Hackett, 1992).

Especially recommended for students who seek close and illuminating discussion of the dialogues are the volumes in the Clarendon Plato Series from Oxford University Press. As relating to the works discussed in the text, these include the following, each an accurate translation with commentary:

51 *Phaedo*, trans. D. Gallop, with introduction and notes (Oxford: Oxford University Press, 1975).

52 *Protagoras*, trans. C. Taylor, with introduction and notes (Oxford: Oxford University Press, 1991).

53 *Gorgias*, trans. T. Irwin, with introduction and notes (Oxford: Oxford University Press, 1979).

54 *Theaetetus*, trans. J. McDowell, with introduction and notes (Oxford: Oxford University Press, 1973).

Secondary literature

As is the case with Socrates, the secondary literature on Plato is vast. For general background, see [4] and [5]. An extremely useful set of introductory discussions can be found in [38], which also contains a helpful bibliography for further study, arranged by dialogue. Two very useful collections of high-quality scholarly articles are:

55   Fine, G. (ed.) *Plato I: Metaphysics and Epistemology* (Oxford: Oxford University Press, 2000).
56   —— (ed.) *Plato II: Ethics, Politics, Religion, and the Soul* (Oxford: Oxford University Press, 2000).

Works [55] and [56] also offer well-organized bibliographies for further study.

Other collections worth consulting, some on more specialized topics in Plato's philosophy:

57   Allen, R. (ed.) *Studies in Plato's Metaphysics* (New York: Humanities Press, 1965).
58   Vlastos, G. (ed.) *Plato I: Metaphysics and Epistemology* (London: Doubleday, 1971).
59   —— (ed.) *Plato II: Ethics, Politics, and Philosophy of Art and Religion* (London: Doubleday, 1971).
60   —— *Platonic Studies*, second edition (Princeton: Princeton University Press, 1981).
61   Wagner, E. (ed.) *Essays on Plato's Psychology* (Lanham, MD: Lexington Books, 2001).

Some other helpful general studies:

62   Crombie, I., *An Examination of Plato's Doctrines*, 2 vols (New York: Humanities Press, 1962, 1963).
63   Gosling, J., *Plato* (London: Routledge and Kegan Paul, 1973).

In addition to [36], which is an especially good place to begin for a full range of topics in Platonic scholarship, other works which develop some of the themes discussed in the text include:

64   Ackrill, J., "Plato and false belief: *Theaetetus* 187–200", *Monist*, 50, 1966, pp. 383–402.
65   Annas, J., *An Introduction to Plato's Republic* (Oxford: Clarendon Press, 1981).
66   Cross, A. and Woozley, A., *Plato's Republic: A Philosophical Commentary* (New York: St Martin's Press, 1964).
67   Cooper, J., "Plato's theory of human motivation," *History of Philosophy Quarterly*,1985, pp. 3–21.
68   Fine, G., "Knowledge and belief in *Republic* V," *Archiv für Geschichte der Philosophie*, 1978, pp. 121–39.
69   Kraut, R., "Reason and Justice in the *Republic*," in E.N. Lee, A.P.D. Mourelatos and R.M. Rorty (eds) *Exegesis and Argument* (Assen: Van Gorcum, 1973), pp. 207–24.
70   Murphy, R., *The Interpretation of Plato's Republic* (Oxford: Oxford University Press, 1951).
71   Nehamas, A., "Confusing universals and particulars in Plato's early dialogues," *Review of Metaphysics*, 1975, pp. 287–306.
72   Williams, B., "The analogy of city and soul in Plato's *Republic*," in E.N. Lee, A.P.D. Mourelatos and R.M. Rorty (eds) *Exegesis and Argument* (Assen: Van Gorcum, 1973), pp. 196–206.

Aristotle

Primary text

Aristotle's complete works are available in a convenient two-volume set:

73   Barnes, J. (ed.) *The Complete Works of Aristotle: The Revised Oxford Translation*, 2 vols (Princeton: Princeton University Press: 1984).

Two very reliable collections of selected works, including all of those most read by students are:

74 Ackrill, J. (ed.) *A New Aristotle Reader* (Oxford: Oxford University Press, 1987).
75 Irwin, T. and Fine, G., *Aristotle: Selections*, trans. with introduction, notes, and glossary (Cambridge, MA: Hackett, 1995).

The glossary of Aristotelian vocabulary in [75] is excellent: well informed, usefully precise, and pedagogically alert. Students will find it especially helpful when conducting primary research in Aristotle's philosophy.

The Clarendon Aristotle Series from Oxford University Press is an excellent series of translations with commentaries and notes for students interested in pursuing Aristotle's philosophy. Some volumes related to themes discussed in the text are:

76 *Metaphysics Z and H*, trans. D. Bostock with commentary (Oxford: Oxford University Press, 1994).
77 *Physics I and II*, trans. W. Charlton with introduction and notes (Oxford: Oxford University Press, 1984).
78 *De Anima*, trans. D. Hamlyn with notes (Oxford: Oxford University Press, 1995).
79 *Categories and De Interpretatione*, trans. J. Ackrill with notes (Oxford: Oxford University Press, 1962).
80 *De Generatione et Corruptione*, trans. C. Williams with notes (Oxford: Oxford University Press, 1982).

Other volumes in the same series are usefully consulted for topics not covered in the text.

Many students have their first extended exposure to Aristotle by reading his *Nicomachean Ethics*. The best translation, which also includes an extremely helpful glossary together with a set of explanatory notes is:

81 Irwin, T., *Aristotle, The Nicomachean Ethics* (Cambridge, MA: Hackett, 1985).

Secondary literature

As with Socrates and Plato, the contemporary literature on Aristotle runs into thousands of books and articles. Much of this literature is technical and unsuited for all but advanced students. There are, however, a number of clear and accessible introductions. The best are:

82 Ackrill, J., *Aristotle the Philosopher* (Oxford: Oxford University Press, 1981).
83 Barnes, J., *Aristotle* (Oxford: Oxford University Press, 1982).
84 Lear, J., *Aristotle: The Desire to Understand* (Cambridge: Cambridge University Press, 1988).
85 Ross, W., *Aristotle* (London: Methuen, 1923).

A classic on the question of Aristotle's development as a thinker is:

86 Jaeger, W., *Aristotle: Fundamentals of the History of His Development*, trans. by R. Robinson, with author's corrections and additions (Oxford: Oxford University Press, 1948).

Some useful anthologies include:

87 Barnes, J., *The Cambridge Companion to Aristotle* (Cambridge: Cambridge University Press, 1995).

[87] is especially useful for students on some topics and contains a full bibliography for further study.

88 Barnes, J., Schofield, M., and Sorabji, R. (eds) *Articles on Aristotle. 1: Science* (London: Duckworth, 1975).
89 —— (eds) *Articles on Aristotle. 2: Ethics and Politics* (London: Duckworth, 1976).
90 —— (eds) *Articles on Aristotle. 3: Metaphysics* (London: Duckworth, 1979).
91 —— (eds) *Articles on Aristotle. 4: Psychology and Aesthetics* (London: Duckworth, 1975).
92 Moravcsik, J., *Aristotle: A Collection of Critical Essays* (Notre Dame, IN: University of Notre Dame Press, 1968).
93 O'Meara, D. (ed.) *Studies in Aristotle* (Washington, DC: Catholic University Press, 1981).
94 Sherman, N. (ed.) *Aristotle's Ethics* (Lanham, MD: Rowman and Littlefield, 1999).

Other works which develop themes introduced in the text include:

95 Ackrill, J., "Aristotle on *Eudaimonia*," *Proceedings of the British Academy* 60, 1975, pp. 339–59, and in A.O. Rorty (ed.) *Essays on Aristotle's Ethics* (Berkeley: University of California Press, 1980), pp. 15–34.
96 —— "Aristotle's definitions of Psyche," *Proceedings of the Aristotelian Society*, 1972–3, pp. 119–33, and in [91], pp. 65–75.
97 Annas, J., "Aristotle on virtue and happiness," *University of Drayton Review*, 19, 1998–9, pp. 7–22.
98 Cooper, J., *Reason and Human Good in Aristotle* (Cambridge, MA: Harvard University Press, 1975).
99 Dahl, N., *Practical Reason, Aristotle, and Weakness of the Will* (Minneapolis: University of Minnesota Press, 1984).
100 Gotthelf, A., "Aristotle's conception of final causality," *Review of Metaphysics*, 1976, pp. 226–54.
101 Irwin, T., "Aristotle's discovery of metaphysics," *Review of Metaphysics*, 1977–8, pp. 210–29.
102 —— "Aristotle's conception of morality," *Proceedings of the Boston Area Colloquium in Ancient Philosophy* I, 1985, pp. 115–43.
103 "The metaphysical and psychological basis of Aristotle's ethics," in A. Rorty (ed.) *Essays on Aristotle's Ethics* (Berkeley: University of California Press, 1980), pp. 35–54.
104 Kraut, R., "The peculiar function of human beings," *Canadian Journal of Philosophy*, 9, 1979, pp. 467–78.
105 —— "Two conceptions of happiness," *Philosophical Review*, 88, 1979, pp. 167–97.
106 —— *Aristotle on the Human Good* (Cambridge, MA: Princeton University Press, 1989).
107 Owen, G., "*Tithenai ta Phainomena*," in S. Mansion (ed.) *Aristotle et les problèmes de méthode* (Brussels: Louvain, 1961), pp. 83–103.
108 Shields, C., *Order in Multiplicity: Homonymy in the Philosophy of Aristotle* (Oxford: Oxford University Press, 1999).

Hellenistic Philosophy

Primary text

The best single source for Hellenistic philosophy is:

109 Long, A. A. and Sedley, D. N., *The Hellenistic Philosophers* Vols. I and II (Cambridge: Cambridge University Press, 1987).

The first volume contains accurate translations of the principal sources of Hellenistic philosophy and is accompanied by incisive introductory commentary. The second volume provides the texts in the original Greek and Latin, and offers a useful bibliography.

Other reliable translations, some covering the entire period, others dedicated to individual schools or authors, include:

110 Annas, J. and J. Barnes, ed. and trans., *Sextus Empiricus: Outlines of Scepticism,* second edition (Cambridge: Cambridge University Press, 2000).
111 Hallie, P., ed. and Etheridge S., trans., *Sextus Empiricus: Selections From The Major Writings On Skepticism, Man, and God* (Indianapolis: Hackett, 1985).
112 Inwood, B. and Gerson, L., ed. and trans., *Hellenistic Philosophy,* second edition (Indianapolis: Hackett, 1998).
113 Inwood, B. and Gerson, L., trans., *The Epicurus Reader* (Indianapolis: Hackett, 1994). Inwood, B. and Gerson, L., trans. with intro., *The Stoics Reader: Selected Writings and Testimonia* (Indianapolis: Hackett, 2008).
114 Mates, B., trans. with notes and commentary, *The Skeptic Way: Sextus Empiricus's Outlines of Pyrrhonism* (Oxford: Oxford University Press, 1995).
115 White, N. P., trans., *Epictetus: The Handbook (The Encheiridion)* (Indianapolis: Hackett, 1983).

Secondary literature

There are a growing number of encyclopedia entries and accessible monographs covering Hellenistic philosophy. Some useful place to begin:

116 Balzty, D., 'Stoicism,' *Stanford Encyclopedia of Philosophy* (http://plato.stanford.edu/entries/stoicism/)
117 Voigt, K., 'Ancient Skepticism,' *Stanford Encyclopedia of Philosophy* (http://plato.stanford.edu/entries/skepticism-ancient/)

Three useful companions are:

118 Algra, K, J. Barnes, J. Mansfeld, and M. Schofield, eds., *The Cambridge History of Hellenistic Philosophy* (Cambridge: Cambridge University Press. 1999)
119 Bett, R., ed., *The Cambridge Companion to Ancient Scepticism* (Cambridge: Cambridge University Press, 2010).
120 Inwood, B., ed., *The Cambridge Companion to the Stoics* (Cambridge: Cambridge University Press, 2003).

These monographs offer more extended discussion, intended for novices rather than scholars:

121 Long, A. A., *Hellenistic Philosophy: Stoics, Epicureans, Skeptics,* second edition (London: Duckworth, 1986).
122 O'Keefe, T., *Epicureanism* (Chesham, UK: Acumen, 2010).

Index

accident: see essence and accident
akrasia (weakness of will): 48–53, 93,
   154–156
   Aristotle's treatment of: 154–156
   introduced and explained: 48
   Socrates' treatment of: 49–53
Alexander the Great: 167
ante rem vs. *in rebus* realism: 88, 101, 106
   introduced and explained: x, 114 n. 63
analysis: ix, 36, 40–47
   Aristotelian: 141, 156–163
   Platonic: 63–64, 66, 68, 88–97
   Socratic impulse for: 36–38, 40–47, 58
   Stoic: 200–201
   and the univocity assumption: 49
Anaximander: 4–6
appearance: 10, 102, 171, 224–225
   and phenomenal propositions: 214–215,
     221
   Protagoras on: 27
   senses of: 226, 231 n. 47
a priori vs. *a posteriori* knowledge: 5, 7, 14,
   16, 25, 38, 61, 67–68, 69, 79, 112
   n. 17
   introduced and explained: 31 n. 4
Arcesilaus: 167, 210
aretê: see virtue
Aristotle: x, 2, 63, 87, 117–119, 183, 203,
   212
   criticism of Plato: 88, 199–120,
     126–127, 143
   four causes, introduced and explained:
     124–127
   four causes, defended: 127–128
     efficient cause: 126, 127, 128,
      130–131, 137, 140
     final cause:126, 131–140
     formal cause: 126, 128–130, 142,
      143
     material cause: 128–130, 131, 140
Function Argument (FA): 147
functional determination thesis: 148
happiness (*eudaimonia*): 145–146, 150,
   156
homonymy: 133, 156–163
hylomorphism: 128

ataraxia: 209, 212, 217
   introduced and explained: 171
atomism: 21–25, 134, 139, 176, 216

Carneades: 167, 211
categories: 122–124
change
   generation vs. alteration: 16, 18
   impossible: 16–17, 20
Chrysippus: 183, 186, 195, 206
Cleanthes: 183, 185, 186
compresence of oppposites: 76–78
   see also: flux, diachronic vs. synchronic
Cratylus: 76

Democritus: 22–29, 134, 139, 216
Descartes: 177, 213
determinism: 193
   determinism vs. fatalism: 193
   and freedom: 194–197
divine command theory of morality: 42,
   44–45

elenchus: see Socrates, elenchus
emotions: 198–201
   Emotions of the Sage (ES): 201
   Stoic analysis of: 198–200
Epicureanism: 169–170
   on fear of death: 175–172
   hedonism: 174–175, 180, 230 n. 19
   sources for: 172–173
Epicurus: 16, 169, 170, 171, 172, 174, 180
equipollent arguments: 217–218, 221, 222,
   224
   introduced and explained: 213
essence and accident: 43, 68, 117, 120–121,
   128–129, 148–149, 185
ethical intuitionism: 115 n. 99
Euthyphro: 35, 36, 39, 41–45, 81, 88, 153,
   156
   Euthyphro's Problem (EP): 41–45
extensional adequacy: 41, 42–43, 45, 55
   introduced and explained: 59 n. 7

family resemblance: 161
fatalism: see determinism

flux: 10–12, 70, 75–77, 82
  diachronic vs. synchronic: 11–12, 76–77
Forms: 68–69, 85–88
  compresence of oppposites: 76–78
  existence of: 72–85
  Form of the Good: 97–100
  Form of Justice: 88–97
  as objects of knowledge: 73–78, 82–85
  participation in: 81, 87, 120
  as properties: 108
  problems for: 106–111
  self-predication: 80, 87,108
  and Third Man Argument (TMA):
    106–111

generation: 18, 88, 126
  see also change
  ex nihilo: 22, 128, 164 n. 10
Gödel: 105

happiness: 144, 169, 175, 176, 190, 193
  being vs. feeling: 149–150, 153
hedonism: 49–50, 145–146, 169–170, 176
  Epicurean: 170, 173–175, 179–180, 182,
    184, 202, 208, 230 n. 19
  introduced and explained 49–50
  see also pleasure
Heracleitus: 9–13, 28, 70, 73–77, 78, 82,
    87
Herodotus: 27, 28
homonymy: 133, 148, 156–163
  see also univocity
  core-depenent homonymy: 162–163
Hume: 185, 230 n. 26
hylomorphism: 128

infinite: 5, 20–21, 107, 178

justice: 94–97

Leibniz's Law: 79, 81, 93, 108
Leucippus: 21
logos: 12, 184–186, 192, 198
  multiply ambiguous: 12
Lucretius: 172, 177, 178, 180

manifest image: 1, 6, 10, 13, 20, 25, 106,
    163
materialism: 2, 3, 141, 142, 176–181
Meno: 39, 40, 65, 66, 156, 210
  Meno's Paradox of Inquiry (MPI): 63–68
monism: 1–4, 22, 216
  see also value monism
Müller-Lyer lines: 226, 227

nature: 2, 10, 117, 171, 176, 184, 188, 216
  living in accordance with: 185–191, 200,
    201–204
nothing: 15
  nothing from nothing (nihil ex nihilo):
    17–18, 22, 128, 164 n. 10
  thinking nothing: 15, 17

oikeiôsis: 185–191, 202, 204
  Oikeiôsis Argument (OA): 188–189
Oracle at Delphi: 53

Parmenides: 13–18, 23, 36, 61, 128, 129,
    164 n. 10, 164 n. 12
paradox: 48
  Meno's Paradox of Inquiry (MPI): 63–68
  Socratic paradoxes: 47–53, 154–155
  Zeno's paradoxes of motion: 19–21, 48,
    107
parsimony: 3–5, 138
perception: 21, 23, 27, 67, 69, 77, 112 n.
    17, 169, 213, 216
  and common sense: 3, 4, 14, 20
  Conventionality of Perception Argument
    (CPA): 23–25, 28, 216
  intellectual perception: 102–103,
    105–107, 230 n. 19
Plato, see also Platonic dialogues
  cave: 105–106
  compresence of oppposites: 76–78
  Forms: 61, 68–69, 72–85, 85–88
  line: 104
  Third Man Argument (TMA):
  tri-partite psychology: 91–94
Platonic dialogues
  dating techniques: 111 n. 5
  Socratic vs. Platonic: 111 n. 5, 111 n. 6
  Apology: 55, 57, 58 n. 1, 58 n. 2
  Charmides: 38
  Crito: 54–58
  Euthyphro: 41–45, 73, 99, 153, 156
  Meno: 39, 41, 63–68, 78, 151, 156
  Parmenides: 107–110
  Phaedo: 58 n. 1, 63, 82, 84, 103, 140
  Protagoras: 49–50
  Republic: 63, 82, 89, 105, 158, 160, 168,
    210
  Theaetetus: 69, 70
pleasure: 48–53, 98, 145–146, 169, 173,
    176, 179–180, 203
  see also hedonism
  Aristotle on: 149–150, 212
  Epicurus on: 170, 173–175, 179–180,
    182, 184, 202, 208, 230 n. 19

impulse for (cradle arguments): 188
Stoics on: 188–189, 205
true vs. false pleasures: 171
properties: x, 3, 29, 68, 77, 79, 101, 108,
121, 222
intrinsic properties introduced and
explained: 112 n. 27
Protagoras: 25–30, 69, 71–72
Argument for Protagorean Relativism
(APR): 27
measure doctrine: 27–30, 70–72
psychological egoism: 49

recollection, doctrine of: 65
relativism: 69–72, 85, 145
Plato's rejection of: 69–92
Argument for Protagorean Relativism
(APR): 27
Russell: 167

skepticism:
see also: Scepticism, Hellenisic
Movement:
doxastic vs. epistemic: 214
Skepticism, Hellenistic Movement: 169,
170–171
Apraxia Objection (AO): 225
and belief: 215, 217, 221, 227–228
equipollent arguments: 213, 217–218,
221, 222, 224
Pyrrhonism: 212
skeptical tropes (or modes): 216–222
sources for: 210–21
zetetic: 211, 212, 218, 223, 228
sense perception: see perception
Sextus: 210, 211, 212, 214, 216–218, 221,
225, 227
Socrates: 35, 87, 153–155, 157, 170, 189,
197, 210
aporia: 37
and akrasia: 49–53
and analysis: 42
and civil disobedience: 54–58
elenchus: 37–39, 55, 58, 59 n. 4
ignorance: 35, 46–47, 62, 64
impulse for analysis : 36, 45, 58, 156,
159, 161
in prison: 140
irony: 46–47, 59 n. 20

Socratic paradoxes: 47, 59 n. 23
sources for: 58 n. 2
trial of: 35, 53
Sophists: 25–30, 119
challenges of: 30–31
soul and body: 63
dualism: 65–66, 141
hylomrophic approach: 140–144
Plato: 141, 176
materialism: 176–178
Stoicism: 169, 170
causation: 194–197
determinism: 193–197
oikeiôsis: 185–191, 202, 204
preferred indifferents: 197, 205–207
sources for: 182–185
virtue: 170, 181, 184, 185–191, 197,
20–205, 207
substance: 122
primary substance: 122–124

teleology: 131–140, 141, 144, 184, 186
Thales: 1–6, 31 n. 2, 126
time: 5, 122, 160, 178

univocity assumption: 58, 64, 156, 161, 163
introduced and explained: 40
and homonymy: 156–163

value monism: 182, 184, 197, 200–205,
207, 208,
virtue: 39–41, 63–65, 94, 184
Aristotelian conception of: 150–153
and knowledge: 48
as only good: 202–207
Stoic conception of: 170, 181, 184,
185–191, 197, 20–205, 207
unity of: 59 n. 23

weakness of will: see akrasia
What-is-F-ness Question: 27, 38, 39, 40,
58, 59, 69, 96, 157
Wittgenstein: 161

Xenophanes: 6–9, 13, 30, 36, 64, 68

Zeno of Elea (Presocratic): 18–21, 48, 107
paradoxes of motion: 19–21, 107
Zeno of Citium (Stoic): 167, 183–185, 206

Planning Care for Children
in Respite Settings

of related interest

Karina Has Down Syndrome
One Family's Account of the Early Years with a Child
who has Special Needs
Cheryl Rogers and Gun Dolva
ISBN 1 85302 820 7

When I'm Away From Home
Jean Camis
ISBN 1 85302 898 3

**Transition and Change in the Lives of People
with Intellectual Disabilities**
Edited by David May
ISBN 1 85302 863 0

The Child's World
Assessing Children in Need
Edited by Jan Horwath
ISBN 1 85302 957 2

User Involvement and Participation in Social Care
Research Informing Practice
Edited by Hazel Kemshall and Rosemary Littlechild
ISBN 1 85302 777 4

Planning Care for Children in Respite Settings

'Hello, This is Me'

Helen Laverty and Mary Reet

Jessica Kingsley Publishers
London and Philadelphia

First published in the United Kingdom in 2001 by
Jessica Kingsley Publishers Ltd
116 Pentonville Road,
London N1 9JB, England
and
325 Chestnut Street,
Philadelphia, PA 19106, USA.

Copyright © 2001 Helen Laverty and Mary Reet

Library of Congress Cataloging in Publication Data
Laverty, Helen, 1961-
Planning care for children in respite settings : hello this is me / Helen Laverty and Mary Reet
p. cm.
Includes bibliographical references and index.
ISBN 1-85302-936-X (pbk : alk paper)
1. Handicapped children--respite care. 2. Handicapped children--Respite care--Planning. I. Reet, Mary, 1960- II. Title.
HV888. L38 2001
362.1'989285889--dc21
2001029761

British Library Cataloguing in Publication Data
A CIP catalogue record for this book is available from the British Library

ISBN 1 84310 002 9

Printed and Bound in Great Britain by
Athenaeum Press, Gateshead, Tyne and Wear

For all those families.

This book is dedicated to Verity,
who will never be measured
by what she cannot do.

Acknowledgements

We would like to acknowledge the invaluable help of Caroline Smith and to thank her for her support, encouragement and common sense, and most of all for her commitment to the model in practice. Helen would like to thank Annie and John for living the model with her. Mary would like to thank Paul and her family for their support during a year when she found out for herself about having extra special needs.

Contents

Introduction   9

Chapter 1: Family-Centred Care?   15

Chapter 2: 'Hello, This is Me'   29

Chapter 3: Assessment: The Key to Accurate
            Care Planning   43

Chapter 4: Planning   55

Chapter 5: Implementation   69

Chapter 6: Evaluation   85

Chapter 7: Making the Model Work   93

Chapter 8: Health and Social Policy   109

Chapter 9: 'Listen to Me, I am a Grown-Up!'   123

APPENDIX 1: 'THIS IS ME'   141
APPENDIX 2: 'HELLO, THIS IS ME'   149
APPENDIX 3: THE MILLENNIUM CHARTER
              FOR CHILDREN'S HEALTH SERVICES   157
REFERENCES AND FURTHER READING   159
INDEX   169